Bound by Recognition

Bound by Recognition

Patchen Markell

PRINCETON UNIVERSITY PRESS

PRINCETON AND OXFORD

Copyright © 2003 by Princeton University Press
Published by Princeton University Press, 41 William Street,
Princeton, New Jersey 08540
In the United Kingdom: Princeton University Press, 3 Market Place,
Woodstock, Oxfordshire OX20 1SY

LIBRARY OF CONGRESS CATALOGING-IN-PUBLICATION DATA

Markell, Patchen, 1969–
  Bound by recognition / Patchen Markell.
    p. cm.
  Includes bibliographical references and index.
  ISBN 0-691-11381-5 (alk. paper) — ISBN 0-691-11382-3 (pbk. : alk. paper)
    1. Equality. 2. Justice. 3. Multiculturalism. 4. Difference (Philosophy)
  5. Group identity. 6. Recognition (Philosophy) 7. Agent (Philosophy)
  8. Individuality. 9. Democracy. I. Title.

JC575.M37 2003
320′.01—dc21   2002193062

British Library Cataloging-in-Publication Data is available

This book has been composed in Sabon

Printed on acid-free paper. ∞

www.pupress.princeton.edu

Printed in the United States of America

10 9 8 7 6 5 4 3 2 1

For Ann and George

And if it is good to be recognized, it is better to be welcomed, precisely because this is something we can neither earn nor deserve.

—HANNAH ARENDT

Contents

Acknowledgments

THIS BOOK HAS BEEN A LONG TIME IN THE MAKING, and I have had the good fortune to accumulate debts to many institutions and people while writing it.

It has been a pleasure to complete this book in the Department of Political Science at the University of Chicago, not least because of the Department's commitments to intellectual adventurousness, to cultivating conversations that stretch across the boundaries of subfields, and to treating young faculty as peers. While at Chicago I have also found my way into several other vital communities, including the Center for Gender Studies (and particularly the Late Liberalism Project housed there); the interdivisional Political Theory Workshop; the Center for the Study of Politics, History, and Culture at Wilder House; and the editorial committee of *Public Culture*. I thank all my colleagues in these places, faculty and students alike, for their warm welcomes and intellectual companionship. I also thank the Department of Political Science and the Division of the Social Sciences for their generosity with leave time and research funding.

At Harvard University, where this book began to take shape, I owe thanks for intellectual stimulation and financial support to the Department of Government, the Minda de Gunzburg Center for European Studies and the Program for the Study of Germany and Europe, the Committee on Degrees in Social Studies, and the Center for Ethics and the Professions. I'm also grateful for the financial support provided during graduate school by the United States Department of Education's Jacob K. Javits Fellowship Program and the Mellon Foundation's Dissertation Research and Writing grants.

Portions of this book, and some closely related ideas, have been presented at many conferences and workshops over the years, and I thank the audiences at all of the following places for their thoughtful responses. At the University of Chicago: the Political Science Department; the Rhetoric and Poetics Workshop; the Late Liberalism Project; and the Society of Fellows' conference on "Agency." At Harvard University: the Gender and Politics and Feminist Political Theory colloquia; the informal graduate political theory workshop; the Junior Fellows' Seminar at the Center for Ethics and the Professions; and the conference on "Multiculturalism and the Struggle for Recognition" at the Center for European Studies. Elsewhere: Northwestern University's Department of Political Science and Center for the Study of Law, Culture, and Society; the

Departments of Political Science at the University of Washington, Wesleyan University, and the New School for Social Research; the UCLA Clark Library and Center for 17th and 18th Century Studies; the Chicago-area chapter of the international Conference for the Study of Political Thought; and a number of panels at the Annual Meetings of the Northeastern Political Science Association, the Midwest Political Science Association, the Western Political Science Association, and the American Political Science Association.

An earlier version of chapter 3 was published as "Tragic Recognition: Action and Identity in *Antigone* and Aristotle" in *Political Theory* 31, no. 1 (February 2003). Some brief passages, mainly in chapter 2, first appeared in different form in "The Recognition of Politics: A Comment on Emcke and Tully," in *Constellations* 7, no. 4 (December 2000). Thanks to Sage Publications and Blackwell Publishers, respectively, for permission to reprint this material. I am also extraordinarily grateful to Ruth Walz for permission to use her photograph on the cover of this book.

I am especially grateful to the many people who have read and commented on part or all of the manuscript over the years, or with whom I have had important conversations about these issues. Needless to say, these people are not responsible for whatever mistakes and missteps remain in the final product: Terry Aladjem, Danielle Allen, Arthur Applbaum, Ike Balbus, Seyla Benhabib, Lauren Berlant, Chris Brooke, Cathy Cohen, Bill Connolly, James Der Derian, Carolin Emcke, Peter Euben, Michaele Ferguson, Andrea Frank, Jason Frank, Jill Frank, Nancy Fraser, Bob Gooding-Williams, Peter Gordon, Kirk Greer, Elaine Hadley, Kevin Hawthorne, Charles Hirschkind, Bonnie Honig, Michael James, Chris Kelty, Alan Keenan, Will Kymlicka, Richard Kraut, Jacob Levy, Eric MacGilvray, Saba Mahmood, Ian Malcolm, George Markell, Kirstie McClure, Pratap Mehta, Sara Monoson, Sankar Muthu, David Owen, Jennifer Pitts, Beth Povinelli, Jen Rubenstein, Michael Sandel, Bill Sewell, Karen Shelby, Christina Tarnopolsky, Michel-Rolph Trouillot, James Tully, Miguel Vatter, Dana Villa, Candace Vogler, Michael Warner, Lisa Wedeen, Alex Wendt, Stephen White, Iris Young, Linda Zerilli, Karen Zivi, and three anonymous press readers. At Princeton University Press, Ian Malcolm has been a wise and patient editor, whose input has been invaluable during the final revisions, and whose confidence in the project has helped keep me going. I am also indebted to Dale Cotton, my production editor at Princeton; to Pamela Schnitter for designing the book; to David Allen for copyediting; to Sylvia Coates for preparing the index; and to Kirk Greer for research and editorial assistance.

I cannot help mentioning some people twice. Special thanks are due first to the three members of my dissertation committee—for the usual reasons, but in this case also for indulging what must have seemed like an improbably eclectic project. Michael Sandel read the whole manuscript carefully and helped me see where I had buried issues instead of confronting them. Seyla Benhabib helped inspire this book, not least by making Hegel's thought seem alive with tension and promise; I am deeply grateful for her invaluable comments on my work and for her steadfast and ongoing support. And Bonnie Honig, whose own work on democratic agency also helped inspire this book, was incredibly generous with her time and energy, reading countless pages of drafts and spending hours at a time helping me distill my hunches into something stronger. I continue to learn from our conversations and from her example.

My first formulation of these ideas now seems inseparable from my friendship with a few other political theory graduate students, late of the unforgettable Six Marie Avenue, including Chris Brooke, Sankar Muthu, Jennifer Pitts, and most of all Michaele Ferguson. Each of these friends has left important marks on this book; just as important, they sustained me while I wrote it, and still do. New friends in Chicago, including Lauren Berlant, Beth Povinelli, Alex Wendt, Lisa Wedeen, Jacob Levy, Iris Young, Michael Dawson, and especially Candace Vogler have not only improved this book but also helped me keep my confidence, balance, and sense of humor. Danielle Allen has been talking with me about these issues for several years and has read some parts of this book more times than she probably cares to count, offering insight and support at every turn. For even longer, Jill Frank has been an irreplaceable interlocutor, whose own ways of approaching Aristotle, democracy, reading and writing, conversation, and friendship have been an inspiration.

I owe a different sort of debt to some of my teachers from Berkeley, including Fred Dolan, Jeremy Waldron, the late Michael Rogin, and especially Hanna Pitkin. None of them was directly involved in this project, yet it would not exist if I had not been drawn into this profession by the examples they set, and it would not have quite the shape it does if I did not still write with them in mind, or turn to their books when I lose my way.

I cannot begin to measure my debt to Andrea Frank. Our conversations about politics, philosophy, and everything else have been going on for nearly two decades. I thank her for helping me think through the issues in this book, for helping me find my sense of vocation when it gets too deeply buried in professional paperwork, for her creative spirit, for her love, and for our future.

This book is dedicated to my parents, who taught me to care about words, ideas, and the world.

Bound by Recognition

The Problem of Recognition

WALKING ALONG A CROWDED AVENUE, you see a friend and call out her name: suddenly, a pocket of intimacy forms in an otherwise anonymous public space. Standing in a long line at the immigration office, you find yourself grateful for your Canadian passport, which you know will make it easier for you to extend your employment in the United States. You roll back the metal gates in front of your shop window, which now displays (next to the list of South Asian languages spoken inside) a new assortment of items prominently bearing the American flag. Sitting down with a calculator, you and your partner wonder whether it will be possible to get a home loan together at a decent rate without being married. A young man watches as you slowly board the bus, and then offers you his seat. Driving down a street in a predominantly white neighborhood, you are pulled over again by the police, suspended in mistrust while the officer runs your identification and plates. You recall how several of your male co-workers unexpectedly declared that they think *you'll* be the next woman in the office to have a baby. You wait for the volunteer to find your name on the voting rolls. You add a new accomplishment to your curriculum vitae. You hold a stranger's gaze for a second too long, checking for and inviting desire.

Life is given texture by countless acts of recognition. From everyday interactions to the far-reaching deliberations of legislatures and courts, people are constantly asking the interconnected questions: Who are you? Who am I? Who are we? In answering these questions, we locate ourselves and others in social space, simultaneously taking notice of and reproducing relations of identity and difference. And in this way, we orient ourselves practically: we regularly decide what to do, and how to treat others, at least partly on the basis of who we take ourselves, and them, to be. For better or for worse, the distribution of affection, loyalty, esteem, consideration, rights and obligations, and many other social goods is closely tied to our assessments of identity, both personal and collective. At one level, there is no reason to regret this fact, and in any case probably no way to escape it, for recognition helps give our lives depth and continuity, and a world completely lacking the signposts of identity would be unnavigable. At the same time, many of the relationships established and maintained through recognition are unjust, often severely so. If recognition makes the social world intelligible, it often does so by stratifying it, subordinating some people and elevating others to positions of privilege or dominance. This book is about the social and political dynamics of recognition, about how recognition becomes a medium of injustice, and about what it would mean for relations of identity and difference to be structured more justly.

Although these are perennial issues, the theme of recognition has become particularly prominent in social and political theory over the last decade and a half, due largely to three intersecting developments. First, during this period, mainstream political theory began to take notice of the distinctive demands for justice raised by political movements organized around ethnicity, race, language, culture, gender, and sexuality. Second, the events of 1989 seemed to place problems of identity and difference—ethnic conflict, religious fundamentalism, regional secession movements, immigration and citizenship, and nationalism—at the center of global politics. And, third, many theorists began to approach these issues through the concept of recognition, drawing more or less directly on the philosophy of Hegel, who coined the phrase "the struggle for recognition" (*Kampf um Anerkennung*) and gave the concept its most influential philosophical treatment. By the end of the last decade, scholars had even begun to talk of a general shift away from a "politics of redistribution," focused on the satisfaction of interests and the distribution of material goods, and toward a "politics of recognition," focused on securing equal respect and esteem for the diverse identities borne by members of pluralistic societies.[1]

Out of this intersection of contemporary politics with Hegelian philosophy came a distinctive theoretical approach to problems of injustice on the terrain of identity and difference, which received one of its most famous statements in Canadian philosopher Charles Taylor's catalytic essay "The Politics of Recognition," which was first published in 1992. There, Taylor drew on Hegel, among many others, to work out an account of the larger meaning and conceptual underpinnings of the demands for recognition made by members of oppressed and marginalized social groups. The first step in this reconstruction was to bring recognition into view as a distinctive but neglected human good. Since we are socially situated creatures, Taylor argued, we are profoundly vulnerable to the ways in which we are perceived and characterized by others. "The thesis is that our identity is partly shaped by recognition or its absence, often by the *mis*recognition of others," he wrote; "and so a person or group of people can suffer real damage, real distortion, if the people or society around them mirror back to them a confining or demeaning or contemptible picture of themselves." Correspondingly, receiving recognition of one's identity from others is a "vital human need," a precondition of effective agency.[2] The second step was to establish a norm of equality governing the distribution of recognition, and here Taylor turned explicitly to Hegel's incisive analysis, in the *Phenomenology of Spirit*, of the self-defeating tendency of asymmetrical structures of recognition such as the master-slave relationship. For Hegel, as Taylor said, "the struggle for recognition can find only one satisfactory solution, and that is a regime of *reciprocal* recognition among *equals*."[3] On this basis, Taylor argued that modern polities must extend public recognition to all their citizens, both as human beings in general and also as the bearers of particular social identities.[4]

It is easy to understand why this general approach to recognition has become influential. It expresses an attractive ideal, envisioning a world in which people could all find their own identities accurately and respectfully reflected in the mirror of their shared social and political life—a world in which, as Rousseau put it, "each sees and loves himself in the others so that all will be better united."[5] At the same time, it offers a concise interpretation of a ubiquitous and deep-seated form of injustice, called "misrecognition," which consists in the failure, whether out of malice or out of ignorance, to extend people the respect or esteem that is due to them in virtue of who they are. Taken together, these two components of the standard approach to recognition constitute a powerful and appealing elaboration of the idea of democracy as self-determination or self-rule.[6] Democracy, on such a view, is always a matter of recognition: citizens must be able to understand the rules and decisions to which they are subject as in some sense expressions of their own wills. And the idea of democracy thus understood is also betrayed by persistent forms of identity-based inequality, which make it more difficult for members of subordinated groups even to understand themselves as full members of the supposedly sovereign "people," much less to experience political decisions as in any substantial way their own doing.

But is this the best way to flesh out the idea of democracy? Must a world of greater justice and equality also be a world of mutual transparency, a world without alienation, a world in which we can be confident of our invulnerability to all powers that we do not ourselves control? There are at least two important and interrelated grounds for concern about this vision. The first picks up on an important strand of political thought—stretching from the exemplary tales of the ancient Greek tragedians, to Tocqueville's eloquent account of the intertwining of promise and danger in democracy, to Arendt's meditations on the unpredictability of human interaction—which has steadfastly warned against overambitious efforts to rescue social and political life from its own fragility. For these authors, such efforts go wrong at the level of what we might call social and political "ontology": they rest on distorted pictures of basic features of the human world, mistaking the irreducible conditions of social and political life for pathologies that might someday be overcome.[7] Correspondingly, from this perspective, the crucial questions to be asked about the politics of recognition are ontological. What would the world have to be like for its vision of successful mutual recognition to be possible, or even intelligible? Does the ideal of recognition rest on a coherent and persuasive picture of, for example, the relationship between identity and human agency? Or does the pursuit of recognition, for all its democratic good intentions, actually blind us to certain ineliminable, and perhaps also valuable, aspects of our own situation?

The second ground for concern about the standard approach to recognition follows the lead of a different but equally important line of political thought. At least since Marx's attack upon the false universality of eighteenth-century declarations of individual rights, radical social critics have often argued that mainstream responses to injustice are superficial: at best, they simply misunderstand deep-seated structures of inequality and relations of power; at worst, they actually help to create or reinforce them. Of course, Marx's critique was directed at notions of rights that purported to be what we would now call "difference-blind," but there is good reason to raise the same concerns in relation to certain kinds of difference-conscious politics, too.[8] From this perspective, the crucial questions to be asked about the politics of recognition concern its presuppositions about the nature and sources of injustice in relations of identity and difference. Is "misrecognition" best understood as the failure to see and/or respect the identity of the other? Or does that characterization of the problem mislead us about the structure of this sort of injustice, and, consequently, about what it would mean to overcome it?

These two concerns may seem to point in very different directions, for if the first strand of thought cautions against excessive theoretical and political ambition, the second insists, ambitiously, that prevailing understandings of injustice are insufficiently deep or demanding. (Indeed, Marx and Marxism are often thought to exemplify just the sort of utopian arrogance—or "metaphysical optimism," as Isaiah Berlin put it—against which the tragedians and their descendents warn.[9]) As unlikely as such an undertaking might seem, however, this book pursues both sets of questions simultaneously, for at least in the context of recognition, their answers are not only compatible but mutually reinforcing.[10] On the one hand, I shall argue that the ideal of mutual recognition, while appealing, is also impossible, even incoherent; and that in pursuing it we misunderstand certain crucial conditions of social and political life. Foremost among these conditions is the fact of human finitude, which I interpret not in terms of mortality, but rather in terms of the practical limits imposed upon us by the openness and unpredictability of the future—what Hannah Arendt called the "non-sovereign" character of human action.[11] In this sense, the pursuit of recognition involves a "misrecognition" of a different and deeper kind: not the misrecognition of an identity, either one's own or someone else's, but the misrecognition of one's own fundamental situation or circumstances.

On the other hand, I shall also argue that injustice in relations of identity and difference is not simply a matter of improper recognition in the conventional sense—that is, of the proliferation of false or demeaning images of various people and groups. To be sure, this is one important and widespread symptom of injustice, although it is not a necessary one. But this diagnosis does not grasp the problem at its root. It gives short shrift to the underlying forms of desire and motivation that sustain and are sustained by unjust social arrangements, thereby ignoring both the possibility that demeaning images of others are epiphenomenal—that they are supported by structures of desire that are not in the first instance *about* others—and, more troublingly, the possibility that even affirmative images of others could be consistent with, or serve as vehicles of, injustice. In what follows, I offer an alternative diagnosis of relations of social and political subordination, which sees them not as systematic failures by some people to recognize others' identities, but as ways of patterning and arranging the world that allow some people and groups to enjoy a semblance of sovereign agency at others' expense. And here, the concern about excessive ambition converges in a surprising way with the concern about our grasp of injustice, for on this account, injustice in relations of identity and difference is itself a matter of misrecognition in the deeper sense I have just described.

Taken together, these two arguments suggest that there is a profound irony involved in the ideal of recognition: the very desire that makes that ideal so compelling—the desire for sovereign agency, for an antidote to the riskiness and intermittent opacity of social life—may itself help to sustain some of the forms of injustice that many proponents of recognition rightly aim to overcome. This irony makes the pursuit of recognition at best an equivocal instrument of emancipation, replete with double binds. Movements organized around demands for recognition may indeed produce concrete gains for members of subordinated groups. Yet in characterizing injustice as the misrecognition of identity, and in embracing equal recognition as an ideal, they may simultaneously make it more difficult to comprehend and confront unjust social and political relations at their root. In some cases, even apparently successful exchanges of recognition may reinforce existing injustices, or help to create new ones.

Having said that, it is important to emphasize that this book is not a polemic against social and political movements organized to fight injustice in relations of identity and difference. It is not a call for people to abandon particularism in favor of universalism—or vice versa. And it is not driven by a concern about what Arthur Schlesinger called the multicultural "disuniting of America."[12] Two points need to be made here. First, when I discuss the "politics of recognition," I mean to refer to a specific way of making and justifying political and theoretical claims, which can be more or less conceptually explicit, and more or less self-conscious, but which is hardly the only discourse through which left social and political movements have tried to respond to injustice in relations of identity and difference.[13] Indeed, it is important to remember that the "politics of recognition" is not simply a framework through which some activists and scholars articulate demands for justice, but also a discourse through which some other academics and political actors have chosen to understand these demands, sometimes with suspicion and sometimes with sympathy.

And this leads directly to the second point. It has become commonplace in mainstream political theory to speak as though the politics of recognition were practiced exclusively by those people and groups who are already socially marked as "particular." On this view, the politics of recognition is a matter of how much or what kind of recognition *we*—speaking, in the voice of universality, for the "larger society"— ought to extend to *them*. But this way of talking obscures the fact that the politics of recognition is not the exclusive province of any group or movement or political sector. As Hegel knew, it takes at least two to struggle; and those who criticize identity politics and multiculturalism in the name of the unity of the "larger society" are also practicing a politics of recognition, which is marked by the same conceptual and political problems I have just described. There is at least one difference, though: people who are able to identify relatively unproblematically with the "larger society" and its institutions are also typically better able to set the terms under which any exchange of recognition with less powerful and more vulnerable others will occur, making their own desires and needs into nonnegotiable items. So while I do raise concerns about one way in which some on the left analyze and respond to injustice, I also direct this critique at actors who are not ordinarily represented as being engaged in the politics of recognition—including especially the state and those who speak on its behalf, both formally and informally—precisely because these are often the actors who make politics into a matter of recognition in the first place, and whose own demands for recognition, tacit and explicit, create powerful incentives for others to frame claims about democracy, justice, inequality, and subordination *as* recognition claims.

It is also important to stress that to criticize the ideal of recognition in this way is not to call for the abandonment of democratic and egalitarian aspirations. To the contrary, it is to recast those aspirations in a way that does not confuse justice in relations of identity and difference with mutual transparency, or with security from risk, or with the overcoming of all experiences of alienation or even hostility in our relations with others. Following up on the thought that the source of relations of subordination lies not in the failure to recognize the identity of the other, but in the failure to acknowledge one's own basic situation and circumstances, I call this alternative a politics of *acknowledgment* rather than a politics of recognition. In this picture, democratic justice does not require that all people be known and respected as who they really are. It requires, instead, that no one be reduced to any characterization of his or her identity for the sake of someone else's achievement of a sense of sovereignty or invulnerability, regardless of whether that characterization is negative or positive, hateful or friendly (for, as we shall see, positive images can be instruments of subordination, too). It demands that each of us bear our share of the burden and risk involved in the uncertain, open-ended, sometimes maddeningly and sometimes joyously surprising activity of living and interacting with other people.

In the following chapters, I develop these arguments through a series of critical engagements with an eclectic group of social and political thinkers, interspersed with extended case studies of struggles for recognition drawn from literature, history, and contemporary politics. At the center of the book, however, is an unorthodox interpretation and reappropriation of Hegel. As I have indicated, Hegel is usually read as the philosophical godfather of the standard approach to recognition, both by proponents of that approach and by some of its most sophisticated and thoughtful critics. There is a great deal to this reading, but it is also an oversimplification, and part of the agenda of this book is to change the way we understand the relationship between Hegel's philosophy and the politics of recognition. Although one strand of Hegel's thought, and ultimately the dominant one, does align him with the ideal of recognition, another strand actually illuminates the limits of that ideal and suggests an alternative understanding of justice, rooted not in recognition but in acknowledgment. This neglected dimension of Hegel's philosophy ties him, however partially, to an important countertradition of thought about recognition that stretches from Sophocles and Aristotle to Hannah Arendt and beyond. By reading Hegel in the company of these other thinkers, I aim to transform our understanding of the ethical and political implications of his account of recognition, especially in the famous sections of the *Phenomenology* devoted to the struggle for recognition and the master-slave relation. Bringing this dimension of Hegel's thought into the foreground will also let us see where he turns against his own best insights, embracing exceedingly ambitious visions of human reconciliation through mutual recognition, and endorsing unjust social relations in his pursuit of those quixotic goals.

The close attention to Hegel and others notwithstanding, this book is not a contribution to the history of political thought in any straightforward sense. That is not to say it is ahistorical: I proceed mainly through detailed engagements with particular authors and cases, and I have tried to say something interesting and new, however modest, about each of these subjects on its own terms, and with reference to at least some of the specialized literature into whose territory I venture. Still, this is not a history of the concept of recognition, nor is it a thorough investigation of the significance of that concept in the complete works of any single thinker—not even Hegel's, the powerful gravitational pull of his corpus notwithstanding. It is, at best, an episodic history, whose shape has been guided as much by my own thematic preoccupations as by anything else.

It is also important to specify the sense in which this is a work of normative theory. The purpose of this book is not to defend my own set of all-things-considered judgments about well-known policy controversies involving issues of identity and difference—should the provincial government of Québec be allowed to regulate the use of English on signs? Should Britain fund Muslim schools? Should the law recognize same-sex marriages? This is not because I think such political judgments are unimportant, nor because I think political theorists—or anyone else—can't or shouldn't make them. Yet such judgments depend on, among other things, the lucidity of the background vocabulary in which we represent, to ourselves and to each other, the nature of the political problems we face, the stakes of the decisions we confront, and the range of possibilities we possess.[14] And when an often-used vocabulary of this sort obscures as much as it clarifies, political theorists are faced with another set of tasks, at once diagnostic and reconstructive: to bring the obstruction into view; to demonstrate its implications; to understand its sources (for these things are rarely accidents or mere matters of careless thinking); and, in the course of all that, to work toward an alternative and more perspicuous language. It is this sort of background conceptual work—not yet prescriptive, but certainly normative—that I undertake in the following chapters with respect to the idea of recognition.

CHAPTER ONE

From Recognition to Acknowledgment

IN HER CLASSIC STUDY OF MACHIAVELLI, Hanna Pitkin describes the political theorist's "special problem of communication" this way: "In order to be understood, he must speak in terms familiar to his audience, from within a conceptual framework and an understanding of the world that they share. Yet he wants not to convey new information to them, but rather to change the terms, the conceptual framework through which they presently organize their information."[1] Any attempt to overcome the misrecognitions that afflict the politics of recognition as it is conventionally understood faces a version of the same problem. These misrecognitions are not easy to grasp, because they are not simply errors, like false empirical propositions or fallacious arguments. They are more like blind spots built into the "grammar" of a theory or a practice; and as such, they are not immediately visible from within the terms in which the theory operates, or from the perspective made available by the practice.[2] This is why talking, as I do, about the pursuit of recognition as itself an example of misrecognition, or about the difference between recognition and acknowledgment, can sound senseless at first.

The problem is not intractable, however. One way to get a hold upon misrecognitions like these is to focus on their symptoms: unresolved tensions in the operation of a theory, or unexpected disruptions in the course of a practical undertaking. As we shall see, this is an important part of the argumentative strategy of Hegel's *Phenomenology*, which exposes the limitations of various accounts of knowledge by tracing the internal contradictions that emerge when those accounts are put to work. And if there is one way in which this book remains resolutely Hegelian even when Hegel is absent from the page, it is in its diagnostic approach: I proceed by taking up exemplary theories and projects of recognition, listening for the metal-on-metal sound of a theory working against itself, looking for the surprising reversals that signify counterproductive or self-defeating courses of action, and using the leverage generated by these moments of contradiction to create space for a new approach to the politics of identity and difference.

This approach has its limitations. An argument of this sort is most persuasive when it proceeds through an extended and sympathetic engagement with another's perspective. But all of the dense work of exegesis and reconstruction that this requires can tax a reader's patience, and the larger thread of the argument can get lost in the details. In response to these dangers, I begin in this chapter by surveying some of the central concepts and lines of argument that structure this book, and which cut across the individual essays that follow. This will help to explain how each of the later studies fits into the whole; and it will also help situate this book more precisely on the terrain of contemporary political thought. But it is important to stress that this synoptic treatment cannot substitute for the subsequent close readings and case studies, which is where the full sense of my alternative vocabulary, and the evidence of its usefulness, will emerge.

It is worth noting, before diving in, that this methodological problem—the problem of wishing to be able to speak in advance in a language that will only become intelligible retrospectively—foreshadows one of the central substantive ideas that will appear repeatedly in this chapter, and throughout the book: the idea that the key to recognition lies in its *temporality*. By temporality, I do not mean the mere fact that recognition occurs in time, nor do I refer to its pace or speed. Rather, I mean that recognition links an agent's past and present to her future; and that the *politics* of recognition involves a distinctive kind of practical relation to these different horizons of temporality. Attention to this theme, I believe, can help us escape some of the deadlocks into which debates about identity and difference have frequently fallen over the last couple of decades—deadlocks which have their origin in part in a privileging of spatial concepts and metaphors in our thinking about identity and difference. In fact, as I shall argue, social relations of subordination can themselves be understood in terms of the displacement of problems of temporality and their conversion into problems of spatial organization.[3] Put differently, justice and injustice in relations of identity and difference, properly understood, have much to do with the ways in which our relations to each other are shaped by postures we assume in, and toward, time.

SOVEREIGNTY, IDENTITY, AND ACTION

One of the central arguments of this book is that the politics of recognition is characterized by certain important misrecognitions of its own—not misrecognitions of identity, but failures to acknowledge one's own basic ontological conditions—and that these arise from the fact that the pursuit of recognition expresses an aspiration to *sovereignty*. But what could this mean? Sovereignty, after all, is usually understood as a property of states: a state is said to be sovereign when it represents the "final and absolute authority in the political community," able to govern its own territory independently, without the interference of competing powers either inside or outside its boundaries.[4]

In fact, this specific notion of state sovereignty often does play an important role in the politics of recognition, and I shall say more about it later. But the idea of state sovereignty is also only one manifestation of a broader idea of sovereign agency, which can be attributed as easily to persons as to institutions. In this broader sense, sovereignty refers to the condition of being an independent, self-determining agent, characterized by what Hannah Arendt calls "uncompromising self-sufficiency and mastership."[5] The idea is well-captured in Isaiah Berlin's famous account of "positive" liberty, which refers not just to the absence of external obstructions, but to a stronger condition of independence, of something like full ownership of one's life and doings:

> The 'positive' sense of the word 'liberty' derives from the wish on the part of the individual to be his own master. I wish my life and decisions to depend on myself, not on external forces of whatever kind. I wish to be the instrument of my own, not other men's, acts of will. I wish to be a subject, not an object; to be moved by reasons, by conscious purposes, which are my own, not by causes which affect me, as it were, from the outside. I wish to be somebody, not nobody; a doer—deciding, not being decided for, self-directed and not acted upon by external nature as if I were a thing, or an animal, or a slave incapable of playing a human role, that is, of conceiving goals and policies of my own and realizing them.[6]

It may seem counterintuitive to suggest that the ideal of recognition is tied to the aspiration to sovereignty thus understood. After all, interest in the theme of recognition arose precisely out of influential late-twentieth-century *critiques* of the so-called "sovereign self." Some of these critiques focused on the widespread image of the human being as paradigmatically an owner of private property, with an exclusive right to use and dispose of things under his *dominium*, which seemed to underwrite mainstream contractarian approaches to political thought; others focused on models of the self as "unencumbered" or "atomistic," which seemed to treat human beings as somehow existing above and acting independently of their social and historical contexts and bodily matrices.[7] The politics of recognition, by contrast, deals with socially and historically situated subjects, with human beings understood as members of communities and as bearers of particular identities, and with distinctive forms of injustice that operate not merely by systematically depriving already-constituted subjects of resources, but by shaping subjects themselves in ways that produce and perpetuate systematic inequality.

This genealogy is correct, but it misses the point, for the image of the person as an isolated property owner, and the related image of subjectivity as unencumbered, are not the only manifestations of the desire for sovereignty; indeed, one aim of this book is to cultivate an appreciation of the unexpectedly wide range of ways in which that desire can find expression. Contractarian political theories and voluntarist conceptions of the self anchor sovereignty in the notion of *choice*—the former, in the possibility of being subject only to those forms of authority to which you have yourself consented, and whose purpose is to protect your domain of independence; the latter, in the context-transcending power to choose your ends and purposes. The ideal of recognition, by contrast, anchors sovereignty in *knowledge*; that is, in the prospect of arriving at a clear understanding of who you are and of the nature of the larger groups and communities to which you belong, and of securing the respectful recognition of these same facts by others.[8] The idea is that mutual recognition of this sort would eliminate the obstacles of misunderstanding, ignorance, and prejudice that alienate us from each other and ourselves, making it possible for us to act in accordance with who we really are, and to do so with the support rather than the resistance of our fellows. In this way, even as the ideal of recognition brings agents back from the solitude of ownership or the thin air of choice and into the thick of social life, it also preserves, in transfigured form, the basic aspiration behind those images of agency: the aspiration to be able to act independently, without experiencing life among others as a source of vulnerability, or as a site of possible alienation or self-loss.

The same point can be made even more clearly in terms of temporality, for the strategy of choice and the strategy of recognition represent different ways of establishing links among an agent's past, present, and future, which nevertheless overlap in one crucial respect. The idea of the unencumbered self, at least according to its critics, enables agents to assume a posture of confident mastery in the face of the future by granting them the power to break deliberately with the legacy of the past; to slough off its weight, repeatedly, in an ongoing sequence of present choices. This prioritization of the present, its critics charge, is problematically ahistorical: it leaves us unable to account for the moral weight either of unchosen attachments and memberships, or of the historical injustices that continue to structure our present situation, notwithstanding efforts to will them away. The politics of recognition, by contrast, takes account of the weight of the past—but it does so in a very specific way. In this picture, history takes the form of identity, and identity is understood specifically as an antecedently given set of facts about who we are, and indeed as a set of facts which both precedes and *governs* our action, telling us what acting "authentically" means for us.[9] If the assumption that identity precedes action makes it possible to treat identity as the benchmark by which to distinguish successful recognition from misrecognition, the assumption that identity governs action tells us, in turn, why knowing who we are, and being recognized by others, matters. Together, these assumptions about the nature of identity and its relation to action make it possible to imagine successful recognition as a source of profound empowerment, as a social arrangement that would still make it possible for us to face the future with a confident mastery, albeit one that has been achieved by knowing and respecting the past, not by breaking with it.

But is this picture of the relationship between identity and action persuasive, or even coherent? Does the project of anchoring sovereign agency in the knowledge of antecedently given identities make sense? Does the weight of history always come tidily packaged in rules and prescriptions for action? In *The Human Condition*, Hannah Arendt offers a different account of the relationship of action to identity. Rather than treating identities as antecedent facts about people that govern their action, Arendt conceives of identities as the *results* of action and speech in public, through which people appear to others and thereby disclose who they are.[10] Of course, the language of "disclosure"—like the terms "display" and "reveal," which Arendt also uses in this context—might seem to suggest that action merely renders a pre-existing identity visible to others, but Arendt makes it clear that identity itself comes into being through the public words and deeds through which actors "make their appearance" in the world.[11] One important consequence of this is that identity, for Arendt, is not something over which agents themselves have control. Because we do not act in isolation but interact with others, who we become through action is not up to us; instead, it is the outcome of many intersecting and unpredictable sequences of action and response, such that "nobody is the author or producer of his own life story."[12] A second and closely related consequence is that identity is only ever available to be recognized in retrospect, by the storyteller or historian who gives a narrative account of someone's activities, and therefore of who that person has shown himself or herself to be. "This unchangeable identity of the person," Arendt writes, "though disclosing itself intangibly in act and speech, becomes tangible only in the story of the actor's and speaker's life; but as such it can be known, that is, grasped as a palpable entity only after it has come to its end."[13]

This alternative view of the relationship of action and identity is closely tied to Arendt's broader rejection of the aspiration to achieve sovereign agency, which she calls "contradictory to the very condition of plurality" and to the unpredictability to which that condition gives rise.[14] For Arendt, the history of Western philosophy is shot through with misguided efforts to escape the condition of non-sovereignty, sometimes by recommending the "abstention from the whole realm of human affairs" and sometimes by recasting human affairs as matters of making rather than acting, relatively more rule-bound and therefore more easily subject to sovereign governance.[15] From this perspective, it would seem, the pursuit of sovereignty through recognition is yet another expression of the same impulse. If identity can only be reliably known in retrospect, then to wish for recognition is tantamount to wishing for the security of death: "Only a man who does not survive his one supreme act remains the indisputable master of his identity and possible greatness," she says, "because he withdraws into death from the possible consequences and continuation of what he began";[16] and even he is not *really* master of his identity, since he relies upon the "storyteller, poet, or historian" to narrate his life.[17] Indeed, it is striking to note that Arendt herself had a habit of reflecting publicly on the theme of recognition whenever she was invited to speak on the occasion of receiving an award or an honor, and that she expressed increasing discomfort with recognition as she approached the end of her life, almost as if to defy premature eulogy.[18] In the concluding lines of her 1975 Sonning Prize address, given less than a year before her death, she warned against being "seduced by the great temptation of recognition which, in no matter what form, can only recognize us *as* such and such, that is, as something which we fundamentally are *not*."[19]

The point of this brief detour through Arendt is not simply to contrast her ontological assumptions with the ones that underlie the politics of recognition, as if to suggest that theorists like Taylor had simply made philosophical mistakes about the relationship between identity and action, the possibility of sovereignty, and the temporality of recognition. My claim is more radical: that something like this alternative view of action, identity, sovereignty, and recognition is already implicit, but half-buried and disavowed, in the politics of recognition itself. That politics, after all, is in part a response to the experience of vulnerability, to the fact that our identities are shaped in part through the unpredictable responses of other people: this is what makes being recognized by others seem so acutely important in the first place. The trouble is that the politics of recognition responds to this fact by demanding that others recognize us as who we *already* really are. Invoking "identity" as a *fait accompli* precisely in the course of the ongoing and risky interactions through which we become who we are (or, more precisely, who we will turn out to have been), it at once acknowledges and refuses to acknowledge our basic condition of intersubjective vulnerability.[20] This is what I mean in suggesting that the ontological assumptions behind the politics of recognition are not simply unpersuasive but incoherent; and it is also what I mean in claiming that, in its pursuit of sovereignty, the politics of recognition is rooted in a deeper misrecognition, or failure of acknowledgment, of its own.[21]

This is, importantly, *not* a criticism of the politics of recognition in the name of individualism or universalism. Such a criticism would be beside the point anyway, since many of the most influential articulations of the ideal of recognition are, at least in part, both individualist and universalist.[22] In fact, approaching the politics of recognition through the lens of sovereignty may help us understand how unhelpful it is to organize debates about recognition and identity around distinctions between the individual and the collective, or the universal and the particular.[23] Such distinctions lead us to approach recognition in essentially *spatial* terms, as though justice in relations of identity and difference were a matter of getting our normative maps of the world right, of working out the relative weight of claims issuing from different social locations, or from different dimensions of the self—an effort that often enough ends with a rather unsatisfactory affirmation of the need to find some "elusive middle term" that would bridge these boundaries.[24] Here, by contrast, I cast the problem with the ideal of recognition as in the first instance a problem with its temporality—that is, with the way in which it expresses the aspiration to a sort of sovereign invulnerability to the open-endedness and contingency of the future we share with others—and that aspiration cuts across distinctions between individual and collective, universal and particular.[25] Individualism can be as peremptory as some forms of collectivism—for example, if it reduces "individuals" to discrete but more or less uniform creatures, each possessed of a set of preferences or a plan of life which he or she attempts to pursue or enact, but with no place for, say, the experience of being a mystery or a surprise to oneself and others.[26] Likewise, universalism can be as problematic as some forms of particularism, if it conceives of itself merely as the logical application of a rule whose meaning is thought to be known wholly in advance.[27] And, conversely, one can attend to the enormous social and political weight of collectivity and particularity—to the ways in which the conditions of our lives, including the distribution of risk and uncertainty across society, depend on far more than just what we, as individuals, share with everybody else—without thereby treating our identities as practical authorities to which we must defer.[28]

In a similar way, this argument also reaches beyond now-familiar claims about the socially constructed character of identity, which—while largely correct, in my view—also have less critical bite than is sometimes believed. In the constellation of ideas that make up social constructionism, for example, two of the brightest stars are the notions of multiplicity and change: identities are now frequently characterized as "multiple," "complex," "fragmented," or "overlapping"; and as "unstable," "in flux," "contingent," or "shifting."[29] Yet the modifiers that emphasize multiplicity are, once again, all basically spatial, and so do little to challenge the basic structure of the ideal of recognition: on its own, the idea that identities are multiple and complex is perfectly compatible with the thought that identities, in all their complexity, are nevertheless independent and antecedent facts about us that ought to be cognized properly and accorded due respect. The modifiers that emphasize change and instability are a bit more radical. They suggest that all exchanges of recognition will tend to become obsolete as our identities shift over time, and this would seem to deny the possibility of a *finally* satisfactory regime of recognition. But this claim, too, is relatively easily incorporated into the discourse of recognition, and has been by some of its most sophisticated defenders. Axel Honneth, for example, acknowledges that the struggles for recognition he describes are to be understood as "permanent";[30] and James Tully argues eloquently that the politics of recognition should be reconceived as an ongoing activity rather than as a project with a fixed goal.[31] These qualifications are useful, but they do not go far enough, for they leave the notion of successful recognition in place as a regulative idea, a constantly receding horizon toward which our politics nevertheless ought to strive, interminably. They treat recognition as necessarily provisional, but not as necessarily *retrospective*, and so they do not force us to consider the more challenging possibility that the pursuit of recognition, even when recognition is understood in this way as a regulative idea, might be an incoherent and therefore potentially costly enterprise.

I spell out this argument about sovereignty, action, identity, and recognition over the next three chapters. In chapter 2, I begin to explore the contradictions internal to the politics of recognition through a sympathetic but critical engagement with the work of Charles Taylor. While Taylor is one of the most insightful philosophical critics of certain versions of the idea of sovereignty, he also fails to acknowledge the ways in which his own work on recognition reproduces, in a new form, the very aspiration to sovereignty he rightly criticizes—a claim I defend in part by reading Taylor alongside one of his own most important philosophical sources, Johann Gottfried Herder. The following two chapters continue to develop this immanent critique of the politics of recognition while simultaneously spelling out the alternative ontology which that politics both presupposes and denies. In doing this, I make relatively little extended use of Hannah Arendt's work, since her comments about recognition are rare and tantalizingly brief. However, her references and allusions to classical authors, both in *The Human Condition* and elsewhere, suggest a way to elaborate the connections among action, identity, sovereignty, and recognition at which she hints. As I show in chapter 3, the foundations of an alternative perspective on recognition can already be found in Greek tragedy and in Aristotelian poetics and ethics, which were themselves important sources for Arendt.[32] And, as I argue in chapter 4, Arendt was not the only inheritor of this line of thought: read against the background of tragedy, Hegel's often-misunderstood account of the struggle for recognition in the *Phenomenology* can be seen as an incisive critique of the politics of recognition, rather than its founding document.

The Nature and Sources of Injustice

At its best, the politics of recognition is driven by the admirable desire to combat deep-seated forms of injustice in relations of identity and difference. What, if anything, do the foregoing ontological reflections about sovereignty, identity, and action tell us about that political agenda? While it might be tempting to conclude that the problematic ontological assumptions behind the politics of recognition simply render it impotent, this is too simple. The politics of recognition is *not* impotent: its logic, while internally contradictory, is also powerfully appealing, and for this reason, demands for recognition are among the most important mechanisms through which relations of identity and difference are shaped, sometimes for better and sometimes for worse—and, frequently enough, both. Instead, I suggest that the politics of recognition may both misunderstand and in a certain sense be congruent with the injustices it purports to combat. If the assumptions about sovereignty, action, and identity that underwrite the ideal of recognition constitute a misrecognition of a deeper sort—a failure to acknowledge certain fundamental conditions of human activity—the irony is that many instances of injustice in relations of identity and difference can themselves be understood as expressions of a misrecognition of the same kind. This common blind spot does not make the pursuit of recognition unjust per se, nor does it mean that the politics of recognition cannot sometimes produce concrete improvements in the conditions of life of the people it aims to benefit. But it does render even the best-intentioned versions of the politics of recognition ill-equipped to diagnose and respond effectively to the underlying relations of subordination that give rise to systematic, identity-based social and political inequality. And it also makes this politics especially prone to become complicit with injustice, either reinforcing the very problems it hopes to combat, or helping to create new relations of social and political subordination.

But how, exactly, is injustice an expression of this deeper sort of misrecognition? And how does this conception of injustice differ from those expressed or implied by other theorists of recognition? It will be easiest to begin with the latter question. Consider, first, the conventional approach to recognition. On this view, the distinctive injustice of misrecognition involves the failure to extend to people the respect or esteem they deserve in virtue of who they really are. This conception of injustice lends itself especially well to analogies to the maldistribution of wealth; hence, recognition theorists sometimes, though not always, write as though misrecognition were a matter of systematically failing to give some people a good—"recognition"—to which they are entitled.[33] And the reason misrecognition of this sort is thought to be unjust is that it damages the psychic integrity of those who are subject to it, interfering with the development of the forms of self-respect and self-esteem on which healthy human agency depends. Thus Taylor says that misrecognition can "wound" and "cripple" its victims; likewise, Honneth uses the language of "scars" and "injuries" when speaking of the "cultural denigration of forms of life."[34]

This conception of injustice is problematic for several interrelated reasons. First, as I have already suggested, in making the *fait accompli* of identity into the criterion of due or proper recognition, this approach misunderstands the nature of identity and its relation to action. Indeed, it also tends to misrecognize recognition itself: insofar as it conceives of injustice as the unequal distribution of a good called "recognition," it obscures the relational character of acts and practices of recognition, treating recognition as a thing of which one has more or less, rather than as a social interaction that can go well or poorly in various ways.[35] And this, ironically, diverts attention from the role of the powerful, of the *misrecognizers*, in these interactions, focusing on the consequences of suffering misrecognition rather than on the more fundamental question of what it means to commit it. Second, as Nancy Fraser has suggested, there is also something troubling about making psychic deformation into a constituent feature of injustice, for this seems to deny that people may experience severe forms of social and political injustice without finding themselves "crippled" or "scarred" by the experience.[36] And, third, at a deeper level, this emphasis on psychic harm is also an exemplary manifestation of the incoherence of the conventional approach to recognition: even as it invokes an antecedently given identity as the criterion of proper or improper recognition, it also invokes the power of intersubjective recognition to shape and form identity in order to explain why misrecognition is harmful.[37]

Fraser's recent work on recognition and redistribution presents a different and in many respects superior conception of injustice in relations of identity and difference. Against the view that misrecognition involves failing to respect people in virtue of who they are, Fraser argues that misrecognition occurs when "institutionalized patterns of cultural value constitute some actors as inferior, excluded, wholly other, or simply invisible, hence as less than full partners in social interaction."[38] And this, in turn, involves a different understanding of what's unjust about misrecognition, focused less on the integrity of the person than on the shape of social relations. For Fraser, the trouble with misrecognition is not that it necessarily inflicts psychic injuries upon its victims—although she does not deny that it *may* do so—but rather that it creates "externally manifest and publicly verifiable impediments to some people's standing as full members of society."[39] One advantage of this approach, Fraser argues, is that it lets us see the analogy between injustice in relations of identity and difference and economic injustice: both are forms of social subordination, and both violate, in slightly different ways, a single norm of "participatory parity."[40]

Fraser's recasting of injustice as a matter of the patterning or structure of social and political relations is compelling, as is her critique of the claim that misrecognition necessarily involves psychic distortion. At times, however, it becomes unclear how far Fraser's critique really departs from the politics of recognition as it is conventionally understood. On the one hand, Fraser's characterization of misrecognition as a matter of being prevented from participating as a peer in social life sometimes seems merely to *subsume* much of what theorists like Taylor and Honneth mean by misrecognition. On the terrain of identity and difference, she says, what the standard of participatory parity prohibits are "institutionalized value patterns that deny some people the status of full partners in interaction—whether by burdening them with excessive ascribed 'difference' or by failing to acknowledge their distinctiveness."[41] Correspondingly, participatory parity will demand—depending on the case—either the recognition of people's "common humanity" or the recognition of their "specificity."[42] True, on this view we no longer need to appeal to the harm of psychic disruption in order to explain why misrecognition is unjust; at the same time, however, an appeal to the criterion of identity—whether universal or particular—still seems to be required in order to identify instances of misrecognition, and in order to imagine how they might be overcome. What, if not the benchmark of identity, tells us whether an ascribed difference is "excessive," or whether we have failed to acknowledge someone's distinctiveness?

On the other hand, Fraser sometimes seems to press further beyond the politics of recognition. In addition to the recognition of people's common humanity or the recognition of people's specificity, Fraser also entertains the possibility that justice will be well served by the "outing" of the false universality of dominant groups, or by "deconstruct[ing] the very terms in which attributed differences are currently elaborated."[43] These are strategies she has discussed under the rubric of "transforma- tive" as opposed to "affirmative" recognition—although this name is potentially misleading, since it is not clear that transformative strategies involve any kind of *recognition* at all. They are, she says, guided by a "utopian image of a culture in which ever-new constructions of identity and difference are freely elaborated and then swiftly deconstructed," and on her account they are exemplified by queer politics, which—unlike gay and lesbian identity politics—aims to "destabilize all fixed sexual identities" and "to sustain a sexual field of multiple, debinarized, fluid, ever-shifting differences."[44] (I shall bracket the question of the adequacy of these descriptions until later.) At times, Fraser has even expressed a preference for this way of responding to misrecognition, both because transformative remedies seem to avoid the danger of reifying and impos- ing group identity, and because they interact especially productively with radical remedies for economic injustice.[45]

Fraser's effort to bring these two very different approaches under a single theoretical umbrella is admirably inclusive—but I do not think the attempted reconciliation works. To overcome the apparent opposition between affirmative and transformative remedies, Fraser treats them as alternative practical responses to the *same* larger problem, between which we are to choose on wholly strategic grounds.[46] For example, as she explains, her approach is neutral in principle as between two com- peting approaches to the "same-sex marriage" debate—the legalization of same-sex marriage and the deinstitutionalization of heterosexual marriage.[47] On this reading of the issue, the problem of exclusively het- erosexual marriage is a straightforward problem of patterned inequality: some people are being denied social and political benefits that others enjoy. Correspondingly, the choice between affirmative and transforma- tive remedies is a choice between two ways of reintroducing parity into this situation: advocates of gay and lesbian marriage wish to recon- struct our schemes of sexual identity such that same-sex partnerships are treated on a par with straight ones; queer critics of this turn to mar- riage—so Fraser seems to suggest—wish to deconstruct our schemes of sexual identity, achieving parity in mutual destabilization.

But in casting the issue this way, Fraser does not so much reconcile these two approaches as sidestep the underlying conflict between them. Often, the queer critique of the embrace of same-sex marriage has less to do with a distaste for stability and change—as if queerness demanded a perpetual flight from continuity—than with queer theorists' radically different understanding of the problem they take themselves to be com- batting.[48] As Michael Warner puts it, for example, advocates of same- sex marriage take the injustice of present arrangements to lie in the legal restriction of access to an essentially private, intimate, and nonexclusive good called marriage; queer critics of marriage, by contrast, charge that this representation is a "mystification," which obscures the fact that marriage itself is a "public institution, not a private relation," and that it is an institution of privilege that seeks to secure relative sexual autonomy for some people while—indeed, precisely *by*—legitimating the regulation of the sexual lives of others.[49] Fraser's approach brackets this antagonism by focusing exclusively on the *symptoms* of injustice, where these two approaches are likely to converge: whatever else queer theorists and defenders of gay and lesbian identity politics think about marriage, they agree that the institution as it is currently formed represents an inegalitarian patterning of cultural value. This, however, merely defers the fundamental question of why and how social relations come to be patterned in inegalitarian ways in the first place.

Ultimately, then, Fraser does not supply the very thing that is also missing from the conventional approach to recognition that she criticizes: an extended engagement with the deeper question of the *sources* of misrecognition, including the meaning of misrecognition for those who commit or benefit from it. In the standard approach, the existence of misrecognition is largely treated as an unfortunate fact, due perhaps to the persistence of outdated hierarchical belief systems; perhaps to the ignorance of members of majority groups about the worthy features of other cultures; or perhaps simply to some sort of baseline unreasonableness in the pursuit of self-interest.[50] Indeed, it is striking that even a theorist like Honneth, who devotes a great deal of effort to reconstructing the experience of suffering misrecognition and to showing how that experience can become the motivational ground of progressive ethical and political struggle, says so little about the complementary question of the motives, investments, and experiences that sustain misrecognition. This omission is, in one sense, understandable: we might think that what matters is identifying, denouncing, and overcoming misrecognition, not understanding where it comes from or what it means for its beneficiaries. But the issues are not so easily separated: understanding the meaning and sources of injustice is part and parcel of understanding what injustice itself is and why it is objectionable; and it has important implications for the question of how best to respond to it.

The alternative tradition of thought about recognition that I recover in this book has been centrally concerned with this question. The dramas of Sophocles repeatedly track the ways in which certain human aspirations—for self-sufficiency or security, for example—lead people to act tyrannically, and to treat others viciously.[51] Similarly, Hegel himself was, perhaps for obvious reasons, at least as keen an analyst of the motivational structure behind systems of domination as of the first-personal experience of being subordinated. As I argue at length in chapter 4, rather than reducing such systems to matters of sheer malice, unreasonableness, or ignorance, Hegel understands them as expressions of the desire for sovereign agency. That is not to say that such structures actually provide their beneficiaries with the sovereignty they seek, nor that they really consign the victims of subordination to complete abjection or powerlessness: the desire for sovereignty is impossible to fulfill, because it is itself rooted in a misrecognition of the basic conditions of human activity. Rather, subordination insulates some people from the force of the contradiction between the desire for sovereignty and the ineliminable fact of finitude, enabling them to live within that contradiction at other people's expense.[52] Recalling W. E. B. Du Bois's influential analysis of the psychological wage paid by whiteness, we might say that such structures pay an *ontological* wage: they organize the human world in ways that make it possible for certain people to enjoy an imperfect simulation of the invulnerability they desire, leaving others to bear a disproportionate share of the costs and burdens involved in social life.[53]

Once again, the point can be made even more clearly through the notion of temporality, and in this respect Hannah Arendt's work is both a help and a hindrance. While *The Human Condition* is not known for its attention to structures of social subordination, at times Arendt does suggest a link between the desire for sovereignty and the phenomenon of domination: even if our efforts to overcome the human condition of plurality were successful, she says—and for Arendt, recall, plurality is inseparable from finitude and vulnerability in the face of an unpredictable future—"the result would be not so much sovereign domination of one's self as arbitrary domination of all others, or, as in Stoicism, the exchange of the real world for an imaginary one where these others would simply not exist."[54] Here, of course, one of Arendt's characteristic habits of thought shows itself. Just as she often preferred to analyze phenomena that she believed threatened to sweep away the conditions that make public life possible *as such* and for *everyone*—such as totalitarianism or the "rise of the social"—in this passage she considers only the most extreme and unstable versions of the fantasy of sovereignty.[55] But the ways in which people seek to overcome the "weakness" of the human condition are more varied than this: the subordination of *some* others may be a more durable project than the effort to dominate everybody, precisely because it produces and exploits rather than dissolves axes of differentiation in the social world. Indeed, we might say that social subordination can be understood as a means of avoiding or disavowing the open-ended temporality of human action by converting that existential problem of time into the technical problem of the organization of social space.

This approach to injustice has several advantages. First and most obviously, unlike conventional accounts of recognition (and, intermittently, Fraser's), it does not need to appeal to identity, understood as a *fait accompli*, in order to discern injustice. Social subordination, on this view, involves closing off some people's practical possibilities for the sake of other people's sense of mastery or invulnerability; and it is the exploitative character of this relationship, rather than some lack of correspondence between how people are regarded and who they really are, that makes it unjust. Second, even as it follows Fraser's salutary turn from psychic injury to social structure, this conception of injustice also deepens her approach by giving an account of the sources of the patterned inequalities of outcome in social life to which she rightly objects. Third, and perhaps less obviously, it is also important that this account traces injustice back specifically to the pursuit of sovereignty, understood in temporal terms, rather than associating injustice with identity per se.

There is, after all, an extremely familiar story about the sources of injustice in relations of identity and difference—so familiar that it has practically become a reflex. As one version has it: "Persons or objects acquire identities only in contrast to what they are not. The affirmation of an identity entails the production and exclusion of that which is different or the creation of otherness."[56] This story has become familiar because it is truthful: it does capture something about the shape of many relations of identity and difference, past and present; and my own account of injustice is, in a certain sense, an elaboration of it. But this story, at least in this form, has two problematic features. First, it encourages us to worry that the very invocation of identity carries with it the prospect of violence or domination; and this, in turn, often inclines us to think of the constant destabilization of identity as a necessary component of any just politics—even if, as we also often acknowledge, identity remains something we cannot do without. This dilemma (a trace of which can be seen in Fraser's attempt to combine "affirmative" and "transformative" remedies for misrecognition) sometimes generates political theories with distinctly Penelopean rhythms, which assert the necessity of perpetually undoing the identities one is nevertheless bound to construct.[57]

Yet what if the trouble were not exactly with identity, but rather with a specific way of bringing identity to bear upon action; a specific way of using identity to establish connections among an agent's past, present, and future? On the account I develop here, the root of injustice in relations of identity and difference is not identity as such but rather the effort to make identity—the as-yet-unfinished and unpredictable story of one's life—into the ground of an impossible sovereignty over one's own future. Consequently, justice in relations of identity and difference demands neither the recognition of identity nor its fervent dissolution, but rather the reconceptualization of its relation to action, and therefore also of its temporality. After all, retrospective accounts of who we are, and of how we have come to be who we are, can serve a wide range of political purposes beyond anchoring sovereign agency. They can enrich political deliberation by helping agents understand each other's perspectives, or by revealing how little they understand each other; they can be used to startle others (or oneself) into confronting an unseen problem, or reconceiving the stakes of an issue; they can remind people of their own practical finitude by recalling the unexpected twists and turns through which their lives, or the larger stories in which they are enmeshed, have developed. Justice in relations of identity and difference, on this view, depends not on pursuing the greatest possible degree of fluidity or instability in one's identity, nor on trying (vainly) to do away with it altogether, but on acknowledging identity's incompleteness, on being willing to "risk its fate" (to borrow Michael Warner's felicitous phrase) in a field of human interaction that can bring surprising continuities as easily as unexpected disruptions.[58]

The second problem with the aforementioned story about identity and injustice lies in its use of the language of exclusion and otherness. Again, I do not mean to downplay the power of that language to illuminate social and political life. At times, however, this language—which is, once again, basically spatial—can lead us to overlook some of the forms that injustice in relations of identity and difference can take. For instance, when we assume that such injustice is invariably a matter either of the exclusion of otherness or the assimilation of the other to the same, we can only criticize social arrangements that seem on their face to incorporate and respect difference by claiming that such respect is a sham, that it *really* amounts either to the assimilation of difference to sameness or to exclusion masquerading as inclusion.[59] Sometimes that will be true; but not always; and even when it is, focusing on the exclusion or assimilation of difference does not quite get at the heart of the issue.

By contrast, understanding injustice as rooted in a certain kind of temporal posture can help us appreciate the rich variety of spatial strategies through which sovereignty can be pursued, and consequently also the rich variety of spatial manifestations injustice can take. Sometimes agents pursue sovereignty by seeking to assure themselves of the unity of their own identities, and by excluding or assimilating difference. At other times, however, agents may pursue sovereignty by seeking to include difference within an internally articulated totality *without* reducing it to sameness—for example, through the establishment of separate and rank-ordered spheres or positions within society; or through the notion of a functional differentiation of labor; or through the establishment of an official pluralism that at once affirms differences and governs them, reducing a threateningly open field of social plurality to a relatively orderly catalog of identities.[60] These are important distinctions: sometimes the move from an exclusionary to an inclusionary strategy of sovereignty will produce substantial improvements in the conditions of life of members of subordinated groups. In such a case, it would be wrong to say that the change merely reproduces an existing injustice—yet it might also be equally wrong to conclude that the change simply does away with injustice. I discuss two examples of such equivocal changes—Jewish emancipation in nineteenth-century Prussia and mainstream contemporary multiculturalism—in chapters 5 and 6, respectively. As these examples should make clear, conceiving of injustice through the lens of sovereignty makes it possible to take account of the important differences among these social structures without losing sight of what they share—which is not that they exclude otherness, nor that they assimilate the different to the same, but that they privilege some people and subordinate others in the pursuit of an impossible vision of masterful agency, thereby distributing the burdens of our common condition of finitude unequally.

RECOGNITION AND THE STATE

The examples I have just mentioned—Jewish emancipation and mainstream multiculturalism—share an important feature: far from being simple, face-to-face encounters between subjects, *à la* Hegel's stylized story in the *Phenomenology*, both are large-scale exchanges of recognition in which states typically play a crucial role.[61] This is true of many of the political controversies that have been treated under the rubric of recognition over the last dozen years: the dispute about same-sex marriage, for example, is in part a dispute about the forms of partnership that will be officially recognized in law and by state institutions; likewise, debates about the rights of cultural minorities are in part debates about the official distribution of rights and entitlements and the constitutional arrangement of political authority. And it has probably been true about the politics of recognition for as long as there have been such things as states, not least because states, as what Jacqueline Stevens has called "membership organizations," are always in the business of recognizing the difference between insiders and outsiders.[62] But what role, exactly, do states play in the politics of recognition? And what is the relationship between the state's part in the politics of recognition and the notion of state sovereignty?

Generally, treatments of the politics of recognition occupy one of two positions on the question of the state.[63] On the one hand, many theorists don't explicitly discuss the state at all; instead, they implicitly treat institutionalized forms of recognition as expressions of, and ultimately reducible to, more elementary and unmediated exchanges of recognition among persons. (This is manifest in the common, shorthand way of talking about the acts of a state as though they were straightforwardly also the acts of each and all of its citizens, a mode of expression that takes the representative function of political institutions for granted.) By letting the state fade into the background in this way, these accounts treat the state as something like the transparent medium through which people exchange recognition. On the other hand, some Hegelian theorists of recognition, taking their cue not from the *Phenomenology* but from the *Philosophy of Right*, have cast the state in a far more important role, depicting it as a mediating institution that has the capacity to *resolve* struggles for recognition, transcending the conflictual dynamics that characterize social life in the absence of the state by letting us all come to see ourselves as parts of a larger whole. As one Hegel scholar puts it, "what distinguishes the mediation of self and otherness provided in the state [for Hegel] is the ultimate harmonization of social life in which the struggle for recognition is finally overcome."[64]

Neither of these views of the role of the state in the politics of recognition is plausible. The first view of the state as a transparent medium through which elementary exchanges of recognition occur problematically assumes that the people involved in these exchanges are already constituted as a stably bounded group. However, this assumption overlooks the ways in which the state itself gives shape to "the people," not least by establishing rules of membership, and also by actively shaping patterns of affect and identification among its members.[65] In other words, it overlooks the work of recognition that must already have been performed if the state's claim to represent society or the people is to be plausible, much less taken for granted. At the same time, the view of the state as the site of the final overcoming of struggles for recognition is equally problematic. If the first view of the state as a transparent medium assumes the existence of an already-constituted people, this second view of the state likewise treats the state itself as always already sovereign, as independent of the particularity and conflict of social life.[66] The state *must* already possess that sort of privileged position if it is to be able to transcend, rather than simply participate in and perpetuate, political contests over recognition. But the transformative work performed by the institutions of the state in the course of making a "people" is at the same time the work by which the state itself is established and sustained *as* sovereign (however incompletely or imperfectly), creating new relations of political identification and allegiance and displacing or demoting competing ones. To the limited extent that the state "resolves" struggles for recognition, it does so not as a *deus ex machina* that appears from outside the social, miraculously transcending its conflicts once and for all, but by acquiring and maintaining a hegemonic position in the midst of the social.

Each of these views of the state, we might say, misrecognizes a desire or a project as an already-established condition. (Indeed, while neither view is persuasive on its own, when they are taken together each tends to distract attention from the other's inadequacies, in the same sort of shell game that makes the idea of the "nation-state" such a compelling equivocation. The notion that the people is already constituted as a coherent whole that speaks through the institutions of the state imbues the state with the aura of sovereignty it needs if it is to plausibly claim to be an instrument of reconciliation and harmony; conversely, the notion that state sovereignty is a given fact makes it easier for the state's members to identify themselves unproblematically as a coherent people.) In this sense, political invocations of state sovereignty are no different from other recognition claims, which represent identity as an authoritative fact, a *fait accompli*, precisely in the course of the ongoing and open-ended activity through which identities are formed. Indeed, the very idea of the state simply as an object with a certain status or set of properties at a given time—that is, as a state of affairs—is already caught up in a misrecognition of this sort.[67] As Timothy Mitchell has suggested, state and society themselves are not always already "discrete entities"; rather, the distinction between state and society is "a line drawn internally" within a single network of institutions and practices.[68] On this view, the state is a "structural effect" of this internal differentiation of collective life; but that does not mean that the state is an illusion, for this structural effect has real consequences—among other things, it organizes power in a certain way, concentrating certain capacities in specific places, groups, and institutions—which is why the notion of the state as a fundamentally distinct, always-already-sovereign thing appeals to us in the first place.[69]

Thinking clearly about the state and sovereignty therefore requires a kind of dual vision. On the one hand, we need to be able to do justice to the reality and consequences of the state-effect, which will often involve talking about the state as if it were simply a thing or an agent. That, after all, is how many people experience interactions with the state, including people who identify intensely with the state and are therefore heavily invested in its thingness, as well as people who run up against (or are run over by) the power concentrated in state institutions. On the other hand, we also need to be able to understand these effects *as* effects, which requires attending to the activities through which the state is brought into being and reproduced, and particularly to the desires, projects, and aspirations that animate those activities. Here, then, rather than assuming that the state is a transparent medium through which an already-established people relates to itself, or that it is an already-sovereign actor that can transcend struggles for recognition once and for all, I treat the state as a set of social institutions that is also among the central objects of identification onto which people displace, and through which they pursue, the desire for independent and masterful agency. It is, in short, both a participant in and an artifact of the politics of recognition.[70]

One virtue of this approach is that it helps illustrate the limits of certain well-known claims about the obsolescence of the idea of "sovereignty." For example, many analysts of globalization now suggest that, for better or worse, sovereignty has been eroded by the growing power of multinational capitalism, the proliferation of international organizations, the acceleration of transnational flows of people and information, and the weight of ecological problems that transcend the territorial boundaries of modern nation-states.[71] And, in a different vein, many social and political theorists are heeding Foucault's call to "cut off the King's head"—that is, to set aside the concept of sovereignty (which misleadingly portrays power as a repressive force possessed by a privileged person or institution) in favor of the study of the multiple, local, and daily "techniques and tactics" of power that productively order and govern human activity.[72] If states neither are nor ever were sovereign, one might ask, why focus on that outmoded concept now?

These arguments are important, yet neither is quite germane to the way I treat state sovereignty here. The argument from globalization makes a straightforward sociological claim about the extent and limits of the contemporary territorial state's capacity to govern. But this sort of argument has little bearing on the salience of sovereignty as a component of the contemporary political imaginary: the *claim* of states to be sovereign can still have powerful political effects even in the face of its increasing implausibility. Indeed, the very fact that the concept of sovereignty has become an object of intense and normatively loaded debate, provoking everything from celebrations of sovereignty's demise to rearguard actions in its defense, testifies to its continuing power as a category through which our experience of politics is organized. And it is at this level of political culture and identification that I use the concept of sovereignty here: what matters for my purposes is less the actual extent of state power than the fact that, for the moment, sovereignty remains a crucial part of the meaning of statehood, crucial enough that the prospect of the loss of sovereignty can provoke talk of a "crisis of the nation-state."[73]

The Foucauldian objection is more complicated, but ultimately invites a similar response. Importantly, Foucault's argument is intended first and foremost to introduce a shift in our thinking about the operation of power. For him, juridical theories or doctrines of sovereignty are problematic because they imply an incomplete understanding of how power works: by locating power in the king, they suggest that power is something possessed by a "single will" and applied, repressively, to others.[74] On Foucault's account, "escap[ing] from the limited field of juridical sovereignty and State institutions" is thus a condition of the possibility of attending to the other face of power—power as a matter of the ongoing and productive constitution of subjects through mundane and small-scale techniques of governance.[75]

Not all of Foucault's readers have entirely agreed. Some, inspired by his late work on governmentality, have resisted at least part of his injunction to turn away from sovereignty and the state. In *States of Injury*, for example, Wendy Brown charges that Foucault too quickly equates the state with the idea of sovereignty, concluding that "this identification precludes Foucault from including the state as a critical site in the non-sovereign, nonrepressive or 'productive,' microphysical, and capillary workings of power to which he directs our attention." Like Foucault, Brown will have no truck with the notion of sovereignty; unlike him, she thinks that "when we set aside the problem of sovereignty . . . the state comes into view as a complex problem of power, as part of the 'study of the techniques and tactics of domination'" Foucault wishes to promote.[76]

Brown's transformation of Foucault here is tremendously productive. It sets the stage for her subsequent argument, to which my own is deeply indebted, that a politics of identity that looks to law and the state to redress social injuries may depoliticize rather than transform relations of domination, while also "unwittingly increas[ing] the power of the state and its various regulatory discourses at the expense of political freedom."[77] Yet in my view, Brown does not go far enough: the move she elegantly performs with respect to the *state* can and should be reproduced with respect to *sovereignty*. While the juridical doctrine of sovereignty, taken as a description of the nature of power, may well be a false or incomplete representation, it is nevertheless a potent representation within the modern political imaginary—one which, whatever its truth-value, affects the formation of political subjects through exactly those productive mechanisms of power to which Foucault so effectively draws our attention. Indeed, as I shall suggest, it is difficult to grasp the role of the state in the politics of identity and difference *without* taking sovereignty, in this specific sense, into account: as one of the defining projects of the modern state-form, the aspiration to sovereignty is part of what animates the state, helping determine exactly *how* its powers—or, more precisely, the powers that it channels, and out of which it is organized—are deployed.[78] The "king's head" is, we might say, a phantom limb—a nonentity, but a consequential one.

But what are those consequences? What picture of the state's role in the politics of recognition arises from this approach to sovereignty? As I have already indicated, the foregoing argument suggests that characterizations of the state as sovereign are implicated in the same underlying misrecognition—in the sense of a failure of acknowledgment—that I have ascribed to the politics of recognition more generally. However, states' claims to sovereignty are also typically different from other moves made within the politics of recognition in two respects, both of which suggest that these state claims may demand special critical attention. First, they are less often perceived *as* demands for recognition than are, say, the claims of subordinated people and groups, which are already socially marked as "particular" and therefore do not enjoy the privilege of appearing pre- or extrapolitical in the way the idea of state sovereignty, among others, so frequently does. Second, and relatedly, the political encounter between a state and an emergent political constituency demanding an end to some injustice in relations of identity and difference is, typically, highly asymmetrical. This is in large part because the state, while not necessarily truly sovereign in the way it purports to be, nevertheless does command extensive social and political resources; and it does so partly by virtue of the fact that it can usually draw upon a history of relatively stabilized relations of recognition—relations from which it derives authority and power—with other, often much larger and more powerful constituencies. For this reason, it will often be able to set the terms of exchanges of recognition, creating incentives for people to frame their claims about justice in ways that abet rather than undermine the project of state sovereignty.

What this means will depend upon how sovereignty is imagined and pursued at any particular time, and, as I have emphasized before, this may vary. Individual agents can anchor the project of sovereign agency in the idea of context-transcending choice, but they need not do so: they may also anchor that project in the ideal of the reciprocal knowledge of and respect for one's own and others' identities. Similarly, a state can anchor its claim to sovereignty in the thought that it embodies or represents the will of a unified and homogeneous people, but it need not do so: it may also anchor that claim in a picture of the state as an agency that effectively renders "legible," administers, and controls a field of potentially unruly social differences.[79] The first strategy is a familiar part of the ideology of the modern nation-state, and it has many variations, depending upon where the relevant sort of homogeneity is located: in race, ethnicity, culture, religion, language, history, ideas, or some seductive mixture of these; typically, it creates incentives for constituencies protesting injustice to frame their claims in terms that emphasize their fundamental similarity to, or identity with, dominant groups. (The politics of Jewish emancipation, in chapter 5, will provide us with an extended example of this dynamic.) The second strategy, though not a recent innovation, has nevertheless become an increasingly prominent part of the legitimating ideology of contemporary multicultural states, which, often precisely in response to criticisms of the assimilationist tendencies of modern nationalism, has made the recognition of difference into an instrument of, rather than a threat to, sovereignty. And if the nationalist version of the project of sovereignty creates incentives toward assimilation, the multicultural version—as we shall see in chapter 6—creates incentives for people to frame claims about justice *as* claims for recognition on behalf of identifiable groups. That mode of address, after all, furthers the state's project of rendering the social world "legible" and governable: to appeal to the state *for* the recognition of one's own identity—to present oneself as knowable—is already to offer the state the reciprocal recognition of its sovereignty that it demands.

But there is a complication: as I have indicated, while states may be disproportionately powerful actors in many respects, they can no more achieve the sovereignty they seek, and that others seek through them, than can individuals. (This impossibility is already manifest in the fact that states depend upon their subjects, as well as other states, to recognize their sovereignty—a dependence that ironically undercuts the very condition of *in*dependence it is supposed to sustain.[80]) And this contradiction within the project of state sovereignty troubles efforts to secure emancipation from structures of social subordination by appealing to states for recognition, for, as I have suggested, such relations of subordination can themselves be understood as ways of finessing such contradictions, of insulating some agents from the experience of finitude by distributing the consequences of that shared condition unevenly over social space. Thus, even those exchanges of recognition that express a spirit of inclusion—such as Jewish emancipation or contemporary multiculturalism—deal, at best, with the symptoms and effects of subordination, while simultaneously working to reproduce the problematic aspiration to sovereign agency in which those effects are rooted. At times, this may mean that existing relations of injustice will be preserved or even reinforced, albeit cloaked in a superficial layer of reform. Alternatively, even when these exchanges substantially transform relations of identity and difference, improving the conditions of life for at least some members of subordinated groups, such improvements may nevertheless be conditioned on other, sometimes novel ways of stratifying the social world, which still distribute vulnerability and dependence unequally—although, just as the course of a river usually changes slowly, even new relations of subordination will frequently follow the rough contours of old ones, precisely because existing patterns of power influence but do not determine the trajectory of social and political transformation.

Still, it is not only socially subordinate groups who have cause for concern about exchanges of recognition with the state. *Everyone* risks something in such an encounter, though under present circumstances some risk much more than others. To understand why, consider the hypothetical limit-case of a state that recognizes and is recognized as sovereign by all of its citizens equally—an inclusive and egalitarian state that manages and administers identity in such a way that race, sex, nationality, and other familiar axes of social difference no longer underwrite systematic inequalities in the distribution of resources and respect. There is one line of social differentiation, and one form of subordination, that such a hypothetical state could *not* overcome while retaining its claim to sovereignty—and that is the distinction between state and society itself, the founding cut through which one set of institutions is carved out of the web of human interaction and elevated to a position of supposed independence from, and superiority over, the rest. In the end, the putatively sovereign state cannot help us escape the difficulties that plague the politics of recognition, not just because *its* desire for sovereignty feeds relations of subordination that are external to it, but even more soberingly because such a state is itself a relation of subordination, fed by our own desire to find a kind of agency we cannot possess on our own in the experience of belonging to a larger whole. To exchange the uncertain risks and pleasures of activity for the satisfactions of identification with those who rule us: as Tocqueville knew, this is a tempting bargain, and a deadening one.[81]

THE POLITICS OF ACKNOWLEDGMENT

What could justice in relations of identity and difference mean, if not the equal recognition of the identities of all? The alternative tradition of thought I reconstruct in this book points us toward a politics oriented toward what I call *acknowledgment* rather than recognition.[82] Yet this distinction requires some explanation, since in ordinary language the words "acknowledge" and "recognize" are used nearly, if not completely, interchangeably. To conclude this chapter, then, I shall spell out four important features of the conception of acknowledgment that emerges over the course of this book, and which distinguish it from conventional understandings of recognition. And I shall do so in conversation with a few other contemporary political theorists and philosophers who are also trying to open up alternatives to the politics of recognition, or who are using the term "acknowledgment" in distinctive ways, or both.

As I noted earlier, James Tully has recently suggested that we reconceive the politics of recognition as an ongoing process, the value of which lies in the fact that it enables citizens to engage in shared political activity, quite apart from the political "end-states" this activity might produce.[83] This shift, he says, also requires us to reconceive the stakes of this activity. While the end-state model focuses exclusively on the good of recognition, which involves having one's specific identity claims affirmed by others, the activity model highlights the distinctive good he calls "acknowledgment," which consists simply in being treated as a co-participant in an ongoing political process, in being heard and responded to, even when the response to one's claims is partly or wholly negative. While acknowledgment without victory may not seem like much, Tully argues that mere participation in the "game of reciprocal disclosure and acknowledgment" can dispel potentially dangerous *ressentiment*, generate "self-respect and self-esteem," and produce a "sense of belonging to and identification with the larger political society" in the same way that players of a sport, even through their losses, become attached to the game itself.[84]

Tully's effort to recast the politics of recognition as an ongoing activity is welcome and in many respects persuasive. At the same time, it remains unclear whether acknowledgment in his sense is really much different from recognition. The distinction between them is most plausible as long as we stay with the image of political activity as a game, for in the context of games, we are accustomed to distinguishing sharply between activity and outcome, procedure and substance, participation and success. But the maxim "it's not whether you win or lose" only goes so far, especially in politics. It is easiest to suck up a loss when one's very status as a player is not at stake in the game itself; yet because *political* belonging is ultimately worked out precisely on the field of politics, winning or losing—what Tully calls recognition—may sometimes make all the difference to the supposedly prior, procedural question of participation—what Tully calls acknowledgment.[85] Similarly, losing at politics once may leave an actor disappointed but unshaken in his sense of belonging to the community of participants, but after months, years, or decades of *persistent* loss at the game of politics, people may rightly wonder whether they're really being allowed to play in any meaningful way.[86] And the politics of recognition as we have come to know it often operates precisely at these intersections between activity and outcome. Recognition claims are commonly claims about what forms of respect for people's identities are needed if they are to be meaningfully included as participants in the game of politics at all; that is, they are claims about what counts as acknowledgment in Tully's sense. But if being acknowledged turns out to *mean* being recognized—that is, being known and respected in virtue of who one is, so that one can feel oneself fully included in the game of politics—then we are squarely back in the end-state, identity-oriented version of the politics of recognition that Tully—rightly—wants to challenge.[87]

Part of the reason for acknowledgment's semantic slide back into recognition, I think, is that in Tully's use of the word, acknowledgment is still fundamentally about, and oriented toward, others. Against this background, Stanley Cavell's different use of the word "acknowledgment" is especially useful. His conception of acknowledgment is elaborated in the context of the problem of skepticism in our relations to the world and, especially, to other people; and for him, the important contrast is not between recognition and acknowledgment, but between *knowledge* and acknowledgement.[88] For Cavell, we are badly mistaken if we treat practical failures in our relations to others as failures of knowledge, for to cast the issue in epistemological terms in this way is to stake justice itself on an impossibly conclusive resolution of the perpetual problem of skepticism about our knowledge of "other minds."[89] What matters in our relation to another, Cavell suggests, is not knowing something special about him, or knowing him (his pain, pleasure, humanity, character, or very being) in a way that could evade doubt once and for all. What matters, instead, is *what we do* in the presence of the other, how we respond to or act in the light of what we *do* know.[90] *That* is acknowledgment, or its failure: as Cavell says, characterizing Othello's refusal to acknowledge Desdemona, "he knew everything, but could not yield to what he knew, be commanded by it."[91]

Of course, the notion of recognition itself, as developed by Taylor, Tully, and others, already incorporates part of what Cavell means by "acknowledgment." For Cavell, acknowledgment is different from but not opposed to knowledge, for it involves acting on and responding to what we know. And that intersection between the order of knowledge and the order of practice is exactly what political theorists have captured by treating "recognition" as at once a kind of cognition *and* a kind of respect: Axel Honneth's recent argument that recognition involves something "added to the perception of a person"—namely, an "affirmation"—makes this point clearly.[92] But Cavell's move from knowledge to acknowledgment involves more than this. It is not just a move of supplementation, in which something belonging to a different order—the order of normativity—is added to, and articulated onto, knowledge. It is also a move that aims to change our understanding of the relevant "knowledge" itself: of what it means to know, and of what kind of knowledge we need to have in order to take the further step of acknowledging others.[93] And one important part of this change is expressed in Cavell's work by a shift in his characterization of the object and, if you will, the *direction* of that knowledge. At least in some of his formulations, to acknowledge another is in the first instance to respond to, to act in the light of, something about *oneself*; and conversely, the failure of acknowledgment, the "avoidance" of the other, is crucially a distortion of one's own self-relation, an avoidance of something unbearable about oneself.[94] Thus, on Cavell's reading of *King Lear*, what eventually enables acknowledgment is not the discovery of something about the other—about Cordelia or Edgar—but self-insight on the part of Lear and Gloucester.[95]

I have tried to capture this thought—that what draws us to or bars us from a just relation to others is, in many instances at least, not the state of our knowledge of them, but the state of our understanding of ourselves—in the first feature of my use of "acknowledgment": although the presence or absence of acknowledgment may have important implications for others, the direct object of acknowledgment is not the other, as in the case of recognition; it is, instead, something about the *self*.[96] (This change of direction is analogous to the shift I have already described from a conception of injustice that focuses on its significance for those who suffer it, to one that focuses on its meaning for those who commit it.) But this, on its own, is not enough: it is equally important to make clear that acknowledgment is not fundamentally the acknowledgment of one's own *identity*. And here, Cavell's language and examples sometimes invite misunderstanding.

In *The Claim of Reason*, for example, Cavell illustrates the notion of acknowledgment with reference to relationally defined social roles: "if one is to acknowledge another as one's neighbor, one must acknowledge oneself as his or her neighbor"; "one acknowledges one's teacher by acknowledging oneself as his or her student."[97] In these examples, however, acknowledging oneself becomes a matter of recognizing oneself under a certain description, as the bearer of a certain social identity, as if acknowledging yourself as a neighbor sufficed to tell you what to do, how to respond to this other person, who has herself now been fixed in your social imagination as a neighbor (or, in a slightly different example, as a stranger, or an enemy . . .). Yet this slide back into the register of recognition overlooks the possibility that such exchanges of recognition, such cartographic imaginings of the identities of self and other, may *themselves* be strategies of avoidance—that is, that they may manifest a refusal to acknowledge not one's own identity, exactly, but one's own ontological situation.[98] The second feature of my conception of acknowledgment responds to this problem. On my view, what's acknowledged in an act of acknowledgment is not one's own identity—at least not as the politics of recognition conceives of identity: a coherent self-description that can serve as the ground of agency, guiding or determining what we are to do. Rather, acknowledgment is directed at the basic conditions of one's own existence and activity, including, crucially, the *limits* of "identity" as a ground of action, limits which arise out of our constitutive vulnerability to the unpredictable reactions and responses of others.[99] As an avowal of one's own finitude, acknowledgment in this sense is (as Cavell says and as Hegel will dramatically demonstrate) a sort of abdication.[100]

This mention of finitude brings us to the third important feature of my conception of acknowledgment, which can be explained somewhat more briefly. To speak of acknowledging one's own limits rather than recognizing the identity of the other may seem to imply a retreat into the self, a refusal to engage with others out of the conviction that one cannot know anything about them, or that to aspire toward knowledge would inevitably involve domination or distortion.[101] The point here, however, is *not* to insist upon the unknowability of others: to conceive of finitude in these fundamentally epistemological terms would simply return us to the dialectic of skepticism and antiskepticism from which Cavell and others have been trying to detach questions of ethics.[102] Finitude as I conceive it is not epistemological but practical: it is not a matter of knowledge per se, but of what we can expect our knowledge of others to do for us—that is, of whether knowledge of others (or of ourselves, for that matter) can be expected to serve as the ground of sovereign agency, of a posture of mastery and invulnerability in the face of the future. And, importantly, acknowledging this sort of finitude can easily be a matter of having *more* knowledge, not less. While utter strangers can remind us of the unpredictability and contingency of social interaction, so can the people we know best—the people whom we know not as character-types, but as deep, rich, tense, and messy lives in progress. Of course, this does not mean knowing others is always easy, or that trying is always appropriate, or that knowledge can never be placed in the service of, or even constitute, power. Sometimes acknowledgment *might* best be expressed in the admission that you don't know, or in the withdrawal from interaction, or in the acceptance of another's refusal to respond to a curious inquiry. But these are possibilities, not necessities; they demand judgment in particular ethical and political contexts, rather than a priori declarations about the impossibility or injustice of knowledge (or, conversely, about its inevitability or goodness).[103]

Fourth and finally, just as it is important not to treat acknowledgment as an expression of skepticism or as requiring the refusal of interaction, it is equally important not to invest the concept with more ambitious hopes for the redemption of human relations from the full range of experiences that can make social life unpleasant or difficult to bear. To take one instructive example: in a recent critique of the paradigm of recognition, Kelly Oliver has argued in favor of an alternative model of ethics and politics that she calls "witnessing," which overlaps in some respects with what I am calling acknowledgment. For Oliver, witnessing is neither a matter of recognizing the identity of the other, nor of recognizing the identity of the self; instead, it is a matter of experiencing and responding to one's connection to and dependence upon others—including, crucially, bearing witness to, and acting responsibly in the face of, the ways in which one's relation to others has been shaped by injustice.[104] This is a compelling argument; at the same time, Oliver's image of a social world characterized by mutual witnessing is ambitious in ways that undermine her own best insights. In the course of drawing her distinction between recognition and witnessing, for example, Oliver suggests that in a world structured by recognition, relations among people are characterized by, among other things, hostility, conflict, alienation, opposition, domination, oppression, trauma, threat, objectification, the "harsh or accusing stare," war, and sacrifice. By contrast, in a world structured by witnessing, relations among people are characterized by love, compassion, connection, responsiveness, positive attention, the "caress," psychic wholeness, generosity, joy, peacefulness, and democraticness.[105] But do all of the terms in each of these chains of association belong together? And is the first chain straightforwardly opposed to the second?

There is good reason to doubt, for example, that conflict is necessarily a sign of domination or oppression, even if domination or oppression is one way in which people try to resolve conflicts to their own advantage. Indeed, conflict itself may be an important feature of democratic politics, both a byproduct of the flourishing of individuality within a political community and a useful tool of public deliberation. By the same token, sacrifice may be an unavoidable feature of political life in a world characterized by limited resources or simply by substantial disagreement; hostility may be part and parcel of loving relationships, testimony to the intensity of the connection between (or among) people; and alienation may be a healthy attitude and a source of critical insight and leverage for people living—as we all do—under laws that are, at best, only partly of our own making.[106] If Oliver's wager is that all of these supposedly negative features of social life go together, and that they all can be eliminated through witnessing, my wager is that the risk or possibility of *some* of these experiences is not only a permanent feature of social life but also one worth affirming; and that the desire to overcome that risk has itself helped to sustain many serious forms of social and political injustice. So while the cultivation of acknowledgment may be a valuable part of struggles against injustice and subordination in social relations, I do not expect acknowledgment to replace hostility with love or alienation with connection; indeed, I think the modesty of acknowledgment in this regard is also its strength.

Sum

So acknowledgment is in the first instance self- rather than other-directed; its object is not one's own identity but one's own basic ontological condition or circumstances, particularly one's own finitude; this finitude is to be understood as a matter of one's practical limits in the face of an unpredictable and contingent future, not as a matter of the impossibility or injustice of knowing others; and, finally, acknowledgment involves coming to terms with, rather than vainly attempting to overcome, the risk of conflict, hostility, misunderstanding, opacity, and alienation that characterizes life among others. These four features of acknowledgment are, of course, very abstract, and they do not tell us what acknowledgment looks like—but, importantly, there is no general answer to this question, in the same way that there is no general answer to the question of what moderation or justice looks like. Acknowledgment *can* be expressed in a wide range of acts and practices—taking a risk, withdrawing, speaking, listening, welcoming, polemicizing, claiming a right, refusing to claim a right, mourning, celebrating, forgiving, punishing—yet it is reducible to none of these, and none of these is, as such, an instance or mark of acknowledgment: everything depends on how and why they are done, and in what contexts.[107] I shall return to the question of acknowledgment, and its conditions of possibility, in the conclusion; for now, it is time to bring this synopsis to a close and to get the argument under way.

CHAPTER TWO

The Distinguishing Mark
Taylor, Herder, and Sovereignty

> Recognition is par excellence the vehicle of nostalgia. It invests
> in securities, moral, legal, social, political; it parades before us
> the ghosts of all we ever wanted and always failed quite to
> grasp and hold.
>
> — TERENCE CAVE, *Recognitions*

TWO USES OF "RECOGNITION"

IN 1992, THE EMINENT CANADIAN philosopher and political theorist
Charles Taylor published an influential essay on the theoretical foundations of identity politics, which moved deftly between the history of
European philosophy and late-twentieth-century political controversies
over such issues as multiculturalism in higher education and nationalism
in Québec. Taylor proposed that many contemporary social and political movements can be understood as struggles for recognition—that is,
as attempts to secure forms of respect and esteem that are grounded in,
and expressive of, the accurate knowledge of the particular identities
borne by people and social groups.[1]

But what, exactly, *is* recognition? Taylor's essay, like many subsequent theoretical discussions of the same themes, is haunted by a little-
noticed tension between two crucially different uses of the term.[2] Consider the ordinary uses of the word. On the one hand, we frequently use
"recognition" in ways that accent its relationship to knowledge. For
instance, "recognition" can refer to a re-*cognition* of something once
known but lately hidden, forgotten, or absent: I put a name to the face
of an old friend; I remember having been in this place before. Similarly—and more importantly for the purposes of ethics and politics—
"recognition" can refer to a kind of conduct or action that flows from,
and manifests, what we perceive or know of other people or the world.
Recognizing my friend is not just a matter of cognition, for that flash of
familiarity leads me to do things differently: to stop and say hello rather
than walking by in anonymity; to respond with particular generosity to
my friend's appeal for help; or to take special pleasure in her account of
how well her life has gone since our last meeting. In this first sense, then,
recognition brings together cognition and evaluation: it is a matter both

of seeing who someone is and of affirming (or negating) what we see, of letting that knowledge matter to our conduct in one way or another.[3]

On the other hand, we sometimes (though less commonly) use "recognition" to refer not to our awareness of, or responsiveness to, some antecedent state of affairs, but to an act that brings something new into being, or that transforms the world in some way. For example, we say that the chairperson of a meeting recognizes a speaker; but this does not mean that she is merely manifesting her awareness of a status that already really exists—though it may look that way when only one person at a time raises a hand. Instead, the privilege of speaking is itself a product of the chairperson's institutionally authorized act of recognition: by calling on someone, she makes that person into "the one who has the floor."[4] This second sense of "recognition" will be particularly familiar to scholars of international relations, where there has been a long-standing debate about the relationship between the practice of recognition among states and the condition of statehood: while some theorists insist that states are states prior to their recognition as such, others argue that the recognition of a state is more like the chairperson's act of calling on a person to speak: it does not simply perceive and respond to an existing condition, but rather brings "statehood" into being.[5]

The first of these ordinary uses of "recognition," with its accent on cognition, is a prominent feature of Taylor's essay. Unlike toleration, which can be grudging, and is consistent with utter ignorance about the people to whom it is extended, recognition involves respecting people precisely in virtue of, not despite, who they are; and so proper relations of recognition must be founded on accurate mutual knowledge among the people and groups involved. Hence Taylor's emphasis on the notion of authenticity, drawn from Herder, among others. Each of us, Taylor suggests, has an "authentic" identity—"my own particular way of being," as he puts it—and so, too, do the cultures and nations to which we belong.[6] These authentic identities are the forgotten, ignored, suppressed, or distorted truths that movements for recognition struggle to bring into the light of publicity. As Anthony Appiah puts it in a response to Taylor, to be recognized successfully is "to be acknowledged publicly as what [we] *already really are*."[7]

The prominence of this first, cognitive sense of recognition in Taylor's essay has frequently provoked the charge that he embraces a problematic "essentialism" or "primordialism," obscuring the complexity of personal and social identity, and neglecting the ongoing social and political dynamics through which identities are formed and transformed.[8] There is something to this claim, as we shall see—but my aim in this chapter is *not* simply to repeat familiar constructionist attacks on Taylor, for these do not do justice to the complexity of his work, and therefore miss what

is most interesting—and most puzzling—about the politics of recognition.[9] For while Taylor does use "recognition" in its cognitive sense,
referring to an expression of respect grounded in the accurate perception
of an independently existing identity, he also uses "recognition" in its
second, constructive sense, treating recognition not as a knowing but
as a doing, which—like the chairperson's recognition of the speaker—
actively constitutes the identities of those to whom it is addressed.[10] As
Taylor says, "my own identity crucially depends on my dialogical relations with others," and this is why, on his view, misrecognition is such
a serious form of injury: it oppresses by molding identity itself, "impris-
oning someone in a false, distorted, and reduced mode of being."[11]

The point of this observation is not to rescue Taylor from his critics
by finding redemptive moments of anti-essentialism in his work. Nor
do I claim that he has somehow produced a satisfying philosophical
reconciliation of these two senses of "recognition," for although they
exist side by side in Taylor's work, they do so uneasily, and even when
the fault line between them comes close to the surface of his essay, he
does not comment explicitly on the tension, but instead shifts abruptly
from one to the other.[12] Yet I also do not intend to dismiss Taylor on
the grounds of inconsistency. To the contrary, I find Taylor's essay en-
gaging and useful precisely because of the tensions in which it is caught,
for they are philosophically and politically significant tensions, ripe for
interpretation, which can teach us something about the discourse of recognition more broadly. Thus, instead of trying to work out whether
Taylor is *really* an essentialist—the answer to that question will always
turn out to be "yes and no"—I ask: what is the meaning of Taylor's
oscillation between the cognitive and constructive senses of "recognition"? Why does he embrace, at some points, a view of identities as
antecedently given facts about us that, at other times, he seems to disavow? How, if at all, does he try to negotiate this tension? What are its
consequences?

Just as pulling on a loose string can begin to unravel a whole garment,
pursuing these questions through Taylor's work will begin to open up
some of the larger philosophical and political issues that surround the
politics of recognition. The first and most fundamental of these is the
question of the relationship between human agency and identity—which
was one of the issues that drew Taylor to the theme of recognition in
the first place. For Taylor, one of the defining features of human agency
is that we are irreducibly implicated in what he calls "strong evaluation"—that is, we rely, implicitly or explicitly, on discriminations between good and bad objects of desire, or right and wrong courses of
action, that cannot be reduced to expressions of subjective preference, or
to quantitative comparisons of utility.[13] This helps explain why agency is

crucially connected to, even rooted in, identity; for identity is what we draw on and express when we engage in this sort of evaluation. When someone responds to the question "who are you?" by saying "a Catholic" or "a Québécois," Taylor tells us, "what they are saying by this is not just that they are strongly attached to this spiritual view or background; rather it is that this provides the frame within which they can determine where they stand on questions of what is good, or worthwhile, or admirable, or of value."[14] Hence "to know who you are is to be oriented in moral space"; likewise, to have an "identity crisis" is to "lack a frame or horizon within which things can take on a stable significance, within which some life possibilities can be seen as good or meaningful, others as bad or trivial."[15] For Taylor, the politics of recognition responds to this deep connection between agency and identity: you might say that it seeks to overcome a particular, socially induced kind of identity crisis—the kind that arises when the refusal of recognition by some prevents others from living in and acting on the basis of who they are. This sort of misrecognition, Taylor says, "shows not just a lack of due respect. It can inflict a grievous wound, saddling its victims with a crippling self-hatred." Correspondingly, "due recognition is not just a courtesy we owe people. It is a vital human need."[16]

In what follows, I shall argue that the tension between the cognitive and constructive senses of recognition that I have described is the symptom of a serious problem in this view of the relationship between agency and identity. Perhaps surprisingly, I shall also argue that Taylor himself is his own best critic on this point. But to understand why, we will need to place Taylor's recognition essay into conversation with some of his other work, including especially his philosophical essays on language, agency, and identity, as well as his important engagements with the thought of Johann Gottfried Herder, who has been one of Taylor's most important intellectual touchstones. In these contexts, Taylor has argued persuasively that certain important theories of language, mind, action, and politics are underwritten (and undermined) by an attractive but ultimately impossible aspiration to achieve a kind of masterful or sovereign agency. For Taylor, the paradigmatic expressions of this aspiration are those modern theories that conceive of agency as "disengagement," including, among others, designative theories of language, behaviorist models of human action, and, in political thought, "atomist" versions of liberalism. By contrast, Taylor identifies perspectives such as Herder's philosophy of language and the politics of recognition as representatives of an alternative modern tradition that escapes the seductions of sovereignty, affirming instead that human agency is always embedded within, and dependent upon, larger social contexts. Taylor's critique of agency as disengagement is compelling enough, but his effort to reconstruct an alternative tradition is less persuasive. The trouble is that Taylor mistakes one strategy for the pursuit of sovereignty—the strategy of disengagement—for the aspiration *per se*, and so he overlooks the ways in which that aspiration reasserts itself, though in a different form, precisely within accounts of human agency as engaged, including Herder's philosophy of language, as well as his own reconstruction of the politics of recognition.

I begin to spell out this argument in the next section by unpacking Taylor's critique of the aspiration to sovereignty, focusing in particular on his interventions into the philosophy of language. I then turn to one of Taylor's own most important sources, Herder's *Essay on the Origin of Language*, developing a reading of this text, both on its own and against the background of some of Herder's other works, that diverges from Taylor's in two ways. First, I focus explicitly on the theme of recognition in Herder's *Essay*. Although Taylor does not draw this connection himself, Herder's *Essay* turns out to be centered around a mythic recognition scene, which involves the discovery—or is it the creation?—of the "distinguishing mark" that identifies a certain animal to the human being who first speaks its name. The ambiguity of this distinguishing mark, suspended between being the object of an act of cognition and being the result of a constructive act of naming, precisely mirrors the tension between the cognitive and constructive senses of the term "recognition" in Taylor's essay on multiculturalism, and in the discourse of recognition more broadly. Second, by focusing on the ways in which Herder negotiates this tension, I show that his account of language does not overcome but rather reproduces the attractive but impossible ideal of sovereign agency that Taylor rightly criticizes. Finally, in the last sections, I extend this same critique to Taylor's work, tracking unnoticed similarities between his understanding of recognition and Herder's. Profoundly sensitive to the vulnerability and fragility that afflicts human agency by virtue of its intersubjective embeddedness, the politics of recognition—like Herder's account of language—nevertheless responds to that vulnerability not by acknowledging its constitutive place in human life, but by dreaming, against its own best insights, that it might one day be overcome.

Taylor on Agency and Language

Charles Taylor's engagement with multiculturalism and nationalism in the 1990s did not break with, but grew out of, certain long-standing philosophical preoccupations. In his introduction to his two volumes of *Philosophical Papers*, Taylor gives a brief account of the "single rather tightly related agenda" that drives the essays in that collection, which were originally published between 1967 and 1984. His purpose, he says, is to criticize efforts to understand "human life and action" in terms drawn from a certain version of the philosophy of the natural sciences.[17] That version of natural science was characterized by a posture of disengagement toward its objects, which were to be investigated and known not as they are for us, but as they are in and of themselves. Applied to human life and action, this naturalist posture of disengagement helped lead philosophers and social scientists into a range of follies, from Cartesian dualism to utilitarianism, from designative theories of language to reductionist accounts of action, from behaviorism to the effort to create artificial intelligence.[18]

Importantly, Taylor says that he is not setting out simply to refute these theories. He also wants to "give an account of his adversary's motivation in hermeneutical terms"; that is, he wants to understand why naturalism has had such a hold on the modern imagination. His answer is that naturalism rests on "a certain picture of the human agent" that is "deeply attractive to moderns, both flattering and inspiring." That model of the agent idealizes "the ability to act on one's own, without outside interference or subordination to outside authority," and it ties this ability to the "ideals of efficacy, power, [and] unperturbability."[19] Ironically, even as naturalism treats human action objectively, as a matter of laws and necessities, it does so in order to secure a kind of agent- and context-independent knowledge, thereby feeding a modern fantasy of achieving a kind of sovereignty through disengagement.[20]

The implications of Taylor's critique of naturalism are not confined to the philosophy of the social sciences, but extend into political philosophy as well, for, on Taylor's view, certain key aspects of liberalism are also grounded in naturalist ontological premises.[21] As Taylor explains, naturalism's idea of "the disengaged identity and its attendant notion of freedom tend to generate an understanding of the individual as metaphysically independent of society."[22] This premise of the metaphysical independence or self-sufficiency of individuals—what Taylor calls "atomism"—serves, he says, as the foundation for many of the familiar features of modern liberalism, including its contractarianism, its insistence upon the priority of the right over the good, its demand that the state remain neutral among different conceptions of the good, and its proceduralism.[23]

Against atomism, Taylor attempts to draw our attention to "the way in which an individual is constituted by the language and culture which can only be maintained and renewed in the communities he is part of."[24] For Taylor, this shift in ontology need not imply granting political priority to collective purposes at the expense of individual liberty, but it does require understanding the liberal goods of autonomy and freedom as social accomplishments, formed in and supported by the cultures, histories, and institutions of particular political communities.[25] And doing that, he thinks, will involve surrendering or at least moderating the admittedly "flattering and inspiring" image of human agency that atomism and other forms of naturalism present, which offers us the hope of rising above all those particular attachments, casting off our "superstition in some code imposed by tradition, society, or fate," and becoming wholly self-sufficient, independent choosers.[26] The politics of recognition, you might say, emerged as a pluralist variation on this original, "communitarian" critique of liberalism, with the "identity" taking the place of "community" as the preferred vocabulary for thinking about the contexts in which human agents are inevitably embedded.[27]

For Taylor, perhaps the most important manifestation of the fact that we are engaged, embedded agents is that we are language users—a conviction that is powerfully expressed both in his long-standing concern with the politics of Canadian federalism and Québécois nationalism, and in his admiration for Herder, who also placed language at the center of his understanding of human identity.[28] Thus it will be instructive to focus on the details of Taylor's critique of the notion of disengaged agency in the context of the philosophy of language, where that critique takes the form of an attack on designative views of language and meaning.[29]

Designative views of meaning propose that "words get their meaning from being used to designate objects."[30] On this view, Taylor says, "we give the meaning of a sign or a word by pointing to the things or relations that they can be used to refer to or talk about."[31] Of course, Taylor does not deny that "designation" is among the important uses to which words can be put. Yet designative theories of language make this correlation between word and thing into the "fundamental" aspect of language, the very source and essence of meaning.[32] And since the correlation between word and thing is an observable, external relationship, designative theories of language account for meaning in ways that remain entirely indifferent to the first-personal perspective of language users, and which therefore threaten to reduce meaning and understanding to matters of behavior, of the effective production of and response to signals. On these accounts, "a rat who learns to get the cheese by going through the door with the red triangle" might be said to "understand" the triangle rightly, to have gotten its meaning.[33] By contrast, Taylor insists that human language may be distinguished from animal signaling by the phenomenon of "rightness," which "can't be explained in terms of success in a task not itself linguistically defined," but instead requires reference to the first-personal perspectives of language users.[34] Taylor explains:

A creature is operating in the linguistic dimension when it can use and respond to signs in terms of their truth, or descriptive rightness, or power to evoke some mood, or recreate a scene, or express some emotion, or carry some nuance of feeling, or in some such way to be *le mot juste*. To be a linguistic creature is to be sensitive to irreducible issues of rightness.... Whether a creature is in the linguistic dimension in this sense isn't a matter of what correlations hold between the signals it emits, its behavior, and the surroundings—the kinds of things the proponents of chimp language focus on. It is a question of subjective understanding, of what rightness consists in *for it*.[35]

Here, as elsewhere, Taylor's goal is not simply to refute one version or another of naturalism, but also to explain the hold it exercises over us. Taylor offers two explanations of the persistence of designative theories of language. First, such theories are difficult to displace because they accord with our everyday experience of language, in which the relationship of signification seems "built into" our words. The "linguistic dimension" and the experience of "rightness" may indeed make it *possible* for us to use words to designate things, but this fundamental fact tends to fade into "the background of our action"; it is "something we usually lean on without noticing."[36] Second, in keeping with what he says about his broader agenda, Taylor suggests that the invisibility of the "linguistic dimension" is compounded by the fact that designative theories of language serve to reinforce an appealing vision of sovereign agency.[37] For language theorists of the seventeenth and eighteenth centuries like Hobbes, Locke, and Condillac, Taylor says, language "is an instrument of control" which helps us "marshal ideas" and so to gain "knowledge of the world" to which those ideas correspond. In order to serve effectively as an instrument of control in this way, language and meaning "must be perfectly transparent." Happily, if meaning is simply a matter of designation, then this transparency may be within our reach, at least as long as we exercise the proper degree of care in defining and employing words.

> That is why theorists of this period constantly, almost obsessionally, stress the importance of recurring to definitions, of checking always to see that our words are well-defined, that we use them consistently. The alternative is to lose control, to slip into a kind of slavery; where it is no longer I who make my lexicon, by definitional fiat, but rather it takes shape independently and in doing this shapes my thought.[38]

Against this aspiration to mastery, Taylor insists that language can never be a source of sovereignty in this way, and this is so for two reasons. First, as language users, we always find ourselves implicated in a "wider matrix of language" that we did not create and which escapes our governance. "Because the words we use now only have sense through their place in the whole web," Taylor says, "we can never in principle have a clear oversight of the implications of what we say at any moment. Our language is always more than we can encompass; it is in a sense inexhaustible."[39] And, second, because the use of language is itself a form of creative and unpredictable action, language itself "is open to being continuously recreated in speech, continually extended, altered, reshaped" by people who "strai[n] the limits of expression," and who "never fully know" what the results of their innovations will be. Language is "activity, not realized work"; it is "*energeia*, not *ergon*," and as such it cannot be pinned down in the way that designative language theorists had hoped.[40] For both reasons, "the aspiration to be in no degree at all a prisoner of language, so dear to Hobbes and Locke, is in principle unrealizable."[41]

Over the years, Taylor has repeatedly invoked Johann Gottfried Herder as an ally in his struggle against the hegemony of designative theories of language.[42] Taylor argues that Herder brings the "linguistic dimension" of human existence into focus, and thereby marks a momentous transformation in the philosophy of language. Rather than treating language as a matter of effective *signaling*, Taylor says, Herder investigates the hitherto neglected relationship of *signification* itself, asking how words come to stand for things in the first place. By attending to signification, which is usually taken for granted as "the background of our action," Herder helps bring the neglected phenomenon of "irreducible linguistic rightness" into view.[43] To illustrate this point, Taylor quotes extensively from a fable Herder tells in the *Essay on the Origin of Language* about the origin of signification. Yet this fable *also* turns out to be centered around the idea of recognition, and reading it through this lens gives us a view of Herder that is subtly but significantly different from Taylor's portrait.[44] This view of Herder will, in turn, help us make some unexpected connections between Taylor's critique of the aspiration of sovereignty and his work on the politics of recognition.

"Ha! You're the Bleating One!"

In late 1770, the young Johann Gottfried Herder entered an essay in a prize contest sponsored by the Berlin Academy of Sciences on the subject of the origin of language. The contest had its roots in a controversy years earlier between two scholars, Maupertius and Süßmilch, over the question of whether human beings developed language naturally, through the gradual refinement of instinctive, animal cries and sounds, or received it through divine instruction.[45] Herder's *Essay on the Origin of Language* won the Berlin Academy's prize, becoming, for better or worse, "one of the best-known and most important works in the history of the study of language."[46] In the *Essay*, Herder insists, first, that human language is qualitatively different from the "language of nature"—the raw expression of instinct and feeling—that humans once shared with animals,[47] and that the origin of language therefore cannot lie in the gradual development of natural sounds into human words (a position represented in Herder's essay by Condillac rather than Maupertius).[48] But, second, Herder also refuses to infer from this the conclusion he attributes to Süßmilch—that language itself must have been given to mankind through direct divine instruction—for, Herder insists, the notion of receiving instruction already presupposes the existence of the very language it is being invoked to explain.[49] Instead, Herder offers his own account of the invention of the first word, which is centered around the naming of an animal.[50]

Imagine, Herder suggests, a human encountering a lamb. To other animals, the lamb would provoke merely instinctive responses: the "hungry, scenting wolf" and the "blood-lapping lion," for instance, would leap on the lamb and devour it.

> Not so with man! As soon as he feels the need to come to know the sheep, no instinct gets in his way; no one sense of his pulls him too close to it or too far away from it. It stands there, entirely as it manifests itself in his senses. White, soft, wooly—his soul in its reflective exercise seeks a distinguishing mark—*the sheep bleats!* His soul has found the distinguishing mark. The inner sense is at work. This bleating, which makes upon man's soul the strongest impression, which broke away from all the other qualities of vision and of touch, which sprang out and penetrated most deeply, the soul retains it. The sheep comes again. White, soft, wooly—the soul sees, touches, remembers, seeks a distinguishing mark—the sheep bleats, and the soul recognizes it. And it feels inside: "Ha! You're the bleating one!" . . . the sound of bleating perceived by a human soul as the distinguishing mark of the sheep became, by virtue of this reflection, the name of the sheep, even if his tongue had never tried to stammer it. . . . Language has been invented![51]

For Herder, this primordial linguistic act—the act of picking out the distinguishing mark of a thing—is an act of "recognition" (*anerkennen, Anerkenntnis*).[52] And, importantly, Herder's recognition scene expresses the tension between the cognitive and constructive senses of "recognition" in much the same way as does Taylor's essay on the politics of recognition.[53] On the one hand, recognizing the sheep seems to be a matter of correctly perceiving a certain characteristic that already really does distinguish the sheep from other animals, quite independently of our apprehension of that fact: the sheep's bleating, to put it in Taylor's terms, is its authentic identity. In Herder's description, the sheep's bleat-ing "makes an impression"; it "breaks away" from the other character-istics; it "springs out" and "penetrates" the human soul. On the other hand, Herder also assigns an essential constructive role to the human being's act of "reflection," through which he singles out the sheep's bleating *as* the distinguishing mark. The bleating of the sheep would be a meaningless sound absent the "seeking" and "perceiving" of the re-flective human being, who does not merely discover the sheep's name, but *names* the sheep; indeed, this story is in a sense a mythic account of the foundation of the whole practice of naming.[54] But what is the rela-tionship here between the distinguishing mark and the constructive act of naming? Is the sheep always already distinguished by its bleating? Does the human being distinguish the sheep by singling out its bleating? Is it—how can it be—both?

Herder's implicit response to these questions can be found in the way he fits this recognition scene into a larger narrative of the history of language and of humanity more broadly. Herder's plot follows a famil-iar triadic path—past wholeness; present dispersion; anticipated recon-ciliation—and, for Herder, it is an expression of divine providence. (Despite his rejection of Süßmilch's theory of divine instruction, Herder nevertheless did treat language as a divine gift, only in a less direct way: the invention of language, though it happened among and through men, nevertheless happened by virtue of certain divinely granted powers, and in accordance with God's larger purposes.[55]) Later in the *Essay*, for ex-ample, the figure of a providential God helps Herder resolve the question of the relationship between cognition and construction, at least in the *original* act of linguistic recognition. Here, Herder explicitly ties his ac-count of the birth of language to the story of Adam's naming of the animals in *Genesis* 2:19: "And God brought the animals unto the man to see what he would call them, and whatsoever the man called every living creature, that was the name thereof."[56] Herder's elaboration of the biblical passage is illuminating:

> The entire, multisonant, divine nature is man's teacher of language and man's muse. Past him it leads a procession of all creatures: Each one has its name on its tongue and introduces itself to this concealed yet visible god as a vassal and a servant. It delivers to him its distinguishing word to be entered, like a tribute, into the book of his dominion so that he may, by virtue of its name, remember it, call it in future, and enjoy it.[57]

Here, while Adam's act of recognition still seems to have some construc-tive power—"whatsoever the man called every living creature, that was the name thereof"—the outcome of his act of recognition has been or-dained in advance to produce the right result: each animal "introduces itself"; it already "has its name on its tongue" and "delivers its distinguishing word" to Adam, who then pronounces it, recognizing it as what it already, authentically is.

In this first stage in Herder's narrative of language, the cognitive and constructive senses of recognition work in perfect harmony. But the perfect harmony does not last. As a cultural historian, Herder is sensitive to the plasticity of language: differences in experience, differences among individual speakers and from one generation to the next, climate and geography, social convention, jealousy, and even "the mighty goddess of fashion" combine to ensure that language will become pluralized, and that each language will remain subject to transformation over time.[58] This is the root of Herder's well-known pluralism—but however well Herder may grasp the fact of pluralism, he nevertheless represents it as a falling away from the perfection of Adamic language. Unsurprisingly, in the *Essay* and elsewhere, Herder represents this decline through the biblical story of the Tower of Babel.[59] Herder begins his 1764 address "On Diligence in the Study of Several Learned Languages," for example, with an elegy:

> That flourishing age is gone when the small circle of our earliest ancestors dwelt round the patriarchs like children round their parents; that age in which, in the simple and noble message of our revelation, all the world was of one tongue and language. . . . But why do I sketch a lost portrait of irreplaceable charms? It is no more, this golden age.—

> As the children of dust undertook that edifice that threatened the clouds, the chalice of confusion was poured over them: their families and dialects were transplanted to various points of the compass; and a thousand languages were created in tune with the climes and mores of a thousand nations.[60]

Compared to Adamic language, which established a harmonious and immediate bond between humankind and the natural world, the "dead, broken sounds" of postlapsarian speech, as Herder called them in a 1774 commentary on *Genesis*, would hardly be "worth the name of *language*."[61] This mournful recollection of a lost transparency continued to color Herder's understanding of pluralism even in his mature *Outlines of a Philosophy of the History of Man*, where he suggests that the dispersion of peoples and the pluralization of languages fatefully shatters the pretense that language unproblematically connects us to the world, making error and misunderstanding inevitable, and exiling us from the "land of truth."[62]

In the second part of Herder's story, then, construction has parted company with cognition, and left it behind. Still, Herder's story does not end on this melancholic note. Even as he develops this account of the pluralization and transformation of languages, Herder also lays the conceptual ground for the possibility of a future redemption, in which, as he puts it in the *Outlines*, "the *flower of our bud of humanity* will certainly appear ... in a form truly that of *godlike man*, which no earthly sense can imagine in all its grandeur and beauty."[63] What makes this possible for Herder is that the flux of human history is not as complete as it first seems. The differences *between* languages may reveal the underlying arbitrariness of signification, but each language, taken on its own, can be understood as essentially connected to and expressive of the unique character of the *Volk* to which it belongs.[64] Herder freely acknowledges the internal diversity of *Völker* as well as their tendency to change over time, but he now also insists that they are integral wholes, marked by certain distinguishing features, and unified by common histories, forms of life, and standards of value.[65]

These fixed points anchor the possibility of redemption. By positing that each *Volk* has its own "internal character" and "standard ... of perfection," Herder affirms both the possibility of understanding linguistic or cultural change *within* a *Volk* in terms of improvement or decline, *and* the possibility—however difficult—of arriving at a sympathetic understanding of *another* culture.[66] For Herder, this means that people should devote themselves to the study, preservation, and advancement of their own languages and cultural traditions, as well as to the study of other languages, and the understanding of the forms of life they express. Herder himself tried to perform these tasks as, on the one hand, an advocate of the reform and rejuvenation of German language and literature, critical of the dominance of foreign (particularly French) culture at the expense of native German traditions;[67] and, on the other hand, as a translator, armchair anthropologist, and critic of the arrogance and prejudice of European imperialism.[68] This "twofold movement" (as Robert Morton has called it) of cultural introspection and cross-cultural translation is, for Herder, the route through which humankind will ultimately produce a "unity out of multiplicity, order out of disorder, and out of a variety of powers and designs one symmetrical and durably beautiful whole"—all in keeping with the designs of a providential God.[69]

Against the background of this narrative, it becomes much more difficult to claim, as Taylor does, that Herder's account of language *breaks* with the aspiration to sovereignty that animates designative theories of language. Recall that on Taylor's reading, the crucial contribution of Herder's approach to language is that it brings the phenomenon of "linguistic rightness" into view. In a certain sense, this is absolutely true. For Herder, it's meaningful to claim that the primordial namer of the animal *gets it right*, for the name of the animal seems not to be entirely arbitrary, as it would have been for Locke; instead, it is based on the recognition of the "distinguishing mark" borne by the animal itself—in this case, the bleating of the sheep. But while there is rightness in Herder's Edenic scene, there is no *question* or *issue* of rightness: no struggling for the right word, none of the uncertainty about whether one will have been understood (or whether one has understood oneself) that weighs in the moment between our utterance and the other's response; no sense of the tentativeness or fragility of understanding; and no possibility of *mis*understanding at all.[70]

Of course, this is partly an effect of the fact that Herder has written a speculative account of the *first* use of language: Herder's founding speaker does not find himself thrown into an ongoing activity, faced with the challenge of using a gloriously messy linguistic inheritance; instead, he has the privilege of composing—or at least recording—his own dictionary. Moreover, Herder's original scene does not yet involve a plurality of speaking agents, much less a plurality of languages, and so presents no opportunity for misunderstanding or disagreement about meaning to arise in the first place: Adamic language is oddly solitary. But even when Herder introduces change and plurality into his account of language, he does so in a way that is colored by both melancholy and hopefulness, recalling and promising to recapture the easy sovereignty, the unproblematic rightness, of the golden age. If Adam's task was to name the animals in accordance with their distinguishing marks, the analogous but even more challenging task of contemporary humanity is to discover and articulate the essences of *Völker*—to find the words in which the characters of nations can be "captured" or made "recognizable" (*anerkennbar*), as Herder says in *Yet Another Philosophy of History*.[71] And, just as God's careful arrangements ensured that Adam, in the constructive act of naming, only ratified the true names of animals, thereby becoming "the general lord of every thing in nature,"[72] Herder also suggests that the discovery and expression of the unity-in-multiplicity of the menagerie of human *Völker* is similarly underwritten by divine providence.

In short, Herder's story offers a kind of solace for our experiences of misunderstanding, error, and disagreement in language by suggesting that those phenomena have not always been—and need not always be—essential to human life. By plotting the human experience of finitude as a temporary stage on the way between paradise and redemption, Herder reassures us that we are indeed made in the image of God, the very model of sovereign agency:

> The being, who created all things, has indeed placed a ray of his peculiar power, in our feeble frame; and low as man is, he can say to himself, 'I have

something in common with God: I possess faculties, that the supreme, whom I know in his works, must also possess; for he has displayed them in the things around me.' Apparently this *similitude with himself* was the sum of all his works on Earth.[73]

And Herder's case suggests, in turn, that there may be a blind spot in Taylor's own critique of the aspiration to sovereignty. In the context of the philosophy of language, Taylor argues that the aspiration to sovereignty finds paradigmatic expression in the stance of disengagement exemplified by, among others, Locke, Condillac, and modern behaviorist theories. But the example of Herder shows that the wish to become a sovereign agent can manifest itself in "engaged" stances, too: even theorists who have gotten the phenomenon of linguistic rightness into view can be tempted by the desire to *secure* rightness once and for all, to make oneself invulnerable to the misunderstandings, uncertainties, and surprises, pleasant and unpleasant, that characterize human communication. For theorists like Herder, the route to sovereignty lies not through the solitary practice of disinterested observation, but instead through identification with some larger, purposive totality, such as one's community, authentically understood; or, ultimately, God himself. And, as we shall see in the next section, this blind spot in Taylor's account of the desire for sovereignty is not limited in significance to the field of language. For Taylor, the politics of recognition—much like Herder's philosophy of language—is supposed to represent a break with the aspiration to sovereignty, because it corrects liberalism's emphasis on disengaged choice and its corresponding neglect of identity as the ground out of which human agency emerges. Yet, as we shall see, the politics of recognition does not break with the aspiration to sovereignty, but—like Herder's philosophy of language—pursues it by other means.

Sovereignty through Recognition

So far, I have suggested that Taylor's essay on the politics of recognition and Herder's account of the origin of language express the same tension between two senses of "recognition," the cognitive and the constructive. I have also argued that Herder attempts to negotiate this tension by imagining a mythic past and future in which the cognitive and constructive senses of recognition would harmoniously correspond—in which our activity of linguistic construction would always remain faithful to the contours of things as they really are—and that in so doing, Herder becomes a representative of the aspiration to sovereignty, rather than its critic, as Taylor believes. I now want to return to Taylor's work on the politics of recognition and draw out some further similarities between

his account and Herder's. And perhaps the most striking parallel between them is that Taylor plots the history of recognition in the same
triadic form as does Herder, tracing a decline from an original condition
of unproblematic transparency among persons, and imagining a redemptive future in which a similar (though not identical) transparency might
be recovered.

Taylor's narration of the history of recognition begins in a premodern
world in which identities and the forms of intersubjective recognition
that sustain them are fixed and unproblematic—indeed, *so* unproblematic that they are wholly invisible. "In premodern times," Taylor writes—
and it is specifically medieval Europe he seems to have in mind, though
he does not explicitly say so here—"people didn't speak of 'identity'
and 'recognition'—not because people didn't have (what we call) identities, or because these didn't depend on recognition, but rather because
these were then too unproblematic to be thematized as such."[74] Or, again:
"In the earlier age recognition never arose as a problem. General recognition was built into the socially derived identity by virtue of the very
fact that it was based on social categories that everyone took for
granted."[75] In this context, people's "fixed and predetermined horizons
could not be otherwise than confirmed by their world."[76]

As a straightforward historical claim, this is difficult to credit. Even
setting aside ancient Athens, where (as we shall see in the next chapter)
recognition and identity were very much on the agenda, to imagine the
European middle ages as an era thoroughly and evenly penetrated by a
single, internally coherent scheme of social identity—a lifeworld in
which, as it were, *everything* is background—is to mistake a representation of seamless social order for the real thing. Consider an example
Taylor himself uses elsewhere: the medieval notion of society as articulated into three functionally differentiated and hierarchically related
orders—clergy, nobility, and laborers.[77] This scheme was powerful, to
be sure, but it was not the all-encompassing, always-already-taken-for-
granted medium of European life and thought in the middle ages. It had
a history and a politics. It was persistently challenged by popular hereti-
cal movements that resisted the privileges of the established clergy and
the rituals of the church in the name of an alternative spiritual vision
that was at the same time an alternative vision of social order. It was
enforced against these challenges by the ecclesiastical and secular authorities, often violently.[78] To characterize social identity in medieval
Europe as "unproblematic" or "taken for granted" is to gloss over this
and many other cases of uncertainty about, struggle over, and change in
the terms of social identity.[79]

As a piece of stylized history with a philosophical purpose, however,
Taylor's gloss on premodern Europe is important and illuminating,

especially (for our purposes) because it resonates so powerfully with Herder's scene of Adamic naming. In Herder's Eden, the cognitive and constructive senses of recognition work in perfect harmony, as each creature presents itself and its name to Adam to be recorded in the book of his dominion: there is linguistic rightness, but no *problem* or *question* of rightness, and this easy relation to the world is the ground of Adam's godlike, and God-given, sovereignty over nature. Taylor's mythic premodern Europe presents us with the same harmony of cognition and construction. There, social identity and relations of recognition are unproblematic and taken for granted, and so dialogical interaction can never fail to construct people as who, according to the naturally or divinely sanctioned social order, they already really are: there is recognition, but no *problem* or *question* of recognition.

Similarly, just as Herder's Eden is disrupted by plurality and the possibility of misunderstanding, Taylor's era of harmonious (if inegalitarian) recognition has its own fall—modernity. The momentous transformation of the phenomenon of recognition, Taylor tells us, comes with the advent of the modern age, which throws old, established hierarchies into question, giving rise to the ideal of an "inwardly generated" identity that can come into conflict with socially ascribed roles.[80] Here, the constructive and cognitive senses of recognition themselves come apart, supposedly for the first time, making misrecognition among persons possible in the same way that the wrenching apart of signifier and signified after Babel subjected the world to confusion, error, and misunderstanding. Importantly, this development actually has two different dimensions, corresponding to two different aspects of pluralization in modernity, individual and collective: while Taylor often casts the breakdown of the premodern social order in terms of the rise of the modern concern with individual subjectivity, which opens a gap between one's own, personal sense of self and the various socially prescribed and enforced roles in which we find ourselves, a similar dynamic also seems to take place at the level of collective identity: modernity also increases the density of interactions among people belonging to different cultural groups, it so also makes the misrecognition of *collective* identities possible—for example, through colonial rule or forced assimilation.[81] In both cases, as Taylor puts it, "what has come about with the modern age is not the need for recognition but the conditions in which the attempt to be recognized can fail."[82]

And, finally, just as Herder's story of the perfection and decline of language already foreshadowed a redemption to come, Taylor's way of describing the transition from premodern to modern society also sets the stage for the emancipatory politics of recognition, which, on his account, promises to transcend the various forms of misrecognition that have emerged in modernity. In Herder's case, the prospect of redemption was anchored in the premise that each *Volk* bears its own, unique character, which can be recovered, preserved, and developed by its own members, and respectfully studied and sympathetically understood by others. By the same token, for Taylor, the prospect of a future state of successful recognition is anchored in the notion—drawn explicitly from Herder—that each person and each cultural group possesses its own, distinctive identity, which grounds and guides its action; these therefore need to be appropriately recognized (that is, known and respected) not only by the people to whom they belong, but also by the others with whom they share social and political space. Of course, Taylor's anticipated restoration of a condition of successful recognition does not involve anything like a return to premodern European social hierarchies, any more than Herder's future redemption involved a return to a single language. Faithful to his Hegelian roots, Taylor knows that the transformations in the shape of our identities wrought by modern individualization cannot be undone, but can at best be incorporated into a more complex and articulated totality, one in which recognition is distributed equally, not hierarchically. But this egalitarian future, in which formerly neglected, suppressed, and undervalued identities are all properly and publicly recognized, is still a reflection—however transfigured—of Taylor's premodern scene of unproblematic recognition, just as Herder's anticipated unity-in-multiplicity of *Völker* reprises, but does not precisely repeat, the harmony of Eden.[83]

The trouble is that this way of plotting recognition works against Taylor's own insightful critique of the aspiration to sovereignty. For Taylor, as we have seen, human linguistic agency—which exemplifies human agency in general—is marked in crucial ways by finitude: "the language I speak," he says, is something "I can never fully dominate or oversee."[84] At this point, however, it is important to notice that Taylor's account of language includes (but does not clearly distinguish) two importantly different dimensions of finitude. On the one hand, we are not masters of language because language is an *inheritance*, a structure built up out of our own and others' sedimented or congealed activity, which confronts us with a determinate range of possibilities that we cannot simply transform at will. Language understood in this way is one of the media through which we experience the weight of history. On the other hand, we also encounter finitude as linguistic agents because language itself is an ongoing activity, open to the future—it is, as Taylor says, *energeia*, not *ergon*. This dimension of finitude manifests itself in the fact that linguistic agency is constitutively *risky*: the possibility of understanding has as its ineliminable twin the possibility of misunderstanding, although misunderstanding, far from being unequivocally negative, may also be the occasion for painful but productive discoveries about oneself, or the guarantor of much-needed privacy for the people one is failing to understand, or a symptom of the emergence of a novel idiom.[85] Language understood in *this* way is one of the sites at which we run up against other people not *qua* congealed structure, but *qua* interlocutors, whose responses to our utterances cannot be perfectly predicted, either by us or by them.

Yet Taylor's politics of recognition, like Herder's philosophy of language, stands in very different relationships to each of these dimensions of human finitude.[86] Taylor does not deny that language and culture are inheritances not (entirely) of one's own making: his emphasis on the importance of the larger social contexts in which we are situated is meant precisely to counteract the tendency in liberal theory to treat agency as an altogether individual matter. However, when Taylor brings "larger social contexts" back into the picture, he imagines these contexts as coherent totalities, like Herderian *Völker*—indeed, as we have seen, he *must* do so in order to hold out the prospect of a *successful* regime of mutual recognition. This move, however, tends to obscure the second dimension of human finitude—the contingency of social interaction, its openness to the future—which Taylor's own view of language as *energeia* had so elegantly captured. This dynamic is concisely represented by an important passage in one of Taylor's essays on language: "Language is fashioned and grows not principally in monologue but in dialogue," Taylor says—but he then immediately adds: "or, better, in the life of the speech community. Hence Herder's notion that the primary locus of a language was the *Volk* which carried it."[87] The first of these moves, from monologue to dialogue, shatters the pretense that one might achieve sovereign agency in isolation; but the second move, from dialogue to community and *Volk*, reinstates the aspiration to sovereignty in a different form, casting sovereign agency now not as a matter of radically free choice, but as a matter of acting in accordance with who, by virtue of one's membership in a larger whole, one always already is.

Something of the same dynamic can be seen in the closing pages of Taylor's essay on the politics of recognition, in which he tries to steer a middle course between the idea that what recognition demands is that we provide a "favorable judgment" of the value and equality of other cultures "on demand"; and the ethnocentric refusal even to engage another culture until it has demonstrated its excellence in a form we already recognize.[88] Against both of these positions, Taylor suggests that what we owe to the other is a "presumption" of equal worth, one which would draw us toward an engagement with others in which we ourselves might also be transformed, without pretending to know in advance what the outcome of that engagement will be.[89] This stance is admirably modest; indeed, it is a compelling invocation of finitude in the face of multiple varieties of arrogance. But only up to a point. For if Taylor encourages us to remain open to surprise and self-transformation in "the study of any other culture,"[90] he nevertheless grounds this presumption in some other, unquestioned certainties: that our engagements with others are always appropriately understood in terms of "study"; that hermeneutically sensitive study will, over time, result in a progressive fusion and broadening of horizons; and that there *is* some "ultimate horizon from which the relative worth of different cultures might be evident," even if we presently remain "very far away" from that place.[91] But what happens when the surprises you encounter in your interaction with others challenge your confidence in this vision of ultimate harmony—the very vision that is supposed to inspire humility and generosity? Taylor's reversion here to a secularized version of Herder's theory of divine providence limits the force of his invocations of finitude: his critique of arrogance turns out to be conditioned, in the end, on the deferred and displaced, but never quite abandoned, aspiration to sovereignty.[92]

RECOGNITION AS MISRECOGNITION

In the foregoing, I have been trying to highlight the coexistence within Taylor's own work of two competing strands or moments: an attunement to human finitude, which manifests itself in an insightful critique of the aspiration to sovereignty; and a countervailing blindness (shared with Herder) to one crucial dimension of human finitude, which manifests itself in the covert resurrection of the very aspiration to sovereignty that Taylor elsewhere criticizes. To conclude this chapter, I want to return to the tension between the two uses of the word "recognition" with which we began, for I think the movement we have traced—the movement of advancing toward and then backing away from a full acknowledgment of finitude—can help us make sense of that tension, both in Taylor's work and in the political discourse of recognition more broadly.

Taylor's account of the politics of recognition, I suggest, contains both of the competing strands or moments I have described—the acknowledgment and the denial of finitude—and they are represented by the two apparently contradictory senses of the term "recognition" at play in his work. Consider these two uses of "recognition" in reverse order. The notion of recognition as construction—recognition as the intersubjective activity through which identities are formed and transformed—is crucial to Taylor's account of the politics of recognition, because it is his way of registering the fact of our vulnerability to, and dependence on, the ways in which we are perceived and characterized by others. It is, you might say, his way of explaining why the politics of recognition matters in the first place: we ought to care about whether intersubjective interaction goes well or poorly, he tells us, because our very identities are at stake. This aspect of Taylor's account of the politics of recognition brings finitude into the foreground, highlighting the contingency, unpredictability, and riskiness of life among others.

On the other hand, the notion of recognition as cognition is no less crucial to Taylor's account, because this notion helps Taylor explain what it means for intersubjective interaction to go well or poorly, for relations of recognition to be just or unjust. For Taylor, injustice on the terrain of identity and difference is to be understood as misrecognition—that is, as the failure to accurately perceive and/or appropriately respect people as who they already really are. But this understanding of injustice as misrecognition is only intelligible if recognition itself is a matter of the respectful cognition of an identity that is in some sense independent of the vicissitudes of human interaction, of the political play of recognition and misrecognition—for if identities were not independent in this way, they could not serve as reliable benchmarks by which to judge the adequacy of particular recognitive acts or structures. And, as we have seen, it is by positing the existence of such authentic identities that Taylor, like Herder, salvages the aspiration to sovereignty, imagining that the openness and contingency of life among others might someday be overcome in a regime of successful mutual recognition.

The politics of recognition, then, is at odds with itself. Rooted in an admirable awareness of vulnerability and finitude, it nevertheless advances an understanding of justice and injustice that ultimately denies those phenomena in the name of an attractive but impossible vision of sovereign agency. And in this way, the pursuit of recognition comes to be bound up with a certain sort of *misrecognition*—not the misrecognition *of identity* (for that understanding remains within a cognitive framework, in which misrecognition is just a matter of getting someone's identity wrong)—but an even more fundamental *ontological* misrecognition, a failure to acknowledge the nature and circumstances of our own activity. To demand, or extend, or receive recognition, in Taylor's framework, is to participate in the ongoing political activity through which identities are formed and reformed—but it is to do so without lucidity, to do so in the name of an ideological vision of identity as the always already settled criterion of proper intersubjective relations.[93] As I shall suggest in subsequent chapters, this sort of ontological misrecognition has serious political consequences: by leading us to think of recognition and misrecognition as a matter of rightly or wrongly cognizing and respecting an already-existing identity, it distracts us from the real dynamics of many of the forms of social injustice to which the politics of recognition quite rightly seeks to respond; indeed, at worst, it risks inadvertently strengthening those forms of injustice, or inaugurating new ones.

How can we make sense of injustice in relations of identity and difference while sustaining a more adequate sense of human finitude? Doing this will require, in the first instance, a recasting of our understanding of the relationship between human agency and identity. As I indicated at the beginning of this chapter, Taylor's account of that relationship tends to represent identity as the ground of agency: to know who you are is to know where you stand and what matters to you. In this picture, the phenomenon of uncertainty in the face of the future can appear in one of two ways: as a disorienting identity crisis, a "painful and frightening experience" that can even "spill over into a loss of grip on one's stance in physical space";[94] or as the much more modest and unthreatening kind of uncertainty that we express when we concede (as Taylor admittedly often does) that our own accounts of who we are can never be absolute, but are always subject to dispute.[95] But what about the uncertainty that arises out of the fact that we ourselves, like the language we use, are "always also changing and *becoming*"—that, as long as we are alive, we are *energeia*, not *ergon*? While Taylor concedes that identity is inevitably incomplete in this way, he does not let his fact challenge his basic portrait of action as rooted in identity: its upshot, he suggests, is simply that we need to pay attention not only to "where we are" but to "where we're going," to project ourselves into the future on the basis of the best available understanding of who we are and have been.[96] In other words, he does not consider the possibility that the phenomena of change and becoming themselves—and the corresponding uncertainty and incompleteness they introduce into our lives—might require us to take a different sort of stance toward the future, one that involves not just projecting ourselves confidently into it on the basis of who we know ourselves to be, but also preparing ourselves for, and opening ourselves to, the surprises that, as it were, *it* will project into *us*.

Acting well, in short, may involve not just knowing who we are, but also acknowledging what that knowledge can and can not do for us. If a radical identity crisis can be paralyzing, an excessively firm grip on identity—an excessive investment in having your acts reflect and express who you already take yourself to be—can be paralyzing too. Or worse: it can feed modes of action that seek to suppress or manage worldly unpredictability, often by constraining others or compelling them to bear a disproportionate share of the risks of human interaction; it can lead you to simplify your own sense of who you are for the sake of *having* a maximally coherent and stable evaluative orientation; it can lead you to neglect those human goods that cannot be pursued as part of a plan. To explore these possibilities and their political implications in more detail, the next two chapters reconstruct an alternative tradition of thought about recognition that can serve as a counterweight to the conventional approach. In chapter 4, I will try to show how the famous account of recognition in Hegel's *Phenomenology* can be read as part of this alternative tradition. First, however, I turn to an altogether different genre of reflection on human affairs, which takes a strikingly different lesson from the experience of intersubjective vulnerability than do Taylor and Herder.

Tragic Recognition
Action and Identity in *Antigone* and Aristotle

> This unchangeable identity of the person, though disclosing
> itself intangibly in act and speech, becomes tangible only in the
> story of the actor's and speaker's life; but as such it can be
> known, that is, grasped as a palpable entity only after it has
> come to its end.
> —HANNAH ARENDT, *The Human Condition*

RECOGNITION AND *ANAGNÔRISIS*

IN MUCH CONTEMPORARY POLITICAL THOUGHT, "recognition" is cast as
a kind of good, an object of ethical and political aspiration, capable of
emancipating us from the destructive effects of ignorance and prejudice.
In the last chapter, we discovered that this thought sometimes finds expression in the narrative forms that theorists of recognition choose
to employ. Like Herder before him, for example, Taylor projects the
pleasures of successful recognition backward into a mythic past; he diagnoses the failure of recognition in the present; and he anticipates a future
of mutual knowledge and respect in which we recover the recognition
we have lost or been denied.

Yet these theorists were not the first to tell stories of recognition.
Against the background of a long tradition of recognition scenes in
Greek literature—Oedipus's shattering self-discovery; Electra's recognition of Orestes via his footprints and hair—Aristotle famously declared
recognition, *anagnôrisis*, to be one of the constitutive elements of the
best tragedies. Since then, recognition has been a central concept in poetics and has continued to be an important literary device.[1] And, on the
tragic stage, recognition looks startlingly different. While political theorists typically depict successful recognition as a source of satisfaction or
fulfillment, scenes of tragic *anagnôrisis* may also be moments of catastrophic loss, occasions for mourning, provocations to strike out one's
eyes. So tightly intertwined are the satisfactions and dangers of *anagnôrisis* that Jocasta's penultimate words to Oedipus—"May you never
know who you are!"—seem to be meant at once as a curse and as a
blessing.[2]

What do recognition and *anagnôrisis*, so different in valence, have to do with each other? The standard English translation of *anagnôrisis* notwithstanding, "recognition" as used in contemporary political theory and *anagnôrisis* in tragedy are not simply two words for the same thing. But they are not unrelated, either; that is why it will be possible to exploit the contrast between them. On the one hand, recognition and *anagnôrisis* open out onto what we might call common ontological terrain, for both phenomena have something to do with the relationship between action and identity in human life. As we have seen, the ideal of recognition is founded on the notion that what we do, and what others do to us, is rooted in who we are and who we are taken to be; likewise, *anagnôrisis* in tragedy matters precisely because our interactions are shaped by what we know, or what we think we know, about who we and others are. As Aristotle says, *anagnôrisis* is "a change from ignorance to knowledge, and *thus to either love or hate*, on the part of the personages marked for good or evil fortune."[3]

On the other hand, the discourses of recognition and *anagnôrisis* take sharply contrasting stances on the ontological terrain they share. If, as I have suggested, the politics of recognition is animated by a vision of sovereign agency, in which people are empowered by self-knowledge and by the confirming recognition of others to act in accordance with who they really are, tragedy suggests that this aspiration is both impossible and dangerous, because it misunderstands the relationship between identity and action. From a tragic perspective, efforts to achieve sovereign agency are themselves ethically and politically problematic *misrecognitions*—not misrecognitions of the identity of another, as that term usually implies, but failures to acknowledge key aspects of our own situation, including especially our own finitude in relation to the future. Tragic *anagnôrisis*, I shall suggest, brings acknowledgment thus conceived into the foreground, highlighting its difference from, and potential for conflict with, recognition, and ultimately enabling us to reconsider the nature of injustice on the terrain of identity and difference.

Tragedy recasts our understanding of the relationship between human agency and identity by drawing our attention to what I shall call the "impropriety" of action in relation to the choices and identities in which we attempt to ground it. "Impropriety," in this sense, is not meant as a term of condemnation or disapproval. It refers not to a contingent moral failing but to a constitutive feature of human action: the very conditions that make us potent agents—our materiality, which ties us to the causal order of the world, and our plurality, which makes it possible for our acts to be meaningful—also make us potent beyond our own control, exposing us to consequences and implications that we cannot predict and which are not up to us. Our acts, you might say, are always improper in the sense that they are never our property—neither as choosers, nor as the bearers of identities.

As the epigraph to this chapter suggests, this idea of "impropriety" is closely connected to what Hannah Arendt has called the "non-sovereign" character of human action; indeed, one purpose of this study is to bring a loosely Arendtian understanding of the conditions of human activity to bear on the politics of recognition, and also on Greek tragedy.[4] But there is good reason to keep some distance from Arendt's own texts and concepts while doing so. In *The Human Condition*, for instance, the general idea of "non-sovereignty" (which Arendt also sometimes calls "frailty") actually encompasses a number of different phenomena that Arendt herself does not always clearly distinguish, including "unpredictability," which is closest in meaning to what I am calling "impropriety";[5] "boundlessness," that is, the fact that an act can have consequences at a surprising distance from the context in which it was originally undertaken; and "futility," which for Arendt refers to the fact that action itself is intangible and depends upon ongoing narration and remembrance in public if it is to survive its fleeting moment of performance.[6]

Readers of Arendt typically treat these as inseparable aspects of the human condition, and so does Arendt, at least when she is speaking in broad terms about the basic features of human action. Yet Arendt also claims that the historically specific ideal of action that flourished in ancient Greece was disproportionately concerned with the last of these three phenomena. As she puts it:

> Whoever consciously aims at being "essential," at leaving behind a story and an identity which will win "immortal fame," must not only risk his life but expressly choose, as Achilles did, a short life and premature death. Only a man who does not survive his one supreme act remains the indisputable master of his identity and possible greatness, because he withdraws into death from the possible consequences and continuation of what he began.[7]

This, Arendt tells us, was the "prototype of action for Greek antiquity." And because the Greeks were convinced that this mode of action—"summing up all of one's life in a single deed"—could make them sovereign over their own identities, they remained "relatively untouched by the predicament of unpredictability."[8] The only outcomes that mattered, they believed, were within their control. Instead, they worried about futility, about how to ensure that their actions would be remembered after their deaths; and their solutions to this problem included poetry, history, and even politics itself, understood in Periclean terms as the institutionalization of a public space of "everlasting remembrance" of citizens' deeds.[9]

To be clear, the trouble here is not that Arendt romanticizes the Greek city-state, for as others have shown, her treatment of this ideal of action is by no means uncritical. Indeed, one of Arendt's own best-known maxims—that "nobody is the author or producer of his own life story"— suggests that the Achillean belief that one can be master of one's own identity, and the corresponding inattention to the phenomenon of unpredictability, is a fatal conceit, "perhaps a species of hubris."[10] The problem lies not in Arendt's evaluation of "Greece" but in her simplified description of it, which colors her own understanding of the significance of tragedy, and particularly of tragic *anagnôrisis*, in unfortunate ways. Having characterized the Greeks as overwhelmingly concerned with the problem of futility, Arendt herself tends to represent tragedy simply as one example of institutionalized remembrance through storytelling, a way of overcoming the fleetingness of action and holding out the possibility of immortality.[11] Hence, even when she focuses specifically on tragic *anagnôrisis*, she treats this sort of recognition as a matter of the retrospective re-experiencing of a set of events as a "significant whole," which makes possible both its preservation in a lasting narrative, and the reconciliation of the spectators—including those who had participated in the events and are now looking back upon them—to what has happened.[12]

To be sure, these are among the functions of tragedy and tragic *anagnôrisis*; and they are of considerable ethical and political value. But what if tragedy did more than this? What if, in addition to making it possible to remember great deeds and to come to terms with the suffering such deeds involve, tragedy also worked as a mode of critique, through which dramatists drew attention to the limitations of certain specific ways of acting? By declaring the example of Achilles to be *the* prototype of action for the Greeks, Arendt sacrifices an opportunity implicit in her own intermittent citations of Sophocles and of Aristotle's *Poetics*—the opportunity to read tragedy as a response and alternative, from within Greek antiquity itself, to the impossible Achillean pursuit of mastery and self-sufficiency.[13]

Here, then, I read tragic *anagnôrisis* in the spirit of Arendt's own understanding of action, but not according to the letter of her works. On this reading, part of the aim of tragedy is to provoke in us an acknowledgment of action's unpredictability and consequently also of the ineliminable possibility of suffering. More deeply still, it teaches us that the attempt to become master of our own deeds and identity is not only doomed to fail, but risks intensifying that suffering unnecessarily, even demanding that we give our lives for what will turn out to have been an illusion of control. Scenes of tragic *anagnôrisis*, you might say, draw our attention to the ways in which the pursuit of recognition (for that, after all, is what Achilles seeks) involves potentially catastrophic failures of acknowledgment.

SOPHOCLES' ANTIGONE AND ARISTOTLE'S POETICS

To spell out this idea, I turn in the following sections to one vivid example of tragic drama—Sophocles' *Antigone*—along with key portions of Aristotle's philosophical treatment of tragedy in the *Poetics*. The *Antigone*, of course, has often been read through the lens of identity. One standard approach to the play, usually traced back to Hegel, sees Antigone and Creon as representatives of conflicting positions within ancient Greek *Sittlichkeit*, with Antigone acting as a personification of the *oikos*, kinship, and the female, and Creon serving as representative of the *polis*, law, and the male.[14] Jean Elshtain's appropriation of Antigone as a heroine of difference feminism, whose "primordial family morality" can still be taken up in acts of resistance to the tyranny of modern Creons, is a noteworthy example of this approach.[15] Other readers invert this view: criticizing what she sees as the antipolitical character of Elshtain's feminism, Mary Dietz suggests that Antigone's obedient sister Ismene is the real representative of family morality, while Antigone herself is best understood as the bearer of a *political* identity: in her resistance to Creon's tyranny, she acts as "a citizen of Thebes" who represents "the customs and traditions of a collective civil life, an entire political ethos, which Creon's mandate and he himself threaten."[16]

Each of these interpretations shows us something important about the *Antigone*—or, more precisely, each of these interpretations shows us something important about Antigone, for Elshtain and Dietz focus more on the character of Antigone than on the action of Sophocles' play. For Elshtain and Dietz, understanding the *Antigone* is simply a matter of recognizing who Antigone is—member of the family or political actor. Yet the trouble is that while each of these apparently incompatible readings is partly persuasive, neither is *wholly* persuasive, and neither Elshtain nor Dietz accounts for Antigone's uneasy fit with the categories through which they attempt to recognize her. Other readers are more sensitive to Antigone's uncomfortable fit within these categories. In *Antigone's Claim*, for example, Judith Butler takes precisely this issue as her point of departure. Like Dietz, she criticizes the project of making Antigone into the "representative" of kinship; but rather than treating Antigone as the representative of something else—a civic identity, for example—she argues that "Antigone's own representative function is in crisis" by virtue of her implication in "incestuous legacies that confound her position within kinship."[17] Gradually shifting our attention away from Creon's overt prohibition of the burial of Polyneices and the resulting conflict between the principle of kinship and the imperatives of the *polis*, Butler's reading focuses on the ways in which Antigone is always already in violation of established norms of kinship, afflicted with desires that have been rendered unlivable not just by being explicitly prohibited, but by being foreclosed in advance through taboos that are purported to be the conditions of possibility of kinship as such.[18] This approach lets Butler make sense of Antigone's own melancholic, death-bound desire as an effect of the specific social formation of kinship under which she lives;[19] it lets her read the excessiveness of Antigone's grief for Polyneices as a trace of her unspoken or unspeakable grief for all the others she has lost, including Eteocles, Jocasta, and Oedipus;[20] and it lets her eulogize Antigone, elegantly, as a predecessor of those who, in our world, are suspended in a kind of "living death" by virtue of the operation of kinship norms that render some loves unavowable and some losses ungrievable.[21]

Butler's reading of *Antigone* thus represents one powerful way of spelling out the meaning and sources of what I have called action's "impropriety," one which associates that impropriety with the workings of an unconscious heavy with the traces of foreclosed love. As Butler says, noting the instability of reference in Antigone's use of kinship terms, "Antigone does not achieve the effect of sovereignty she apparently seeks, and her action is not fully conscious."[22] Yet the risk in such a psychoanalytic reading, at least on its own, is that it will lead us to treat Antigone's impropriety as, in the end, still a matter of *who* she is—that is, of her character, albeit now understood in a psychologically deeper and sociologically richer way. And *that* would also risk reinforcing, however inadvertently, the political investment in recognition as a source of emancipation: if Antigone is, as Butler suggests, "dying from a lack of recognition," then more or better recognition would certainly seem to be the way to save her.[23]

The trouble here, I think, is that Butler's reading treats impropriety and the unconscious as a matter in the first instance of the weight of an actor's past. Repeatedly, Butler insists that Antigone's punishment "precedes her crime"; that she is "already living the tomb prior to any banishment there"; that she has "already departed from kinship"; that she "meets a fate that has been hers all along."[24] This focus on the weight of the past is not wrong, but it is incomplete. It is equally important to attend to impropriety's sources in the contingency of the future, in the unpredictability of interaction among people who are differently constrained, but never quite determined, by their histories; for it is impropriety in this second, futural sense that is misrecognized and disavowed when claims for justice are advanced as demands for the recognition of an antecedently given identity. From this perspective, we might say that Antigone is dying less from a lack of recognition than from a failure of acknowledgment, one that she herself misunderstands *as* a lack of recognition, and with which she thereby becomes complicit. If the deathboundness of her desire is an indictment of the terms of normative kinship by which she is bound, it is equally an indictment of the strategy through which she responds to her situation—a strategy she shares with Creon (and with Achilles), her differences from them notwithstanding.

In contrast to Elshtain and Dietz, then, and in something like sympathetic counterpoint to Butler, I shall approach the *Antigone* not by trying to determine *who* Antigone and Creon are, or how their identities have already been undone in advance of the action of the play, but by focusing on the ways in which that action itself exceeds or outruns the terms of identity in which these characters try to ground it. In this sense, I shall be following Aristotle's dictum that "the most important of the six [parts of tragedy] is the combination of the incidents of the story," because "tragedy is essentially an imitation not of persons but of action and life" (1450a15–17). But this invocation of the *Poetics* requires one last preliminary comment, for Aristotle's treatise is often taken to be a distortion of tragedy, which "tame[s] its subversive vigor" by insisting that the world of tragedy is, in the end, both intelligible to reason and "intrinsically shaped to human interests."[25] If Aristotle is an antitragic figure, why follow his lead in reading Sophocles?

This is an importance concern. Aristotle's distaste for plots organized around divine caprice or sheer chance, as well as his (inconstant) preference for the drama of averted catastrophe, suggest that he is indeed working to defend tragedy's place in the city by eliding some of its most troubling dimensions.[26] Yet this case is sometimes overstated. In her detailed critique of the *Poetics*, for example, Michelle Gellrich argues that Aristotle, in his drive to render the tragic world intelligible, domesticates tragedy by subordinating action to *êthos* or "character," which determines its nature and direction.[27] In his peculiarly untragic version of tragedy, she concludes, "an action will be of the same quality as the character who conceives it: if the character is good, as Aristotle says he must be, his action will be good."[28] Of course Gellrich is right that such a view—reminiscent of Plato's claim that "the good isn't the cause of all things, then, but only of good ones"—would do violence to tragedy.[29] And it is also true that Aristotelian ethics does aim at the stabilization of conduct through the cultivation of virtuous character. But to stop there would be to miss the force of the equally Aristotelian principle on which I focus in this chapter—that in tragedy, plot and action take priority over character. Just as Aristotle's meditations on the vulnerability of the virtuous and the fragility of happiness in the *Nicomachean Ethics* mark his acknowledgment of the limits of his own ethical project, his claim about the priority of plot to character, I shall suggest, reflects a broader view of human action as at best imperfectly governable by choice or *ethos*, as well as a sensitivity to the fact that willful blindness or sovereign hostility to contingency can be even more disastrous than contingency itself.[30] To say this is, to be sure, to draw a "universal" lesson from tragedy, but it is a lesson that cuts *against* the rationalist fetishization of "coherence and order" Gellrich attributes to Aristotle, aligning him—at least momentarily—with rather than against Sophocles.[31]

In the remainder of this chapter, then, I linger over this momentary alignment, reading Aristotle's maxim about the priority of action in tragedy together with Sophocles' *Antigone*. Aristotle's claim about the priority of action in tragedy, I shall argue, helps bring into focus the ways in which Antigone and Creon both try *and* fail to act in character; at the same time, in this double movement of attempt and failure, the *Antigone* itself elegantly juxtaposes recognition and *anagnôrisis*, shedding light both on the meaning of *anagnôrisis* in Aristotle's poetics and also on its wider ethical and political significance. On the one hand, the *Antigone* stages a paradigmatic struggle for recognition. Its central characters attempt to achieve sovereign agency by acting on the basis of their understandings of who they, and others, are, and by demanding respect from each other on the basis of the identities that animate them. (No doubt it is because Antigone and Creon articulate their identities so forcefully, and so persuasively, that character-based readings of the *Antigone* have been so attractive: these antagonists *want* to be recognized, and they have seduced many interpreters into indulging them.) On the other hand, in keeping with Aristotle's insistence on the ultimate priority of action to character, the movement of the *Antigone* cuts against Antigone's and Creon's pursuits of sovereignty, offering us powerful examples of the impropriety of action, and setting the stage for moments of tragic *anagnôrisis* quite different from the satisfying recognitions Antigone and Creon had sought.

But I am getting ahead of the story.

The Pursuit of Recognition in the *Antigone*

Sophocles' *Antigone* is set in Thebes, after the death of Oedipus and in the wake of the deadly rivalry between his sons, Polyneices and Eteocles.[32] After being exiled by his brother, Polyneices leads an Argive army against Thebes, and the two brothers die at each other's hands.[33] Since the only surviving descendants of Oedipus are the sisters Antigone and Ismene, the kingship of Thebes falls to Jocasta's brother Creon, who faces the task of deciding how to treat the bodies of the fallen warriors. Creon gives Eteocles a hero's burial, but orders Polyneices' corpse left unburied and unlamented, and declares that "anyone who dares attempt the act" of burial "will die by public stoning in the town" (35–36). As the play opens, Antigone tells Ismene of Creon's decree and asks her to help defy the command and bury their brother's body. When Ismene refuses and reminds Antigone of her obligation to obey the city's leaders, Antigone does the deed herself. The outraged Creon condemns both sisters to death. Creon's son Haemon, to whom Antigone is betrothed, protests his father's judgment, but to little avail. Creon relents and releases Ismene, but orders Antigone sealed alive in a cave outside the city. After Antigone, lamenting her fate, has been led away, Creon is visited by the prophet Teiresias, who foretells that Creon's impious acts will be repaid by death in Creon's own family and will bring destruction to Thebes. Frightened, Creon tries to reverse his actions: he rushes to bury Polyneices' corpse and then to free Antigone. But Antigone has already hung herself, and Haemon has already discovered her body. Creon arrives at Antigone's tomb just in time to witness his son's angry, desperate suicide; and when news of Haemon's death reaches his mother, Eurydice, she too dies by her own hand, cursing Creon with her final breath. As the play draws to a close, Creon, acknowledging his guilt, prays for an early death.

The conflict with which this play opens is framed as a conflict over recognition, in which crucial questions of how to act are made to hang on issues of identity. The issue of recognition first arises in connection with the dead Polyneices, whose body is the principal object of controversy in the *Antigone*. This body raises a problem of identity not because there is any doubt about whether the body is Polyneices, but there is a serious question about who Polyneices is—that is, under what description he ought to be recognized. On the one hand, Polyneices is a native of Thebes, a member of the ruling family, the brother of Antigone and Ismene, and the nephew of Creon himself; and under these descriptions, he unquestionably ought to be buried.[34] On the other hand, Polyneices is a traitor, who has just raised an army against Thebes out of jealousy and vindictiveness toward his brother, and this seems to demand that Polyneices be treated differently in death: only the patriot should be buried, while the traitor should be left to rot.[35] And this controversy over Polyneices' identity *matters*, second, because the funeral rites that are at stake are important expressions of respect. Such rites honor and affirm the dead, and they do so precisely through the articulation of the identity of the deceased: the spontaneous lament, the public funeral oration, and the carefully composed elegy all recollect the dead person's character and actions, and the epitaph carved on the funeral monument helps to "secure a degree of personal immortality" for the deceased by delivering at least his name, and sometimes a record of his deeds and virtues, to posterity.[36]

Yet the *Antigone*'s conflict is not only about how to recognize Polyneices. Although his death is the immediate occasion for the conflict between Antigone and Creon, the significance of their confrontation quickly widens, for both ground their obligations toward the corpse not only in their descriptions of Polyneices but also in accounts of their *own* identities. It should come as no surprise that the identities of Antigone and Creon are drawn into the controversy over Polyneices, for funeral ritual is at least as much about the living as about the dead: rites of burial and lament memorialize, but they also help the mourner to work through loss.[37] The linguistic and physical artifacts produced as a part of funeral ritual—laments, eulogies, grave markers—cannot really replace a lost person; but in the production of such artifacts, and through participation in the symbolic systems that govern funeral procedure, mourners work to reconstruct the agency that the traumatic event of death had interrupted. That agency, in turn, is never experienced immediately and abstractly, but only by occupying particular roles and identities in the social world; and since the roles and identities through which different people experience agency may make incompatible demands in a single case, an instance of mourning can quickly become the occasion for broader social conflict. In this way, the struggle over Polyneices turns into a struggle for recognition *between* Antigone and Creon, as they try, unsuccessfully, to compel each other to recognize not just some facets of *Polyneices'* identity, but the legitimacy of their *own* identities—that is, of the locations in the ethical world from which they try to address the personal and civic losses Polyneices' body represents.[38]

Antigone and Creon introduce themselves and begin to articulate these identities in the first two episodes of the play: Antigone's exchange with Ismene, and Creon's speech to the chorus. As Simon Goldhill and others have observed, one of the most important ways Antigone and Creon identify themselves and each other in these speeches is via their contrasting uses of the opposition between *philos* and *ekhthros*, which both characters initially employ with reference to Polyneices.[39] As a concrete noun, *philos* is usually translated "friend"; as an adjective, the same word is rendered as "dear," "beloved," or "loving"; and the related noun *philia* is translated as "friendship" or "love." Correspondingly, *ekhthros*, as a concrete noun, is translated "enemy"; as an adjective it is rendered as "hostile" or "hated"; and the abstract noun *ekhthra* is translated as "hatred" or "enmity."[40] Yet these translations do not do justice to the semantic range of the words, especially in the case of *philos* and *philia*, which could be used in the context of nearly any "positive" reciprocal relationships, including bonds among kin, strategic alliances, the extension of hospitality to strangers, self-love, and the ties of marriage, as well as the class of personal relationships of mutual affection and support that we normally call "friendship."[41] Precisely because of their semantic breadth, these words are well-suited to become the focus of a struggle over the legitimacy and priority of different kinds of social bond. Antigone and Creon make good use of this potential, transforming what is initially a debate about Polyneices into a conflict over the proper sense of *philos* and *ekhthros*—and thereby announcing their *own* deepest commitments to each other, and to the audience.

Antigone's exchange with Ismene, for instance, is framed by the theme of *philia*. In the opening lines of the play, Antigone approaches Ismene with news of Creon's edict: "Have you heard anything?" she asks, "or don't you know that the foes' [*ekhthrôn*] trouble comes upon our friends [*philous*]" (10)? Antigone implies that in denying burial not only to the six fallen Argive commanders but also to Polyneices, Creon has brought an evil appropriate to an *ekhthros* upon a *philos*.[42] But why does she consider Polyneices *philos*? The first and most obvious source of her attachment is *kinship*: when Ismene expresses her surprise at Antigone's plan of disobedience, Antigone justifies herself simply by referring to the fact of family ties: Polyneices is "my brother, and yours, though you may wish he were not." Second, Antigone also indicates that her obligations of *philia* to Polyneices arise from what she will later call the "unwritten and unfailing laws" of "the gods below" (451, 455), which govern reproduction and death.[43] When Ismene declares that she feels compelled to obey the city (65–67), Antigone responds that she regards the underworld as of greater import than the world of the living, and suggests that once she has "dared the crime of piety," she will be able to lie alongside Polyneices, *philos* with *philos* (73–74). Finally, although the gendering of the conflict between Antigone and Creon is more explicit in Creon's speeches, Antigone does some of the work of gender identification in her initial exchange with her sister. Although the contrasting case of Ismene, who submissively cautions her sister to "remember that we two are women" who should not fight with men (61–62), might be taken to be indirect evidence of Antigone's *resistance* to any identification with conventional gender roles, the truth is more complex. The vocabulary of kinship with which Antigone refers to her siblings is itself gendered: the ordinary words for brother and sister, *adelphos* and *adelphe*, literally indicate kinship through the womb (*delphus*), and Antigone calls attention to this mode of kinship when she later calls Polyneices *homosplanchnos*—a less ordinary word that also means "of the same womb" (511).[44] As Charles Segal has explained, this vocabulary "makes kinship a function of the female procreative power," in direct contrast to the patrilineal system of kinship on which membership in the *polis* was based, and from which women were excluded.[45]

Moreover, Antigone's identification with at least some conventional gender roles is later borne out by the manner in which she performs her duties of *philia* to Polyneices. Although she does initially declare her intention to "pile the burial-mound" for Polyneices (80)—a task that was generally performed by men—she does not actually bury the body but merely sprinkles dust on the corpse, "enough to turn the curse," as the guard says (255). Later, just before being led away by Creon's guards, she describes her action in a way that conforms quite precisely to classical norms governing the role of women in funeral rites: "All three of you have known my hand in death," she says, referring to Oedipus, Jocasta, and Polyneices; "I washed your bodies, dressed them for the grave, poured out the last libation at the tomb" (900–902).[46] And, finally, Sophocles describes Antigone's lament over Polyneices' corpse with a familiar, gendered image specifically associated with the mourning of mothers for their children: "the sharp and shrill cry of a bitter bird which sees the nest bare where the young birds lay" (423–24).[47]

If Antigone regards Polyneices as *philos* by virtue of kinship, treats her own obligations to him as a matter of chthonian piety, and expresses a gender identity in the way she grounds and performs these obligations, Creon's early speeches sharply contest this understanding of *philia*. First, although Polyneices is Creon's kinsman too, Creon treats him as *ekhthros*, not *philos*, because for Creon the criteria of *philia* are exclusively political: "He who counts another greater friend [*philon*] than his own fatherland [*patra*], I put him nowhere," Creon announces (182–83), already invoking the principle of patrilineal descent that underlay membership in the *polis* against Antigone's matrilineal vocabulary of kinship. Only the ship of state, "sailing straight," can make it possible for us to "have friends [*philous*] at all," Creon asserts (189–90). For Creon, Polyneices ceased to be a *philos* the moment he raised an army against Thebes, and after she violates the city's laws, Antigone too will be called a "false friend" [*philos kakos*] (652).[48] In identifying himself instead as a citizen and ruler whose deepest commitment is to the all-important law of the *polis*, Creon trumps both the principle of kinship *and* the eternal and unwritten chthonian law that supposedly assigns duties within the family. Unsurprisingly, Creon's exclusively civic conception of *philia* is also rigidly *masculine*. As Creon's polemical use of the word *patra* as a synonym for the *polis* has already indicated, citizenship and rulership are properly the business of men, and only men. The intertwining of gender identity with the distinction between *polis* and *oikos*, already implied in Creon's first speech, runs so deep that Creon, upon hearing the guard's report that Polyneices' corpse has been buried, thinks only to ask "what *man* [*tis andrôn*] has dared to do it" (248). The fact that Antigone has disobeyed thus turns out to be an especially potent threat to Creon's authority: it throws into question not just his authority in this particular case, but his masculinity, the condition of the possibility of his political authority *as such*. In response, Creon's gendering of the *polis* becomes more explicit, insistent, even hysterical: he repeats in different ways and to various people that he will never let himself be conquered, ruled, defeated by a woman.[49] In one remarkable passage, Creon ties together his renunciation of the ties of kinship as grounds of *philia* and the preservation of his own masculinity:

> I am no man and she the man instead
> if she can have this conquest without pain.
> She is my sister's [*adelphês*] child, but were she child
> of closer kin than any at my hearth,
> she and her sister should not so escape
> their death and doom. (484–89)

The portraits that emerge in this way out of Antigone's and Creon's self-identifications, and out of the different stances they adopt toward Polyneices' body, are familiar; they show that the so-called Hegelian tendency to associate Antigone and Creon with *oikos* and *polis* (kinship and the civic, woman and man) *does* capture something crucial in the self-understandings these characters announce in the opening episodes of the play. But to say *simply* that Antigone and Creon "stand for" *oikos* and *polis* would be too quick, for it would take these characters' own projects of self- and other-recognition at face value, ignoring the ways in which their own conduct comes into conflict with the identities they announce.[50] In other words, to stop our reading the play here would be to ignore its action, which, Aristotle tells us, is the "first essential [*archê*], the life and soul [*psuchê*], so to speak, of tragedy" (1450a38–39).[51]

"An Imitation Not of Persons but of Action"

In chapter 6 of the *Poetics*, Aristotle makes a famous claim about the relative importance of the constituent parts of tragic drama: "The most important of the six [parts of tragedy]," he says, "is the combination of the incidents of the story," for "tragedy is essentially an imitation not of persons but of action and life" (1450a15–17). Thus, for Aristotle, "the first essential, the life and soul, so to speak, of tragedy is the plot," while "characters [*êthê*] come second" (1450a38–39); indeed, character is included for the sake of the action rather than the other way around

(1450a20–22).[52] Before we can bring this claim to bear on the themes of action and identity in the *Antigone*, however, we need to answer some daunting preliminary questions. First, what is the relationship between Aristotle's understanding of character (*êthos*) and the notion of identity? Isn't Aristotelian *êthos* a matter of one's specifically *moral* qualities (e.g., courage or generosity) as opposed to the axes of identity and difference that preoccupy theorists of recognition (e.g., sex/gender or nationality)? And, second, is Aristotle's claim about the priority of plot to character just technical advice to poets who wish to compose effective tragedies, or is there some sense in which Aristotle understands action to be "prior" to character in life as well as in the dramatist's craft?

At first, Aristotelian *êthos* may strike us as altogether unrelated to the "identities" articulated by Antigone and Creon, and also to the use of "identity" in contemporary discussions of the politics of recognition, for Aristotle's understanding of *êthos* is typically associated with the specifically moral or ethical qualities of persons he discusses in his ethical treatises, and not with the axes of identity and difference that preoccupy theorists of recognition: courage and generosity are attributes that belong to one's *êthos*; gender and nationality, for example, are not.[53] There is a sense in which this distinction is correct, but it is also overstated: it reads back into Aristotle a sharp divide between ethics and social context that he would not have recognized.

In the *Nicomachean Ethics*, Aristotle does not define *êthos* as such. But in book 2 of the *Eudemian Ethics*, Aristotle says that *êthos* is a "quality" [*poiotês*] that we possess in respect of our "capacities for affections" [*dunameis tôn pathêmatôn*] such as anger, fear, shame, or desire; as well as in respect of the states or habits [*hexeis*] that determine how we experience and respond to those affections (1220b5–20). A quality, Aristotle says elsewhere, is a "differentia" [*diaphora*]; it is simply "that in virtue of which people are said to be such and such."[54] And because the states or habits that differentiate us are "lasting and firmly established,"[55] when we give an account of the *êthos* of a person, we are saying something about what we take to be that person's *persistent* qualities with respect to affection, rather than their momentary attributes. In sum, as Nancy Sherman says, Aristotelian character "has to do with a person's enduring traits; that is, with the attitudes, sensibilities, and beliefs that affect how a person sees, acts, and indeed lives."[56] These enduring traits, in turn, are the objects of *mimêsis* in dramatic characterization, which lets us see not just a man charging across the stage, sword in hand, but—depending upon the characterization—a courageous man, a reckless man, an ill-tempered man, whose action is neither a random happening, nor a whim, but an expression of who he is.[57]

Now, on the one hand, Aristotle's focus on *êthos* as a quality of the

nonrational part of the soul does mean that "external" social characteristics are not necessarily aspects of *êthos* in Aristotle's sense: to depict a
woman, a man, a Theban, an Athenian is not *yet* to depict a person's
character. But, on the other hand, social characteristics *may* be related
to *êthos* in at least two important ways. In the *Rhetoric*, Aristotle suggests that a wide variety of social attributes, including gender, age, noble
birth, wealth, and nationality, may tend to produce distinctive *êthê*, presumably by shaping the ways in which people regularly experience and
respond to desire and other affections.[58] Yet the link between social
characteristics and *êthos* is not only causal. Later in the *Poetics*, when
Aristotle discusses exactly how character ought to be incorporated into
drama, he indicates that the *êthê* of the people depicted should be "appropriate," and the example he offers—not irrelevant to the *Antigone*,
as we shall see—is that while a person may be courageous (*andreios*,
which also means "manly"), such an *êthos* is not appropriate to a
woman (1454a22–24). As this passage reminds us, for Aristotle, people
are not virtuous or vicious in the abstract, but in relation to whatever is
appropriate or fitting to them, as the sort of people they are: this is why
Aristotle insists in the *Nicomachean Ethics* that virtue, as a mean, is
relative to the agent and the situation, and is thus "neither one nor the
same for everybody" (1106a29–33). So, while social characteristics on
their own do not amount to *êthos*, some social characteristics (normatively loaded ones, we might say) are nevertheless necessary constituents
of *êthos*: they form the background against which assessments of the
excellence of character can be made.

These considerations suggest how closely related Aristotelian *êthos*
and identity actually are. In contemporary discussions of the politics of
recognition, after all, "identity" refers not merely to some set of social
characteristics a person bears, but to a set of such characteristics that
are taken to have practical force in both of the ways I have described.
On this view, a person's identity is constituted in part by her location in
a variety of dimensions of social space, and that social context helps
orient her in practice, both causally, by helping to shape the ways in
which she experiences and responds to desire and other affections, and
normatively, by making certain courses of action obligatory and prohibiting others. Thus when Antigone and Creon, through their speeches,
demonstrate how heavily their understandings of their obligations and
responsibilities have been shaped by their respective social positions, it
makes sense to say that these speeches are representations of their *êthê*.
Antigone and Creon present themselves as acting out of the virtue of
philia—but neither one can make sense of *philia* in the abstract, without
reference to the social identities that establish who, for each of them, is
properly *philos*.[59]

This discussion of *êthos*, however, raises a second question about the meaning of Aristotle's claim that action has priority over character in tragedy. As we have seen, Aristotle's view of *êthos* in his ethical writings emphasizes the capacity of *êthos* to introduce predictability, pattern, and order into our activity: as Sherman says, *êthos* shows us "not merely why someone acted this way now, but why someone can be counted on to act in certain ways."[60] This, however, seems to give *character* a kind of priority over *action*—as we might expect from the intellectual grandfather of contemporary virtue ethics, which focuses on the underlying qualities, formed through practice, habituation, and education, that can reliably produce right action. Thus some interpreters have concluded that the perspectives of Aristotle's ethical writings and the *Poetics* are incommensurable.[61] Elizabeth Belfiore, for example, argues that the claim about the priority of action to character in tragedy refers only to poetic technique—first, the poet devises a plot; then, he adds character to the play in order to flesh out the meaning of the action—while in "real-life situations," by contrast, "action is caused by *êthos* and thought."[62] If this is right, it would be pointless to look to Aristotle's claim about action and character for guidance in understanding the world depicted in Sophocles' play: at best, it could help us understand the world of the writer's garret. But Belfiore's distinction is not ultimately persuasive. Consider, again, the passage in which Aristotle first makes his claim about the priority of action to character in the *Poetics*:

> Tragedy is essentially an imitation not of persons but of action and life, of happiness and misery. *All human happiness or misery takes the form of action; the end for which we live is a kind of activity, not a quality. Character gives us qualities, but it is in our actions—what we do—that we are happy or the reverse.* In a play accordingly they do not act in order to portray the characters; they include the characters for the sake of the action. (1450a16–22, emphasis added)[63]

Importantly, Aristotle's claims in the emphasized sentences refer not only to the representation of action and character on the stage, but to action and character *simpliciter*, which suggests that the priority of action to character in tragedy should, somehow, correspond to the relationship between action and character in real life.[64] Aristotle's insistence here that happiness is an activity rather than a quality provides an important clue, for it points us back to certain crucial parts of the *Nicomachean Ethics*, including the discussion of the acquisition of virtue in book 2, and the famous treatment of happiness and misfortune in book 1.[65]

In book 2 of the *Nicomachean Ethics*, Aristotle stresses that the ethical virtues are formed through habituation, even speculating that the words for character (*êthos*) and the ethical (*êthikê*) are derived from the word for habit (*ethos*).[66] Habituation, in turn, consists in repeated activity: as in the arts, we learn virtue by doing, and this is why it is crucially important that we "perform the right activities" (1103a31–33, 1103b23). For this reason, then, the relationship between *êthos* and action in the *Nicomachean Ethics* is not one-sided, but reciprocal: it is not *only* that the virtue of bravery causes or is actualized in courageous acts, for example, but also that bravery itself is formed through the doing of brave deeds (1104a28–b4).[67] But if the relationship between character and action is reciprocal, it is not perfectly symmetrical. Character, we might say, pushes out into the world by shaping the kinds of things we do; *and* it is at the same time formed and reformed by our worldly activity. Yet because action takes place in the world, this circuit of mutual constitution *is not closed*: action, and, by extension, character itself, is exposed to various forms of worldly contingency—a prospect Aristotle himself concedes in book 1, chapter 10 of the *Nicomachean Ethics*, where he suggests that people cannot be called happy without qualification until they are dead, if even then.[68]

What are these forms of worldly contingency that afflict activity, and, through activity, character? First, action projects human beings into a world of causality, initiating sequences of events that, once begun, proceed without necessarily respecting the agent's intentions. This fact of the causality of human action most obviously threatens our capacity to control the *consequences* of our actions, but in a sense it also limits our ability to control the very *content* of our actions, insofar as it prevents us from locating a natural and uncontroversial boundary between our actions and the events that follow from them. Of course, we rely on such boundaries all the time, particularly in the law, where we often need to decide whether an event is to be imputed to an agent as *his act*, for which he may be held responsible. Yet while these conceptions of the limits of responsibility or imputability may *represent* themselves as reflections of some sheerly factual line of demarcation between, say, the willed and the caused, it is, in a way, the very *absence* of such a line that allows imputability to arise as a problem in the first place. Will and agency only become possible sources of injury or damage because they are *not* isolated from a separate world of causes and effects, but are themselves sources of causation—and this absence of a firm qualitative distinction between will and causation makes it difficult to fix, once and for all, the limits of what may be imputed to us as "our" doing.[69] Aristotle confronts this problem in his treatment of responsibility in book 3 of the *Nicomachean Ethics*, which begins with a telling equivocation: an involuntary act, Aristotle says, is one in which nothing is contributed by the "agent or the person acted upon" (*ho prattôn ê ho paschôn,*

1110a3). Here, as in tragedy, doing and suffering, *prattein* and *paschein*, seem to be two sides of the same coin rather than mutually exclusive opposites, and Aristotle's subsequent treatment of responsibility does not ultimately manage to separate them.[70]

The fact that our action inserts us into chains of causality not wholly under our control can, of course, manifest itself in numerous ways, and is perhaps most strikingly visible in cases of natural disaster in which nonhuman forces undermine our plans (and often destroy us altogether) in unpredictable, sometimes even utterly meaningless ways. But the sheer contingency of nature is not quite the stuff of tragedy, at least not directly.[71] Even more important, from the perspective of tragedy, is the fact that human beings act into a world inhabited by a *plurality* of other acting persons: the fact of human freedom, which is the condition of the possibility of effective agency, also limits our practical capacities because it is not exclusively ours but is mirrored in others.[72] Here, again, the point is not only that human plurality limits our control over the consequences of our action, but also that the *meaning* of our deeds is not wholly at our disposal, for the very terms through which we make assessments of significance are not exclusively our own, but intersubjective.[73] The importance of human plurality as a source of vulnerability in human action is acknowledged by Aristotle too, perhaps most prominently in his praise of what Martha Nussbaum has called "relational goods," including, especially, *philia*.[74]

These general features of action share a distinctive structure: they involve the *doubling back* of some human capacity upon itself—a recursivity, in which a source of possibility also operates as its own limitation. If human beings were not themselves parts of the causal order of the world, the will would be impotent; yet the very fact of our implication in the causal order of the world both connects our deeds to chains of events that lie beyond our control, *and* blurs the boundaries between action and event that might help us fix and master the meaning of our actions. Similarly, our capacity to engage in *meaningful* action depends upon the presence of a plurality of others—and, at the same time, the presence of others also subjects us to the uncertainty of others' responses to what we do, on which the meaning of our action partly depends. This peculiar structure of enabling conditions that are always also limitations places human actors in ontological double binds, rendering us dependent on the very forces that, in action, we seek to transcend. This constitutive openness of action to worldly contingency—to what I have called "impropriety"—is, I suggest, the feature of "real life" that ultimately lies behind Aristotle's claim about the priority of action to character in the *Poetics*.[75] To make this portrait of action's impropriety more concrete, however, we need to turn from Aristotle back to Sophocles' play, where we have left Antigone and Creon on the cusp of the deeds that undo them.

THE IMPROPRIETY OF ACTION IN THE *ANTIGONE*

The notion of human beings as constitutively caught in a double bind, rendered vulnerable by their potency, recalls one of the best-known passages in the *Antigone*: the first choral ode, often called the "Ode to Man," which famously describes humankind with the polysemic term *deinos.*[76] As Robert Goheen has noted, *deinos* suggests both "marvellous capability" and "strange danger," a range of meanings well captured in Wyckoff's translation of the first line of the ode: "Many the wonders [*deina*] but nothing walks stranger [*deinoteron*] than man."[77] Indeed, as the ode proceeds, it combines praise for the masterful power of human beings (who cross the seas, plough the earth, snare birds, harness the horses) with a sobering acknowledgment of the risk and uncertainty that attend human activity: "Clever beyond all dreams / the inventive craft he has / which may drive him one time or another to well or ill" (366–67). As we have seen, Antigone and Creon each seek to achieve a kind of masterful agency through recognition, yoking their acts to their own identities (and Polyneices'). The movement of the play, however, bears out the chorus's warning: in action, Antigone and Creon do, and become, more and other than they intend; and ironically, the consequences of this impropriety are intensified and rendered deadly by Antigone's and Creon's own impossible efforts to overcome the vulnerability and uncertainty to which they, like all human actors, are subject.

Antigone's and Creon's acts exceed the terms of the identities of which they are supposedly expressions in two general ways. First, both Antigone and Creon do *more* than they intend. Antigone frames her action as an expression of the pious devotion of sister to brother, and she underscores this identification through her refusal of the vocabulary of politics. Whenever Antigone is confronted with a claim about the city, she replies exclusively in the vocabulary of the family, refusing the possibility of *any* distinction between her brothers, even one more attenuated than Creon's.[78] However, Antigone's expression of family piety has political dimensions she does not acknowledge: despite her refusal of the vocabulary of politics, she finds herself in political space, performing an act that challenges the authority of a tyrant.[79] Similarly, Creon's act turns out to have implications in the realm of family that he, focused exclusively on the *polis*, does not acknowledge. Creon is, after all, not only the ruler of Thebes but also the head of the *oikos* to which Antigone belongs; indeed, he is doubly tied to her both as Jocasta's brother and as the father of her fiancé. But in his encounter with Antigone, Creon notably does *not* explicitly invoke his *familial* authority; instead, he continues to assert the political distinction between Polyneices and Eteocles, just as Antigone repeatedly counters him in the vocabulary of kinship.[80] Similarly, when Haemon arrives on the scene, he invites his father to speak the language of family by offering a conventional expression of filial loyalty, but Creon refuses the invitation, introducing the metaphor of "a soldier posted behind his leader" to describe the proper relation of son to father (640), and thereby swallowing family into *polis*.[81] Yet Creon's act, like Antigone's, exceeds the identity from which it proceeds. Just as Antigone's act of family piety became an act of political subversion, however inadvertent, Creon's defense of political order also turns out to be an assault on his own family, first in the person of Haemon, whose love for Antigone leads him to join her in death, and second in Eurydice, driven to suicide by the loss of her son.

Antigone and Creon do not merely turn out to have done *more* than they intended, however, for their actions place them into conflict not only with what they disavow, but also with their own deepest commitments. Antigone's relationship with Ismene is a telling example of this second kind of impropriety. Although Antigone is willing to suffer death out of loyalty to a blood relative, in the pursuit of her goal she behaves toward her sister—whom, on her own understanding of *philia*, she ought to love—with cold, vindictive hostility. When Ismene tries to warn Antigone that it is foolish to pursue her goal against the irresistible force of the *polis*, Antigone responds: "If that's your saying, I shall hate you first, and next the dead will hate you in all justice" (93–94). And when Ismene shows her belated support for her sister by falsely declaring to Creon that she had been an accessory to the deed, Antigone declines the offer of solidarity, insisting that she "cannot love a friend whose love is words" (543).[82] Similarly, Antigone's action undermines her identification with conventional gender roles: as we have seen, by preparing Polyneices' body for burial, scattering dust on the corpse to symbolize the burial that she herself does not perform, lamenting Polyneices' death, and pouring a final libation, Antigone follows the norms governing female participation in funeral ritual. But Antigone acts amid circumstances that make it impossible for her to conform to *this* traditional role without also *violating* equally central norms of gender. These violations become evident in the course of Creon's hysterical response to her disobedience, which reminds us that the very appearance of women in civic space threatened the constitutive boundary between *oikos* and *polis*. But they are also evident in Antigone's own final speeches, in which she laments that her fate will prevent her from following the conventional trajectory from girlhood to marriage and reproduction.[83] "No marriage-bed, no marriage-song for me," she sings, "and since no wedding, so no child to rear" (917–18, emphasis added).

Creon's acts, like Antigone's, not only exceed but also undermine his own identifications. Just as Antigone's ruthless devotion to her family leads her to treat her own sister cruelly, for instance, Creon's mono-maniacal pursuit of civic order turns him from a leader into a tyrant. After Creon shifts the terrain of his exchange with Haemon from family to city, Haemon criticizes his father's style of rule, at first gently and then with increasing passion and frustration. After reminding Creon of the murmurs of support for Antigone among the citizens of Thebes, Haemon warns his father: "do not have one mind, and one alone," for "whoever thinks that he alone is wise" will, "come the unfolding, sho[w] his emptiness" (705–9). Here already we have a pointed sugges-tion that Creon is betraying his own values, since he himself had earlier mocked Antigone for acting in isolation from the rest of the city (510); Teiresias will confirm the suggestion by insinuating that Creon is not a king but a "tyrant" (1056), and by forecasting the devastation that Creon's misrule will bring, not only upon his family, but upon the entire city (1080–84).[84] And, just as Antigone's action exceeds and frustrates her identification as a woman, Creon's deeds, though meant to secure his masculinity, actually undermine it. For Creon, as we have seen, mas-culinity is closely tied to political rule, and therefore (he insists) to the rejection of the normative force of kinship. But consanguinity was what brought him the political power through which he expresses his man-hood: he rules Thebes by virtue of being Jocasta's *adelphos*—the very same relation in which Polyneices and Antigone stand. His disavowal of the import of kinship leads to the death of his own son, Haemon, in a violent rush of blood (*haima*). As Creon is graphically reminded of the blood ties he had repressed, his fragile economy of identification and disavowal collapses like a house of cards. "So insistent earlier on the separation of gender roles and scornful of the female," Segal observes, "Creon now performs the characteristically (though not exclusively) fe-male role of lamenting over a 'child,'" expressing the anguish and bitter-ness that his edict had tried and failed to keep out of public view.[85]

Although there is a fearful symmetry between, on the one hand, Anti-gone's and Creon's initial acts, and on the other hand, the deviations and reversals that afflict them, it is crucial to attend not only to the irony of these outcomes but also to the mechanisms by which they occur, for Sophocles does not represent Antigone's and Creon's reversals as the inexorable results of cosmic necessity, divine justice, or other extrahu-man forces; rather, he suggests that they are the contingent results of the unpredictable interactions among a plurality of persons. It is true, of course, that Antigone speaks as though she knew from the beginning what the consequences of her act would be: "I know that I must die, how could I not?" she asks (460). But while Antigone *does* die by the end of the play, her death does not in fact occur in the way she expects, nor does it have the significance she anticipates. When Antigone first announces her intention to bury Polyneices, and her willingness to die doing it, she has just told Ismene that the punishment for the burial is to be death by stoning at the hands of the citizenry of Thebes—a form of punishment "felt to be particularly appropriate for traitors," and which, crucially, relied on the cooperation of the citizens who were to carry out the sentence.[86] Importantly, Antigone believes she will die with honor (95–97), a claim she later repeats in her exchange with Creon (502–3), whom she taunts by suggesting that the citizens of Thebes are really sympathetic to her, and approve of her action, but are muted by fear (504–5).[87] But Antigone does not die by stoning—she dies at her own hand, after having been confined to a living death in a cave.

Why does Creon change his mind? Perhaps he realizes that he will not need to rely on the shaky loyalty of the citizens to carry out *this* punishment; perhaps, as his own casuistical speech suggests, he thinks the fine distinction between death and living death will absolve him, and Thebes, of responsibility for yet another death in the royal family (773–80).[88] But Creon's decision also seems to respond to his sense that Antigone threatens his status as a man (and, relatedly, as a ruler), a sense that is sharpened in the course of their increasingly strident confrontation at 441–525,[89] and further heightened by the intervention of Haemon, whose efforts to moderate his father's anger seem only to intensify his gender panic.[90] The punishment Creon finally chooses for Antigone responds to this threat by mimicking the conventional enclosure of women within the *oikos*, as Antigone herself notices, calling the cave her "marriage-chamber" and her "hollowed-out house" (891–92).[91] Whatever Creon's motivation, from Antigone's perspective, this change of plans is catastrophic, for it seems to deprive her of the *glorious* death she had originally anticipated. Unwitnessed, she fears, her death will not be mourned and remembered: when the chorus suggests consolingly that she will still win fame in death (836–38), she objects that they are mocking her (839–41), and as she is led away, she laments that she will die "with no friend's mourning" (844).

Creon's "fate," too, proceeds in and through the contingencies of human action. Indeed, perhaps the most powerful image that the *Antigone* offers of the capacity of actions to exceed the intentions and control of agents comes near the end of the play, as Creon tries to undo what he has done. After confronting Teiresias, who finally gives Creon an account of his crimes and foretells the destruction that await him and his city, Creon yields, and tries to stave off his fate, announcing that he has "come to fear it's best to hold to the laws of old tradition to the end of life" (1113–14). Some of what happens next we witness or learn through the reports of a messenger before Creon does, but the special force of the sequence of events emerges if we examine it in strict chronology and from Creon's perspective. First, as the messenger recounts, Creon and the chorus went to bury Polyneices' corpse, hoping to reverse the pollution that the exposed body had brought upon the city (1197–1200). It's not clear whether Creon accomplishes this in time to turn the curse or not, since Teiresias has said that other cities, whose hearths have been polluted by the animals that fed on the exposed corpses, are already preparing to make war on Thebes (1080–84). With no time to speculate, Creon and his rescue party proceed toward Antigone's tomb, from which, at a distance, they hear the "keen lament" of Haemon's voice (1208). Antigone has already hanged herself, and while Creon was busy burying Polyneices, Haemon found the tomb and discovered her fate. When Creon finally reaches the burial chamber, he finds Haemon mournfully embracing Antigone; Haemon says nothing to his father, but lashes out at him with his sword, and then turns his weapon on himself, dying in a bloody embrace with Antigone (1220–40). At this point, the messenger leaves Creon and the rest of the party to attend to the bodies and rushes back to the palace, where he informs Eurydice (and us) of all the preceding events; she leaves the room without a word, followed in short order by the messenger, who is concerned that her silence "may portend as great disaster as a loud lament" (1251–52). Creon arrives shortly thereafter—and just as he is confessing his crimes to the assembled chorus, the messenger returns to announce that Eurydice, too, has taken her own life (1282–83). Once Creon has given it life, we might say, his action breaks the bonds of intention and identity and goes off on its own, interacting in unpredictable ways with the actions of others, and wreaking havoc. Creon rushes from the house to the deserted plain to the rocky cave and back to the house, all in a desperate attempt to chase down and subdue his errant deed, but the act and its reverberations always remain one tragic step ahead of its agent. In the case of the messenger's early departure from the tomb, the deed, or at least its "signification," is *literally* a step ahead of the doer.[92] Here, the character of the messenger vividly personifies the gap between the actor's performance of a deed and the imitation or recollection of the deed in which its significance is expressed, offering tragic confirmation of Arendt's observation that "nobody is the author or producer of his own life story."[93]

ANAGNÔRISIS AND ACKNOWLEDGMENT

We are now in a position to return, finally, to the theme of tragic *anagnôrisis*, and its relationship to the concept of recognition. Aristotle first defines the concept of *anagnôrisis* in chapter 11 of the *Poetics*, in the course of elaborating the nature and components of the tragic plot: "A recognition is, as the very word implies, a change from ignorance [*agnoias*] to knowledge [*gnôsin*], and thus to either love or hate, in the personages marked for good or evil fortune."[94] Aristotle proceeds (both in this chapter and later) to list some examples of recognition, including the recognition of Odysseus by his scar (1454b25–8); Electra's recognition of Orestes by "reasoning" in Aeschylus's *Choephori* (1455a4–6); and Oedipus's recognition that he himself is his father's killer (1452a32–3). It is tempting to conclude on the basis of these examples that *anagnôrisis* in the *Poetics* has the same sense that it did in the contemporary politics of recognition: after all, the examples all seem to suggest that recognition is the recognition *of an identity*, either one's own or another's.[95] This is not altogether wrong, but it is misleading. A somewhat different view emerges if we situate the concept of recognition within Aristotle's larger account of the structure of tragedy and tie it back to the account of *êthos* and action discussed earlier.

First, it is important to acknowledge that for Aristotle, recognition is closely linked to another component of what he calls "complex" tragic plots, *peripeteia* or "reversal"; indeed, Aristotle says that the "finest form" of recognition is the one accompanied by reversal (1452a32–33). Reversal, in turn, is a particular form of change (*metabolê*) in the fortune or circumstances of an actor; specifically, it is a change that takes place through a relatively abrupt shift in the trajectory of the action.[96] The presence of such abrupt shifts or reversals in the action, in turn, can be understood as Aristotle's way of spelling out what it means for the events that make up a tragic plot to occur "unexpectedly and at the same time in consequence of one another" (*para tên doxan di' allêla*, 1452a4), which is a feature that he says characterizes the most effective tragic plots.[97] But what does it mean for events to occur "unexpectedly and at the same time in consequence of one another"? Obviously, this phrase could refer to what happens in straightforward cases of the ignorance of identity: Oedipus kills Laius and sleeps with Jocasta, not knowing that they are his mother and father; and everything that follows from that is, for Oedipus, tragically "unexpected." Yet the *Poetics* and the *Antigone* also suggest that there is another, deeper meaning to *para tên doxan di' allêla*; that, even when we have all the names right, what I have called the "impropriety" of action—its exposure to an unpredictable and uncontrollable future—can *also* introduce a crucial gap between our expectations and our action.[98] Aristotle's original claim about the order of priority of action and *êthos*, and our parallel understanding of the impropriety of action with respect to identity, thus turn out to be intimately connected to recognition: action's impropriety is the one of the central occasions for tragic *anagnôrisis*.

This way of situating *anagnôrisis* suggests a different account of its meaning, as well as of its ethical and political force. If the priority of action over *êthos* and identity is an occasion for reversal and thus for *anagnôrisis*, then perhaps the "shift from ignorance to knowledge" involved in *anagnôrisis* is best understood not only as the discovery of someone's true identity, but also and more fundamentally as what I would call an "ontological" discovery, a shift from ignorance to knowledge about the real conditions of one's own existence and activity, and especially about the very relationship between *êthos* or identity and action. On this account of tragic *anagnôrisis*, to be sure, *anagnôrisis* may indeed take place through the discovery of something about who one is—or, in any event, who one has become under the weight of action and its consequences. But what differentiates this sort of *anagnôrisis* from recognition as Antigone and Creon pursued it is that this sort of *anagnôrisis* does not satisfyingly consolidate and strengthen a practical identity—a coherent set of commitments and values that enables an agent to know what to do. Instead, this sort of *anagnôrisis* comes *after* action, shattering without yet reconstituting the coherence of the identificatory scheme with which the agent has tried to govern his activity. Tragic *anagnôrisis*, we might say, is the acknowledgment of finitude under the weight of a (failed) effort to become sovereign through the recognition of identity.

This understanding of tragic *anagnôrisis* is borne out by the text of the *Antigone*, for while the *Antigone*'s struggles for recognition do indeed fail, the play nevertheless contains moments of "successful" (though unhappy) *anagnôrisis* in this sense. The first such moment comes, appropriately enough, at the end of the first choral ode, and the agent through which the *anagnôrisis* occurs is neither Antigone nor Creon but the chorus itself. Earlier, I noted that the so-called "Ode to Man" moderates its praise of human mastery with an acknowledgment of the risks that attend human activity, which can lead people "one time or another to well or ill" (366–67). Immediately after this qualification, however, the chorus makes an attempt to tame the force of this uncertainty by splitting these two possibilities apart and assigning them to "two distinct kinds of people," those who "hono[r] the laws of the land and the gods' sworn right," and those who "dar[e] to dwell with dishonor" (368–71).[99] This distinction enables the chorus to dissociate themselves from people of the latter sort, declaring confidently that they will never let such people share their hearth or their thoughts (373–75), a move that echoes Antigone's and Creon's own earlier efforts to organize the world into *philos* and *ekhthros*. But Sophocles, as if to underline the radical implications of the notion of humanity as *deinos*, immediately calls into question the chorus's effort to draw an easy distinction between its friends and its enemies, for at this moment, Antigone is led onstage by the guard, who is about to present her to Creon as "the woman who has done the deed" (384). Antigone's appearance brings the ode to an end and suddenly collapses the chorus's confidence: "My mind is split at this awful sight," it declares; "I know her. I cannot deny Antigone is here" (376–78). This *anagnôrisis* is not the *satisfying* recognition of the identity of another; instead, it undermines the chorus's recognitive distinction between someone who is *deinos* in a good, just, orderly way and someone who is *deinos* in an uncanny, terrible, dangerous way, leaving it caught between the desire to deny, and the evident impossibility of denying, what is before its eyes.[100]

This moment of acknowledgment anticipates Antigone's and Creon's own *anagnôriseis*. It is tempting to think that these will find expression in straightforward confessions of guilt, as for instance when Creon, frightened by Teiresias's prophecies, accepts the chorus's counsel and rushes off to bury Polyneices and free Antigone. But the trouble is that there is no corresponding confession involving Antigone herself: the only parallel episode comes near the end of Antigone's self-lament, and is more equivocal than Creon's plain reversal: "Should the gods think that this [i.e., her punishment] is righteousness, in suffering I'll see my error clear," she says. "But if it is the others who are wrong, I wish them no greater punishment than mine" (926–29). To say that she admits her guilt here would be to overstate the case, for she only professes uncertainty about whether the gods will find her righteous or culpable.[101]

Yet to suppose on these grounds that only Creon experiences a moment of *anagnôrisis* is both to overlook something important about Antigone's words *and* to misunderstand what this moment of tragic acknowledgment involves. In the first place, we must be careful to avoid a false choice between an Antigone who straightforwardly confesses her guilt and an Antigone who remains as resolute as ever to the end. In fact, both are untrue to the text. Both Antigone's self-lament *and* her admission of the *possibility* that the gods will judge her guilty represent real transformations of Antigone's earlier rigidity. In her opening speeches, Antigone had defiantly welcomed the prospect of death (70–72), but now she *mourns* her fate, and in so doing, explicitly acknowledges that her act has deprived her of the very goods she pursued, including *philia* and motherhood (878–81, 918). In fact, by conceding that the question of the real significance of her act is out of her hands and rests instead with the gods, Antigone expresses a more sophisticated acknowledgment of human finitude, of the gap between identity and action, than a simple avowal of guilt would have indicated. After all, even after Creon changes his tune, he is no more master of his fate than he had been earlier; in fact, his worst suffering is still to come. Creon's real moment of *ana-*

gnôrisis in this sense comes *after* the deaths of his son and wife. As he laments his fate and prays for a quick death, Creon's own words reflect his belated awareness not of his wrongdoing, exactly (for he has already seen *that*), but of the gap between his intentions and his actions: "Take me away at once," he pleads, "the frantic man who killed my son, against my meaning" (1339–41). What Antigone and Creon have acknowledged, in different ways, is a version of the predicament described by the chorus in its famous closing words (1343–52): to avoid the catastrophes that action's improprieties bring, we would need to possess as actors a kind of knowledge that we acquire only in retrospect, and too late.

Tragedy thus leaves us with a contrast, even a conflict, between the recognition of the identity of the other, and the acknowledgment of the circumstances or conditions that surround one's own activity. Tragedy does not, of course, suggest that human beings can live in the utter absence of recognition, nor does it suggest that there are no genuine and valuable goods to be found in the many human relationships that are sustained by exchanges of recognition. But in its account of the relationship of action to identity or *êthos*, tragedy helps us understand both why a perfect regime of recognition is impossible, and, more importantly, why this impossibility is not only a regrettable limitation but itself a condition of the possibility of agency—the flip side, as it were, of freedom. To will truly successful recognition, on this view, is to exchange one sort of social death for another, sacrificing the uncertainty of the plural, futural social world for the final word, the perfect subjection, of the eulogy—an exchange Antigone herself is willing to make.

But that is not the only lesson of the play. Throughout this chapter I have stressed the moments of symmetry between Antigone and Creon, but it is important to acknowledge that this symmetry is only partial. Creon, after all, *survives* his catastrophe, though undoubtedly scarred and perhaps chastened, while Antigone *dies*: it matters—it is a matter of life and death—that this play occurs against an all-too-familiar background of profound social and political inequality, most obviously between men and women, but also, as Butler's reading shows, between people who can occupy the roles and terms laid out by normative systems of kinship with relative ease, and those who cannot. In fact, it is inequality of just this sort that makes it tempting to read the play through the language of contemporary theories of recognition, for such theories seem to give us a principle according to which we can condemn this inequality, and which we can use to help imagine an alternative.

This, I think, would be a mistake, and the notion of acknowledgment can help us see why. As I have suggested in chapter 1, the politics of recognition parses this sort of inequality as a matter of the unfair distribution of respect, rooted in the failure to grasp *who* a person or a group really is. There is something to this. Identity-related injustices do often manifest themselves through the reproduction and dissemination of distorted characterizations of people and groups. But are these characterizations the root or the symptom of injustice? Are they genuine cognitive mistakes that might be corrected through the production and dissemination of truer pictures of who we and others are? Or are they more deeply motivated representations, representations that have less to do with the people who are their putative objects than with the aspirations or desires of those who hold them?

An analysis of injustice centered around the concept of recognition can tell us, for example, that Creon—like many men—holds false and demeaning views of women; or that he unfairly belittles kinship as a mode of human relationship (and it might be able to tell us similar things about the Greek model of normal kinship and its exclusions). But it cannot help us understand the way in which Creon's actions are driven by his own panicked defense of a position of privilege within a hierarchical social order. An analysis of injustice centered around *anagnôrisis* understood as acknowledgment, by contrast, might help us get at the underlying structures of desire that animate systematic relations of inequality, for it suggests that social relations of subordination and the images and representations that accompany them may be supported in part by the (impossible) aspiration to achieve sovereign agency. Might those relations be understood as ways of shoring up that aspiration, as ways of insulating some people from the force of its impossibility precisely be leaving others to bear the weight of the contradictions, reversals, and failures that forever frustrate the desire for mastery? Something of this thought seems to me to lie behind Sophocles' implicit critique of Creon's tyrannical tendencies, as well as of the abusiveness Antigone displays toward her sister—a sort of smaller-scale tyranny, commensurate with Antigone's subordinate position in the larger scheme of Theban society and politics. But these are still only intimations. To deepen them, we turn now from tragedy to Hegel.

CHAPTER FOUR

The Abdication of Independence
On Hegel's *Phenomenology*

> To the question: 'What is Now?', let us answer, e.g. 'Now is
> Night.' In order to test the truth of this sense-certainty a
> simple experiment will suffice. We write down this truth; a
> truth cannot lose anything by being written down, any more
> than it can lose anything through our preserving it. If *now,*
> *this noon*, we look again at the written truth we shall have to
> say that it has become stale.
> —HEGEL, *Phenomenology of Spirit*

HEGEL'S TWO VOICES

THE PRECEDING CHAPTERS have left us with two sharply contrasting
views of the significance of the concept of recognition for political thought.
On the one hand, the politics of recognition, eloquently defended by
Taylor and others, takes recognition to be a crucial human good. On
this view, a just social and political order is one in which people mutually recognize each other in all their diversity, thereby overcoming the
crippling restrictions on some people's agency that result from unequal
or asymmetrical distributions of recognition. On the other hand, tragedy, with its distinctive understanding of the relationship between action
and identity, offers us important reasons to think that such an ideal is,
in principle, unfulfillable, and these reasons fit with and extend Taylor's
own insightful critique of the pursuit of sovereign agency in the context
of the philosophy of language. From this second perspective, the pursuit
of the sovereign satisfaction of recognition is itself a form of misrecognition, a failure to acknowledge the ways in which human agency is conditioned by such basic circumstances as plurality, which exposes action
(and hence also identity) to an unpredictable future, at once limiting our
control over what we do and who we shall become, and also making
possible the distinctive pleasures of life and action among others. One
late-twentieth-century view; one ancient Greek: so far we have circled
around but not confronted the monumental figure of Georg Wilhelm
Friedrich Hegel, surely the most influential theorist of recognition in
modern European philosophy, author of the famous accounts of the

"struggle for recognition" and the "dialectic of master and slave" in the *Phenomenology of Spirit* of 1807.[1] How does Hegel fit into this picture?

Typically, Hegel is aligned with the first of the these two approaches. Indeed, he is often cast as the intellectual grandfather of the contemporary politics of recognition. On this reading, Hegel is a key source both of the norm of equal recognition, and of the vision of a just social order as one in which diverse individuals and groups are bound together by mutual recognition into a whole that does not suppress difference. This general way of understanding Hegel's conception of recognition is shared by theorists with widely different political orientations, and by generalists as well as Hegel specialists. Francis Fukuyama's 1992 book *The End of History and the Last Man*, for example, famously proposed that modern liberal democracy might have brought human history to an end by completely satisfying the basic human longing for recognition. Alluding to Hegel's *Phenomenology*, Fukuyama argued that "the problem of human history can be seen, in a certain sense, as the search for a way to satisfy the desire of both masters and slaves for recognition on a mutual and equal basis," and, encouraged by the events of 1989, he suggested that the worldwide triumph of liberal democracy might mark the conclusion of this search.[2]

Charles Taylor's essay on the politics of recognition, published the same year, implicitly challenged Fukuyama's assumption that demands for the recognition of ethnic and cultural identities simply represented an irrational regression away from the "universal and homogeneous" forms of recognition achieved by modern liberal democracy.[3] Still, while Taylor's defense of thicker and more diverse forms of recognition was in one sense a forceful critique of liberal self-congratulation, Taylor ultimately remained in agreement with Fukuyama about the underlying meaning of the Hegelian account of recognition. For Taylor as for Fukuyama, Hegel's philosophy grounds a principle of mutual and equal recognition and challenges us to find social and political forms that will realize that principle, finally satisfying—for everyone—the basic human need to be seen and respected by one's fellows. Glossing his own earlier interpretation of the *Phenomenology* in his massive and influential treatise on Hegel's philosophy, Taylor concluded: "The struggle for recognition can find only one satisfactory solution, and that is a regime of reciprocal recognition among equals."[4]

Recent developments in Hegel scholarship have bolstered this general approach. A new wave of interest in Hegel's view of recognition, which began mainly among German scholars but has now spread to the English-language literature, has produced a number of important studies of the concept, which trace it back through Hegel's pre-*Phenomenology* Jena manuscripts to its origins in Fichte's philosophy, and forward into such later works as the *Philosophy of Right*.[5] These scholars often define themselves, explicitly or implicitly, in opposition to an earlier wave of interest in Hegel's concept of recognition which began in pre–World War II France, driven in substantial part by Alexandre Kojève's influential 1933–1939 Paris lectures on the *Phenomenology*.[6] Scholars of the new wave such as Robert Williams and Axel Honneth argue that Kojève and his students, especially Sartre, tended to reduce the very idea of recognition to one of its concrete instantiations—the master-slave relationship—thereby falling into a kind of philosophical misanthropy in which social relations are always and only dominative and alienating, and in which the only authentic stance is that of the solitary existential hero.[7] By contrast, these more recent interpreters insist that Hegel's theory of recognition offers an *affirmative* account of the contours of a just social and political order, one that can transcend the inequality and asymmetry of the master-slave relationship in a "community of mutual recognition."[8]

In many respects, this general way of approaching Hegel's conception of recognition is correct. For example, as we shall see, it is true that Hegel's story of the master-slave relationship is not in any straightforward sense a philosophical anthropology, a portrait of human nature as essentially driven toward the enslavement and subjugation of others. Instead, just as these readers of Hegel have said, it is a diagnosis and critique of social relations of domination, undertaken in the name of equality and mutuality. It is also true that Hegel, especially in his mature political philosophy, understood himself to be offering an account of a set of social and political institutions that could satisfy the demand for equal and mutual recognition, binding people together without eliminating individuality or difference. But at this point, difficulties arise. It is easy to suppose, as most readers do, that these two elements of Hegel's thought fit easily together, that his vision of equal and mutual recognition is the natural complement to or extension of his critique of domination. Yet the truth is more complicated: properly understood, Hegel's diagnostic and critical account of the struggle for recognition and the master-slave relationship actually stands at odds with his own vision of a community of mutual recognition. Indeed, as I shall argue, Hegel's thought actually echoes and deepens (even as it ultimately betrays) the critical perspective on recognition implied by Taylor's account of language and agency and more fully elaborated in Greek tragedy.[9]

Now this argument can only make sense if what I have been calling "Hegel's account of recognition" is not actually a single, seamless thing. And part of the purpose of these chapters is to tease apart two different voices in Hegel's account of recognition, which Hegel himself tries but fails to bring into harmony.[10] The first of these voices is Hegel's "diagnostic" voice. It is the voice of Hegel the phenomenologist, whose great skill lies in the ability to notice and represent, often dramatically, the ways in which determinate theoretical perspectives, forms of knowledge, modes of action, and social orders fall into contradictions even on their own terms—a skill Hegel shared with Sophocles (though the pleasures of Hegel's poetry are more austere).[11] While it does not disappear in the later works—it recurs in the ascending dialectic of abstract right, morality, and *Sittlichkeit* in the *Philosophy of Right*, for example[12]—this voice is most clearly audible in Hegel's *Phenomenology of Spirit*, perhaps because the explicit agenda of the *Phenomenology* was to offer an alternative to those "dogmatic" and "abstract" modes of philosophizing that treat truth as a bare result, cut off from the difficult path through reversal and contradiction by which it is achieved. Such approaches, Hegel famously claims in the preface to the *Phenomenology*, "lack the seriousness, the suffering, the patience, and the labour of the negative," whereas phenomenology will "surrender to the life of the object" it studies, letting itself and its readers become implicated in the adventures and misadventures of spirit it traces, the better to learn their lessons (10, 32). And it is this first, diagnostic voice that is predominant in Hegel's account of the struggle for recognition and the master-slave relationship.

The second of these voices is Hegel's "reconciliatory" voice. It is, you might say, the voice of the *system*—the voice that promises us that at the end of this journey there lies the prospect of a homecoming, of finally arriving at a state in which contradiction, division, suffering, and other manifestations of negativity have been not necessarily eliminated, but at least *redeemed* as moments of an intelligible, internally articulated, encompassing whole.[13] It is also present in the *Phenomenology*—in the preface's image of the movement of philosophy through negativity as a "self-restoring sameness," for example (10)—but this voice is most clearly audible in the later works. If the ascending dialectic through abstract right, morality, and *Sittlichkeit* in the *Philosophy of Right* is an example of Hegel's diagnostic voice, the subsequent unpacking of *Sittlichkeit* itself through the categories of family, civil society, and state is performed in Hegel's reconciliatory voice: it is an account of an institutional whole that incorporates and redeems what is worthwhile in the perspectives on "right" that were left behind in the move to *Sittlichkeit*.[14] It is this voice in which Hegel offers his affirmative account of the basic structures of a community of equal and mutual recognition, and it is this voice which still echoes in contemporary neo-Hegelian versions of the politics of recognition.

I cannot pretend to give anything like a thorough account of the relationship between these two voices in Hegel's thought as a whole. But I shall try to show that, at least with respect to the idea of recognition,

Hegel's diagnostic voice cuts against his reconciliatory voice in two important and persuasive ways, which he himself did not consistently acknowledge. (In this sense, my reading of Hegel in this chapter and the next runs parallel to my simultaneous appropriation and critique of Taylor in chapter 2.) Notice, first, that theorists who make recognition into a social and political ideal implicitly adopt an especially ambitious version of Hegel's reconciliatory voice. They suppose that equal and mutual recognition is something like a precondition of genuine agency, a state or condition that can be secured *in advance of action*, rendering the action that follows it truly free, or authentically one's own. Yet while it is true that action always emerges out of an enabling background of relations of recognition that have made us who we are, Hegel, in his diagnostic voice, echoes the tragic insight that action forever outruns the relations of recognition out of which it emerges, and that recognition is therefore inevitably *belated*:[15] it cannot insulate us against the surprises and reversals of action, in which we lose ourselves, sometimes pleasantly, sometimes catastrophically.[16]

Of course, one could respond to this first conflict between Hegel's voices by denying that Hegel himself, when he talked of "reconciliation," really had anything so ambitious in mind as a *final* state of satisfaction that would inaugurate a new epoch of unalienated activity. Instead, we might conclude, Hegel knew full well that successful recognition could never be anything more than retrospective, and that reconciliation itself was not a state that could be achieved once and for all. He took reconciliation via recognition to be something more like a perpetual project, at best provisionally complete, and subject to constant revision under the pressure of changing circumstances.[17] This, after all, is one way of reading the force of Hegel's famous meditations on the relation of philosophy to politics at the end of the preface to the *Philosophy of Right*, where he declares—echoing, with a touch of melancholy, the chorus's gnomic utterances about the belatedness of wisdom in the closing lines of the *Antigone*—that philosophy "always comes too late" to give instruction as to how the world ought to be.[18]

This is an attractive interpretation, but it is not enough, because it doesn't quite capture the full force of the belatedness of recognition. The upshot of that insight is, if you will, qualitative rather than quantitative: it is not just that we shall have to settle for a sequence of provisional approximations of successful recognition, but that recognition itself is not the kind of thing we thought it was; and that we therefore go wrong in investing our ethical and political hopes in the idea of successful recognition, even if that idea remains purely regulative.[19] And this brings us to the second important contribution of Hegel's diagnostic voice. As we have seen, we often invest political desire in the ideal of recognition by imagining mutual recognition as the antidote to important forms of social and political inequality and subordination. However, Hegel develops an account of the nature of relations of subordination in which the pursuit of recognition is *part of the problem rather than part of the solution*. On this account, such social relations are to be understood not in terms of the failure of recognition, but in terms of the failure of *acknowledgment*—that is, the failure to acknowledge one's own finitude, rooted in the condition of human plurality. But because this failure of acknowledgment is precisely the same failure involved in the pursuit of sovereign agency via recognition, the effort to overcome subordination by pursuing a community of mutual recognition is not just fated to be an ongoing project: it misses the point, and worse. Such pursuits are not only futile; in many instances, they are the very instruments by which we insulate ourselves from the weight of our finitude, displacing our aspiration to sovereign agency onto a larger whole with which we identify. In other words, even at their best, such pursuits of recognition attenuate subordination without adequately addressing its roots; at their worst, they express and intensify the dominative impulses they purport to overcome.

This is all very brief and abstract; in this chapter and the next, I spell it out in more detail. Chapter 5 will read Hegel against himself, appropriating his own diagnostic voice to analyze a case that he (and some of his interpreters) take to be an instance of unequivocally emancipatory recognition, and thus evidence of the possibility of reconciliation: the case of Jewish emancipation in early-nineteenth-century Germany. In this chapter, however, I focus on recovering Hegel's diagnostic voice and reconstructing his understanding of the dynamics of subordination, without assuming that this analysis feeds neatly into the reconciliatory ideal of a community of mutual recognition. This reconstruction will center around a re-reading of Hegel's account of the struggle for recognition and the dialectic of master and slave, for the appropriation of Hegel in the service of an ideal of mutual recognition rests on a fundamental and widespread misunderstanding of just what it is that goes *wrong* at the inaugural moment of the master-slave relationship. To lay the ground for that reading, however, I begin not with the struggle for recognition, but with Hegel's thinly veiled treatment of Sophocles' *Antigone* in the *Phenomenology*, which will help us understand the continuities between Hegel's diagnostic perspective on recognition and the line of thought I have been developing in the last two chapters.

The *Antigone* in the *Phenomenology*

By the time the young Hegel began his schooling in Stuttgart, German intellectual life was already feeling the force of a powerful wave of Hellenism, inspired in part by Winckelmann's famous celebration of the "noble simplicity and tranquil grandeur" of classical sculpture.[20] Hegel, swept up, was to remain engaged with the legacy of ancient Greece, and in particular Greek tragedy, for the rest of his life, from his earliest days translating Sophocles in *Gymnasium*, to his late lectures on aesthetics in Berlin.[21] His early writings from Bern and Frankfurt often invoke Aeschylus's *Oresteia* in particular as a model of ethical and social reconciliation, but in his late Berlin lectures on aesthetics, he declared Sophocles's *Antigone* to be one of "most magnificent and satisfying" works of art he knew, and it is this play above all others that Hegel singles out for extended if oblique treatment in his 1807 *Phenomenology of Spirit*.[22]

What is the significance of Hegel's reading of tragedy, and especially of the *Antigone*, for the concept of recognition? This question is rendered especially complicated by the fact that, even within the bounds of the *Phenomenology*, Hegel's engagement with the *Antigone* is caught in the tension between his two voices. In his diagnostic voice, Hegel takes up and extends some of tragedy's fundamental ontological insights into the conditions of human agency, building those into a subtle analysis and indictment of unjust social relationships. At the same time, despite the potential of Hegel's own view of social subordination to serve as a tool for understanding and criticizing patriarchal power (both as it is represented in the *Antigone* and in Hegel's own time), Hegel himself refuses to apply his own critique of subordination to gender relations; instead, both in the *Phenomenology* and in the later *Philosophy of Right* (where Antigone makes another notorious appearance), Hegel ratifies the exclusion of women from public life—a move that is driven, I shall suggest, by the theoretical requirements of his own aspiration to imagine a community reconciled through mutual recognition. We shall return to the issue of Hegel's patriarchalism later in the chapter. Here, however, I want to focus on the ontological lessons that Hegel, at least in his diagnostic voice, takes from tragedy. Hegel's reading of the *Antigone* in the *Phenomenology*, I shall suggest, zeroes in on the theme of the impropriety of action—which, as we have seen, is the key to Sophocles' implicit critique of the politics of recognition. Indeed, the structure of reversal through which the impropriety of action is manifest both in the *Antigone* and in Hegel's retelling of it turns out to be exemplary of the larger narrative structure and argumentative method of the *Phenomenology*—and this point will help us interpret his story of the struggle for recognition and the dialectic of master and slave.

Hegel's engagement with the *Antigone* in the *Phenomenology* comes at the beginning of the division of the book devoted to "Spirit." The previous sections of the *Phenomenology* narrate the travails of a subject who seeks to achieve self-certainty, alternately via knowledge and via action, but whose efforts in this direction merely reveal, at each stage, the inadequacy of its present self-understanding or practical posture, provoking a succession of refinements in the subject's self-conception and mode of action. The section on "Spirit" inaugurates a new stage in this movement: it marks the moment at which the subject begins to understand itself, and its ways of knowing and acting, as irreducibly situated within a larger social context.[23] In keeping with this transition, the very *name* of Hegel's protagonist changes: it is no longer an individual "consciousness" or "self-consciousness" but "spirit" whose rocky, conflictual experience Hegel now traces. And the first episode in this part of the story concerns the manifestation of "spirit" that had long been regarded by German men of letters as the very model of simple harmony and unalienated existence: the social order of ancient Greece.[24] The lens through which Hegel approaches ancient Greece is, in turn, Sophocles' *Antigone*.

To suggest that Hegel's reading of the *Antigone* actually focuses our attention precisely on the improprieties of action—on the ways that Antigone and Creon *fail* to smoothly act out the identities they bear— certainly resists the conventional wisdom about his interpretation of the play. On most accounts, Hegel's major contribution (for good or ill) to the history of the interpretation of the *Antigone* is his claim that there is in some sense an ethical symmetry between Antigone and Creon, a claim that pits him against Goethe and others who see Antigone as a heroine, an exemplar of virtue, and a model of resistance to the tyranny represented by Creon.[25] For Hegel, by contrast, Antigone and Creon, by virtue of the social roles they play, represent valid, but partial and one-sided, ethical principles: Antigone stands for the rights of kinship; Creon, for the rights of the city. But if this is Hegel's view, it would seem to conflict with the account developed in chapter 3 of the impropriety of action, since it identifies Antigone and Creon as the representatives of two coherent social identities. In an important critique of Hegel, Patricia Mills makes just this claim, arguing that Hegel too easily reduces Antigone and Creon to their identities as female and male representatives of the family and the state, failing to see the ways in which Antigone in particular "breaks out of the confines of her assigned sphere."[26] This is true enough as a claim about Sophocles' play; but it is more problematic as a claim about Hegel, because it neglects the internal structure of Hegel's interpretation, and thus also the larger argumentative strategy of the *Phenomenology*.

As I have already suggested, the *Phenomenology of Spirit* is Hegel's most dramatic work of philosophy.[27] Hegel's methodological preface, though dryly entitled "On Scientific Cognition," quickly shatters any expectation that we are about to read a standard exposition of a philosophical system. Dogmatic philosophies, Hegel says, promise edification through the application of a single true principle to a variety of themes or problems; but this he dismisses as "monochromatic formalism" and even "insipidity" (9, 10). Real insight cannot be satisfied with a bare result, but must also grasp "the process through which it came about," and that involves narrating the experience of consciousness as it moves from ignorance toward knowledge, a journey filled with unexpected turns and reversals (2, 33). Moreover, the narrator of this story is tricky: he uses strategies ranging from polite invitation to rhetorical subterfuge to cultivate identification with the protagonist, all the better to ensnare the reader in the same conflicts and surprises, and thus the same despair and disappointment, to which consciousness is subject.

But this means that the *Phenomenology* demands to be read with a sense of cautious anticipation, honed by familiarity with the movements of reversal that Hegel's text repeatedly traces. Statements that, in a different sort of book, might justifiably be taken to represent the author's own position on an issue may turn out, a few pages later, to be tragically mistaken. Yet discussions of Hegel's interpretation of the *Antigone* often suffer from a lack of attention to just this feature of the *Phenomenology*'s method. Interpreters freely quote passages drawn from throughout the discussion of Greek *Sittlichkeit* as though they all straightforwardly represented Hegel's views, without considering the conceptual movement that takes place over the course of those pages. Likewise, Hegel's readers quote material from throughout the discussion as though it were all related to the *Antigone* in the same way, without attending to the distinctive position, both conceptually and textually, that Sophocles' drama occupies within Hegel's treatment of Greek ethical life.[28]

Hegel's discussion of Greek *Sittlichkeit* has three distinct parts: the first part includes the paragraphs numbered 446–63 in Miller's translation; the second part includes paragraphs 464–72; the third—which I shall not discuss until later in this chapter—extends from 473–76. In the first section, Hegel presents a stylized reconstruction of the ancient Greek social world. This world is organized around a parallel series of distinctions between different but complementary "powers"—family and city, divine law and human law, unconscious and conscious, and female and male—which fit together, in a peaceful and mutually reinforcing way, into a single harmonious totality. Of course, as we have seen, these distinctions do correspond roughly to the categories of identity through which Antigone and Creon define themselves in the opening speeches of Sophocles' play, and this fact would seem to support the view that for Hegel, Antigone and Creon are the *proper* bearers of coherent social identities.[29] Here, however, our sense of caution about Hegel's narrative strategies ought to be sounding its alarm. When Hegel says that the ancient Greek ethical world was characterized by "a stable equilibrium of all the parts"; when he suggests that in it, identities and their bearers fit together without remainder (277); or when he calls Greece "an immaculate world, a world unsullied by any internal dissension" (278), should we understand him to be speaking in his own voice? Are we really supposed to understand these comments to be straightforward expressions of approval and approbation of the organization of identity in the Greek ethical world—especially in light of what we already know about the subsequent action and *dénouement* of the *Antigone*?

Quite to the contrary: there is a sharp break in Hegel's discussion of Greek *Sittlichkeit* between his initial description of the harmonious internal organization of the Greek world and his subsequent account of the ultimately catastrophic introduction of discord and conflict into this world through the performance of particular deeds. In the second part of his discussion, Hegel personifies the social identities that he had articulated in his initial characterization of Greek ethical life, introducing concrete individuals who bear those identities and (attempt to) act them out. But this movement from identity to action is not smooth and harmonious, as we had been led to expect; instead, the introduction of the particular person and the deed "disturbs the peaceful organization and movement of the ethical world" (279), leading eventually to its downfall and the emergence of a different "shape of spirit" (289).

But what, exactly, makes action disruptive in this way? Here, Hegel's account becomes ambiguous. The answer clearly has something to do with the unknown or unanticipated meanings and consequences of human deeds. Action, Hegel says, gives rise to a contradiction between the "known and the unknown" (280) such that agents do not know the full character of what they are doing in advance, but only discover "the developed nature of what [they] actually did" through the consequences and reactions their deeds evoke (283). However, there are at least two ways of understanding this phenomenon. At times, it seems that on Hegel's reading the trouble is *simply* that Antigone and Creon, in their decisive and self-assured efforts to act on the basis of their social identities, have blinded themselves to one of the two constituent parts of Greek *Sittlichkeit*. "That consciousness which belongs to the divine law sees in the other side only the violence of human caprice," Hegel writes, "while that which holds to human law sees in the other only the self-will and disobedience of the individual who insists on being its own authority" (280).[30] Each character's tragic downfall thus amounts to the reassertion of those "powers" he or she refuses to recognize: "the two laws being linked in the essence, the fulfillment of the one evokes the other and—the deed having made it so—calls it forth as a violated and now hostile entity demanding revenge" (283). On this reading, the problem is (as Robert Williams glosses it) simply that "each character has a false consciousness, a one-sided grasp of the whole which leads him/her to identify entirely with his/her particular social role and its duties while denying validity to the claims of the other."[31]

This is surely part of Hegel's story—indeed, it is the part of his story that prepares the way for his reconciliatory voice, which will read the development of *Geist* as the unfolding and making-explicit of a content that is in some sense already given. But there is—there must be—more to it than this, because this account leaves us unable to account for the structure of Hegel's interpretation. On the one hand, if the point of Hegel's account was merely that Antigone and Creon both possess incomplete understandings of the social totality in which they are situated—Antigone, representative of the family, refuses to acknowledge the legitimacy of the *polis*; Creon, representative of the *polis*, is blind to the demands of the *oikos*—then it would be unclear why this tragedy reaches as deep into the structure of Greek ethical life as it does, rather than merely being a story of the *personal* flaws of these individuals, whose action, guilt, and downfall could be understood as the mechanisms of self-correction through which, in a larger sense, the "stable equilibrium" of the whole is maintained. It would be unclear, in short, why the "deed" would expose the inadequacy of the harmonious structure of Greek *Sittlichkeit* that Hegel describes in the first section of his account, driving that shape of spirit to "vanish" and be replaced by another (289). And, on the other hand, it will not do to say in response that Antigone's and Creon's deeds were merely the symptoms of some deeper substantive conflict between the two "powers" into which Greek *Sittlichkeit* was organized, for *that* response moves too far in the opposite direction, leaving it unclear why the action of concrete persons was necessary to expose this structural contradiction: why couldn't the issue already have been explained in the first section of Hegel's discussion, in which he describes the internal structure of Greek ethical life?

Given the structure of Hegel's reading, the trouble must be located precisely at the point of articulation *between* the categorical organization of Greek *Sittlichkeit* and the concrete deeds through which Antigone and Creon attempt (and fail) to instantiate those categories—or, in other words, at the point of intersection between identity and action. The reason the contradiction at the heart of Greek ethical life cannot be discerned in the absence of the "deed," I suggest, is that that contradiction is in its deepest sense *not* a contradiction between two substantive powers that already exist—*polis* and *oikos*, male and female. It is, instead, a contradiction between the very idea of Spirit as a self-subsistent ensemble of substantive powers, on the one hand, and the phenomenon of action, which is at once the medium through which those powers have their life and the site of unpredictability through which their supposed harmony is perpetually disrupted (283). Action does not just *reveal* this contradiction: it *is* (one pole of) this contradiction. This, I take it, is what Hegel means by the otherwise mysterious proposition that action is in some sense the source of the very law it violates:

> On the contrary, action is itself this splitting in two, this explicit self-affirmation and the establishing over against itself of an alien external reality; *that there is such a reality, this stems from the action itself and results from it.* (282)[32]

But this means that Hegel's account of the antithesis of the known and the unknown points neither to a contingent problem with the mental states of Antigone and Creon, nor to some underlying structural contradiction between the powers into which Greek *Sittlichkeit* was organized, but rather to a persistent condition of human action.[33] By focusing in this way on what I have called the impropriety of action—indeed, by making it the engine of this episode of the *Phenomenology*—Hegel thus remains faithful to Aristotle's suggestion that tragedy is, in a certain sense, *about* the priority of action to the conceptions of character or identity in which we attempt to ground it, but which can never quite succeed in insulating us from the riskiness and unpredictability of life among others.[34]

This reading finds further, indirect support in other parts of the *Phenomenology*, for this is not the only episode in the *Phenomenology* that closely mirrors the structure of complex tragic plots. Just as tragic agents are subject to catastrophic reversals, Hegel's particular shapes of subjectivity are repeatedly caught in shattering contradictions that arise when they attempt to act, and especially to *interact* with others, on the basis of self-conceptions through which they hope to achieve a kind of self-certainty. It's significant, for example, that the whole movement of the *Phenomenology* is initiated by the effort of the character called "consciousness" to *write* and *speak* what it knows, or anyway what it thinks it knows—that is, to *do* something from within its epistemological framework (which Hegel calls "sense-certainty") (59–60). And what goes wrong in *that* case anticipates what goes wrong in the case of Antigone and Creon in a fundamental way. When consciousness, in the mode of sense-certainty, tries to write or say what it knows, all it can do is use indexicals like "now" and "this"—but those, Hegel indicates, become "stale" as soon as they are uttered (60).[35] Here, as in tragedy, it is the *future* that relentlessly undoes subjectivity's pretenses to certainty or sovereignty;[36] and here, as in tragedy, the horizon of the future is closely tied (however dimly) to the fact of human plurality, for what originally provokes consciousness to action is that *someone*, hidden behind Hegel's passive construction, *asks* it to say what it knows (59).[37]

A similar pattern is evident in the first part of Hegel's difficult discussion of what he calls "individuality real in and for itself," which is itself a portion of the chapter on "Reason," located between the chapters on "Self-Consciousness" and "Spirit" (236–46).[38] Here, Hegel is concerned with one particular conception of individuality, which sees the individual as the bearer of what Hegel calls a "determinate original nature," which the individual seeks to express in action (238). (Terry Pinkard, glossing this in terms of "sincerity," suggests that Hegel was probably thinking of seventeenth- and eighteenth-century models of the *honnête homme*, or of Rousseau's self-presentation in the *Confessions*; but, notably, the language of "authenticity" whose origins Taylor finds in both Rousseau and Herder seems equally appropriate.[39]) Yet the individual who attempts to act on the basis of this self-understanding merely displays its inadequacy. This conception of individuality supposes that the "determinate original nature" of the person and the expression of that nature in action constitute something like a circular totality: on the one hand, the action gets its guarantee of sincerity or authenticity from the fact that it merely expresses or makes explicit an original nature that is given in advance; on the other hand, it is only in the action that one first discovers what that original nature is—that, after all, is why it is necessary to *act*.[40] Yet this "circle" (like the "circle" of *êthos* and action in Aristotle) is in fact no circle at all; and what interrupts it is the contingency of action—specifically, the contingency generated by the fact of human plurality. What my act will turn out to have been, Hegel observes, depends not only on the purpose I possessed in advance, but also on the "counter-action of other forces and interests," including "other individualities"—in short, it depends on the unpredictable responses and reactions of others (234–44).[41] And with this discovery, the conception of individual agency as the expression of an authentic nature collapses.

In each of these cases, as in Hegel's reading of the *Antigone*, subjectivity's trouble arises from the contradiction between its commitment to epistemic and practical sovereignty on the one hand, and its experience of vulnerability in action on the other. This, I suggest, is the deepest sense in which the *Phenomenology* might be said to be "tragic"—not, as is usually assumed, because it contains moments of ethical conflict between opposed but equally valid powers (though that is also sometimes true), but because, at least in its diagnostic voice, it shares with tragedy a keen appreciation of the contingency of human interaction and of the dangers involved in our efforts to deny or suppress that contingency. With this reconstruction of Hegel's diagnostic technique in mind, I want to turn now to Hegel's accounts of the struggle for recognition and the master-slave relation, for as I shall suggest, the same contradiction between the aspiration to sovereignty and the experience of the impropriety of action is also at play in those parts of his text, though in ways that have not been fully appreciated.

THE ABDICATION OF INDEPENDENCE

The contemporary reappropriation of Hegel in the service of the politics of recognition, I suggested earlier, rests in substantial part on a *misreading* of Hegel's famous parables of the struggle for recognition and the dialectic of master and slave. Neo-Hegelian theorists of recognition, rightly attracted by Hegel's incisive critique of unjust relations of recognition, assume (as Hegel himself sometimes seems to) that this critique leads naturally into an affirmation of the principle of equal recognition as the appropriate response to social structures of subordination. That reading, however, misses the force of Hegel's diagnosis and critique of such structures, which raise questions not merely about the mode of distribution of recognition (unequal or equal) but also about the value and dangers of the pursuit of recognition *as such*. To spell this out, we need to return to the beginning of Hegel's account of the struggle for recognition, paying close attention to the similarities between the structure of that account and the structure of tragic reversal we have found in other parts of the *Phenomenology*.

Hegel's parables of the struggle for recognition and the relation of master and slave make up part of the cluster of episodes grouped under the chapter heading "Self-Consciousness"; indeed, "self-consciousness" is the name that Hegel gives to his protagonist(s) in this portion of the story, because the immediately preceding episodes (grouped together in a chapter called "Consciousness") have revealed to subjectivity that its relation to the world actually hinges on its relation to *itself*, thereby turning its attention back onto its own character as an acting and knowing being (104). Importantly, however, the struggle for recognition is not the first episode in the chapter on self-consciousness; instead, the struggle arises out of the failed effort of self-consciousness to secure certainty of itself, of its own independence, through the satisfaction of material desires. At first, self-consciousness believes itself to be independent, but finds this claim threatened by the sheer fact of its corporeality, which renders it subject to material forces and bodily needs beyond its control (104–10).[42] In response to this threat, self-consciousness tries to confirm its independence through the *consumption* of whatever it encounters as "other"; consequently, its initial posture toward the world is characterized by "desire" (109), and specifically the assimilatory desire of what Kojève brilliantly called "the being that eats."[43]

Consumption, however, turns out to be a poor strategy for "preserving" a sense of one's own reality, since consumption does not so much master objects as destroy them. The destruction of an object throws self-consciousness back upon itself, leaving it devoid of that external confirmation of its independence that it had sought and, fleetingly, grasped. (We should be reminded here of the way in which consciousness, using indexicals, always finds its truth to have become "stale" as soon as it has been spoken: the same sense of the immediate obsolescence of satisfaction permeates this part of Hegel's story.) For the consumer, satisfaction begets only renewed desire, and a renewed dependence upon objects of nature; and from this frustrating cycle, self-consciousness learns that it cannot find lasting satisfaction through the consumption of material objects.

What *can* offer the satisfaction self-consciousness seeks? Hegel's answer is packed into a difficult sentence: "On account of the independence of the object, therefore, it [self-consciousness] can achieve satisfaction only when the object itself effects the negation within itself" (109).[44] In the case of the satisfaction of material desires, self-consciousness had performed a "negation" by consuming an object: it made the other over into "nothingness," thereby demonstrating its power over the object and preserving its independence (109). But this kind of negation was self-defeating because it destroyed the very object that was supposed to confirm the independence of self-consciousness. If an external object is to provide more than fleeting self-certainty, it must somehow both be negated in its independence and yet continue to exist: its dependence on self-consciousness must be demonstrated in some manner other than sheer destruction. As Pinkard puts it, "its dependence must be such . . . that it *makes itself* dependent on the subject." And the only sort of thing which can "abdicat[e]" its own claims to independence in this way is . . . another self-consciousness.[45] At the moment self-consciousness discovers that it can "achiev[e] its satisfaction only in another self-consciousness," the stage is set for the encounter of selves that gives rise to the struggle for recognition (110).[46]

Self-consciousness begins its encounter with another self-consciousness in the same position from which it began its encounter with the material world: certain of its own absolute independence and sovereignty. "Self-consciousness is, to begin with, simple being-for-self, self-equal through the exclusion of everything else . . . what is 'other' for it is an unessential, negatively characterized object" (113). Yet just as the resistance of the material world threatened the independence of self-consciousness, the presence of *another* self-consciousness making an equivalent claim of self-sovereignty also renders self-consciousness's knowledge of its own independence uncertain. Each responds to this intolerable situation in much the same way self-consciousness had reacted to its dependence on the material world: by stubbornly seeking to reaffirm its sovereignty through the destruction of the other. Since this response is now no longer one-sided but mutual, the first interaction between self-consciousnesses takes the form of a "life-and-death struggle." In this struggle, each self-consciousness tries to eliminate the external threat to its sovereignty by "seek[ing] the other's death," but each also demonstrates its own independence by its willingness to sacrifice its own mere material existence (114). What better demonstration of self-sovereignty, after all, than the decision to risk self-destruction?

Here, however, Hegel alters the trajectory of his story. He stops short of killing off one self-consciousness, since—as he explains to his readers—the consummation of the "trial by death" would "d[o] away with the truth which was supposed to issue from it" (114). After all, even the winner of the struggle to the death would have destroyed the very object through which it had sought confirmation; this sort of negation of the other, like the consumption of an object, would only be an "abstract negation," not a negation "which supersedes in such a way as to preserve and maintain what is superseded" (114–15). However, the latter kind of negation—a negation which must be performed *by the other itself*—can be achieved if one self-consciousness *surrenders* to the other. Hegel therefore introduces such a surrender into his story, which launches the next episode in his narrative of self-consciousness, in which

> one [self-consciousness] is the independent consciousness whose essential nature is to be for itself, the other is the dependent consciousness whose essential nature is simply to live or to be for another. The former is master [*Herr*], the other is slave [*Knecht*]. (115)[47]

Now, the relationship of master and slave might seem to constitute a stable social form in which the recognition of self-consciousness's independence can be secured, if only for the victor: "here, therefore, is present this moment of recognition, viz. that the other consciousness [the slave] sets aside its own being-for-self [its independence], and in so doing itself does what the first [the master] does to it" (116). But this structure of recognition *also* turns out to be unstable. From the perspective of the master, the recognition of the slave proves unsatisfying, because while the master had sought recognition by another self-consciousness, he[48] has found recognition only through a person who has been debased and objectified, and whose recognition thus cannot *count* for the master in the way that he had hoped.

> In this recognition the unessential consciousness is for the master the object, which constitutes the *truth* of his certainty of himself. But it is clear that this

object does not correspond to its Notion, but . . . has in reality turned out to be something quite different from an independent consciousness. What now really confronts him is not an independent consciousness, but a dependent one. He is, therefore, not certain of being-for-self as the truth of himself. (116–17)

So far, this should all be fairly familiar—yet at this point things become complicated, because Hegel's explanation of the failure of the relation of master and slave to satisfy the desire for recognition often gives rise to misunderstandings. It is clear that the problem lies in the *asymmetry* of the relation of master and slave: this outcome, says Hegel, is "one-sided and unequal" (116). But what, *exactly*, is lacking in this structure of recognition?

The most obvious answer, and by the far the most common, is simply that while the slave has done something for the master—recognized his independence—the master has not done the same for the slave: as Taylor says, "slave is forced to recognize master, but not vice versa"; or, in John McCumber's phrase, "one consciousness (the bondsman) does all the recognizing and the other (the master) gets all the recognition."[49] On this reconstruction, the moment of recognition ought to have been an even exchange in which each self-consciousness saw and therefore respected the dignity of the other; and on this reading, Hegel's critique of the master-slave relation amounts to a call for the master to *complete* the exchange by reciprocally recognizing the independence of the slave, which would, of course, amount to the abolition of the master-slave relation itself.[50] And when Hegel's view of recognition, read this way, is lifted from the sociologically stripped-down scene of the *Phenomenology* and brought into modern debates about multiculturalism and identity, it seems to support the contemporary discourse of recognition and its promise of a satisfying moment of full, proper recognition, in which identities are completely visible and relations among persons are untainted by disrespect.

This account is problematic, however, because it leads us to think of "recognition" as a kind of cognitive act that, first and foremost, has the *other* as its object. If the master "gets all the recognition," this means both that the master is the recipient of the slave's recognition, and that the slave's recognition is essentially about the master and focused on his *identity*—in this case, his identity *qua* independent, sovereign being. But is this really what has happened? Consider again the asymmetrical act of surrender to which Hegel refers. Strictly speaking, it is incorrect to say that this act is performed *by* the slave, for that role does not yet exist, nor does the role of master; rather, the relationship of master and slave is itself made possible—though not inevitable—by the asymmetrical surrender of a character whose social identity, like that of its opponent, is, at the moment of the act, still indeterminate.[51] Moreover, on Hegel's account, the self-consciousness that submits does not do so *because* it has come to see the truth of the other's claim to sovereignty. Rather, this character has *itself* been transformed by the realization that "life is as essential to it as pure self-consciousness" (115). Having acknowledged its own dependence on organic life, it is filled by "the fear of death," which makes it "trembl[e] in every fibre of its being" (117).[52] This self-consciousness submits, in short, *because it has confronted its own finitude*, and this experience has led it to abandon its futile aspiration to demonstrate its sovereignty at all costs. The act of "recognition" Hegel describes here is thus in the first instance a self-negation, an *abdication* of self-consciousness's *own* claim to absolute independence, which then has as its secondary and indirect consequence the (momentary and fleeting) satisfaction of the other's desire.[53]

It is important to be clear about what "finitude" means in this context.[54] It would be easy to suppose, given the association Hegel sets up here between finitude and the fear of death, that the self-consciousness who surrenders does so because it has confronted its finitude in the sense of its *mortality*. On this reading, Hegel—in momentary conjunction with Kierkegaard and Nietzsche—becomes one of the forerunners of twentieth-century existentialism, with its characterizations of human being as "being-towards-death," and its critiques of the various forms of inauthenticity in which we "evade" the fact of our mortality.[55] This is not exactly wrong: mortality is an important dimension of finitude, and awareness of mortality is an important part of Hegel's story. But it is not quite what's at stake here. After all, Hegel's self-consciousnesses have *already* confronted mortality in their earlier decision to enter a "life-and-death struggle," a struggle in which each "stak[es] its own life" in order to demonstrate its freedom and universality and to secure its self-certainty by negating a threatening other (113–14). *That* decision—rather than the decision on the part of one self-consciousness to surrender—is reminiscent of the stance Arendt associates with Achilles in *The Human Condition*: the conscious embrace of death in a final, glorious deed, one that could make of one's life—including one's death—into a work of art.[56]

But as we have seen, Hegel, no less than Arendt, is critical of this stance, which cannot really satisfy its promise. This is manifest in Hegel's abrupt shift from a scene of imminent death to a scene of fearful surrender. This fearful surrender, then, represents not the confrontation with mortality *per se*, but the realization of the futility of a certain way of *responding to* mortality—namely, by treating it as an occasion for the assertion of masterful agency. Indeed, Hegel's lesson here seems to be that the idea of mortality *on its own* is an insufficient figure of human finitude, for it leaves plenty of room for the sovereign ideal of "mastering death by aristocratic self-will."[57] And if this is right, then I suspect what is important about the fear of death in this scene is less its association with mortality than the fact that it takes place in the midst of a confrontation with an unpredictable and threatening *other*—that is, that the occasion for the fear of death is the experience of intersubjectivity. From this perspective, self-consciousness's fearful surrender is indeed a confrontation with mortality, but it is a confrontation of a very specific kind, for it is inflected by an acceptance of human plurality.[58] The self-consciousness that surrenders risks a relation to the other—an uncertain relation, which might turn out to be dominative, or generous, or deadly—because, in its estimation, that relation is the condition of the possibility of life.

On this reading, Hegel's account of the struggle has deep affinities with tragedy's critique of the pursuit of sovereignty through recognition. First, Hegel's account, like tragedy, and like the other episodes in the *Phenomenology* discussed earlier, is structured around a significant reversal, one that throws into question the self-understanding and practical posture with which both self-consciousnesses begin the episode. The standard reading of Hegel assumes that the trouble with the master-slave relationship is simply that it represents maldistribution of some social good—the recognition of one's independence or identity—which ought to be distributed equally. But Hegel's point is more radical: he suggests that the very desire that animates the struggle for recognition is impossible to fulfill, that the "good" to which it is devoted is not really what we ought to be after; consequently, the asymmetry and thus the inadequacy of the relation of master and slave lies in the fact that only one of the two parties has acknowledged this, admitted the impossibility of satisfying its own claims, and conceded its own dependence. And second, as this language suggests, the affinity with tragedy is not only structural, but also substantive. By focusing our attention on self-consciousness's renunciation of its claim to sovereignty, as opposed to the recognition of the independence or identity of the other, Hegel reproduces the move we have traced in the *Antigone* and the *Poetics* from the recognition of identity to the acknowledgment of one's own fundamental condition: self-consciousness's abdication has more in common with the *anagnôriseis* of Antigone and Creon than with the satisfying recognitions they (like Hegel's two self-consciousnesses) had originally pursued.[59]

SUBORDINATION, OR THE WEIGHT OF CONTRADICTION

Yet Hegel also takes tragedy's critique of the pursuit of recognition a step further. Even as he echoes the by now familiar point about the *futility* of the desire for sovereignty through recognition, Hegel also (and more ominously) ties that desire to the phenomenon of social subordination; and to understand this connection, we need to turn from Hegel's account of the struggle for recognition to his account of the master-slave relation that results from self-consciousness's surrender. This, of course, is almost certainly the most widely known episode in the whole of the *Phenomenology*. Still, the interpretation and appropriation of this episode has largely focused on Hegel's account of the reversal through which the master turns out to be a dependent rather than an independent consciousness, and through which the slave, despite his subjection, acquires a kind of limited independence through his work upon the physical world. These parts of the story, which highlight the vulnerability of power, the irrepressible agency of the dominated, and the centrality of material labor to that agency, have for good reason proved resonant among analysts of modern colonial slavery and its legacy, as well as among Marxist theorists, postcolonial theorists, and feminists.[60] Here, however, I want to focus on a somewhat different point suggested by Hegel's story, which has less to do with the agency of the oppressed than with the investments and desires that sustain social and political subordination. That view, as we shall see, is importantly different from the implicit view of subordination underlying the contemporary discourse of recognition.

From this angle, what is most intriguing about Hegel's account of master and slave is that, *despite* his claim that it is contradictory and cannot ultimately satisfy the desire that animates it, this social relationship does not simply collapse under the weight of its own incoherence. The transition from the account of master and slave to the next episode in the *Phenomenology*, on "stoicism, skepticism, and the unhappy consciousness," does not involve either the self-undermining and eventual disappearance of the institution of slavery, or the overthrow of the masters by slaves who have empowered themselves by their patient labor. Instead, Hegel's account of stoicism, skepticism, and the unhappy consciousness describes a series of practical and epistemological postures that could plausibly emerge against the background of the experience of "bondage" itself, a series that is set in motion by the stoic retreat from physical enslavement into the unshackled freedom of pure thought.[61] But this raises an important question about the nature and force of the "contradiction" Hegel has diagnosed in the master-slave relationship: if this social form is incapable of satisfying the desire that drives it, what accounts for its persistence? Why and how does the master *survive* the apparently catastrophic "reversal" to which he is subject in Hegel's text?

Here, it will be useful to consider a little-discussed but brilliant (and brilliantly Hegelian) line from another analysis of subordination—Marx's

Capital. Relatively early in volume 1 of *Capital,* in the middle of the chapter on "Money, or the Circulation of Commodities," Marx recalls that "we saw in a former chapter that the exchange of commodities implies contradictory and mutually exclusive conditions." He then adds: "The further development of the commodity does not abolish these contradictions, but rather provides *the form in which they have room to move*."[62] The language of giving a contradiction "room to move" is illuminating, because it highlights the difference between a logical proof and a social form: a social form, precisely because it has spatial and temporal extension, can be structured in ways that accommodate contradictions, organizing opposed forces in ways that permit them to exist together. The contradiction between universal and particular, for instance, might be given "room to move" if it is plotted onto some other dimension of social space, mapping "universality" onto one concrete group of people and assigning "particularity" to others. Such accommodations may be more or less fragile or temporary, but they do at least defer the destructive force of the contradictions they address.

In *Capital,* Marx's recurring example of this phenomenon is the development of the money-form, which accommodates the contradiction between the commodity as exchange-value (which implies its equivalence to other commodities) and the commodity as use-value (which implies its qualitative difference from other commodities). Exchange depends on this contradiction at the heart of the commodity, because on the one hand, exchange is supposed to be the exchange of goods of equivalent value; yet precisely insofar as two commodities are equivalent in value, the motivation to exchange them must rest on some qualitative difference between them, a difference that contradicts the notion of their equivalence. The money-form provides this contradiction with "room to move" by singling out *one* commodity as the bearer of *qualitative* distinctiveness—the money commodity—so that the rest may be treated as unproblematically comparable and exchangeable (and thereby be reduced to exchange-values). Here, a contradiction that is in some sense internal in principle to each and every commodity is accommodated or managed by assigning each of its poles to a distinct subset of actually existing commodities.[63]

The master-slave relation in Hegel's *Phenomenology* works in the same way to accommodate contradictions, though without resolving them. Although Hegel does not at all deny the role of interpersonal violence and fear in his (stylized) system of mastery and slavery, for him the key to that system seems to lie in the fact that it places master and slave in strikingly different relations to the material world. Here, Hegel is effectively reprising self-consciousness's original attempt to sustain its sense of its independence through the satisfaction of its physical desires—but now with a twist. In that episode, the effort to win sovereignty was undermined by the fleetingness of consumption's pleasures, which exposed the ongoing dependence of self-consciousness on an intransigent material world: put flatly, it had to *work* before it could eat, repeatedly. In Hegel's parable, the master-slave relationship splits apart these two moments of the ongoing dialectic of desire, structuring social relations such that some people—the slaves—do the hard work of acquiring and preparing parts of the material world, while others—the masters—do nothing but consume what the slaves produce:

> What desire failed to achieve, he [the master] succeeds in doing, viz., to have done with the thing altogether, and to achieve satisfaction in the enjoyment of it. Desire failed to do this because of the thing's independence; but the lord, who has interposed the bondsman between it and himself, takes to himself only the dependent aspect of the thing and has the pure enjoyment of it. The aspect of its independence he leaves to the bondsman, who works on it. (117)

The master-slave relation thus accommodates the contradiction between dependence and independence by spreading it out over social space, making one person bear the disproportionate weight of the fact of human dependence on the material world so that another person, equally disproportionately, can experience the pleasures of nature without suffering the burden of labor. This arrangement thus reflects back to the master something like the image of himself as sovereign that he had originally sought, insulating him from the experience of his own dependence—though not *eliminating* that dependence, which haunts the master-slave relation and constitutes one of its points of vulnerability.

Yet dependence on the material world is not the only form of finitude from which the master is thereby insulated. Just as this self-consciousness had, long ago, found its certainty of its own independence challenged by the resistance of the objects of nature to its will, it had more recently found itself threatened by the presence of another self-consciousness— that is, it had found itself running up against the unpredictability introduced into human affairs by the phenomenon of intersubjectivity. And, correspondingly, just as the presence of this other self-consciousness makes it possible for the first to finesse the problem of its own contradictory relation on the material world by establishing social distance between production and consumption, the presence of the material world simultaneously makes it possible for the first self-consciousness to finesse the problem of its own contradictory relation to the other by creating a kind of distance between master and slave. If the primordial social identities of master and slave consisted in nothing other than "victoriousness" and "surrender"—if to live in one of these identities meant nothing more than to repeat, unendingly, the face-to-face encounter with the other—then the master-slave relation would represent nothing but a prolongation of the struggle it is supposed to resolve. However, the existence of an object to be worked on—of what Hegel calls the "thing"— enables the master to relate to the slave "mediately"; that is, in terms of their differently defined roles in relation to the objects of nature (115). These roles give substance to the social identities of "master" and "slave" and lend relative stability to the intersubjective world, making it possible for the master to experience his own status—like the slave's—as a reflection of who he always already is, rather than as the political (and therefore fragile) effect of an ongoing practice of subordination.

Of course Hegel's account of the master-slave relation hardly constitutes a complete explanation of any actually existing practice or institution—whatever its resonances, it is still a minimalist parable and not a fully worked-out social theory. But it does contain some suggestive ideas about the nature and sources of injustice in relations of identity and difference. The most fundamental of these is that, on Hegel's account, identity-based social subordination is *not* fundamentally rooted in the failure of the powerful to notice some fact about the worth or value of the subordinated—though the denial of such worth or value may be certainly be part of the practice of subordination. Instead, these practices are rooted in the failure of the powerful to acknowledge something about *themselves*—specifically, in their failure to acknowledge, to bear the full weight of, the fundamental human condition of finitude. But this immediately suggests two further points about the implications of Hegel's account of subordination for the politics of recognition. First, while the politics of recognition is, in many of its forms, admirably devoted to the goal of overcoming injustice, it tends to treat injustice simply as a systematic failure to cognize and respect the identity of the other. In so doing, however, it fails to acknowledge the possibility that those failures of cognition and respect are differently and more deeply motivated failures, driven in the first instance by the project of securing one's own independence or sovereignty rather than by ignorance of, or mere malice toward, others. Second, and even more problematically, Hegel's account suggests that the pursuit of recognition itself may be implicated in the formation and maintenance of unjust relations of social power. In Hegel's story, the trouble with the one-sidedness of the act of abdication that ends the struggle for recognition is not only that it leaves the self-consciousness who becomes master in a condition of ontological ignorance, doomed to pursue a fantasy of sovereignty he cannot attain; it is also that the strategies he employs in pursuit of that impossible fantasy involve the subjection and unfreedom of others. The pursuit of recognition *is* the failure of acknowledgment; and in this instance, the failure of acknowledgment founds a structure of subordination.

HEGEL'S ANTIFEMINISM AND POLYNEICES' SHIELD

For a somewhat more concrete example of the ways in which the pursuit of recognition can feed relations of subordination, one need look no further than Hegel himself. Although my emphasis so far has been on showing how Hegel's analyses of the struggle for recognition and the master-slave relation provide us with useful theoretical tools with which to understand and criticize injustice, I also suggested earlier that Hegel himself ultimately betrays his own best insights in this matter in his treatment of the role of women in modern social and political life, and that this betrayal is not merely an accidental prejudice, but is closely connected to Hegel's project of reconciliation through recognition. To spell this out, we need to return briefly to the final part of Hegel's reading of the *Antigone*, postponed earlier.

It is not hard to imagine how the account of subordination we have found in Hegel's story of the struggle for recognition and the master-slave relationship might be extended to the forms of gender relations Hegel ascribes to ancient Greek ethical life, and which we glimpsed in Sophocles' *Antigone*. As we saw in the last chapter, part of what informs Creon's intransigent stance toward Antigone is a certain gender panic: in a world in which political office is the exclusive province of men, Antigone's defiance of Creon is simultaneously an attack on his political authority and a threat to his masculinity, and he reacts by reaffirming, with frightening and deadly intensity, the hierarchical relationship between public men and private women. The view of subordination spelled out here suggests that Creon's hyperbolic defense of his masculinity, like the broader social structure from which it flows (and which it exaggerates), must be understood not as a mere expression of sexist attitudes or prejudices—the trouble is not, or not *just*, that Greek culture was marked by an ingrained set of false beliefs about the capacities or moral status of women—but as a structure of power that paid a kind of ontological wage to men, organizing the social world in a way that enabled them to experience themselves (however tentatively or imperfectly) as sovereign agents. The assignment of men and women to different spheres of life served this purpose by enabling men to deflect the experience of finitude, grasping that experience as the contingent and therefore in principle controllable consequence of the misbehavior of women, and not as an ineliminable condition of their own agency.[64]

Hegel's own treatment of Greek ethical life even hints at such an extension. In the third and final part of that episode of the *Phenomenology*, Hegel steps back from the particular deeds and fates of Antigone and Creon and considers the broader significance of the story for the understanding of Greek *Sittlichkeit*. This is the part of the episode in which Hegel infamously refers to "womankind" as "the eternal irony of the community," but that reference, on its own, is not (yet) obviously an endorsement of the hierarchical structure of Greek ethical life. In fact, Hegel's point seems at first to be quite consistent with the analysis and critique of domination I have suggested: "womankind" only *becomes* the "eternal irony of the community," he tells us, because of the activity of the community itself, which "creates for itself in what it suppresses and what is at the same time essential to it an internal enemy— womankind in general" (288).[65] The perpetual (re)subordination of women, Hegel seems to be saying, is the activity through which the community "gets an existence," repeatedly working to shore up a sovereignty that it can never *quite* secure by tracking the threat to that sovereignty to a specific social location, and thereby rendering it manageable, however imperfectly.[66] But, notoriously, rather than following through on the normative potential of this diagnosis, Hegel instead takes up Creon's mantle in the *Philosophy of Right*, suggesting that the confinement of women to the family is a reflection of the "natural determinacy of the two sexes," and offering Antigone herself—now stripped of her transgressive character—as an exemplar of family piety.[67] Elaborating the justification for the exclusion of women from the state in an infamous part of his treatment of the family, he distinguishes between the rationality of men and the affectivity of women, whose lack of intellectual rigor makes them singularly unsuited for political life: "when women are in charge of government," he concludes, "the state is in danger, for their actions are based not on the demands of universality but on contingent inclination and opinion."[68]

What accounts for Hegel's failure to follow through on the potentially radical implications of his own view of subordination? Often, Hegel's well-known endorsement of sexual inequality is treated as an unfortunate but philosophically inconsequential reflection of commonplace nineteenth-century ideologies of gender, or of Hegel's personal prejudice, in any case not closely connected to the rest of the substance of his political thought. The consequence of this is that when critics (rightly) attempt to engage in immanent critique, using Hegel's best insights against his own worst moments, they often underestimate how deeply such an immanent critique must cut.[69] But Hegel's ideology of sexual inequality is actually substantively tied to his political thought, and in particular to his efforts, in his reconciliatory voice, to arrive at a satisfactory arrangement of mutual and equal recognition among the (male) citizens of the political state.[70]

The connection is already anticipated in Hegel's treatment of Greek ethical life in the *Phenomenology*, as we can see by considering in somewhat more detail his characterization of "womankind" as the "eternal irony of the community." Womankind, that passage continues,

> changes by intrigue the universal end of the government into a private end, transforms its universal activity into a work of some particular individual, and perverts the universal property of the state into a possession and ornament for the Family. Woman in this way turns to ridicule the earnest wisdom of mature age which, indifferent to purely private pleasures and enjoyments, as well as to playing an active part, only thinks of and cares for the universal. She makes this wisdom an object of derision for raw and irresponsible youth and unworthy of their enthusiasm. (288)

It is easy to assume that when Hegel talks here about "womankind" he has Antigone in mind: after all, she purports precisely to stand for the particular, the private, and so on.[71] But on closer examination, the fit becomes considerably more awkward. "Womankind," Hegel says, changes the universal into the particular "by intrigue"—but Antigone does no such thing, either in Sophocles' play or in Hegel's reading of it.[72] She is guileless: she simply carries out what she takes to be her obligation to her brother, untroubled by the isolation in which Ismene's demurral leaves her, apparently unconcerned about being discovered, neither evasive nor apologetic when captured. "Womankind," Hegel says, "changes" the universal end of the government into a private end; "transforms" the character of its activity; "perverts" its property into an ornament for the family. None of this language, which, like the word "intrigue," suggests corruption more than flat disobedience, has much resonance with Antigone, who seems less intentionally subversive of than cold to the *polis* and its ends, activities, and property. And, finally, "womankind," Hegel says, "makes this wisdom [devoted to the universal] an object of derision for raw and irresponsible youth and unworthy of their enthusiasm." This, it seems, is something like a specification of the methods of intrigue "womankind" employs: she subverts the universal by undermining the emergent commitment of "youth" to the universal—and of course, as Hegel indicates a few lines later, "youth" means *male* youth, "the manhood which, while immature, still stands within the sphere of individuality" (288). This is an image of the corruption of young men by manipulative women, and while it corresponds rather precisely to Creon's paranoid fantasies of Antigone as a plotting viper who exploits Haemon's "lust" to mislead him, it is not particularly appropriate as a characterization of the Sophoclean Antigone herself, who does not achieve her effects through the manipulation of another, but just *acts*.[73]

Of course, there is no shortage of figures of women in Greek literature who fit Hegel's characterization of "womankind" much more closely than Antigone—as Detienne and Vernant put it, "whenever cunning plotting or fraudulent manoeuvring is concerned the Greek likes to believe it is a matter for a woman"[74]—and it is worth entertaining the possibility that Hegel, if he was thinking of any specific character at all, had someone else in mind. One possibility comes from a scene in Aeschylus's *Seven Against Thebes*, which recounts the story of the deadly conflict between Eteocles and Polyneices that immediately precedes the action of the *Antigone*.[75] In this, the final part of the so-called shield scene, Eteocles, defending the city against his brother and an accompanying band of Argive warriors, discovers that it will be Polyneices himself whom he shall have to fight to the death at the seventh gate to the city. The messenger who brings this news describes this "very violent Polyneices":

> He bears a new-made, rounded shield
> and a twofold device contrived thereon:
> a woman leading modestly [*sôphronôs hêgoumenê*] a man
> conducts him, pictured as a warrior,
> wrought all in gold. She claims she is Justice,
> and the inscription reads: I will bring him home
> and he shall have his city and shall walk
> in his ancestral house. (ll. 642–48)

She *claims* she is Justice, but of course Eteocles doubts it, and so, in effect, does Hegel. He regards the whole quarrel between the brothers as a manifestation of the threat posed by the "merely particular" to that which is universal, namely, the city: *both* brothers are willing to put the city itself at risk for the sake of what is effectively a family feud, a private conflict between individuals (286). *This* Justice, then, is thus a fitting example of Hegel's figure of "womankind," for her leadership of the man, insofar as that man represents Polyneices himself, precisely "perverts the universal property of the state into a possession and ornament" for one brother at the expense of the other; moreover, she accomplishes this by guiding a "raw and irresponsible youth," and not, as in the case of Antigone, by her own exertion of force. There is *intrigue* on Polyneices' shield.

Whomever Hegel had in mind, the crucial point is that his figure of womankind is in fact a *double* figure: not just a woman, but a woman paired with the young man whom she corrupts, drawing him away from the universal and toward the particular. And the importance of this figure becomes clearer when we reach the *Philosophy of Right*, which attempts precisely to explain how it is possible to achieve reconciliation through recognition—that is, how it is possible for the members of civil society and the state to recognize each other and themselves both as the bearers of particular identities and interests, *and* as members of an overarching totality that neither threatens nor is not threatened by the differences among its members. Hegel's account of this possibility hinges on the mutual interpenetration of the institutions of state and civil society, which simultaneously root political life in the flourishing diversity of private interests and opinions, *and* elevate private individuals to universality.[76] So, for example, Hegel's "corporations"—something like updated medieval guilds, reconstituted in accordance with the modern division of labor—act both as bulwarks against the abuse of individual persons by the state, *à la* the "associations" so highly valued by Tocqueville, *and* as the sites of emergent universality, where individual actors first learn to think and act with, and on behalf of, others.[77] Similarly, "public opinion," particularly as manifest in the Estates, plays a dual role: on the one hand, it checks corruption in the state by enabling the independent criticism of political officials by the public; on the other hand, it serves as the "most important means" by which political officials can "educate" the public (in part through spectacular displays of "wit and eloquence"): "it is from this [public assembly of the Estates] above all that the people can learn the true nature of their interests."[78]

Of course, it is never made entirely clear *how* these institutions are supposed to perform the dual and, apparently, contradictory functions Hegel assigns to them, which has provoked critics from Marx onward to worry that Hegel's "mediations" of the contradiction between universal and particular are nothing more than new "embodiments" of that contradiction.[79] But the image of the woman and the young man, together with Hegel's account of sexual difference in the *Philosophy of Right*, I suggest, are devices of representation that work to establish at least the *possibility* of such a reconciliation of universal and particular. By representing "particularity" itself through a *double* figure (rather than making either "womankind" alone or the young man alone into the signifier of particular interest) Hegel facilitates the simultaneous overcoming *and* preservation of particularity in the state, for one half of the pair, "womankind," can be represented as the bearer of extreme, intransigent, uneducable particularity—particularity of the sort that might threaten to overwhelm the mediating institutions of civil society and the state—and this, in turn, enables the particularity represented by men to be conceived as, at least in principle, capable of being brought into harmony with the universal.

Indeed, this seems to be the political import of Hegel's famous contrast, in his discussion of the family, between the modes of education of women and men: "Woman are educated" he says, "who knows how?—as it were through the atmosphere of representational thought, more through living than through the acquisition of knowledge [*Erwerben von Kenntnissen*], whereas man attains his position only through the attainment of thought and numerous technical exertions."[80] And this difference in mode of education seems to qualify men but not women for membership in civil society and the state, for it is precisely the through the acquisition of "knowledge" (*Kenntnis, Kenntnissen*) about their own interests and affairs that members of civil society, via their participation in mediating institutions like the Estates, are educated to, and reconciled with, universality.[81] In this way, the diffuse and non-specific possibility of an irremediable conflict between particular interests and the demands of universality gets mapped onto specific areas of social space—the potential intransigence of the particular gets converted into the natural ineducability of *women*—thereby rendering the threat manageable. The challenge of (male) particularity, which on Hegel's account had been the downfall of ancient Greek ethical life, can be accommodated by (or can be represented as being accommodated by) the mediating institutions of the modern state and civil society—as long as women are kept in the family. Hegel's account of sexual difference and his exclusion of women from political life thus serves as something like an ideological warrant for his claim to have shown the possibility of reconciliation through mutual recognition. Here, as in the institution of mastery and slavery, the pursuit of recognition is tied, nonaccidentally, to the maintenance of social relations of subordination.

RECOGNITION BEYOND THE *PHENOMENOLOGY*

Earlier, I noted that the revival of the Hegelian ideal of equal recognition has been driven in part by important developments in Hegel scholarship, including especially the reconstructive work of Axel Honneth, Robert Williams, and others who seek to displace the parable of master and slave from the center of our understanding of Hegelian recognition. Especially since my account here has relied heavily on the *Phenomenology of Spirit*—an emphasis that both Honneth and Williams suggest has historically been behind the reduction of recognition to domination[82]—I shall conclude this chapter by explaining why the reading I have given here, while more equivocal than either Honneth or Williams about the ethical and political meaning of the norm of recognition, nevertheless avoids some of the pitfalls against which they quite rightly warn.[83]

One of the most persuasive and insightful parts of Williams's reconstruction of the concept of recognition is his distinction between the general conceptual structure of recognition, on the one hand, and the widely varied social forms in which that general structure can be instantiated. The trouble with Kojève and Sartre, Williams argues, is that they mistook a "determinate shape of recognition" for recognition as such, reducing recognition to one of its possible instantiations—and one of its least successful, most unpleasant instantiations at that.[84] By recovering the distinction between general structure and concrete instance, Williams argues, we can grasp the affirmative possibilities inherent in the concept of recognition, possibilities like love or membership in a state, which transcend the conflict, struggle, and domination characteristic of the master-slave relationship.[85]

This is right; but it is important to notice that nothing in the account I have given here *reduces* the idea of recognition to a single concrete social relationship. Instead, I have tried to show, at the level of basic conceptual structure, how the pursuit of recognition itself is a failure of acknowledgment of just the sort that nurtures a wide variety of relations of subordination; and I have suggested that Hegel's account of master and slave, though it does have *resonances* with Greek and Roman slavery, modern colonial slavery, and relations of personal domination in medieval Europe, is best understood as a parable that illustrates certain general features of social domination, and not as a single concrete form.[86] This does not mean that every instance of recognition is equivalent to the master-slave relation, or even that every instance of recognition is necessarily and only unjust, but it does call into question the notion that an ideal of equal recognition can constitute an adequate response to social and political injustice on the terrain of identity and difference, and at least gives us cause to treat subordination as a persistent possibility in relations of recognition—even those (as we shall see in more detail in the next chapter) that we are likely, on balance, to affirm.

Of course, as I indicated earlier, part of the reason that Williams and Honneth think it is so important to avoid reducing recognition to the master-slave relation is that, in their view, this sort of reductionism has also led theorists, Sartre in particular, to retreat into a posture of "ontological separation"—the posture of the silent, aloof, and solitary existential hero who shuns social interaction as inevitably corrupting and inauthentic.[87] Williams and Honneth are right, I think, to point to the ethical and political problems with this posture, but it is also crucial to notice that the account I have given here does not entail—indeed, it actively resists—such aloofness. On my reading, the crucial connection between the pursuit of recognition and social subordination lies in the fact that the pursuit of recognition involves a failure of acknowledgment of one of the basic circumstances of human action—the fact that action is always, ultimately, *interaction*, and that this interaction introduces an ineliminable contingency into life among others. This circumstance is, in a certain respect, a limitation on our agency, at least as long as agency is understood in terms of sovereignty—but it is also the enabling condition of agency and freedom themselves. The Sartrean hero who pursues authentic existence by fleeing from the intersubjective world would be doomed to failure, oscillating endlessly between the impossible aspiration to become master of his own existence and the nauseating awareness of his situatedness in an intersubjective world that exceeds his control.[88]

If anything, Williams and Honneth overcompensate for the errors they identify in Sartre. Rather than moving from the isolation of the existential hero to the unpredictable world of genuine intersubjectivity, they overshoot, seeking to identify social forms in which we can experience, through identification and recognition, the satisfactions of sovereignty that are denied to us as individuals. (In this sense, their critiques of Sartre run precisely parallel to Taylor's critique of atomism and naturalism, which we discussed in chapter 2.) Honneth, for example, criticizes Sartre for treating human existence as the incessant and merely negative transcendence of any of its possible determinations: since the Sartrean human has no identity that can, or needs to be, recognized by others, Sartre treats all concrete forms of intersubjectivity as more or less disguised modes of alienation, objectification, or subjugation.[89] By contrast, Honneth argues, Fichte and Hegel were able to see human subjects as the bearers of stable personal identities, and so they were able to imagine intersubjectivity as the possible site of *successful* communication and mutual recognition:

> If, on the contrary, [Sartre] had possessed the conceptual means to understand subjects as self-identical personalities, then the interactive encounter would not have appeared to him as a struggle for the maintenance of the pure transcendence of the for-itself but rather as a struggle for the mutual recognition of the self-understandings that subjects by their very nature bring with themselves into every interaction. That, however, was the great insight which Hegel, spurred by Fichte, reached: he was able to interpret interactions as being such forms of the struggle for recognition which contained within themselves the potential for their own resolution because subjects were fully capable of reaching agreement concerning the mutual recognition of their claims to selfhood.[90]

But by casting the choice between Sartre and Hegel as a choice between total alienation on the one hand and the complete transcendence of opacity on the other, Honneth misses the character of genuine intersubjectivity just as much as Sartre does. As Hegel, Aristotle, Sophocles, and

Taylor have suggested in different ways, "the self-understandings that subjects by their very nature bring with themselves into every interaction," while real and important, nevertheless are not the sole or most important measure of justice, for in interaction itself, we become more and other than we take ourselves to be. And if the roots of subordination lie, as Hegel suggests, in the failure to come to terms with that circumstance of agency, then what justice demands is less the recognition of people as who they already really are than the acknowledgment of our own condition.

Finally, it is important to note that the (Hegelian) critique of the (equally Hegelian) ideal of recognition I have developed here is substantially different from the more familiar but less persuasive arguments that the ideal of recognition simply sacrifices individuality at the altar of the collective, or that it assimilates difference, amoebalike, into an utterly homogeneous totality. A great deal of sophisticated and persuasive work has been done to defend Hegel's philosophy in general, and his conception of recognition in particular, against these accusations.[91] However questionable Hegel's account may be in its particulars, his *aim* is indeed to show that, as Frederick Neuhouser puts it, "the values of individuality and social membership are not to be thought of as competing or mutually exclusive ideas," and to outline the basic features of a social order that does justice to both concerns;[92] similarly, as Robert Williams argues, Hegel's conception of the whole as an *internally articulated* totality means that it is perfectly able, in principle, to incorporate and preserve rather than eliminate difference.[93] What is at issue here, however, is neither individuality nor difference per se, but *action*—and specifically, the notion of action as a site of contingency and surprise, which can be put at risk as much by individualism as by communitarianism, and as much by internally articulated conceptions of social order as by undifferentiated ones. Hegel's antifeminism is a good example: as Williams rightly points out, Hegel's assignment of women to the family is *not* a radical exclusion of women from ethical life altogether. Instead, it is, as we have seen, precisely a way of accommodating and preserving difference within a larger totality—but one that systematically restricts and confines some members of that whole in the service of the aspirations and self-image of others.[94]

Still, there is one sense in which the account I have developed here is open to the charge of incompleteness. So far, my main emphasis has been on working out the conceptual structure of Hegel's diagnostic and critical approach to relations of recognition; and I have begun to suggest that Hegel, in his reconciliatory voice, betrays some of his own best insights into the connections between the pursuit of recognition and social domination. But in doing so, I have been drawing mostly on texts that deal either with direct dyadic encounters between subjects (like the stylized struggle for recognition) or encounters mediated by nonmodern social institutions (like the ethical world of ancient Greece), and I have touched only briefly and in a roundabout fashion on Hegel's view of those modern social institutions—including, especially, the state—that he thinks are necessary to achieve reconciliation through recognition.[95] In the next chapter, therefore, I turn to a case study in the politics of recognition that differs from the examples dealt with here in three ways. First, it is a case that appears in Hegel's own work but which I also treat at length as a matter of real social and political history. Second, it is a case that involves the mediation of relations of recognition by the modern state. And, third, it is a case that seems, on its face, to be unequivocally *emancipatory*, unlike the confinement of women to the family. That case—Jewish emancipation in nineteenth-century Germany—will give us another, even more challenging opportunity to put these Hegelian conceptual tools to work.

CHAPTER FIVE

Double Binds

Jewish Emancipation and the Sovereign State

> *Herr von Schrötter sent for me . . . and asked me, since he*
> *thought I must be quite familiar with the Jews, whether I*
> *knew a way to strike them dead—bloodlessly, but all at once.*
> —KRIMINALRAT F. BRAND

THE MEDIATING POWER OF THE STATE?

BETWEEN THE LAST DECADES of the eighteenth century and the continent-shaking revolutions of 1848, the lives of Jews in Europe's German-speaking lands were fundamentally transformed by a series of measures designed to end or weaken the restrictions that had long excluded Jews from the mainstream of social and political life. Although these measures were gradual and often halting, this period is rightly called the era of emancipation; and the movement for reform had already made substantial progress by 1821, when Hegel, in a famous note to the *Philosophy of Right*, declared that the exclusion of Jews from civic life was the "highest folly" and that the emancipatory measures that granted Jews civil rights were "wise and honourable."[1]

Hegel's endorsement of Jewish emancipation is brief, but it is forceful, and it has become an important piece of evidence in some recent efforts to show the compatibility of Hegel's thought with liberalism and/or pluralism.[2] For example, in his monumental book *Hegel's Ethics of Recognition*, Robert Williams uses the case of Jewish emancipation to buttress his claim that Hegel succeeds in salvaging the ideal of recognition in his mature system. A large part of Williams's purpose is to defend Hegel's conception of recognition against the charge that it eliminates or suppresses "otherness," and while Williams sometimes seems to have in mind a relatively apolitical sense of "otherness" as ontological distinctness,[3] Williams also argues that Hegel's conception of recognition respects "otherness" in the sense that term has come to have within debates about multiculturalism and pluralism: his state is not "totalitarian" but "genuinely pluralistic and inclusive,"[4] and he invokes Hegel's defense of Jewish emancipation to demonstrate this claim. "Hegel's state," Williams argues, "in recognizing the humanity of the Jews, does not simply affirm Jews in an abstract, anonymous identity within the whole; it would also affirm Jews as coequal others in their difference. . . . Hegel's state, as an articulated unity and totality, would affirm and preserve difference in its difference."[5]

Against the background of Sophocles' story of the tragic collision between Antigone and Creon, or Hegel's parable of a struggle between self-consciousnesses, what is especially striking about Williams's argument is its use of the notion of the *state*. In Sophoclean Thebes, no overarching institution exists to adjudicate the conflict between *oikos* and *polis*; in Hegel's parable the politics of recognition is played out face to face. In the contemporary political world, by contrast, struggles over recognition are paradigmatically struggles over the shape and behavior of encompassing political institutions. To be sure, political theorists often talk of people or groups seeking to win recognition from "the larger society," or from "their fellow citizens," but this is typically shorthand for some alteration of law or public policy; indeed, those who claim recognition may never meet the vast majority of those to whom their appeals are ultimately addressed. And for Williams, as for many Hegelian theorists of recognition—and indeed for Hegel himself, at least in his reconciliatory voice—the presence of state seems to make all the difference to the politics of recognition.

Why would this be so? In the *Phenomenology*, as we have seen, Hegel's account of the struggle for recognition ends at an impasse. Indicting the inequality and asymmetry with which the struggle ends, Hegel draws attention not to one party's failure to see and respect the identity of the other, but instead to one party's failure to acknowledge its own fundamental condition of dependence and to abandon its impossible quest for sovereign agency. In this context, Hegel's implicit endorsement of a norm of mutual self-acknowledgment seems to undermine, not support, the project of equal recognition. On Hegel's account, social relations—in this instance, the relation of master and slave—only become possible because one of the two parties to the struggle does not surrender but preserves his aspiration to achieve independence, arranging social relations in ways that mirror back to him (however imperfectly or temporarily) the self-image he desires, and at the same time forcing the other to bear, disproportionately, the weight of the finitude he disavows. Recognition, here, rests on the failure of acknowledgment.

Yet this problem might be resolved if there were some regime or form of recognition consistent with the *mutual* acknowledgment of finitude. And this is precisely the role played by the concept of the state in Hegel's theory of recognition. Just as, in contractarian thought, the state serves as an institution of mediation that protects people against the consequences of unregulated social conflict, Hegel's idea of the state represents an alternative resolution of the struggle for recognition in which, in effect, *both* self-consciousnesses acknowledge their dependence on others by coming to see themselves as members of a larger political community, whose institutional expression is the state.[6] In a *Zusatz* to the *Encyclopaedia of the Philosophical Sciences*, in which he retells the story of master and slave in refined form, Hegel assures us that "the fight for recognition pushed to the extreme indicated here can only occur in the natural state, where men exist only as single, separate individuals; but it is absent in civil society and the State because here the recognition for which the combatants fought *already exists*."[7] In short, as David Duquette puts it, "what distinguishes the mediation of self and otherness provided in the state [for Hegel] is the ultimate harmonization of social life in which the struggle for recognition is finally overcome."[8]

This view of the state as a site of reconciliation may be appealing, but is it convincing? At first glance, these brief statements seem to suffer from one crucial problem: they move directly from a condition of unmediated conflict to one in which the mediating work of the state has always already been accomplished. But to do this, as I have suggested in chapter 1, is to treat the state like a *deus ex machina* that appears from outside the social, which—by virtue of its sovereign elevation above the conflicts of social life—can serve as a mediating institution. And this begs crucial questions. How, if at all, does one set of institutions acquire such a sovereign status in the first place, and how does it sustain that status over time? *Can* the state lift itself out of the fray of social struggle in this way, or does it always remain a party to the conflicts it purports to transcend? These questions come into especially clear view when dealing with controversies over membership and belonging, as in the case of Jewish emancipation, for with respect to those who are not, or who are not yet, or who might cease to be citizens, the state *cannot* reassuringly be redescribed as the ethical substance in which "we" have always already found ourselves. In such cases, the definition of that "we" is precisely what is at issue.

In this chapter and the next, I develop a different view of the role of the state in the politics of recognition. Rather than treating the state as an already-sovereign institution that can transcend struggles for recognition once and for all, I suggest that the modern state is instead one of the central objects of identification onto which persons displace, and through which they pursue, the desire for independent and masterful agency. This phenomenon of displacement through identification is already evident in Hegel's account of the master-slave relation: there, as we have seen, the social role of master—a relation misrecognized as an identity—helps to insulate its bearer from the self-contradictory nature of his own aspiration to absolute independence. The same phenomenon is also visible in the *Antigone*, where Antigone's and Creon's efforts to achieve mastery are mediated by their intersubjectively constituted social roles: it is *as* bearers of those identities, not as agents *simpliciter*, that they seek recognition. Identification with the modern state, I shall suggest, is not radically different from these other forms of identification: as a bearer of the displaced aspiration to sovereign agency, the state participates in and reconfigures, but by no means transcends, the conflictual and potentially unjust dynamics of recognition.

Unlike many considerations of the problem of membership, however, my purpose here is *not* to make the now familiar point that the formation and consolidation of sovereignty inevitably results in exclusion.[9] This is not to deny that many of the components of modern practices of sovereignty, from territorial boundaries to racialized rules of national membership, have been unjustly, often violently exclusive. But that claim, important as it is, does not yet represent the strongest possible challenge to the notion that the state can stand above and resolve struggles for recognition, for it tempts us to consider the state only at what its defenders would consider its worst. Here, instead, I focus on the ways in which states also seek to establish and preserve sovereignty precisely in moments of political *inclusion*. Without suggesting that inclusion and exclusion are no different, I tease out the complex, equivocal consequences of such moments of inclusion-through-recognition even for its apparent beneficiaries.

To do this, I work not from the top down—by following the conceptual development of the notion of the state in the *Philosophy of Right*, for instance—but from the bottom up. The question of whether the state represents a real resolution of struggles for recognition or what Marx calls "the semblance of a resolution which [Hegel] declares to be the real thing" requires us to consider how that resolution works, or fails to work, in specific cases.[10] For this reason, I take up the example upon which Williams relies to demonstrate the success of the Hegelian state's transcendence of struggles for recognition. It is certainly true that Hegel's endorsement of Jewish emancipation distinguishes him from the most vicious anti-Semites of his day. Nevertheless, Williams, eager to vindicate Hegel's conception of the state, is too quick to celebrate emancipation as an unequivocally progressive accomplishment. Focusing only on emancipation's universalist moment, he neglects the role this very universalism played in the formation of a putatively sovereign nation-state, both in Hegel's system and in history. Indeed, Williams mentions the historical context of Hegel's famous footnote only briefly, describing the Prussian emancipation Edict of 1812 as a declaration "that the Jews were to receive full equality of civil and political rights in Prussia."[11] But as we shall see in detail the next sections, the edict did both less and more than this; moreover, its rationale (like Hegel's praise of it) was less purely principled than Williams implies, and its consequences for the Jews it emancipated were much less straightforward than he acknowledges. Far from being a simple "release" or *Freigabe* that "affirms Jews as coequal others in their difference," Jewish emancipation (both in history and for Hegel) was part of the process of nation- and state-building in Prussia and other German lands; and even as it liberated Jews from some restrictions, it also subjected them to novel forms of subordination precisely in order to secure the sovereign self-image of Germans—albeit indirectly, by facilitating identification with a supposedly sovereign state.

BEYOND "ON THE JEWISH QUESTION"

Later in the nineteenth century, of course, Hegel's most famous student and critic had already adopted a different, less sanguine posture toward Jewish emancipation. In "On the Jewish Question," Marx uses this issue to launch a broad critique of what he called merely "political emancipation"—that is, the abolition of explicit forms of political privilege grounded in differences of social status such as religious affiliation or property-ownership—which he associates with eighteenth-century revolutionary liberalism's universalist discourses of rights. Without rejecting Jewish emancipation or advocating a return to the segregation of previous centuries, Marx nevertheless argues that political emancipation frees people only in an abstract and formal way, declaring differences in social status to be politically irrelevant while doing nothing to alter the social relations of power those differences express.[12]

Marx's argument has been extremely influential. Among other things, it has served as one important starting point for Wendy Brown's recent critiques of rights discourse and the state. Drawing explicitly upon "On the Jewish Question," Brown has argued that appeals to law and the state to redress identity-related injustice may "inadvertently redraw the very configurations and effects of power that they seek to vanquish," while also "unwittingly increas[ing] the power of the state and its various regulatory discourses at the expense of political freedom."[13] Brown's compelling account has helped inspire my own attempt to rethink the role of the state in the politics of recognition, and in many respects the present chapter follows her lead. Nevertheless, I am less confident than Brown about the usefulness of Marx's "On the Jewish Question" here. This is not simply a matter of Marx's infamous and disturbing use of anti-Semitic tropes in the second half of "On the Jewish Question"; Brown is right, I believe, that we should not let that deter us from a substantive engagement with the essay.[14] Rather, at crucial moments

Marx's essay suffers from a cramped understanding of the role of the state in the politics of identity and difference, and this contributes to his striking insensitivity to the distinctive forms of alienation and subordination to which German Jews were subject in the age of emancipation. And while Brown herself is subtler than Marx in these matters, a more deeply critical reading of "On the Jewish Question" might still push her own critique of the state in an importantly different direction.

To review briefly: Marx's argument begins with a critique of Bruno Bauer's 1843 essay "Die Judenfrage." Bauer's essay was itself a critique of a piece published the preceding year by an otherwise forgotten conservative writer named Carl Hermes, whose purpose was to defend an ultimately unsuccessful neomedieval plan to roll back Jewish emancipation and resegregate Prussian Jews, restoring the Christian character of the state.[15] Bauer accepted Hermes's premise—that there was a fundamental contradiction in the idea of a Christian state granting Jews equal rights—but drew the opposite conclusion: that true freedom required the abolition of all connections between political status and religious belief, Christian as well as Jewish.[16] Marx, in turn, charges that Bauer put too much faith in the capacity of such political measures to produce complete, "human" emancipation, a charge he substantiates by pointing to the fact that in the nominally secular United States, religion "not only continues to *exist* but is *fresh* and *vigorous*."[17] This, for Marx, could only count as evidence of continued unfreedom, for he regards "the existence of religion" as "the existence of a defect," a disavowal of our own powers and a projection of these onto an alien entity which is really nothing but a misrecognized product of our own consciousness.[18]

But the problem is not merely that political emancipation fails to achieve human emancipation. Worse, political emancipation may actually *entrench* the very forms of inequality and relations of power from which we seek to be freed. To make this point, Marx broadens his frame of reference from religion to consider the relation of the political state to the various distinctions and forces that operate in civil society. As Marx puts it, in undertaking political emancipation

> the state abolishes, after its fashion, the distinctions established by *birth, social rank, education, occupation* when it declares that birth, social rank, education, occupation are *non-political* distinctions; when it proclaims, without regard to these distinctions, that every member of society is an *equal* partner in popular sovereignty. . . . But the state, none the less, allows private property, education, occupation to *act* after *their* own fashion, namely as private property, education, occupation, and to manifest their *particular* nature.[19]

What is true of religion is true of other social powers too: political emancipation not only leaves them in place but, in calling them "non-political," disguises their status as forms of power and makes it more difficult to address them politically.[20] Moreover, this depoliticization and entrenchment is not accidental; instead, it is driven by the modern state's own imperatives of legitimation. As Marx adds, immediately after the passage just quoted: "far from abolishing these effective differences, [the state] only exists so far as they are presupposed; it is conscious of being a political state and manifests its universality only in opposition to these elements."[21] In other words, as Brown puts it, "the state is premised upon that which it claims to transcend and requires that which it claims to abolish"; it can only legitimate itself as a "neutral and universal representative of the people" by reinforcing the forms of social power that serve as its foil.[22]

The problem is that Marx's essay is caught between two different understandings of what it means for the state to "presuppose" that which it purports to abolish; that is to say, it is caught between two different approaches to the relationship between state and civil society. At times, Marx's argument here, as in his "Critique" of Hegel's *Philosophy of Right*, is, in a precise sense, deconstructive. It shows that the distinction between the political state and civil society is not a "fixed antithesis" but an insecure historical accomplishment—insecure, because the admittedly real institutional separation between state and civil society always belies a deeper relationship of interdependence between these two spheres, which renders the very boundary between them unstable.[23] This interdependence is, in part, a matter of history: civil society and the state, Marx suggests, are not always already independent entities that had only to be untangled through political emancipation; rather, the modern political state and civil society were *first constituted as such* through one and the same founding act of division—what Marx calls the "political revolution" that did away with feudalism.[24] Yet precisely because they were first brought into being as two sides of a single cut, the separation between civil society and the political state can never quite be made final, and so their complex relationship of interdependence-in-opposition is not only historical but also ongoing. Civil society's material, ideological, and affective dynamics continue to sustain and shape political life even while keeping it under a shadow of particularism; the institutions (and organized violence) of law and the state continue to sustain and shape civil society while also keeping it under a shadow of regulation. What is crucial here is that by treating state and civil society as mutually constitutive in this way, *this* version of Marx's argument suggests that the state does much more than merely entrench existing relations of power in civil society: the project of establishing and securing the independence of the state actively transforms the character of social life, and vice versa.

Yet even as Marx criticizes dogmatic treatments of the state-civil society distinction, he also deploys that distinction in "On the Jewish Question" in ways that foreshadow his own most dogmatically reductionist pronouncements about the state.[25] Now inverting rather than deconstructing liberalism's embrace of the political state and political emancipation as a source of universality, Marx calls political life and citizenship "abstract," locating the "real" instead in civil society. He declares that *human* emancipation will have occurred when "the real, individual man has *absorbed into himself* the abstract citizen," suggesting, again, a kind of priority of civil society's "reality" over its mere shadow in the state.[26] And, most importantly, contrary to the notion of state and civil society as mutually constitutive, Marx writes as though political emancipation merely removes impediments to the operation of a civil society whose own logic had been there all along: the political state, Marx says, lets private property and other social structures "*act* after *their* own fashion"; it represents the "consummation of the materialism of civil society"; it removes the "bonds which had restrained the egoistic spirit of civil society."[27] (Indeed, one way to read this essay is as an opportunistic use of the "Jewish Question" to broach other, supposedly more fundamental issues: hence, in the course of the article, the question of Jewish emancipation quickly becomes a question about religion in general; and from there it is further displaced to problems of political economy such as private property, first merely by analogy—private property and "religion," like education, occupation, and birth, being among the various forces that make up civil society—and then, in the second half of the essay, through the exploitation of commonplace associations between Jews and "huckstering," "egoism," and the worship of money, which Marx now calls the "*supreme practical* expression of human self-estrangement."[28])

Economism aside, the trouble with this approach is that it seriously constrains Marx's view of the role of the state in relations of identity and difference. If, as I have suggested, Hegelian theorists like Williams are too optimistic about the capacity of the state to resolve struggles for recognition once and for all, Marx often suffers from the opposite problem: he too quickly reads the state *out* of those struggles, locating power instead in the elsewhere of civil society and casting the state merely as a second-order expression of human alienation that reinforces, but does not otherwise shape or constitute, potentially unjust relations of identity and difference. (A trace of this problem shows itself in Brown's appropriation of Marx, too: for her, the state "veils," "consecrates," "presupposes," "naturalizes," "entrenches," and "reinforces" the distinctions and forms of power that operate in civil society, but there seems to be nothing in its legitimating ideology that demands any more substantive intervention into the field of identity and difference.[29]) One symptom of this too-quick turn away from the state is that Marx—again, in a surprising convergence with Williams—often writes as though political emancipation were unproblematic, as far as it goes. Just as Williams describes the Prussian emancipation edict simply as a declaration of equal rights for Jews, Marx takes at face value the notion that Jewish emancipation represents a straightforward divorce between the state and religion—a withdrawal of the state from direct intervention into the field of belief, which nevertheless does nothing to undermine people's addictions, rooted elsewhere, to this particular opiate. Indeed, for Marx, as for Brown, the trouble with political emancipation seems to lie in its success: the social power that operates in civil society will be depoliticized precisely to the extent that the state *achieves* the separation from civil society upon which its legitimacy depends.[30]

But Jewish emancipation, as I have already suggested, was hardly so simple. Far from merely declaring Jewishness to be irrelevant to political membership, emancipation was at once a removal of restrictions on Jewish life and an active effort to reshape Jewish, and German, identity. Indeed, the policy was shot through with tensions that arose from the fact that it was designed in substantial part to secure an impossible sovereignty for the state; and many of the most troubling consequences of the policy for Jews arose less from the fact that it succeeded in making the state neutral (for it did not) than from the fact that it made Jews bear, disproportionately, the weight of its own failure to achieve its quixotic goals. In this case, in other words, the consequences of political emancipation were far more varied than simply reinforcing an existing relation of power by depoliticizing it. In some respects emancipation reinforced existing patterns of social subordination; in other respects it eliminated them; in still other respects it created new patterns of subordination and asymmetrical dependence; and in many ways it transformed the identities of all the parties involved. Bringing this into view, however, will require reading the case of the Jewish question through the lens of national identity and state sovereignty, treating the state as one among many sites of, and players in, politics, not as a distraction from it, or as its consummation. And to do that, we need to spend more time than either Marx or Williams does with the historical details of this fascinating and equivocal instance of recognition.

"A WAY TO STRIKE THEM DEAD"

On November 25, 1808—a little more than two years after the disastrous defeat of Prussian forces at Jena, which Hegel witnessed while completing the manuscript of the *Phenomenology*—the influential Jewish community of Königsberg addressed a letter to Friedrich Wilhelm III, appealing for, among other things, the freedom of marriage, greater freedom of residence, and the right to acquire property in land. The opening lines of their letter suggested, subtly, that an exchange of recognition might be in order:

> Your eternal royal Majesty's noble and wise orders and reforms fill every subject of the Prussian state with love, awe, and joyful anticipation; therefore, the members of a people that has lagged behind [in enthusiasm] because it has felt itself beset and neglected, do venture to have resort to your eternal royal Majesty's good sentiments, full of hope and confidence.[31]

The Jewish community's appeal was hardly the beginning of the movement to emancipate German Jews from the web of archaic legal and administrative restrictions that guided their lives.[32] Since the publication of Christian Wilhelm von Dohm's essay *On the Civic Improvement of the Jews* in 1781, Jewish emancipation had become a prominent topic of public discussion and a favored cause of political reformers across German-speaking lands.[33] The following year, Habsburg emperor Joseph II issued an Edict of Toleration that removed a number of restrictions on Austrian Jews for the sake of making them "more useful to the state."[34] To the west, by 1791, the Revolutionary assembly had extended the principles of the Declaration of the Rights of Man and of the Citizen to all French Jews,[35] and the ideological force of the French Revolution, supplemented by the force of Napoleon's armies, helped generate emancipatory legislation in western and southern German territories during the first decade of the nineteenth century.[36]

On March 11, 1812, Friedrich Wilhelm finally issued an "Edict concerning the Civic Conditions of the Jews in the Prussian State."[37] The edict declared Jews legally resident in Prussia to be "natives and citizens of the Prussian state" (*Einländer und Preußische Staatsbürger*) and announced that these Jews would enjoy "the same civic rights and freedoms as the Christians," including the right to obtain academic posts and local public offices (though the question of service in other public offices was deferred); the right to practice previously restricted crafts and trades; the freedom from special taxes; the liberty to pass on property to all their children (not just the first and second sons); the freedom to marry and divorce without special permission; and freedom of residence in the cities and the countryside.[38]

By all available accounts, the edict was received by Prussian Jewry with jubilation.[39] The day after its adoption, the elders of the Berlin Jewish community wrote to Prime Minister Hardenberg that they had received this "most invaluable kindness" with profound joy, and promised to undertake the "greatest efforts" to make themselves worthy of their new status through "genuine loyalty and unconditional obedience" to the Prussian state.[40] The representatives of the Königsberg community followed suit, offering the king the assurance that they would seek "to merit the confidence that his Majesty has demonstrated in raising us to the status of real citizens of the state."[41]

By sweeping away thickets of unjust legislation that had helped keep Jews confined to certain occupations, restricted them to certain regions, towns, and neighborhoods, artificially constrained the size of their families, and left them generally poorer than their Christian neighbors, the Edict of 1812 and similar legislation gave Jews in Germany a new measure of dignity. These reforms doubtless also contributed to the general skyrocketing of the Jewish standard of living in Prussia over the next several decades, though broader patterns of economic transformation, as well as the emigration of poorer Jews to America and elsewhere, also helped. The improvement was marked: In 1816, David Sorkin reports, only 38.3 percent of the Jewish population of Hamburg earned enough to pay taxes; in 1848, the number had risen to 93.2 percent.[42] As Rürup insists, the Edict of 1812 "was a remarkable law, which to this day must be valued as one of the great documents of the history of emancipation in Europe."[43]

Yet Jewish emancipation in nineteenth-century Prussia meant much more than merely removing onerous burdens from a defenseless minority. As the members of the Königsberg community knew when they answered the king with a pledge of loyalty, emancipation legislation was not conceived merely as the fulfillment of liberal principles of fairness or equality, nor was it simply the gift of an indifferent king who expected nothing in return. The law secured recognition for the Jews, yet it also secured recognition for Prussia by placing Jews into a new relationship with the state; it lifted restrictions on Jewish life, but it also served as a tool through which the state could mold its Jewish population into a shape consistent with the requirements of modern government—by which, that is, it could perform the work of *identifying* Jews as citizens, *and* identifying *itself* as sovereign.[44] As Salo Baron wrote: "Jewish emancipation was as much a historic necessity for the modern state as it was for the Jews."[45]

From the beginning of the movement for Jewish emancipation in Germany, the issue of the status of German Jews was almost universally understood to be an issue about facilitating the transformation of Germany's Jewish population and, consequently, its dissolution into the nation at large. The title of Dohm's pamphlet—on the "civic improvement" (*bürgerliche Verbesserung*) of the Jews—set the terms of the debate for decades to come. Advocates of reform, like Dohm, argued that "everything with which one reproaches the Jews"—dishonesty, egotism, exploitative huckstering, fanatical isolation from Christian society—"is caused by the political conditions in which they presently live,"[46] and advocated a combination of equalized legal status, occupational restructuring (to move Jews out of lending and peddling and into the "productive" occupations of crafts and agriculture), and state-directed education to overcome these circumstances.[47] Opponents of emancipation, on the other hand, insisted that the undesirable characteristics of Jews were innate and therefore difficult, if not impossible, to reform.[48] Even prominent Jewish advocates and defenders of emancipation—who were, it must be noted, mainly well-educated and successful Jews from a few large urban centers—operated on the same terrain. The contributors to the innovative Jewish journal *Sulamith*, for instance, argued for Jewish "reform" and "regeneration" as, in Sorkin's words, "an act of reciprocity to the agent of emancipation,"[49] and the same journal published critiques of the influence of Polish rabbis on German Jewish children, complaining that the easterners were "'infecting' the language of German youth with their despicable *Jargon*."[50] In Reinhard Rürup's terms, "integration into civic society . . . could not be imagined otherwise than as a process of assimilation to the mentality and life-style of the non-Jewish majority."[51]

In order to understand the terms of this exchange, we need to look more closely at the image of Jews that lay behind the demand for assimilation as a condition of emancipation. German perceptions of Jews were complex, but for the purposes of this discussion, we can isolate two important sources of anxiety about the Jews. The first was the concern that, in their extreme parochialism, distinct customs, adherence to the Mosaic law, and messianic hope for political redemption, the Jews constituted a distinct "state within a state."[52] As with the demand for assimilation in general, this concern was shared by proponents and opponents of emancipation, who disagreed not about *whether* Jews were dangerously parochial, but only about *how* this condition could be overcome. Dohm himself wrote constantly about the "segregation" and "separation" of the Jews from their Christian neighbors, but thought that the government could "dissolve" this distinct nation into "the great harmony of the state" by granting Jews citizenship rights.[53] Dohm's frequently quoted words—"the Jew is a human being even more than he is a Jew"—occur not (as is sometimes suggested) in the context of a defense of universal human rights, but rather in the course of a psychological argument about how the state might most effectively weaken the parochial ties among Jews and convert them into loyal German citizens. "The Jew is a human being even more than he is a Jew," Dohm writes, so

> how could it be possible for him not to love a state in which he was able to freely hold and enjoy property, where his taxes were not higher than those of other citizens, and where he too could acquire honor and respect? Why should

he hate people who are no longer separated from him by hurtful privileges, people with whom he has equal rights and equal duties? . . . gratitude [for this good fortune] would make him into a patriotic citizen. He would regard the fatherland with the tenderness of a previously unrecognized [*verkannt*] son who was only installed in his familial station after a long exile. *These human feelings would speak more loudly in his heart than the sophistic deductions of his rabbis.*[54]

Opponents of emancipation, on the other hand, feared that the emancipated Jew would always belong to a "state within a state," and that emancipation would merely make it easier for him to extort and manipulate his Christian neighbors for the selfish aggrandizement of his own people.[55]

This concern about Jewish parochialism was clearly at work in the discussions within the Prussian government that led up to the Edict of 1812. In a letter to Friedrich Wilhelm in November 1808, Minister Schrötter tried to persuade the king of the wisdom of a comprehensive reform of Prussia's legislation concerning the Jews. Emphasizing the contributions that wealthy Jews could make to the Prussian treasury and that other Jews could make to the strength of the Prussian military, Schrötter reminded the king that the state must first "recognize Jews as citizens [*als Bürger anerkennen*] before it demands that they fulfill civic duties."[56] In Schrötter's opinion, such an exchange of civil rights for civil obligations would also "completely abolish the existing separation between Jews and Christians." Emancipating the Jews would "undermine and abolish their nationality, and gradually . . . produce a situation in which they will no longer to seek to form a state within a state."[57] (This sort of "abolition," one suspects, is what Schrötter had in mind when, in the process of preparing an early draft of the 1812 edict, he supposedly asked a Prussian security official whether he "knew a way to strike [the Jews] dead—bloodlessly, but all at once."[58])

The Edict of 1812 itself contained provisions designed to effect this denationalization of the Jews. Though emancipation was technically immediate and unconditional, the edict also required that newly emancipated Jews fulfill a number of obligations and threatened them with loss of their status as citizens if they did not comply.[59] These included the adoption of fixed, Western-style surnames, the use of German "or another living language" in the conduct of business and legal affairs, the use of German or Latin characters in their signatures, and the registration of their identities with the authorities.[60] (Early drafts of the legislation had also contemplated requiring that Jews abandon distinctive clothing—their "national dress"—and that Jewish men shave off their beards.[61]) The Edict even performed a sort of denationalization through its language: by referring to Jews in its introductory paragraph as "persons of the Jewish faith" (*jüdische Glaubensgenossen*), it signalled its intention to transform Jews from members of a *Volk* or *Nation* into individual subscribers to a religious creed.[62] Perhaps most importantly, the edict dealt a "heavy, though not fatal, blow" to the traditional Jewish community by depriving rabbis and community elders of all legal jurisdiction and authority, and putting Jewish affairs almost entirely under Prussian law.[63] The edict thus helped usher in a vastly transformed rabbinate whose responsibilities were remarkably similar to those of the Protestant clergy:

> The rabbi was no longer to be the judge of a community governing itself according to religious law, as he had been prior to emancipation, but was to be a religious leader alone. The rabbinate's institutional locus was no longer the law court but the school and the temple. The rabbi was to be concerned solely with his congregants' spiritual welfare. He was to be a minister to souls, a "*Seelssorger*," whose office could best be discharged through the edifying sermon and education.[64]

(This, one should note, casts a different light on Marx's own insistent framing of the "Jewish Question"—three decades after the edict—as a *religious* question, a question of the alienating grip in which people are held by theological mystifications. What Marx does not see is that the very notion of Judaism as a mode of belief or as one faith among others—interchangeable, in that sense, with Christianity and equally representative of "religion in general"—was itself in important ways a product of the initial work of political emancipation, which did not just entrench Jewish religious consciousness by privatizing it, but transformed the meaning of Jewishness itself, working to convert it *into* a matter of religious consciousness, and doing so in the service of the project of nation-state sovereignty.[65])

At the same time, there was a second component to German anxieties about Jews, which may seem to stand in tension with the first. Jews were threatening not only because of their parochialism—their tendency to cluster together in separate communities governed by, and devoted to, the Mosaic law—but also because of their supposed rootlessness. The idea of Jews as rootless had been a commonplace in the European imagination at least since the appearance in the Middle Ages of the earliest versions of the legend of the "Wandering Jew," often called Ahasverus, who was supposedly condemned to roam the earth after having struck or mocked Jesus on the road to Cavalry.[66] The force of the legend must have derived in part from its correspondence to the actual circumstances of some European Jews, including itinerant individuals who never received permission to settle in a community (about 10 percent of German Jews at the beginning of the era of emancipation)[67] as well as whole families who found themselves displaced by war, pogrom, or the whim of the local prince.[68]

Of course, in the seventeenth and eighteenth centuries, European states had counted on a variety of Jewish cosmopolitanism—the international connections of prominent "Court Jews"—to keep their treasuries full during costly wars and other financial crises.[69] But by the nineteenth century, the prospect of a continuing migration of poorer Jews from Poland and elsewhere in eastern Europe led the authorities to seek to stabilize and defend Prussia's territorial boundaries.[70] To this end, the Edict of 1812 made use of an important distinction between "Prussian" and "foreign"—*fremd* or *ausländisch*—Jews. Despite (or perhaps because of) a long tradition of German-Jewish congregations employing Polish immigrants as rabbis and cantors, as well as a history of wealthy German Jews employing poorer and less-educated immigrants as domestics and laborers, the Edict of 1812 categorically prohibited foreign Jews from working as rabbis, synagogue officials, tutors, domestic workers, or laborers, and threatened Prussian Jews who employed foreigners with fines and prison sentences.[71] There is evidence that these provisions were taken seriously by the authorities: a few months after the announcement of the edict, Hardenberg issued a set of instructions which required that the police assemble and maintain reliable lists of Jewish citizens, that Jewish citizens report all births, marriages, divorces, and deaths to the authorities so that these lists could be kept current, and that every Jew be prepared to prove his citizenship to the authorities by presenting a state-issued certificate upon demand.[72]

These two concerns about the Jews—parochialism and cosmopolitanism—form a telling ideological pair: they testify to the central role played by the goal of constructing and defending the sovereignty of the nation-state in the movement for Jewish emancipation. Parochialism and cosmopolitanism stand in equivalent relationships to the idea of the nation-state: parochialism threatens national identity by pulling the loyalties of citizens down and in, as it were, toward exclusive subgroups within the state; cosmopolitanism threatens national identity by pushing the loyalties of citizens up and out, toward persons and groups outside the state. Fichte's famous remarks about the Jews in an early essay on the French Revolution tellingly synthesize these two anxieties. There, Fichte called the Jews "a mighty state stretche[d] across almost all the countries of Europe, hostile in intent and engaged in constant strife with everyone else," and warned:

> Are you not reminded here of a state within a state? Does the obvious idea not occur to you that the Jews constitute citizens of a state to which you do not belong, a state that is sounder and stronger than all of yours? If you grant

them civil rights in your state as well, they will trample all your other citizens underfoot.[73]

In Fichte's depiction, the danger the Jews present comes from neither cosmopolitanism nor parochialism alone; rather, Jews threaten because it is precisely in their segregation and withdrawal from German national life that they maintain their spiritual and material connections to a larger community, one which "stretches across . . . Europe." Of course, Fichte was no friend of emancipation: he famously said that he could only imagine giving Jews civil rights if one were first "to cut off all their heads one night and replace them with others that do not contain a single Jewish idea."[74] But if the emancipators' fantasies of state sovereignty were considerably less bloody, they were nevertheless animated by similar anxieties about the Jews, and they aimed at similar results.

HEGEL, EMANCIPATION, AND SOVEREIGNTY

Against this background, Hegel's defense of Jewish emancipation takes on a considerably different cast. To be sure, as Williams suggests, there is reason to believe not only that Hegel's discussion of Jewish emancipation in the *Philosophy of Right* was a sincere defense of civic equality, but also that it was inspired by his distaste for some of the cruder forms of German nationalism and anti-Jewish sentiment then circulating, and perhaps even by some specific events.[75] The textual history of this discussion is illuminating in this regard, though it provides only circumstantial evidence. The basic outlines of what would become the *Philosophy of Right*—completed in 1820 and published in January 1821—were already present in the version of the *Encyclopaedia of the Philosophical Sciences* that Hegel published in Heidelberg in 1817, and beginning in the 1817–1818 academic year, Hegel developed his political thought in annual lectures on "Natural Right and Political Science." In that first year's lectures, Hegel did claim—in a marginal comment in the course of his account of international law—that the exclusion of Jews from the state was "unnecessary," a comment that seems to be a weak antecedent to the later defense of Jewish emancipation. But the comment was not repeated the next year, and it was only in the lecture course that began in the winter semester of 1819, and then in the text of the *Philosophy of Right* itself, that Hegel included a prominent discussion of religious toleration and Jewish emancipation near the beginning of his elaboration of the idea of the state.[76] One plausible interpretation of this change is that Hegel was responding in part to events of the summer of 1819, when a wave of destructive anti-Jewish riots swept across German-speaking lands. The climate of public discourse in Germany had been growing increasingly anti-Semitic in part through the pronouncements of the Heidelberg professor J. F. Fries, who had published a vicious attack against the idea of Jewish citizenship in 1816; this review essay was apparently so popular that it was reprinted as a separate pamphlet the same year, and was "read aloud in beerhouses."[77] Fries's superficiality and demagoguery had already been the primary target of Hegel's polemic in the Preface to the *Philosophy of Right*; and the note to section 270 certainly reads like a rejoinder to Fries's brand of anti-Semitism.

The trouble is that Hegel's own characterizations of Judaism in texts ranging from the youthful theological writings of the 1790s to the mature lectures on the philosophy of religion and history are often negative; sometimes crudely and harshly so, sometimes more moderately. To many readers, these writings have seemed hard to square with his apparent commitment to emancipation. Yet this will only seem like a puzzle if we assume that what Yirmayahu Yovel calls "aversion to Judaism" and "support of civil equality" are inconsistent with one another in the first place—and this is not obviously the case.[78] As we have seen, in the discourse surrounding Jewish emancipation in Hegel's time, civil equality was conceived first and foremost as a device for the reform and/or elimination of actually existing Judaism, and there is nothing particularly puzzling about how someone could support emancipation in those terms *and* polemicize against Jews in the same breath. Indeed, if we focus less on the mere fact that Hegel said negative things about Jews, and more on the substance of his negative characterizations; and, likewise, if we suspend the assumption that the defense of emancipation as a political strategy is necessarily a defense *of* Jews or Judaism, it will become clear how closely Hegel's thinking about Jews and Judaism follows the pattern laid down by Dohm and other advocates of emancipation.

In his theological essays of the 1790s, including "The Positivity of the Christian Religion" and especially the vitriolic "Spirit of Christianity and its Fate," Hegel makes Judaism the primary representative of "positive" religion—that is, religion based upon obedience to authority, rather than upon ethics.[79] The Jewish nation, Hegel thinks, is held together by obedience to a law conceived as the word of a jealous and infinite God entirely external to the human world. Because Judaism makes the impassable separation of God and humankind into its foundational principle, it remains blind to the possibility of a reconciliation between the human and the divine, which Hegel thinks was exemplified in the becoming-finite of God in the person of Jesus and in Jesus' expression of love for humankind through his self-sacrifice. Repeatedly characterizing the Jewish nation as "slavelike" in its religious and practical attitudes,[80] Hegel infamously interprets the historical sufferings of the Jewish people as the consequences of this basic theological deficiency:

The subsequent circumstances of the Jewish people up to the mean, abject, wretched circumstances in which they still are today, have all of them been simply consequences and elaborations of their original fate. By this fate—an infinite power which they set over against themselves and could never conquer—they have been maltreated and will be continually maltreated until they appease it by the spirit of beauty and so annul it by reconciliation.[81]

Of course, Hegel's view of Judaism underwent a transformation between these early essays and his later lectures on the philosophy of religion; yet the change should not be overstated. Hegel did moderate the tone of his account of Judaism; he did place Judaism within a narrative of the development of religious concepts; and he did, for this reason, come to find certain things about Judaism admirable, such as the "courageousness" of the Jewish people.[82] But Hegel's view of the limitations of Jewish theology was not substantially altered, nor was his view of its ultimate anachronism and the necessity of its supersession. As the religion of "sublimity," Judaism was still characterized as postulating an absolute gulf between God and humankind, and Jews were therefore seen as relating to God like "the servant [Knecht] vis-à-vis the Lord [Herr]."[83]

This characterization of Judaism has political significance for Hegel in two different but related ways. First, at the level of figuration, Hegel's descriptions of Judaism seem to represent the disavowal, and the projection onto a discrete group, of the condition of dependence or finitude. Indeed, it is remarkable how closely Hegel's description of Jewish theology mirrors his account of the self-renunciation and submission of the slave in the *Phenomenology of Spirit*. The similarity begins with Hegel's use of terms like *Sklaverei* and *Knechtschaft* to describe the condition and attitude of the Jews in his early essay on "The Spirit of Christianity,"[84] but it is not limited to his vocabulary; it extends even into the details of his characterization of Judaism as the "religion of sublimity" in his lectures on the philosophy of religion. As we have seen, Hegel describes the experience of self-consciousness in the *Phenomenology* as a "fear of death, the absolute Lord," which has made it "trembl[e] in every fibre of its being" and shaken "everything solid and stable . . . to its foundations."[85] Likewise, in the Jewish religion, Hegel says, the experience of the worshiper is the experience of "fear of the Lord," and he stresses that "it is no earthly Lord that is feared, but fear of the invisible, i.e., of the *absolute power*," before which "everything that belongs to our earthly nature, everything ephemeral and contingent, is given up."[86] This submission before God is exemplified for Hegel by the story of Job, whose "renunciation" of his own demands, his repentance in dust and ashes, constitute his "recogni[tion]" of the sovereignty of the Lord.[87] And Hegel further associates the experience of human finitude with Judaism by stressing the Jewish theme of the unrepresentability of God. In "The Spirit of Christianity," Hegel recounts the story of Pompey entering the Israelites' temple: "After Pompey had approached the heart of the temple, the center of adoration," says Hegel,

> and had hoped to discover in it the root of the national spirit, to find indeed in one central point the life-giving soul of this remarkable people, to gaze on a Being as an object for his devotion, on something significant for his veneration, he might well have been astonished on entering the arcanum to find himself deceived so far as some of his expectations were concerned, and, for the rest, to find himself in an empty room.[88]

As we saw in the preceding chapter, such disavowal and projection can serve as a strategy for preserving the desire for masterful agency in the face of mounting evidence of its impossibility: to identify others as the site or source of finitude, and to arrange social relations in ways that seem to confirm that ideological diagnosis, is to deflect the force of one's own experience of dependence, giving the contradiction between that experience and one's own desire "room to move," and making independent or sovereign agency seem once again possible. And this seems to be precisely the function of Hegel's characterizations of Judaism. The prohibition against the making of graven images, which requires that the arcanum in the temple remain empty, is precisely an acknowledgment of the finitude that the *Phenomenology of Spirit* seemed to teach us that we must accept—but because it is here associated with a particular religion, it holds out the possibility of a transcendence of human finitude at a different and higher stage of religious development. Thus, by contrast with Judaism, in which "humanity's relationship to God takes the form of a heavy yoke, of onerous service," Hegel says that "*true* liberation"— and a reconciliation of finite and infinite—"is to be found in Christianity, in the Trinity."[89]

Indeed, the figure of Judaism plays a similar role in some of Hegel's political writings. In the 1802 essay "The German Constitution," for example, written during the death throes of the old Holy Roman Empire of the German Nation, Hegel is preoccupied with diagnosing the weakness and anachronism of the old empire and with spelling out the conditions of effective statehood. Hegel argues that the fragmentation of the empire into a multitude of powers, provinces, and Estates had destroyed the sovereignty of the whole, and insists that Germany would only truly be a state if the "political authority" were "concentrated in one centre" of decision and execution, and if this center were "secure in itself and immutably sanctified in the person of a monarch."[90] The essay thus prefigures Hegel's mature doctrine of sovereignty, which, as he says in the

Philosophy of Right, consists the state's "absolute self-determination"—
that is, in the fact that the various powers of the state may all be traced
back to a "single self" that is absolutely free to determine itself, and which
is made actual in the person of the monarch.[91] "The German Constitution" is hardly optimistic, but it finds a certain perverse solace in its final
paragraph, observing that, however difficult the achievement of sovereignty may be, and however much force may be required to subdue and
tame the unruly forces of civil society, Germany is at least not "capable
of intensifying its stubborn insistence on particularity to the degree of
madness encountered in the Jewish nation, which is incapable of uniting
with others in common social intercourse."[92] By making Jews into the
example *par excellence* of political fragmentation in this way, Hegel at
the same time salvages the possibility that non-Jewish Germans might
be something more than irredeemably particularistic: the fantasy of a
state through which people might experience sovereign agency, however
vicariously, is sustained here by the projection of finitude onto the Jews.

All that is at the level of figuration; but Hegel's characterizations of
Jews as the bearers of finitude also take on political significance in a second
and more immediately practical way, for they are also closely related to
Hegel's justification of Jewish emancipation. In "The Spirit of Christianity," Hegel begins his account of the nature of Judaism through a sketch
of the life and character of Abraham, whose "spirit" Hegel says "is the
unity, the soul, regulating the entire fate of his posterity."[93] And in
Hegel's portrait of Abraham, the theological spirit Hegel attributes to
Judaism—its tendency to relate to both God and world as an irreducibly
external force—is indistinguishable from the spirit of social and political
spirit of separatism Hegel *also* attributes to Judaism. Just as Abraham
(and thus his descendents) are cut off from God, Abraham also "steadily
persisted in cutting himself off from others," a tendency he made "con-
spicuous by a physical peculiarity imposed on himself and his posterity."[94] Abraham, like his nation, "always was and remained a foreigner,
yet not so far removed from them [other people] and independent of
them that he needed to know nothing of them whatever, to have nothing
to do with them"—precisely the circumstances that made the so-called
Jewish Question possible in modern Europe.[95]

Hegel continued to describe Jews as parochial and separatist well beyond his youthful writings. "They have a religion of their own," he says
of Jews in his 1817–1818 lectures on natural right and political science,
"which also contains a political ingredient in that they cleave to their
religion and in conformity to it hold apart from all other peoples and
may not even eat or drink with a non-Jew."[96] And, like his contemporar-
ies, Hegel regarded this national parochialism of the Jews as a threat to
the sovereignty of the state: "If . . . several nations constitute one state,"

Hegel says, referring explicitly to the Jews as a source of such plurality, "the state retains a certain weakness, which is only eliminated after centuries of amalgamation."[97] Correspondingly, in his defense of Jewish emancipation, Hegel avoids making his case on grounds of abstract principle.[98] Conceding that "it may well have been contrary to formal right to grant even civil rights to the Jews, on the grounds that the latter should be regarded not just as a particular religious group but also as members of a foreign nation [*Volk*]," he argues, like other defenders of civic equality, that the most prudent and effective way of overcoming Jewish parochialism is through emancipation.[99]

Here, Hegel echoes Dohm with striking precision. As we saw, when Dohm claimed that "the Jew is a human being even more than he is a Jew," this was not an argument from humanitarian principle, but the basis for a psychological argument that emancipation would make the voice of "humanity" speak more loudly in the Jewish heart than "the sophistic deductions of his rabbis." Likewise, Hegel here insists that "the Jews are primarily human beings," but this is only the point of departure of a strategic argument about the preconditions of assimilation. As Hegel puts it: "The Jews are primarily human beings; this is not just a neutral and abstract quality . . . for its consequence is that granting of civil rights gives those who receive them a self-awareness as recognized legal persons in civil society, and it is from this root, infinite and free from all other influences, that the desired assimilation in terms of attitude and disposition arises."[100] Ultimately, for Hegel as in the discourse of emancipation at large, civil equality for the Jews is demanded not by abstract principle but as part of the state's own project of securing self-recognition through the confirming recognition of others. As Hegel puts it, if the Jews had not been granted civil rights, they "would have remained in that isolation with which they have been reproached, and this would rightly have brought blame and reproach upon the state which excluded them; for the state would thereby have failed to recognize [*verkannt*] its own principle as an objective institution with a power of its own," i.e., one capable of inspiring patriotic identification those whom it treats as citizens.[101]

THE CONTRADICTIONS OF EMANCIPATION

Both in Hegel and in history, then, Jewish emancipation represented something much more complex and equivocal than the generous inclusion of a previously scorned and demonized minority. Yet the point of this account of emancipation, it must be stressed, is not to show that emancipation was merely a ruse of state, or that German Jews would have been better off unemancipated. Nor is my purpose to lament the ways in which emancipation transformed the conditions of Jewish existence in Europe, as though pre-emancipation German Jewry represented some sort of authentic expression of cultural particularity that was steamrolled in the name of a universalizing and homogenizing modernity. To put things in those terms would be to remain within the framework of recognition I have been trying to displace, for such an argument would rest, tacitly, on a wish to have Jewish identity *properly* recognized by the state rather than being sacrificed at the altar of state sovereignty. (Such dissatisfaction with assimilatory modes of inclusion is one root of contemporary multicultural politics, which I will consider in more detail in the next chapter.) Such an objection also supposes that emancipation *succeeded* at producing "the desired assimilation" of which Hegel spoke—but as we shall see, some of the most insidious consequences of emancipation arose less out of its success than out of the ways in which it did not, and could not, completely achieve its purposes.

As Hegel's analysis of recognition has suggested, the struggle for recognition is constitutively marked by contradiction: in the very act of demanding the recognition of our independence or mastery from others, we betray our dependence or finitude, putting the lie to our own self-descriptions. In Hegel's story, this contradiction originally manifests itself in the self-undermining consequences of self-consciousness's efforts to consume or destroy the other, which ironically shatters the very mirror in which a confirming reflection was sought. A similar contradiction afflicted the effort to secure the sovereignty of the state through the emancipation of German Jews, as we can see by considering a phenomenon we might call the ambivalence of the state toward the Jewishness of the Jews.

One instance of this ambivalence can be found in the fascinating story, reconstructed in detail by Michael Meyer, of the controversy over religious reform in Berlin in the years following the edict.[102] Although the edict was hardly the first impetus for religious reform—the eighteenth-century Haskalah, or Jewish enlightenment, had already occasioned conflict between modernizers and traditionalists into many Jewish communities—the success of emancipation did prompt some Jewish reformers to redouble their efforts.[103] In 1812, for example, David Friedländer, the radical disciple of Mendelssohn, argued that the transformation of Jewish religious life was necessary both to preserve the goodwill of the state and to sustain Judaism itself as an ongoing tradition under modern conditions; to this end, he proposed a far-reaching reform of traditional Jewish religious services, including substantial changes in prayers and songs, and the abandonment of Hebrew in favor of German.[104] But even less radical reform efforts met strong resistance from traditionalists, and so the reformers responded in part by organizing alternative religious services in private homes in Berlin. Such rumblings of reform might have been expected to win the approval of the Prussian government, since they seemed to confirm the hypothesis that emancipation would contribute to the *Verbesserung* of German Jewry; yet Friedrich Wilhelm responded in 1815 by reaffirming an old ordinance "expressly forbid-[ding] the assembly of Jews outside of the synagogue."[105] The synagogue, wrote the king,

> is the established location for the assembly of Jews for religious services. Should the religious service there be held in a language comprehended by only a few of those present, the congregation must persuade their rabbis to get rid of the incomprehensible language and introduce the national language; but they cannot expect that another assembly-place outside the synagogue be established, any more than a portion of the Catholic congregation can separate itself from the established assembly for religious services on the grounds that Latin is used in the mass and in other religious activities. This is not intolerance; it is just to hold fast to the order needed to prevent the sectarianism that would arise out of such separations.[106]

The reformers were not yet defeated, but after a drawn-out sequence of maneuvers in which the reformers and traditionalists fought over loopholes and competed for influence with various state agencies, the king finally put an end to the affair, declaring even more strongly that "the religious service of the Jews shall take place only in the local synagogue and only according to the time-honored rite, without the slightest innovation in language, ceremonies, prayers, and songs, wholly in accordance with ancient tradition," and charging his interior minister to "permit absolutely no sect to arise among the Jews in my state."[107] With this order, Friedrich Wilhelm effectively threw the power of the state behind the entrenchment of the very identity his own policy of emancipation had supposedly been intended to dissolve.

Even more striking instances of ambivalence were already visible in some of the terms of the Edict of 1812 itself. On the one hand, the edict moved to dissolve the legal distinction between Jew and Christian—to recognize them equally (only) as Prussians. On the other hand, the same edict took pains to ensure that Jews could always be recognized *as Jews* by the authorities. Since Prussia did not yet have a *universal* institution of citizenship, the certificates of citizenship that native Jews were issued under the edict were easily distinguishable from the documents with which non-Jews demonstrated their membership in the Prussian state,[108] and "the Jews" continued to be a distinct object of concern for the police.[109] The same contradictory dynamic shaped Prussian policy concerning names. As we have seen, the edict required Jews to assume Western-style surnames as a condition of retaining their newly won citizenship;

this, along with its other provisions, was intended to ensure—in Humboldt's words—"that everyone who does not have to ask for religious purposes should remain uncertain whether or not someone is a Jew."[110] Yet as early as 1816, Friedrich Wilhelm became concerned about the increasingly common practice of Jewish parents giving their children "Christian" first names, and he issued a series of orders to his ministers over the next several years demanding that they correct the situation. "For some time," the king wrote to the Minister of the Interior and Police in 1825, "the Jews have been adopting names which mean that they can no longer be recognized as Jews. This must be prevented if possible, since I do not want to permit Jews to pretend to be Christians"[111] These instances of ambivalence, I suggest, reflect a constitutive contradiction at the heart of the project of securing the sovereignty of the state, a contradiction of the same sort Hegel diagnoses in the *Phenomenology*: on the one hand, Jewishness (otherness) must be eradicated, in this case through a peaceful act of inclusion; on the other hand, in order for the consequent recognition of the sovereignty of the state to be more than momentary and ephemeral, the institutions of the state must maintain a vigilant surveillance of the Jews to be sure that they are conforming to the terms of their emancipation—and such a surveillance requires that Jews be recognizable. The imperative of emancipation becomes, paradoxically, that *the state must see at all times that each Jew has ceased to be Jewish.*

Yet the force of this contradiction was borne, disproportionately, by the Jews themselves. Rather than collapsing under its own weight, the project of sovereignty was transformed into an ongoing affair, and the persistent failure to secure that sovereignty once and for all was represented as a consequence of the characteristics of Jews rather than a consequence of the impossibility of the project. The trouble, in this ideological picture, is that no matter how successful their assimilation, Jews seem always to be on the edge of slipping back into rootlessness or parochialism: hence the extraordinary popularity of the actor Albert Wurm's famous depiction of a Jewish woman "who wished to entertain her guests by rendering one of the well-known poems from the German classics. The Jewess makes a tremendous effort to sustain the standard of High German in pronounciation and intonation. At the beginning she does indeed succeed. In the process of the performance, however, she gets carried away and reverts to the common Judendeutsch she has been trying so hard to avoid."[112] Hence, also, the common characterizations of "successfully" assimilated Jews as deceivers who have assumed a German shell only for the purposes of masking their selfish designs. In 1861, for instance, Johannes Nordmann insisted that while "the Jews may outwardly and involuntarily accept the authority of a non-Jewish state,"

this acceptance can never penetrate to their innermost selves: "they cannot do otherwise than preserve the Jewish community *in their hearts* as
a state within a state."[113] Such images of the Jew hidden behind the German extended the moment of sovereignty into the indefinite future: if
some trace of Jewishness always remained undevoured, the satisfaction
afforded by consumption would be inexhaustible.[114]

Such expressions of ambivalence powerfully shaped the experience of
many German Jews of their own identities. The psychic conflicts experienced by emancipated Jews have been objects of extensive literary, philosophical, and psychological reflection, and I will only mention one
well-known discussion of the theme: Hannah Arendt's treatment of "the
Jew as pariah."[115] In a famous passage, Arendt described the paradoxical
situation of the emancipated Jews who attempted to live according to
the state's injunction that they be "Jews yet at the same time not Jews."

> They did not want and could not belong to the Jewish people any more, but
> they wanted and had to remain Jews—exceptions among the Jewish people.
> They wanted to and could play their part in non-Jewish society, but they did
> not desire to and could not disappear among the non-Jewish peoples. Thus
> they became exceptions in the non-Jewish world. They maintained they were
> able to be "men like others on the streeet but Jews at home." But they felt
> they were different from other men on the street as Jews, and different from
> other Jews at home in that they were superior to the masses of the Jewish
> people.[116]

"The majority of assimilated Jews," Arendt concluded, thus "lived in a
twilight of favor and misfortune and knew with certainty only that both
success and failure were connected with the fact that they were Jews."[117]
Arendt documented the inner turmoil that this twilight state inspired in
her portrait of Rahel Levin Varnhagen, the Berlin *salonière* who went
from social assimilation to baptism to a reassertion of her Jewishness.
At twenty-one, Rahel had written to David Veit: "Do what I will, I shall
be ill, out of *gêne*, as long as I live; I love against my inclinations. I
dissemble, I am courteous . . . but I am too small to stand it, too small.
. . . My eternal dissembling, my being reasonable, my yielding which I
myself no longer notice, swallowing my own insights—I can no longer
stand it."[118]

This psychic conflict was not only personal; it assumed political significance in a variety of ways—for example, by closing off possible
avenues of solidarity between Prussian and "foreign" Jews. As Steven
Aschheim has shown, one strategy by which German Jews negotiated
the split identity produced by the imperatives of state sovereignty was
to project supposedly "Jewish" pathologies onto subsets of the Jewish
population. The groundwork of this strategy is already laid in the terms

of the Königsberg community's letter to Friedrich Wilhelm, which admits that "there may have existed and may still exist among us individuals who are unworthy of your eternal royal Majesty's grace," but tries to distance itself from those others, who of course ought to be treated harshly. The most frequent objects of this insistent projection were poorer and more vulnerable eastern Jews, either from the Prussian province of Posen (which had been severed from Prussia at the time of the edict of emancipation and had not been subject to its provisions even once it was recovered, probably because it was home to a great mass of poorer Jews) or from Poland, Galicia, Lithuania, and Russia. Despite the restrictions on the employment of "foreign" Jews in the Edict of 1812, eastern Jews continued to migrate west into Prussian and German territory after emancipation, and in sharply increasing numbers beginning in the 1870s and 1880s. Their presence was problematic not merely for the Prussian state, which sought to keep its boundaries secure, but also for assimilated German Jews. As Aschheim writes:

> Increasingly, East European Jewry, bordering Germany and constantly infiltrating her space and consciousness, became the living reminder to German Jewry of its own recently rejected past. The Eastern Jew was the bad memory of German Jewry come alive and an ever-present threat to assimilationist aspirations. At the same time he was a convenient foil upon which German Jews could externalize and displace what were regarded as negative Jewish characteristics.[119]

The Edict of 1812 encouraged this disidentification of Prussian Jews with their eastern neighbors in ways both obvious and subtle. Not only the restrictions on the employment of foreign Jews, but also the requirements concerning the use of German, helped to undermine communication and identification between Prussian Jews and *Ostjuden*, who continued to use Yiddish and Hebrew well after Prussian Jews had made German their dominant language.[120] In one of the most telling examples of the political consequences of the split between German and eastern Jewry, the debate over emancipation was replayed on a smaller stage in a series of controversies over the voting rights of immigrant Jews in religious elections between the turn of the century and World War I. In an ironic turn, Orthodox and Zionist factions defended the easterners while liberal Jewish leaders led moves for the disenfranchisement of foreigners. And they did so precisely on the grounds that these new arrivals were insufficiently cultured and did not possess sufficient "identification with the German *Volk*."[121]

RECOGNITION'S DOUBLE BINDS

Throughout this chapter I have been concerned with exposing the neglected costs of Jewish emancipation. These costs, we have seen, included the coercive transformation of Jewish life and culture; the fragmentation of personal identity; efforts to resolve this psychic conflict through the projection of the worst Jewish stereotypes onto poorer and more vulnerable eastern Jews; the weakening of relations of social and political solidarity with these more recent immigrants; and the imposition upon German Jews of a fateful dependence on the continued good will of the state. To insist that we confront these costs, however, is not to deny the considerable benefits that were secured through emancipation, nor is it to make a claim in either direction about how these competing considerations balance. Instead, my aim has been to show something about the relationship between these costs and the role of the state in the politics of recognition, for this will help us notice the risks that exchanges of recognition pose in our own time, and it should lead us at the very least to temper our enthusiasm about even those exchanges of recognition we are prepared to affirm.

It is important to notice, first, that the costs of Jewish emancipation I have identified do not fit easily within the terms in which we conventionally think about the risks of the politics of recognition. Often, under the influence of Taylor's original essay on the subject, we tend to classify struggles for recognition into two groups: those concerned with what Taylor called "equal dignity" and those concerned with "difference."[122] The first group encompasses demands for the abolition of various forms of second-class citizenship—for the recognition of our common humanity, you might say—and it is associated with Enlightenment universalism and its contemporary legacy. The second group encompasses demands for the affirmative recognition of particularity, and is associated with the romantic language of authenticity and *its* contemporary legacy. And one tempting response to foregoing account of Jewish emancipation would be to claim that this history demonstrates precisely what critics of liberal universalism have long asserted: that a difference-blind universalism can easily turn out to represent to a false universalism, one that perpetuates the hegemony of a dominant culture by demanding that minorities assimilate to its terms, "forcing people into a homogeneous mold that is untrue to them."[123]

That thought, of course, found ample expression among early-twentieth-century German Jews who were dissatisfied with the terms of liberal assimilationism. It helped drive the revival of Hasidism as well as the related articulation of a "romantic cult of the Ostjuden" onto cultural and political Zionism.[124] But while there was certainly loss involved in the cultural transformations that emancipation wrought, there is loss involved in *every* cultural transformation, and I am not prepared to claim that life behind the gates of the Frankfurt *Judengasse* or in the *shtetl* represents authentic Jewish existence. As I suggested in chapter 2, these invocations of authenticity typically retrace the same lines of sovereign desire that drive the assimilationism they reject. More importantly, as I have suggested in this chapter, such objections mischaracterize Jewish emancipation itself, and thereby fail to grasp its deepest costs. Those costs did not involve getting Jewish identity wrong. Instead, they involved the creation of unjust relations of inequality, asymmetrical dependence, and exploitation among people, groups, and institutions— between the Jews and the state; between the Jews and those "unmarked" Germans for whom identification with the state was relatively unproblematic; and between different groups of Jews. And the policy from which those costs arose was not simply a policy of assimilation, for it expressed conflicting and equally irreducible imperatives toward assimilation *and* toward the preservation of Jewish distinctness. It was, we might say, simultaneously an instance of the politics of equal dignity *and* an instance of the politics of difference; and through this contradictory combination, Jews themselves were made to bear the disproportionate weight of the state's own impossible pursuit of sovereignty.

Such dynamics will remain invisible as long as we treat the state as the always-already-sovereign institution that can resolve struggles for recognition once and for all. Yet they will also remain difficult to discern as long as, with Marx, we treat the state merely as the agent through which existing identities and relations of power in civil society are depoliticized. And here, in conclusion, it may be worth speculating briefly about the meaning and sources of Marx's limited view of the state in "On the Jewish Question." As we have seen, Marx describes the state in that text as a site of abstract universality, which acquires its status as universal precisely in *distancing* itself from the particularity of civil society. Yet in putting matters this way, Marx has already begun to forget the lessons he had learned in the course of his own critique of Hegel's *Philosophy of Right*, undertaken earlier the same year. Such abstract universality, after all, is no more acceptable to Hegel than to Marx. Hegel worries, for example, that the unrestricted play of particular interests in civil society would produce extremes of "extravagance and misery,"[125] and his youthful critique of the formalism of the "rights culture" of the old German Empire, in which the state exists only in the act of ceding authority to the "individual parts" that make up the whole, is strikingly similar to Marx's description of the illusory, unreal character of life in the political state, which "overcomes" civil society only by "acknowledg[ing] it again, re-establish[ing] it, and allow[ing] itself to be dominated by it."[126] This is why the state, on Hegel's account, cannot merely separate itself from civil society but must *both* "release" particularity by making room for subjective freedom in civil society and, as he says, harmonize particular identities and interests with the universal "so that both they themselves and the universal are preserved."[127]

In his critique of Hegel, Marx had tried to show that the various institutional mechanisms through which this reconciliation of universal and particular in the state was supposed to occur merely repeated the contradiction Hegel had set out to overcome.[128] In this brief moment, at least, Marx seemed to speak in a version of the diagnostic and critical voice Hegel himself had adopted, however intermittently, in the *Phenomenology*. In "On the Jewish Question," by contrast, Marx attends only to the state *qua* abstract and neutral—and this leaves him unable to account for the more complicated (and contradictory) dynamics of state action in the case of Jewish emancipation. Might Marx's reluctance to persist in his earlier and more radical mode of critique have something to do with the fact that he increasingly envisions his project as a materialist inversion of Hegel's own effort at reconciliation? That he sought not to criticize the concept of sovereignty *per se*, but rather to preserve the vision of sovereign agency by relocating it outside the state, in a revolutionized social life where we will no longer experience our own powers as alien forces?[129] Mere months after the publication of "On the Jewish Question," in his notebooks on James Mill, Marx describes an idealized scene of production in which each finds self-confirmation by laboring to satisfy others' needs. There, he says, "our productions would be as many mirrors from which our natures would shine forth."[130] With that, however, acknowledgment is overtaken, again, by the desire for recognition.

CHAPTER SIX

The Slippery Slope
Multiculturalism as a Politics of Recognition

> *The utopian, immanent, and continually frustrated goal of the
> modern state is to reduce the chaotic, disorderly, constantly
> changing social reality beneath it to something more closely
> resembling the administrative grid of its observations.*
> —James Scott, *Seeing Like a State*

Recognition beyond Monoculturalism

When the conservative German politician Friedrich Merz suggested
in late 2000 that foreigners should be required to adopt a German *Leitkultur*—a "guiding" or "defining" culture—Foreign Minister Joschka
Fischer responded acidly that "the problem is some Christian Democrats
like Mr. Merz are still living in the 19th century."[1] Fischer's retort suggests one way of thinking about the relevance of the case of Jewish
emancipation, and others like it, to contemporary political life: perhaps
what such cases show us is not the limits of the politics of recognition
as such, but rather the dangers of a specific version of that politics, one
constrained by outdated and pernicious assumptions about the necessarily monocultural character of political membership.

In nineteenth-century Prussia, after all, the project of establishing the
sovereignty of the state was closely intertwined with the project of sustaining a culturally homogeneous national community, whose homogeneity would reflect and undergird the unity of will attributed to the
sovereign; it was for this reason that debates about the merits of Jewish
emancipation were always framed by the imperative of dissolving Jewish
particularity into an undifferentiated German *Volk*. Having learned
where *that sort of thing leads,* this story goes, many contemporary societies have become increasingly tolerant, even welcoming, of cultural difference; and here, the idea of *multicultural* recognition—which is, after
all, the version of the idea recognition to which Taylor, Tully, Honneth,
and others have given voice—has played a positive role, exposing the
inadequacy of ingrained monoculturalist assumptions and helping express an alternative ideal that would, finally, do justice to oppressed and
marginalized people and groups.

In this optimistic reading, such a shift—from a form of recognition that erases difference to one that respects it—promises to escape the double binds that structured Jewish emancipation. Hegelians might even be inclined to say that it completes the unfolding of the concept of recognition itself, vindicating Hegel's reconciliatory aspirations precisely by leaving behind the baggage of nineteenth-century nationalism that weighed him down. But if the case of Jewish emancipation does nothing else, it should encourage us to dig deeper before settling into whiggish self-satisfaction, for this is also how the defenders of emancipation conceived of their own historical role: they were progressive men ushering a medieval kingdom into modernity, for whom the Jews served a what David Sorkin has called the "testing ground" of "Enlightenment ideals."[2]

It is noteworthy, for instance, that this optimistic story about multicultural recognition misrepresents the nature of the problem with Jewish emancipation, casting it simply as a matter of an impulse toward homogeneity. As we have seen, emancipation was not exactly a device of assimilation, nor exactly a device of differentiation, but a contradictory combination of the two, whose structure reflected its role in the pursuit of an attractive but impossible project of sovereignty. And if the trouble lay in the pursuit of *sovereignty* rather than in the pursuit of homogeneity, then it should seem less obvious that a shift from monoculturalism to multiculturalism will straightforwardly overcome the complications that afflicted earlier modes of recognition, for as we have seen, the idea of sovereign agency is relatively flexible, and can be pursued in a variety of different ways.

In this chapter, I read specifically multicultural exchanges of recognition as instruments through which many contemporary states and their citizens attempt to reconstruct sovereign agency in an era marked both by pronounced anxiety about "difference" in liberal societies, and by a heightened sensitivity to these societies' own histories of injustice in relations of identity and difference.[3] I also argue that, insofar as multicultural recognition serves the pursuit of sovereignty in this way, its capacity to respond productively to injustice will be importantly limited, though it may still result in genuine improvements in the conditions of life of some of the people and groups it aims to benefit. In this way, the present chapter represents both an extension of the lessons of the case of Jewish emancipation into a contemporary context, and a return to some of the political concerns that originally occasioned Taylor's essay on the politics of recognition, and which have helped sustain the revival of the discourse of recognition in the intervening decade.

The focus of the argument, however, will not be on the merits and disadvantages of particular multicultural policies, but rather on the conceptions of culture and cultural identity that typically stand in the background of theories and practices of multicultural recognition, for it is at this prior level that much of the decisive work of the discourse of multiculturalism occurs.[4] Recall, for example, that in Taylor's essay on the politics of recognition, "culture" is represented as the expression of the unique, authentic identity of a distinctive "people" or *Volk*.[5] Taylor draws this conception from Herder, but it also echoes the view of culture that became dominant in anthropology beginning in the early twentieth century, though that view is now widely criticized among anthropologists. On this view, as William Sewell summarizes it (though without endorsing it), culture is a "concrete and bounded world of beliefs and practices";[6] to have a cultural identity, in turn, is to belong to a particular cultural world, which shapes what its members value and how they act. And to recognize someone as the bearer of a cultural identity is, correspondingly, to respect or esteem him or her not merely as an individual but also as a member of a culture-bearing group, for whom being himself or herself in the fullest sense involves hewing to a certain distinctive "way of life."[7]

Given what I have said earlier about the "cognitive" sense of the term "recognition," and the corresponding view of identity, in Taylor's work, it should come as no surprise that I am suspicious of this view of culture and cultural identity. The idea of identity as a given fact about us that finds expression in our action, I have suggested, reifies the ongoing, unpredictable, and eminently political activity through which we become who we are, reducing it to a *fait accompli*; similarly, this conception of culture reduces cultural activity—what James Clifford has called "complex historical processes of appropriation, compromise, subversion, masking, invention, and revival"—to a matter of knowing and acting out one's place within a distinct, coherent, and continuous world of meaning.[8] Still, my aim is not to repeat these well-known criticisms of the classic anthropological conception of culture, but instead to understand *why* such a conception has so much staying power, both in academic work and in broader public discourse, even in the face of decades of critique, and even among authors who seem at other times to acknowledge its inadequacy. Why do many discussions of justice and injustice in cultural relations continue to be framed, at least intermittently, in terms of an encounter among the members of distinct, coherent totalities called "cultures"—rather than, say, in terms of an encounter *within* culture, conceived not as a self-enclosed whole but as a (striated, articulated) medium of practice and interaction?[9] What is the appeal of this picture? What unacknowledged work might it be doing for us? And what dimensions of the politics of multicultural recognition does it thereby obscure?

In this chapter, I address these questions in part through an extended consideration of Will Kymlicka's subtle and influential defense of multiculturalism. This approach requires some explanation, both because

Kymlicka makes no explicit use of Herder or of the ethnographic tradition in formulating his account of culture, and because the concept of recognition plays a much less central role in his thought than it does in Taylor's.[10] Nevertheless, two features of Kymlicka's work make it especially useful here. First, as we shall see, his philosophical justification of what he calls the "right to culture" is grounded decisively in the liberal idea of choice, and so also in a picture of culture as something that is constantly being remade through the reflective decisions of those who participate in it. For this reason, it is especially surprising when, in the course of elaborating this justification, Kymlicka winds up being pulled toward a different picture of culture as the distinctive way of life of a group, which precedes and determines its members' activities. What better place to diagnose the surprising resilience of the Herderian-anthropological view of culture than in the work of a thinker who does not exactly propound it, but rather gets caught up in it despite himself?

The second reason Kymlicka's work is especially useful is that it is at once conceptually sophisticated and rhetorically sensitive. Typically, commentators treat his writings as exemplary works of political philosophy or social theory, arguing about, for example, the logical coherence of his deduction of the right to culture, or the adequacy of his well-known distinctions among types of ethnic and national minority and forms of group-differentiated rights. This is appropriate enough; yet Kymlicka's writings are also works of persuasion, which attempt to influence policy and public opinion, and whose assumptions, examples, and arguments are meant both to justify multiculturalism philosophically *and* to respond to the "deeply felt anxieties" multiculturalism arouses among some of his colleagues and fellow citizens, anxieties which, he says, often drive "otherwise sensible and intelligent people" to "invoke apocalyptic scenarios of segregation and violence . . . as if we were on some slippery slope to civil war or apartheid."[11]

Here, I shall argue, the notion of recognition becomes directly relevant to Kymlicka's work. Although his philosophical defense of multiculturalism does not rely on the concept, his attempts to defuse his audience's affective aversion to multiculturalism—which, as we shall see, involve advancing certain reassuring claims about the desires of cultural minority groups—effectively involve him in the *performance* of an exchange of recognition between subordinated and dominant groups. And ultimately, I shall suggest, this is closely related to the first point about culture. By understanding the terms of the exchange of recognition in which Kymlicka is involved, we can also understand the tensions in which his philosophical account of culture is caught, because that philosophical account is influenced—and driven into difficulties—by the imperatives he faces as a political rhetorician and a broker of recognition. Approaching the concept of culture as a device of representation within an exchange of recognition, then, will help us grasp the unacknowledged political work performed by the Herderian-anthropological view of culture (together with the liberal views of culture and agency that it shadows); and it will help bring into view the limits of such an exchange as a way of responding to injustice in cultural relations.

KYMLICKA AND THE RIGHT TO CULTURE

Will Kymlicka's account of multiculturalism has been elaborated in a series of essays and books spanning more than a decade, but with its center of gravity in the 1995 monograph *Multicultural Citizenship*.[12] There, Kymlicka offers a subtle liberal defense of institutionalized multiculturalism, grounded in a reconstruction of the importance of culture to the flourishing of individual freedom. The forms of official state recognition of minority cultures Kymlicka defends include rights of self-government, exemplified by the special constitutional status of Québec within Canada and by the political autonomy exercised by indigenous peoples of North America; the state sponsorship and public funding of "cultural practices"; provisions for the use and teaching of immigrant languages; religious or cultural exemptions from laws that may unfairly burden minority groups; efforts to counteract the disproportionate weakness of minority groups in legislative bodies through redistricting or guaranteed representation; revisions to school curricula "to give greater recognition to the historical and cultural contributions of ethnocultural minorities"; and others.[13] Such measures, Kymlicka argues, are necessary responses to the serious injustices that have too often been inflicted on cultural minorities by Western states, including economic discrimination, the denial of political rights, physical segregation, forced assimilation, mass expulsion, and genocide.[14]

How does Kymlicka defend this position? Here we need to return, briefly, to the liberal-communitarian debate out of which this argument first emerged. That debate, at least in what Charles Taylor called its "ontological" register, centered around the question of the relationship of the self to its ends or purposes.[15] As we saw in earlier chapters, critics like Taylor charged that liberal political theory was committed to a "flattering and inspiring" but ultimately fantastic conception of the sovereign self defined exclusively by the context-transcending power to *choose* its purposes; against this model of the self as atomistic or unencumbered, these critics insisted that persons are also constituted by *unchosen* attachments and ends, acquired by virtue of our embeddedness in social and historical context.[16] Kymlicka's response to this critique is, in effect, that the communitarian critics have been arguing against a straw man. Liberalism is perfectly capable of acknowledging the ways in which human agents are situated within historical and intersubjective horizons without abandoning its fundamental commitment to the value of individual freedom; unlike communitarianism, however, liberalism refuses to grant ultimate authority to the social and historical contexts whose constitutive force it nevertheless acknowledges.[17]

In the debates of the 1980s, the term "community" was the usual one-word stand-in for the "social and historical context" in which human beings are embedded. In the 1990s, by contrast, a new interest in forms of pluralism within and among political communities fueled the partial displacement of that term by "identity" and "culture." This transposition of the liberal-communitarian debate into a new register generated two opposed positions about the relation of culture to agency. One position, understanding agency purely in terms of autonomy, sees culture (precisely because of its nonvoluntary nature) as at best morally neutral, and at worst a source of unjust constraint.[18] Another position holds that culture *enables* agency, conceiving of "agency" now not as autonomy or choice, but as the realization and expression in action of an antecedently given identity, which an agent possesses by virtue of her membership in a larger cultural community.[19]

Yet the conceptions of "agency" and "culture" involved in these two positions are deeply problematic. In fact, as I suggested in chapters 1 and 2, the apparently opposed views of agency at play here are actually two different versions of the same understandable but impossible aspiration to sovereignty. And, by the same token, both the view of agency as sheer autonomy and the view of agency as the expression of an antecedently given identity tend to be paired with the Herderian-anthropological view of "cultures" I have described, though in different ways. In the former case, such a view makes possible to dismiss culture as a monolithically constraining force that acts upon us from the outside, and which we would be better off without; in the latter case, such a view makes it possible to embrace culture as a monolithically obliging force that constitutes us, seamlessly, as the bearers of particular identities that tell us what we value and what we ought to do.

Given Kymlicka's desire to steer a middle course between two equally problematic visions of the relationship between context and agency— one that equates agency with the total transcendence of context, and another that reduces agency to the performance of authoritatively given roles—we might expect him, when he makes the jump from the older debates about liberalism and communitarianism to the newer debates about multiculturalism, to be equally wary of oversimple and problematic conceptions of culture, agency, and the relationship between them. And at first, this seems to be the case. On Kymlicka's account, the value of culture lies in the fact that culture serves as what he calls a "context of choice." As he puts it, "freedom involves making choices amongst various options, and our societal culture not only provides these options, but also makes them meaningful to us."[20] This claim certainly seems to involve a rethinking of culture: since culture does not just constrain us but, first and foremost, enables choice, culture itself must not be some monolithic totality; and indeed Kymlicka often characterizes culture as a dynamic and open system, made up of multiple strands, and subject to creative transformations via the activities of the people who participate in it.[21] This claim also seems to involve a rethinking of agency, since it situates agency in a cultural context, suggesting that we only come to be agents by virtue of our immersion in a language and history that we did not choose, and which forms the horizon of our possibilities: here, agency does not consist in absolute autonomy, but arises instead precisely out of autonomy's (partial) bounding or limitation. In this view, the relation between culture and agency is dialectical—they are reciprocally constitutive—and there is thus no position from which something like "sovereignty" might be claimed, for each of these terms is understood to be, at some level, irreducibly dependent upon the other.

Yet as Kymlicka presses his case for multicultural citizenship, he seems to retreat from this subtly dialectical view of culture and agency as reciprocally constitutive and dependent. A crucial turn in the argument comes when, after offering his initial account of culture as a context of choice, Kymlicka makes an important observation: so far, he says, he has shown that "meaningful" freedom is impossible except against *some* cultural background—but the kinds of injustices that his account of multicultural citizenship hopes to address do not involve people being deprived of culture as such; instead, they involve the destruction of some cultures, or their assimilation by others. An adequate response to these injustices, he concludes, demands an answer to a further question: why do members of a minority group have a right not just to culture in general, but to "their *own* culture"?[22]

This way of posing the question is noteworthy. After having shown that human agency exists *in*, not outside or in opposition to, culture, one might have expected Kymlicka to ask: How does culture come to be a medium of injustice? What distinguishes decent from indecent patterns of human interaction within culture? Instead, Kymlicka subtly but decisively shifts the scene of justice and injustice off of the terrain of culture itself, recasting politics as an encounter *among* the representatives of several individuated cultures; in which the challenge is to ensure no agent is unfairly denied "access" to whichever of those cultures is his or her own. This way of thinking about culture is an unstable amalgamation of the liberal language of property and possessive individualism and the communitarian language of encumbrance: on the one hand, it treats culture as an external good to which we either do or do not have "access," in the way that we have access to money, or a museum, or a file cabinet;[23] on the other hand, since culture is supposed to serve not as an object of choice but as the background *to* choice, the idea of a particular culture as "one's own" suggests—it *has* to suggest—not just that I possess my culture but that it possesses me. And the instability of this language becomes increasingly acute as Kymlicka tries to answer his own question.

So—to return to Kymlicka's vocabulary—why *do* people have rights to their own cultures? Why not expect minorities to assimilate to a majority culture, as long as members of the majority culture welcome them and assist them? Kymlicka has two answers. The first has to do with cost: although people "do genuinely move between cultures," Kymlicka says, it is sometimes impossible to do so, and "even where successful integration is possible, it is rarely easy. It is a costly process, and there is a legitimate question whether people should be required to pay the costs unless they voluntarily chose to do so."[24] Kymlicka does not say exactly where the costs of moving from one culture to another lie, but he suggests that they are proportional to the degree of *difference* between the two cultures' languages, histories, modes of social organization, and levels of technological development.[25] The more dramatic these differences, apparently, the less overlap between the ranges of options the cultures offer their members, and the greater the likelihood that moving from one culture to the other will require a substantial change in one or more aspects of a person's way of life. Yet on this reconstruction, the decisive fact about culture for Kymlicka's purposes turns out to be not that cultures serve as contexts of choice, but rather that each culture rules certain options out, and thereby offers its members a bounded and determinate range of choices.

This sense of culture as a source of determination, and therefore differentiation, also comes to the fore in Kymlicka's second defense of the right to one's own culture. It is also unreasonable to demand assimilation, Kymlicka says, because of "the role of cultural membership in people's self-identity," which means that "the bonds to one's culture are 'normally too strong to be given up.'"[26] Kymlicka's example of the resilience of cultural identification—the development of Québécois national identity after 1960—is telling. Québec's rapid period of liberalization, Kymlicka says, might have been expected to weaken the bonds of cultural identity, since "Québécois society now exhibits all the diversity that any modern society contains—e.g., atheists and Catholics, gays and heterosexuals, urban yuppies and rural farmers, socialists and conservatives, etc."[27] But, he observes, the effect of liberalization seems to have been the intensification of Québécois identity, as well as its transformation: in the face of diversification, Québécois identity came to be centered around language, rather than around the "rural, Catholic, conservative, and patriarchal" culture that dominated Québec before the Quiet Revolution.[28] But Kymlicka's example does more than just demonstrate the strength of cultural identification. Like his first response about the difficulty of switching cultures, this example also shifts our attention from the choices a culture enables to the options it rules out—from its flourishing internal diversity to its relatively hard edges—for that, as the increasing prominence of the French language demonstrates, is where identification coalesces.

Both of these positions, then, press Kymlicka toward the uncomfortable conclusion that the normatively important work of culture is done by culture *qua* determining force: a right to one's own culture, it seems, depends on culture being just the sort of thing Herder and the anthropologists had thought. Kymlicka's response to this difficulty is to introduce a distinction between "the existence of a culture" and "its 'character' at any given moment" (which is itself the successor to a distinction he proposed in an earlier work between the general "structure" of a culture and its particular "character").[29] On this new account, it is the "existence" of a culture with which people rightly identify, which they have a legitimate claim to preserve, and which is ultimately the source of its differentiation from other cultures; the "character" of a culture, by contrast, is a diverse, ever-shifting palette of choices, which, as a good liberal, Kymlicka thinks ought to be left alone to change and evolve, without special protection from the state.

This seems to let Kymlicka have his cake and eat it too: on the one hand, the "character" of the culture, where people live and act, can be represented as a site of freewheeling autonomy, while all the work of differentiation and identification can be magically performed by some mysteriously separate property called the "existence" of the culture, which, just by virtue of its separateness from the culture's character, would seem to pose no threat to the autonomy of the culture's members. Yet, as James Johnson has persuasively argued, this distinction is artificial and unpersuasive.[30] It understands the "existence" of a culture and its "character" to be altogether separate things, rather than *aspects* of a single dynamic movement of mutual constitution—which is like trying to separate Wittgenstein's duck from his rabbit. Even from Kymlicka's own perspective, the distinction is problematic, for it is not clear how the "existence" of a culture, understood as something separate from the particular ways in which that culture guides and patterns the activity of its members, could ever be an object of passionate identification, as his account requires, or a "context of choice," as his account also requires.

Unless culture somehow exists in and through its character—that is, in and through the particular pattern of possibilities it enables *and* inhibits—then the "existence" of distinct cultures loses its connection to human agency, and that connection is what is supposed to make culture matter in the first place.

In short, while Kymlicka sets out to find a middle route between two equally problematic views of culture and its relation to agency, what he produces is an uncertain equivocation between these two extremes, which he attempts to manage, unsuccessfully, by splitting culture apart into a site of pure choice and a site of differentiation and distinction. What accounts for this equivocation? What centrifugal forces pull Kymlicka's synthesis apart? Part of the trouble, I suspect, has to do with Kymlicka's ongoing attraction to the image of agency as reflective choice among a field of alternatives, which draws him ineluctably back toward an opposition between choice and constraint, thereby also making the work of constraint done by culture into a problem to be solved (or disavowed) rather than an unavoidable condition to be affirmed. But the problem is only partly philosophical. As I shall suggest in the next sections, this unstable equilibrium between the idea of culture as a field of choice and the idea of culture as a source of constraint can also be understood as the philosophical trace of the political scene into which Kymlicka's work intervenes. This unstable equilibrium between choice and constraint, we have seen, arises in part out of Kymlicka's decision to present the politics of culture as taking place among individuated cultures rather than within the medium of culture. Yet at the level of political rhetoric and representation, this way of locating the politics of culture, and the opposition between choice and constraint to which it gives rise, turn out to be *resources* for Kymlicka, not problems. They help him present multiculturalism as a solution to certain half-spoken crises in the self-understanding and self-identifications of his liberal audience. But to understand this, we need to back up and approach Kymlicka's work afresh, this time as a work of political persuasion.

THE RHETORIC OF MULTICULTURALISM

As I suggested earlier, one of the distinguishing features of Kymlicka's work is his exemplary sensitivity to the concerns of an (anticipated or projected) audience. To persuade his readers to accept his account of minority rights, he makes use of a wide variety of argumentative strategies, from reconstructing a philosophical justification for the right to culture, to making sociological claims about the likely effects of multicultural policy in order to ward off possible objections, to reminding his readers of forgotten episodes in recent political history in order to transform their view of the present. But who makes up Kymlicka's audience? Although its exact contours are not fixed, either across his writings or within a single text, in the works under consideration here Kymlicka tends to speak to an audience made up mainly of liberal academics and intellectual and political elites in what he variously calls "Western democracies," "liberal democracies," "liberal states," and "modern societies," who find themselves "confronted with minority groups demanding recognition of their identity, and accommodation of their cultural differences."[31] Sometimes, as in the 1998 book *Finding Our Way*, which grew out of a series of papers written for the Department of Canadian Heritage, he seems to presume an even broader audience, something like his fellow Canadian citizens in general, though, again, this often seems to mean those Canadians who are confronted by, and nervous about, multiculturalism.[32]

What do we learn about the members of this implied audience from Kymlicka's work? First, we learn that as liberals, they are committed to freedom, and indeed they can "only endorse minority rights in so far as they are consistent with respect for the freedom or autonomy of individuals."[33] Sometimes, this is an explicit philosophical stance, but it is also typically expressed in, and sustained, by the shape of the societies in which these people live, for liberalism is both a set of principles and a corresponding set of political, social, and cultural forms.[34] Second, we learn that the members of this audience are, by and large, genuinely concerned with avoiding a repetition of the historical injustices in which their own societies have frequently been involved. This, at any rate, seems to be Kymlicka's good-faith wager: early in *Multicultural Citizenship*, for example, he explains the purpose of his undertaking by invoking the damage that has been done—from genocide to forced assimilation—in the name of the misguided "ideal of a homogeneous polity."[35] But, third, we also learn that this audience often worries that multiculturalism will undermine political unity and stability—and this fear has indeed been a ubiquitous feature of public discourse around multiculturalism over the last dozen years.[36] As Kymlicka puts it, "critics of differentiated citizenship worry that, if groups are encouraged by the very terms of their citizenship to turn inward and focus on their 'difference', then . . . nothing will bind the various groups in society together, and prevent the spread of mutual mistrust or conflict. . . . Citizenship would be yet another force for disunity, rather than a way of cultivating unity in the face of increasing social diversity."[37]

Kymlicka's arguments take these three features of his audience into account in a number of ways. He responds to the first feature by framing his defense of the right to culture in terms of the idea of freedom, and also by providing an extensive account of the history of liberal approaches to minority rights, which he hopes will demonstrate that multiculturalism is not a "recent and illiberal deviation from long-established liberal practice" but a "legitimate component of the liberal tradition."[38] He responds to the second feature by representing multiculturalism itself as a way of acknowledging historical injustices and resisting their recurrence:

> Adopting multiculturalism is a way for Canadians to say that never again will we view Canada as a 'white' country (and hence deny entry to Asians or Africans, as both Canada and Australia did earlier this century); never again will we view Canada as a 'British' country (and hence compel non-British immigrants to relinquish or hide their ethnic identity, as both Canada and Australia used to do). It is a way for Canadians to explicitly denounce those historical practices, and to renounce forever the option of returning to them.[39]

And, finally, Kymlicka responds to the concern about political unity by arguing that fears about the divisive effects of group rights are often overstated.[40] In the case of self-government rights—that is, the more substantial forms of legal and political autonomy extended to "national minorities" like the Québécois or aboriginal groups, as opposed to immigrants—Kymlicka concedes that group-differentiated citizenship may threaten social unity under some circumstances, and laments that liberal theory "has not yet succeeded in clarifying the nature of [the] 'peculiar sentiment'" which could hold multinational states together. But he reassures his readers that the other two categories of rights he favors pose no threat to the unity and stability of the state. "The demands of immigrants and disadvantaged groups for polyethnic rights and special representation rights," he says, "are primarily demands for *inclusion*," and are therefore more likely to help hold the polity together than to tear it apart. Indeed, he concludes that the overstated fear of fragmentation "often reflects an underlying ignorance or intolerance" of ethnocultural groups.[41]

Kymlicka's effort to respond to concerns about fragmentation is admirable. Yet we should hesitate at Kymlicka's equivocation between "ignorance" and "intolerance," because these two terms actually imply two very different strategies for addressing the fear of fragmentation. The diagnosis of ignorance suggests that the appropriate response is simply to correct the ignorance: "Minority groups aren't really like that." The diagnosis of intolerance, by contrast, has the potential to turn the question about fragmentation back upon the people who pose it, making what had seemed to be a question about the characteristics of ethnocultural groups into a question about the desires of the people who fear them, and about the mechanisms through which that fear is translated into a social relation of subordination. Or, to put it in more familiar terms: the diagnosis of ignorance points toward a failure of recognition, the diagnosis of intolerance points toward a failure of acknowledgment.

There is good reason, even on Kymlicka's own account, to think that some of the most serious and persistent forms of injustice in ethnocultural relations may be rooted in the failure of acknowledgment rather than in the failure of recognition. In *Finding Our Way*, for instance, he notes the "near hysteria" that accompanies much of the public debate over multiculturalism, in which "otherwise sensible and intelligent people . . . invoke apocalyptic scenarios of segregation and violence"—generally a sign that we are in the space of fantasy rather than a space of pure cognition.[42] He repeatedly expresses surprise that so many Canadians were persuaded by the hyperbolic claims of two extraordinarily "ill-informed" and poorly supported critiques of multiculturalism, whose claims contradicted what should have been "obvious."[43] He notes that the shape of Canadian anxieties about Muslims is "virtually identical" to older anxieties about Catholic immigrants—"every new wave of immigration brings its own stresses"—but while he takes this repetition as a sign of hope that Muslims will eventually find themselves as accepted as Catholics are today, one could equally take such an unceasing rhythm of periodic xenophobia as evidence that something more than a lack of information about the newcomers is at work.[44]

Still, while Kymlicka mentions in passing that immigrants in America and Canada may suffer intolerance as a result of displaced anxieties about race, the Québécois, and Aboriginals, and while he admits in *Finding Our Way* that some Canadian opposition to multiculturalism may be rooted in attitudes of "xenophobia, racism, and prejudice," he finds little to say about these psychic and affective structures. Instead, he treats them more or less as anachronistic habits and attitudes that somehow survive alongside the liberal norms that they contradict.[45] Observing that "the real xenophobes never supported multiculturalism in any case," he directs his attention instead to the problems of ignorance and "good-faith uncertainty," indulging rather than interrogating the demand for a reassuring characterization of what minority groups really want.[46]

The result is a flood of descriptions of the desire of the multicultural other. "Most polyethnic demands are evidence that members of minority groups want to participate within the mainstream of society," Kymlicka says. Or again: "The philosophy underlying polyethnicity is an integrationist one, which is what most new immigrant groups want." And again: "It has become clear that the overwhelming majority of immigrants want to integrate . . . moreover, they care deeply about the unity of their country." And again: "The desire for such polyethnic rights is a desire for inclusion which is consistent with participation in, and commitment to, the mainstream institutions that underlie social unity." And again: "These groups are demanding inclusion into the dominant national culture."[47]

These are sweeping generalizations, which make awfully quick work of the problem of knowing the desire of an enormous and heterogeneous population. To take just the United States, this population includes people from many different countries of origin; of different religions; with different educational backgrounds; of varying economic and professional status; some of whom return, episodically or permanently, to their countries of origin; who may remain in territorially concentrated ethnic enclaves or disperse more widely; who may retain their first language while learning English, or abandon their first language, or learn and speak little English at all; who may or may not identify themselves as "hyphenated Americans"; who sometimes seek citizenship and sometimes do not; who may seek citizenship for instrumental reasons as well as out of identification or loyalty; who may relate in very different ways to the economy, local political bodies, national political institutions, military and intelligence agencies, social welfare agencies, civic organizations, churches, schools, the media, and cultural institutions; and whose relationships to these institutions may be mediated not only by "ethnicity" or "immigrant" status but also by gender, class, sexuality, and other intersecting axes of "difference." Still, my point is not to offer a different set of generalizations about immigrant desire. Instead, I want to ask what work these reassuring claims might be doing even for Kymlicka's good liberal audience—not the "real" xenophobes whom Kymlicka seems to dismiss as irredeemable, but the audience that is posited as being committed to freedom and appropriately appalled by historical injustices committed in the name of cultural purity. Is *this* audience moved only by information, and not by desire, fantasy, or ideology? Are Kymlicka's propositions about the characteristics and desires of immigrants merely cognitive in significance? Or is there an exchange of recognition going on here too, whether Kymlicka intends it or not?

Negotiating the Slippery Slope

Here, we can finally return to the tension, played out earlier, between culture conceived as a site of choice and culture conceived as a site of constraint. Committed, as a liberal, to valuing culture only insofar as it contributes to freedom, Kymlicka nevertheless finds himself driven to ground the right to one's own culture precisely in its least liberal features. This sort of unexpected dependence upon the very forces one aims to transcend, I now want to suggest, is not an idiosyncratic feature of Kymlicka's work; it is, instead, a persistent structure of liberal thought, and of liberal ethical and political experience. This is why many of the most thoroughgoing liberals are perennially troubled by such phenomena as authority, tradition, culture, and coercion, even when they accept their ultimate necessity.[48] It is why liberal education, which is supposed to produce autonomy but is bound to begin in subjection, remains a vexed topic. It is why some rationalist liberals are ambivalent about, when not outright hostile to, passion and emotion. None of this, I should emphasize, counts against liberalism as such, though it may point to its insufficiency. What matters is how liberals negotiate the resulting tensions, and in particular on whether they bear the weight of those tensions themselves, or resolve them on the backs of others.[49]

With this general idea in mind, consider, again, the concern of Kymlicka's liberal audience about the relationship of multiculturalism to political unity and stability. As Kymlicka puts it in an especially vivid passage, "one of the most common objections to granting minority rights is that it would lead us down a 'slippery slope', in which more and more groups will demand more and more rights, leading to the eventual disintegration of society." He then adds that "this slippery slope concern presupposes that ethnocultural groups do not fall into identifiable types, with specific and finite needs and aspirations, but rather are totally amorphous, capable of radical changes in their demands from day to day."[50] Of course, that would be a surprising thing to think about the very groups who are also represented, in liberalism's anxious moments, as the bearers of a threateningly illiberal traditionalism.[51] But it would not be a particularly puzzling thing for liberal agents to see and fear in themselves, given the premium they place on reflection, revision, and choice—and given that, on Kymlicka's account, liberalism is not just a philosophical position but a social and cultural formation marked precisely by thinness, by flourishing internal diversity, and by the fact that it does not just permit but facilitates revision of one's deepest ends.[52] Indeed, concern with what Kymlicka calls "the ties that bind" in liberal societies long predates the contemporary wave of concern over multiculturalism: one need think only of Hegel's ambivalent representations of civil society as a site of subjective freedom that is also a centrifugal force, or of Durkheim's effort to soothe fears of anarchy by explaining the sources of solidarity in modern, individualist societies.[53]

One way of understanding these hyperbolic representations of multiculturalism as a source of social dismemberment, then, is as displacements of a dissatisfying uncertainty about the sources of political identity and stability that has its roots elsewhere, and which may in one form or another be endemic to liberalism.[54] Yet there is another way of reading the "slippery slope." Recall that Kymlicka's liberal audience is characterized not only by a concern with political unity, but also by a consciousness of the implication of their own societies in various historical injustices: this sensitivity renders them receptive to multiculturalism, which, as Kymlicka puts it, is a way of saying "never again." Such expressions of shame and regret have in fact been important parts of many public performances of multicultural recognition, perhaps most obviously in cases of official apology and public commemoration, but not only there.[55] As Elizabeth Povinelli has shown, such consciousness of injustice plays an important rhetorical role in Australian multiculturalism: both in the written opinion of Australia's landmark Aboriginal land rights case and in the public discourse around Aboriginal rights, for instance, confessions of the shame of colonialism served to anchor the recognition of native title.[56] And, as we have seen, the left responded to Friedrich Merz's call for immigrants to adopt a German *Leitkultur* by invoking of the horrors of the German past.

In this light, I suggest, the anxious image of the slippery slope can also be understood as an expression of this liberal audience's fragile desire for redemption from their own past, in which, as Povinelli puts it, "the nation would . . . be able to come out from under the pall of its failed history" and "betrayed best intentions."[57] The imagined prospect of an "infinite" emergence of new groups and new demands would prolong the process of atonement, never quite releasing these liberals from the obligation of discomfort in their own historical skins. And not only their *historical* skins: perhaps even more threatening than the prospect of a permanent stain on the historical record is the possibility that the wrongs in which liberal societies are implicated are not just past but present and ongoing; that their members may become tied to injustice despite their good intentions not merely at the moment of their birth or naturalization, but daily; and that the justice might therefore require sacrifices that cut deeper than the explicit renunciation of the acts of past generations. From one perspective, Joschka Fischer's declaration that Merz was still living in the nineteenth century can be read as a stinging rebuke; but from another perspective, it can be read as wishful thinking in the face of the evident breakdown of the hopeful liberal chronology of injustice and justice.[58]

In each of these cases, the displaced concern in question can, and often does, find expression in hostility toward multiculturalism and its constituencies. But it can also find expression in *sympathy* toward multiculturalism and its constituencies, as long as these are represented in ways that salve rather than aggravate liberal anxieties. This is just what Kymlicka aims to do. Since "progress on the rights of minorities will only come about if we effectively tackle this 'slippery slope' view," he argues, "we need to show that ethnocultural groups do not form a fluid continuum, in which each group has infinitely flexible needs and aspirations, but rather that there are deep and relatively stable differences between various kinds of ethnocultural groups."[59] Ironically, it is this rhetorical imperative, which arises out of liberalism's resolute affiliation with the idea of culture as a site of choice, that draws Kymlicka back toward the anthropological idea of cultures (minority cultures, anyway) as bounded, coherent ways of life that determine their members' activities.

Something of this impulse can already be seen, I think, in Kymlicka's explicit definition of "cultures" or, as he says, "societal cultures." A societal culture, Kymlicka says, is "an intergenerational community, more or less institutionally complete, occupying a given territory or homeland, sharing a distinct language and history"; in turn, "a state is multicultural if its members either belong to different nations (a multination state) or have emigrated from different nations (a polyethnic state)."[60] And this way of defining "culture," which makes cultures roughly equivalent to territorially concentrated "nations," suggests a relatively tidy world of discrete cultural communities, unriven by potentially disconcerting multiplicities or ambiguities of identity. By depicting societal cultures as "complete"—that is, as providing their members "with meaningful ways of life across the full range of human activities, including social, educational, recreational, and economic life"—Kymlicka implies that cultures do not normally overlap or intersect: each of us belongs to one, and only one, culture.[61] Moreover, Kymlicka's definition of "culture" quite deliberately excludes certain forms of difference that might "cu[t] across national and ethnic lines." Kymlicka says: "I am not including the sorts of lifestyle enclaves, social movements, and voluntary associations which others include within the ambit of multiculturalism," such as "associations and movements of gays, women, the poor, the disabled." [62] By abstracting away from these cross-cutting differences, Kymlicka helps limit the number of groups that might seem eligible to make multicultural rights claims, and he also makes his generalizations about what ethnic and immigrant groups want seem more plausible.

Still, Kymlicka does insist that the term "societal culture," on his definition, is quite different from the "thick, ethnographic" sense of "culture" often used in other academic disciplines, in which it refers to "the sharing of specific folk-customs, habits, and rituals."[63] But that turns out to be true only of a certain subset of societal cultures; namely, "modern liberal" ones, where "the rights and freedoms guaranteed to liberal citizens" have already done the work of breaking down thick, traditional modes of cultural solidarity.[64] When it comes to the minority groups who make demands upon these larger, liberal societies, by contrast, things look somewhat different. Recall, for example, Kymlicka's reassuring claim that the desire for polyethnic rights just *is* a desire for inclusion on the part of members of minority cultures. To make this claim plausible, Kymlicka is compelled to treat the meanings of the practices that are to be accommodated by multiculturalism as relatively simple, more or less fixed, and easily ascertainable. A case in point is his brief description of the well-known French "headscarves affair," in which a school administrator disciplined three teenaged Muslim girls who wore headscarves to school, setting off a heated national debate about secularism, citizenship, immigration, and gender.[65] Kymlicka offers the case of the girls as one in a series of examples of demands made by "ethnic groups . . . for exemptions from laws and regulations that disadvantage them, given their religious practices," which Kymlicka says "are intended to help ethnic groups and religious minorities express their cultural particularity and pride without it hampering their success in the economic and political institutions of the dominant society."

> For example, Jews and Muslims in Britain have sought exemption from Sunday closing or animal slaughtering legislation; Sikh men in Canada have sought exemption from motorcycle helmet laws and from the official dress-codes of police forces, so that they can wear their turban; Orthodox Jews in the United States have sought the right to wear the yarmulka during military service; and Muslim girls in France have sought exemption from school dress-codes so that they can wear the *chador*.[66]

Under this description, the meaning of the "headscarves affair" seems straightforward enough. The act of wearing the headscarf in school is nothing more or less than an expression of membership and pride in one's own culture; a fulfillment of the obligations that culture has assigned you. Likewise, the demand for recognition of the right to wear the headscarf is evidence of nothing other than the desire to be included in mainstream French institutions without thereby having to violate those obligations.

Notice what has happened: in these cases, at least on Kymlicka's reading, liberals who belong to a thin, modernized culture find themselves faced by actors who do still seem to claim—or, better, to be claimed by—a connection to a culture in the thicker sense.[67] Here, we might say, the conceptual opposition between culture as a site of choice and culture as a site of constraint has been mapped onto the two parties to multicultural politics. And that move reprises the strategy we have already seen at work in other cases of the politics of recognition, in which a contradiction is given "room to move" by being spread out over social space. The tension that could not be resolved philosophically—by splitting the existence of a culture off from its character, for instance—is now translated into a political encounter: the self-identified liberal agent confronts his own disavowed anxieties, borne symbolically by the people and groups who make demands upon him. Here, however, as long as those demands are phrased properly—that is, as long as they are phrased in ways that restore the liberal agent's sense of sovereign agency, assuring him that his concerns are misplaced—an exchange of recognition can occur.

Thus, for example, the representation of minority groups as possessing relatively stable "needs and aspirations"—including, centrally, the desire to be integrated into mainstream institutions while retaining certain traditional practices and other recognizable marks of particularity—helps to preserve Kymlicka's audience's sense of sovereign agency in the face of the felt threat of uncontrollable social dispersion by positioning them, and the states that represent them, as the observers and administrators of cultural identity.[68] It is important to note that this involves a subtle transformation of the idea of sovereign agency from its earlier manifestation in the case of Jewish emancipation. Given a monoculturalist assumption about the necessary homogeneity of "the people," the pursuit of sovereignty might involve perpetual (and unsuccessful) attempts to consume or assimilate difference into an undifferentiated whole; similarly, a classically liberal logic of sovereignty might work by enforcing a sharp boundary between the public sphere of politics and the private sphere of intimate relationships and nonpolitical associations, thereby attempting to confine the expression of particular identities to certain well-specified locations.[69] Multicultural exchanges of recognition, by contrast, demand neither the overcoming of difference, nor its confinement to the private sphere; but they do require that it be observable and manageable: in short, recognizable. They aim to secure the sort of sovereignty James Scott associates with the administrative state, which does not sweep away difference but instead measures it, maps it, categorizes it, renders it "legible"—and, sometimes, enforces certain limits on the acceptable expressions of cultural difference.[70]

At the same time, the representation of minority groups as finite in number and relatively stable in their desires helps to preserve Kymlicka's audience's sense of sovereign agency in a second way, for it also sustains the fantasy of a moment of complete redemption from liberal societies' own unjust histories. If injustice is historical; and if multiculturalism is a way for members of dominant groups to renounce unjust historical practices; and if we know with reasonable confidence which people and groups were affected by those practices; and if we know, as Kymlicka assures us in passing, that these people and groups "genuinely appreciate" the symbolic gesture of saying "never again" to those pieces of history;[71] then perhaps the multicultural exchange of recognition itself will also represent liberalism's consummation by releasing it, finally, from its illiberal past—illiberal both in the sense that it involved injustices today's liberals cannot abide, and in the sense that its shame is experienced as an unchosen burden. And in fact, this version of the idea of sovereignty fits neatly with the first idea of sovereignty as the supervision and administration of difference, for such a moment of redemption also promises to free liberal agents from their lingering discomfort with the exercise of power in the present.[72]

The Limits of Multicultural Recognition

Earlier, I said that one of the central purposes of this chapter is to understand the resilience of a certain problematic view of culture in contemporary political discourse. Why are debates about cultural justice so often framed in terms of an encounter *between* distinct cultures or their representatives? Why the persistence of the Herderian-anthropological view of culture even in the face of widespread criticism? By now, I hope that an answer to that question has become clear. This way of framing cultural politics, and this way of understanding "culture," are not just neutral philosophical or sociological premises on the basis of which the politics of multicultural recognition is built. Instead, they are themselves deeply involved in the politics of recognition, and they are supported even in the face of their apparent implausibility by certain distinctively liberal forms of the desire for sovereign agency. Such representations of culture are already acts of recognition, and also failures of acknowledgment.

What are the political costs of framing issues of justice and injustice in culture in terms of multicultural recognition? It is important to be clear here: I do not mean to say that the forms of multicultural policy Kymlicka endorses are flatly pointless or counterproductive. In fact, I think that many of them, like Jewish emancipation, are likely to provide some real benefits for at least some of the people and groups they are meant to aid. Yet the same policies, particularly when they are justified and publicly defended in the way Kymlicka does, may also have important, neglected costs. In particular, such multicultural exchanges of recognition risk overlooking—indeed, they risk drawing attention away from—some of the deeper relations of power and forms of subordination that underlie the very injustices they are meant to combat. As we have seen, the two views of culture between which Kymlicka equivocates—culture as a resource we have, and culture as a way of life that has us—both locate the politics of culture *outside* of culture. Cultural injustice, on these views, consists in being wrongly denied access to one's own culture, or being wrongly prohibited from acting in accordance with one's cultural identity: these forms of injustice are *about* culture, but they also stand apart from it. And for this reason, even as they give us reasons to condemn injustice, they also leave us with an impoverished understanding of the nature and sources of the injustices we condemn.

Consider an example mentioned earlier: the French "headscarves affair." As we have seen, Kymlicka treats the act of wearing the headscarf
in school as a straightforward enactment of the girls' cultural particularity. He has to do so, both in order to make this act seem like the sort of
thing that ought to qualify for a cultural right, and in order to be able
to represent the act of wearing the headscarf in a reassuring manner as
evidence of the girls' desire for inclusion into mainstream institutions.
Indeed, this imperative even seems to affect the way Kymlicka describes
the event: in his summary, the girls "sought exemption from school
dress-codes so that they can wear the [headscarf]";[73] yet according to
more extended accounts of the controversy, it seems that the girls simply
wore the headscarves to school one day and did not drop them to their
shoulders upon entering the classroom, as school policy required.[74] Kymlicka's summary not only confidently assigns intentionality to the girls;
it also distances the act of wearing the headscarf from its central place
in the story, replacing it with an unspecified act of petitioning or appealing for permission. The effect of this move is to drain the act of wearing
the headscarf itself of political significance: "seeking exemption" becomes the political act, while "wearing the headscarf" becomes the implicitly nonpolitical cultural practice the political act seeks to enable, a
simple piece of North African cultural particularity that has been carried
over into France.

Yet this seems rather question-begging, for part of what made this
such an *affair* was the often contradictory density of meanings the headscarf seemed to contain, particularly in the face of the relative absence
of the voices of the girls themselves from the public debate.[75] Was the
act of wearing the headscarf *simply* an expression of cultural belonging?
Was it a repetition of the patriarchal norms of Muslim families? Was
it an act of political resistance directed against a xenophobic French
establishment, or an authoritarian school administrator? Was it an act
of fundamentalist opposition to French secularism?[76] In the end, what
seems most striking about these acts is precisely the fact that they provoked such a wide range of hyperbolically self-confident claims by
others to recognize the intentions of the girls who performed them. The
"meaning" of the acts, we might say, lay not in the girls' minds—they,
even more obviously than Antigone and Creon, were unable to exercise
sovereignty over the meaning and consequences of their deeds—but in
the chains of interpretation and reaction the acts provoked, strung along
the various lines of power, racial, patriarchal, colonial, and religious,
that structure but do not determine the lives of North African immigrant
women in France.

Indeed, the anxious confidence of those who participated in this
frenzy of recognition suggests that these were not, or not only, empirical

claims about what the girls had intended. Like the displacements I described earlier in this chapter, they were also efforts to consolidate the self-understandings of the speakers as masterful agents according to one or another logic of sovereignty. As such, they were as much *about* the speakers themselves (or their privileged objects of identification, like "the French nation") as about the girls. And from this perspective, what was objectionable about these declarations was not that they failed to recognize the true desires or intentions of the girls, but that they played out larger projects of sovereignty quite literally on the heads of young Muslim immigrant women, thereby participating in the larger structures of power that already rendered these women relatively vulnerable, though not powerless. Such injustices—failures of acknowledgment rather than failures of recognition—do not take place in a political sphere that is about, but also separate from, some closed system called "culture." They take place in the medium of culture itself, which, as a mode of relationship among persons, comes to be patterned by the character of our relations to each other and, crucially, ourselves.

One of the consequences of multiculturalism's abstraction from such relations is that it may obscure or reproduce existing patterns of subordination—or, more subtly, help to inaugurate new ones. Even when, in the moment, multicultural recognition does provide some concrete gains for particular people or groups, it also leaves its beneficiaries subject, as emancipated Jews were, to the perpetually needy and often suspicious gaze of the state and its normative citizens, dependent on their continued good will, and vulnerable to sudden swings in the national mood that can provoke transformations in the organization of social and political privilege. Bonnie Honig has subtly traced such a dynamic in her analysis of the twinning of xenophilia and xenophobia in American political discourse: rather than merely opposing xenophobia, she shows, xenophilia indulges and thereby sustains the impulse to convert a broader problem of democratic consent into an issue about foreigners, thereby feeding xenophobic reactions to that subset of real immigrants who do not or cannot live up to the expectations set by xenophilic discourse."[77] Similarly, as Gillian Cowlishaw has shown, the failure of Australian Aboriginal peoples to respond to acts of recognition, including the recognition of native title, in the ways white Australians had expected and desired— that is, their failure to bring the Australian redemptive story to its appropriate conclusion—has provoked a shift in Australian public talk away from the issue of Aboriginal self-determination and toward sometimes authoritarian invocations of the need to rescue Aboriginals who will not, apparently, rescue themselves.[78]

Another consequence can be seen in the ongoing conflicts between feminism and struggles for cultural justice. In a recent essay, subtitled "an update from the multiculturalism wars," Kymlicka reports that he and other liberal multiculturalists now find themselves fighting battles on two fronts at once: critics still object that multiculturalism threatens political unity and social stability, but this familiar point has now been joined by a second line of criticism, which focuses on what he calls "the way particular policies may entail an unjust distribution of the benefits and burdens associated with identity and culture."[79] The most important version of this criticism has come from some feminist theorists, who have argued that the provision of group rights or other forms of accommodation to minority cultures may reinforce the oppression of women.[80] And for Kymlicka, it seems, this criticism is especially unsettling, for multiculturalism and feminism ought to be natural allies in the struggle to replace difference-blind liberalism with a "more inclusive conception of justice."[81]

Kymlicka considers these problems sequentially and in isolation from each other. Yet the manner in which he engages the first concern about the unity and sovereignty of the larger society actually renders his multiculturalism all the more vulnerable to the second concern, about its potential to strengthen rather than overcoming relations of subordination. This is so in two ways. First, as we have seen, Kymlicka's response to the concern about unity is to make reassuring claims about what minority groups want, claims that are facilitated by a representation of "cultures" as discrete, stable ways of life. But it is precisely this way of representing "culture" that makes multiculturalism seem most threatening to some feminists, for it depicts cultures as simply *requiring* certain practices or courses of action; if those practices or courses of action involve the subordination of women, then the "culture" itself, the thing that lends those practices their obligatory force, will come to seem like a source of injustice, driving a wedge between feminism and multiculturalism.[82] And this is not just a discursive effect: when policies of multicultural accommodation tie the distribution of rights and resources to the maintenance of existing cultural forms or practices, or recognize powerful subgroups within a culture as its "authentic" representatives for legal or political purposes (thereby reinforcing their status), real political conflicts may arise between the project of mitigating cultural domination and the project of feminism.[83]

There is a second point of potential interference here as well. So far, I have spoken as though the set of people who object to multiculturalism on nationalist grounds and those who object to it out of concern with the rights of women did not overlap; but that is a simplification: the icon of the oppressed woman trapped by the terms of a stultifying culture, and therefore available to be liberated by the firm hand of a Western state, has often served as a potent instrument of national fantasy.[84]

Importantly, this does not mean that such images of oppression are altogether false, or that those for whom feminism and nationalism come to be imbricated in this way are merely exploiting feminist politics for coarser purposes, though that may sometimes be true. But such alliances, intended or unintended, between feminist politics and national fantasy are nevertheless problematic: they risk infusing a strong element of sovereign arrogance into feminists' interpretations of cultural practices and their claims about other women's interests, which makes neither for good judgment nor for effective politics, much less for justice.[85] To defend multiculturalism by indulging rather than questioning liberal citizens' anxieties about political unity and stability, I think, also risks reinforcing this sort of nationalization of feminism, in which the question of how to achieve justice for women in culture is colored by, and sometimes even reduced to, the question of how to shore up a threatened sense of national political identity in liberal societies.[86]

Ultimately, however, the most fundamental cost of this approach is that it acquiesces in a stifling model of the nature of agency and its relationship to culture, or to "identity" more generally. As I argued in chapter 2, Taylor's critique of the liberal model of agency as sheer autonomy rightly charged that model with aspiring to an attractive but impossible sort of sovereignty, yet Taylor's own view of agency as the expression of one's own authentic identity merely reproduces the aspiration to sovereignty in a different form, anchoring that sovereignty not in choice but in the knowledge of one's position in a larger social totality. Kymlicka's view of the relation between culture and agency, I have argued here, hesitates uncertainly between these without finding a third way. And the trouble is that both of these approaches to agency fail to come to terms with one of the most fundamental conditions of human action, which Arendt, Sophocles, Hegel, and others have all, in different ways, brought into the foreground: the fact our choices and our identities are constitutively open to an unpredictable future, whose unpredictability arises in substantial part from the fact that we do not act in isolation but as agents among others.

That condition could be experienced as a site of promise and possibility, though not one that comes with any guarantees. Yet by making the protection of the state, the distribution of resources, and the institutionalization of rights dependent upon one's recognizability as the bearer of an identity, the politics of multicultural recognition risks subjecting the very people whose agency it strives to enhance to powerful forces of normalization, binding them ever more closely to who they are, and heightening their indifference, or even hostility, toward other possibilities of existence. This does not mean that multicultural recognition is just like all the other exchanges of recognition we have tracked in this book. Compared to the eliminationist violence of the struggle to the death, or the kinder, gentler death-strokes of coerced assimilation, or the deep (though not bottomless) abjection of slavery, it is the very image of justice. And in some circumstances exchanges of recognition may well be the best realistic political option for people facing serious trade-offs between the social death of nonrecognition and the stifling force of successful recognition. But however accommodating a regime of recognition may be; however much it may "let difference be," or even insist on it; what it cannot accommodate—what it cannot and does not acknowledge—is the *doing*, the action into an open space and future shared with others, that takes us beyond what we are, and beyond recognition.[87]

Toward a Politics of Acknowledgment

> *The reason consequences furiously hunt us down is not merely*
> *that we are half-blind, and unfortunate, but that we go on*
> *doing the thing which produced these consequences in the first*
> *place. What we need is not rebirth, or salvation, but the*
> *courage, or plain prudence, to see and stop. To abdicate. But*
> *what do we need in order to do that? It would be salvation.*
> — STANLEY CAVELL, "The Avoidance of Love"

THE RHYTHM of the foregoing story about recognition, misrecognition, and acknowledgment is tragic. It is not a story of monstrous or ignorant people. It is a story of people who, understandably, respond to the experience of intersubjective vulnerability in overly ambitious ways—that is, in ways that do not acknowledge but instead try to overcome some of the basic conditions of human activity—and who thereby find themselves working against their own purposes; or achieving some of those purposes but at a substantial and unavowed cost to themselves or others; or both. But if this story is tragic, and if one of tragedy's lessons is that some conditions are beyond our power to transform, then it is reasonable to ask whether all of this amounts to anything more than a counsel of despair. Perhaps, for all the blindness in which it implicates us, the desire for recognition and the politics that flows from it—including its injustices—are ineliminable features of human life. Perhaps what I have been calling acknowledgment is just the last vestige of the old dream of an existence beyond ideology. Is what one of Sophocles' choruses says of the house of Labdacus—that "no generation can free the next"—true of us all?[1]

Yes and no. There is nothing—certainly nothing in this book, and, I would wager, nothing at all—that will deliver us once and for all from the problematic circuits of desire that sustain the politics of recognition. If the condition to which the politics of recognition responds cannot be overcome, and if it is nevertheless entirely understandable that people should want to do so, then it seems likely that the pursuit of recognition, however quixotic, will remain a permanent temptation. In this sense, there is no redemption; not even from the wish for redemption.[2] Yet even tragedy, insofar as it moved people, did not merely leave *everything* as it was. As scholars of fifth-century-B.C. Athens have increasingly emphasized, the Greek tragedies are not just texts but artifacts of a political culture in which the practice of spectatorship, as well as more active participation in the official festivals in which tragic performance took place, were thought to be a vital part of civic education—and not merely because tragedy reinforced existing social and political ideologies, but also because it created space for critical reflection upon them and upon the larger tensions that animated political life.[3] The hope, as Peter Euben puts it, seems to have been that "the actors watching the play can, because of their experience in the theater, resist the play of forces that consume the characters on stage."[4] Is a similar hope available in this case? What difference, if any, might lucidity about the ideal of recognition make?

This conclusion is a meditation on these questions, at once tying together some threads of the foregoing argument and pointing toward some new lines of inquiry. My guiding rubric—"the politics of acknowledgment"—must not be misunderstood. Such a politics consists in the first instance in a distinctive, yet still fairly general, account of the meaning of justice in relations of identity and difference, one that is rooted in the ontological picture, and the diagnoses of *in*justice, that I have laid out over the course of the book. This interpretation of justice cannot, all on its own, settle political controversies or prescribe courses of action. But it can have other, subtler effects. It can change our view of the nature of the problems we confront; it can alter our sense of what courses of action are open to us in the first place; it can lead us to see hitherto unnoticed dangers in some political options and to discover unappreciated promise in others. It can, in short, do the sort of work Stephen White has called "prefiguration," providing us with a broad orientation, a set of emphases, presumptions, sensitivities, and rules of thumb that we bring with us into politics but which by no means fully determine the judgments we make once we are there.[5]

One way to spell out what is distinctive about this interpretation of justice is to note the ways in which it departs from the commonplace that justice is a matter of giving to each what he or she is due.[6] The politics of recognition can quite unproblematically be understood as an elaboration of this familiar maxim, for it sees injustice as a failure to extend people the good—recognition—that they deserve in virtue of who they are. The politics of acknowledgment, by contrast, stands in a more complex relation to the idea of justice as due distribution. It, too, responds to the phenomenon of undue inequality—of some people having more than their share of social goods, or enjoying unwarranted privileges at others' expense. But it does not *equate* injustice with this sort of inequality; rather, it treats such inequality as the symptom or outcome of an underlying injustice that is not itself a matter of failing to give what is due.

Recall Iris Young's critique of the "distributive paradigm" in *Justice and the Politics of Difference*. There, Young argues that inequalities of distribution are themselves often generated by structures and institutions that a distributive framework cannot bring into view.[7] From her perspective, the problem is not merely that distributions are produced by institutions and structures; it is also that justice itself, properly understood, concerns phenomena that cannot be treated distributively. Being enabled or constrained, for example, is a function of people's positions within social relations, not merely of how much of some thing people possess.[8] Likewise, our very sense of what counts as a "good" can be shaped in unjust ways by relations and institutions that operate, as it were, prior to the work of distribution (the devaluation of certain kinds of labor, for example, which often coincides with the categorization of such labor as "women's work").[9]

Young's arguments focus on the *objects* of distribution, showing that certain goods or values cannot be treated distributively; but one could equally focus on the *agents* among whom questions of justice arise. Just as, for Young, the distributive approach presupposes that we know what the various goods are and how much of them there is to go around, the principle of giving what is due likewise presupposes that we have already determined who the relevant parties to a distribution are—that is, that we have recognized them, both in the sense of having picked them out, and in the sense of having ascertained enough about their identities to be able to judge what, in the way of respect or esteem, they are owed. But the question of justice on the terrain of identity and difference can not be addressed this way, because it concerns the quality of the recognitive relations through which identity itself is brought into being and reproduced. This means two things: first, every attempt to specify the set of agents to whom an issue of justice pertains will itself, as an act of identification and recognition, be a potential site of injustice; and as such will demand a kind of critical scrutiny that cannot appeal to a distributive principle.[10] And, second, even among agents who already have standing within a jurisdiction, every appeal to the identity as a settled criterion of distribution will likewise be a potential site of (nondistributive) injustice, both because existing patterns of identity and difference may bear the traces of past wrongs, and even more fundamentally because those people for whom justice is a live issue are not done becoming who they are; or, better, who they will turn out to have been.

Prior to the practice of giving people what they are due, then, is a more fundamental kind of justice, which does not yet take place directly between two (or among several) determinate people. It *cannot*, because it involves precisely the acts and practices through which we open ourselves to, or avoid, the presence of others.[11] I mean this not in the sense of going out or staying home (though under some circumstances that could be a choice with existential implications), nor in the sense of opening ourself to what is distinctive about the other instead of assimilating him or her to the same (though that is one mode in which avoidance occurs), but in the sense of accepting that the existence of others—as yet unspecified, indeterminate others—makes unpredictability and lack of mastery into unavoidable conditions of human agency. Such acknowledgment is a crucial part of justice, yet it is not something we owe or give directly to others. It cannot be. At most, as I have said, others are its indirect objects and beneficiaries, and not some particular others but any others at all, since part of the point of acknowledgment is to expose ourselves to surprise appearances and unexpected developments.[12]

One of Hannah Arendt's comments about recognition can serve as an illustration: near the beginning of her speech to the American Academy of Arts and Sciences in 1969, on the occasion of being awarded the Emerson-Thoreau Medal, she commented that "if it is good to be recognized, it is better to be welcomed, precisely because this is something we can neither earn nor deserve."[13] Welcoming, here, refers to the risky inclusion of another in a shared activity, without reference to her identity, or state of character, or degree of merit. And, importantly, this "without" does not signify that the act of welcome is grounded in an appreciation of someone's universality rather than her particularity; it is not the "without" of liberal abstraction. To welcome someone says more about the welcomer than the welcomed: it represents a slackening of the urge to convert an uncertain activity into a predictable process by setting and enforcing strict boundaries to participation.[14] Equally importantly, it does not necessarily indicate that the welcomer is full of warmth toward the welcomed. Arendt, we may presume, had indeed felt such warmth in the greeting of her audience, but precisely by redescribing the academy's prize as an instance of *welcoming*, Arendt attempted to evade, if not exactly to refuse, the proferred recognition: do not take my presence here, she seems to reply, as a commitment to do and speak in ways that will confirm your good feelings about me and yourselves.[15]

Understood in these terms, the idea of acknowledgment generates at least one important rule of thumb for thinking about issues of justice and injustice in relations of identity and difference. If acknowledgment is not something people give directly to others, but is in the first instance something people perform in relation to themselves and their condition, then we should abandon the presumption that justice in these contexts will always consist in granting *more* recognition to members of subordinated groups. A different, if not quite opposite, presumption seems appropriate: faced with a relation of privilege and subordination, look for ways to dismantle or attenuate the privilege itself before (or while also) working to include a determinate group of previously excluded people under its protection. Sometimes less may be more.

Although it seems straightforward enough, this point is difficult to make within the paradigm of recognition, because that approach tends to misrecognize privilege as the inequality of distribution of the good of recognition. Consider two examples, drawn again from the work of Will Kymlicka. In *Finding Our Way*, Kymlicka discusses the problem of accommodating religious diversity in public calendars, and he considers two possible solutions to the present exclusion of all but Christian holidays from official recognition. First, drop one Christian holiday and "recognize one important holiday from each of the other two largest religions." Second, "eliminate all religious holidays from the public calendar, including Easter and Christmas, and then allow everyone to take off, say, five days of their own choosing, in accordance with their own religious beliefs (or secular desires)."[16]

Kymlicka opts decisively for the first option. Although he admits that the second might, technically, be more fair, he argues that it would be "regrettable" for nearly everyone, because it would "mean an end to the shared public holidays around which people can plan social events." Perhaps more importantly, "rather than enhancing the status of Judaism and Islam, it would simply diminish the status of Christianity."[17] The first concern seems implausible: social events spring up all the time without official recognition to help them along. Indeed, it would be interesting to see what new cross-faith patterns of social interaction such a transformation might spur. The second issue strikes me as the crux of the matter, and here it seems to me that the diminishment of the status of Christianity as a privileged state religion ought to be exactly the point. From the perspective of the politics of recognition, such a diminishment appears to be denying someone a good; from the perspective of the politics of acknowledgment, it is denying someone a mild but real form of institutional privilege.

A similar point can be made about Kymlicka's treatment of nonnormative sexualities. In *Finding Our Way*, he extends his model of multicultural accommodation to groups that are not strictly "ethnocultural" but which, in his view, are nevertheless sufficiently like ethnocultural groups to be treated like them, including gays and lesbians. On his view, what most gays and lesbians want and need is "public affirmation of their identity through, for example, gay marriages and positive portrayals of gay lives in school texts." Here, the queer critique of neoethnic gay and lesbian politics barely appears: it is presented as a form of separatist nationalism, with an unrealistic agenda of large-scale withdrawal from the "larger society" into a territorially concentrated gay ghetto.[18] What is omitted from this picture, however, is the queer critique of normative heterosexuality as a system of privilege, as well as any thought that justice in these matters might demand fairly radical transformations in the shape of sexual culture, ranging from the decoupling of the distribution of various socioeconomic resources from marital status, to the work of cultivating a more widespread acceptance of the vulnerability involved in sexual life.[19]

Indeed, in each of these cases, the idea of acknowledgment is especially useful because it can help us understand *why* a relation of privilege and subordination continues to be misrecognized as a mere inequality in the distribution of a good. In the case of sexuality, Michael Warner puts the argument elegantly, suggesting that the very idea of normal sexuality is sustained by a failure to acknowledge some of the "least reputable" dimensions of one's own being, including, especially, the fact that sex is typically "an occasion for losing control," and therefore a possible source of shame.[20] If this is right, then part of what sustains the image of a field of tidy sexual subcultures, available to be recognized, may be the investment in the notion of sexuality as orderly, a disavowal of the marked impropriety of our own desires, which we "typically do not know . . . until [we] find them."[21]

Something similar might be said about Christianity, and indeed about any dominant identity that is unchosen, or that carries substantial historical weight, or that is in any other sense not easily at your disposal. If there is a loss of control involved in sexuality, there is also a loss of control in being attached by history (or by skin color, or by political membership) to a church (or a social system, or a state) with at least some of whose past or present operations you do not wish to be identified, but from which you cannot easily detach yourself. Neither disavowal nor guilt will do: both postures reassert the ideal of the sovereign agent, one by inventing a world in which the injustice does not exist; the other by pretending to have been its cause. Acknowledgment, here, means accepting these attachments, not in a spirit of resignation, but as one's points of departure in this world, which is the world where justice must be made, or avoided.

All this talk of acknowledgment may sound naïve. After all, acknowledgment sounds negative or privative in character. It demands that we refuse something, restrain an impulse, forego an advantage, evade a recognition. Yet, the thing being refused or evaded also seems to be something we cannot do without: recognition; or, indeed, identity itself. Isn't there a basic need for identity as a stabilizing mechanism in human affairs, a source of orientation that lets the world have meaning for us? Could justice possibly demand that we do without *that*? What could motivate such self-effacement, even if it were possible? Here, I want to try to tackle these questions through a brief consideration of some of the recent work of Ernesto Laclau, which is structured by a version of this problem.

For Laclau, politics is built around an ineliminable paradox. On the one hand, as an infinite field of differential relations, "the social," like language, lacks an internal principle of order through which the identity, or meaning, of its constituent parts could finally be fixed.[22] Indeed, the attempt to perform such fixation has historically been responsible for the grievous injustices committed in the name of false universals—i.e., principles which purport to represent the social as a whole but which do not, and cannot. On the other hand, even though "society," in the sense of a closed, coherent totality, is an "impossibility," Laclau also observes that "the impossibility of an object does not eliminate its need."[23] Closure and fixation are both impossible and necessary, because "a discourse in which meaning cannot possibly be fixed is nothing else but the discourse of the psychotic."[24]

Consequently, for Laclau, democratic politics itself must live in the space of this contradiction. To avoid the specter of psychosis, politics must always attempt to fix meaning, to fill the "empty place" of the universal by constructing chains of equivalence among various political actors, which would enable "the objectives of a particular group [to be] identified with the society at large."[25] (The paradigmatic case is Marx's representation of the proletariat as the class with "radical chains," whose sufferings represent "wrong in general."[26]) But since these fixations will always be ideological, and will therefore also always risk injustice, a democratic politics must have a second element as well, which Laclau sometimes describes as a "recognition" of the ultimate impossibility of eliminating the gap between universal and particular; or as the "making visible" of the unavoidability of "nonclosure"; or as the "affirmation" of openness, incompletion, and contingency.[27] Democratic politics becomes "the ambiguous practice of trying to fill that gap [between universal and particular] while keeping it permanently open."[28]

I find this description of politics appealing in several respects. It is sensitive to the possibility that political life might be structured by ineliminable tensions. It refuses to offer a recipe for political redemption. It takes seriously the idea of the openness of the future, treating democratic politics as a perpetually incomplete and provisional task rather than a form that can be achieved once and for all.[29] Still, I am not content to treat acknowledgment simply as the negative pole in an unending circuit of the fixing and unfixing of identity, for this sort of formulation seems to me to accept, too quickly, the imperative of fixing meaning as an invariant condition of the political itself, which lends these descriptions of politics what, in chapter 1, I called their Penelopean rhythm: political agents must always be working to unmake their formulations of identity as soon as they have made them, if not sooner.

Consider, again, Laclau's claim about the necessity of closure. "The operation of closure is impossible but at the same time necessary," he says, because "without that fictitious fixing of meaning there would not be meaning at all"; the result would be "the discourse of the psychotic."[30] But is this plausible? Is the fantasy of the complete fixation of meaning really the condition of the possibility of any meaning at all? Does the slightest bit of uncertainty augur total breakdown? It is noteworthy that Laclau often invokes Wittgenstein in support of his characterization of the impossibility of closure in the linguistic field; yet, as Aletta Norval has suggested, Laclau's insistence on the necessity of pursuing closure even in the face of its impossibility is decidedly un-Wittgensteinian.[31] If Wittgenstein helps us see that meaning *cannot* be completely fixed, he is also constantly reminding us that serviceable forms of meaning nevertheless continue to emerge out of local, contingent patterns of language use, and that their operation does not depend upon on the illusion of certainty. The idea that it does is, as he puts it, "is like a pair of glasses on our nose through which we see whatever we look at. It never occurs to us to take them off."[32]

What if, in this spirit, we refused to treat the need for closure and fixation—the need for recognition, in my terms—as an exclusively ontological imperative? Without assuming that this need can ever be completely overcome, we could nevertheless investigate the contingent—and therefore potentially alterable—social and political conditions that give rise to this necessity, rendering it now more acute, now less, and thereby tightening or loosening the political paradox Laclau describes. As we have already seen, the appeal of the use of identity categories for members of socially subordinated groups is determined in part by the political situation in which they find themselves—i.e., faced with the possibility of an exchange of recognition with a sovereign state; which is in command of extensive resources; which is itself already the effect of a certain set of recognitive exchanges; and which has its own investment in making the language of politics into a language of recognition. This may be a genuine dilemma—but it is at least in part a social and political dilemma, not an ontological one. (It is also a dilemma that is shared to a greater or lesser degree—though not with exactly the same terms—by *every* citizen of contemporary large-scale adminstrative states.) One thing that might help sustain the politics of acknowledgment, then, would be an inquiry into the social and political conditions that intensify the felt need for recognition, and an attempt to transform those, where possible.

I will come back to this issue. For now, let me note that one advantage of working to loosen the terms of Laclau's dilemma in this way is that it would also make it possible to understand acknowledgment as being manifest in acts and practices that do not look merely negative. That image—the image of acknowledgment as a relentless unfixing—is simply the shadow of the imperative of recognition: these two are "locked in a dialectic of insistence and counterinsistence," as James Conant says (glossing Cavell on skepticism and antiskepticism).[33] Consider the example of Wittgenstein again: if the *Philosophical Investigations* is an attempt to overcome, therapeutically, our "bewitchment" by certain pictures of the nature of language, meaning, rules, and so forth, it is significant that Wittgenstein does not generally proceed by taking up propositions and refuting them, or by demonstrating the impossibility of a certain kind of knowledge.[34] More often, he points to or brings to view certain phenomena, and particularly certain linguistic possibilities, that we lose sight of in our preoccupation with a certain ideal of what language "must" be.[35] His catalogues of the rich variety of language games and uses of words, and the playful counterexamples with which he confronts his interlocutor, operate not merely to show the futility of a certain urge to master language once and for all, but also to give some intimation of the kinds of linguistic agency that exist outside the language games of knowing and doubting:

> We can easily imagine people amusing themselves in a field by playing with a ball so as to start various existing games, but playing many without finishing them and in between throwing the ball aimlessly into the air, chasing one another with the ball and bombarding one another for a joke and so on. And now someone says: The whole time they are playing a ball-game and following definite rules at every throw.

> And is there not also the case where we play and—make the rules up as we go along? And there is even one where we alter them—as we go along.[36]

The work being done here is not so much the work of unfixing as the work of *unfixating*; and the possibility to which it points is not a blurring of boundaries or a psychotic dedifferentiation, but meaningful action, undertaken now with a different posture toward the future.

A similar point might be made about the relation of acknowledgment to identity. In theories of recognition, as we have seen, the function of identity is to ground action. People give accounts of who they are both so that they can get clear about how to act, and because others, in their responses to these accounts, should (if all goes well) treat them with the respect or esteem they deserve, and which they need, if they are to be secure in their self-understandings, and if they are to be able to act in accordance with their identities without interference. The structure of the situation may vary—Antigone recognizes Polyneices as her brother, for instance, though he is not alive to reciprocate—but even there, the point of the recognition and of the identity that is its object is to decide a course of action. That is who he is, so this is what she must do. Identity is a rule.

But consider some of the other things an account of identity might do for someone, or might be expected to provoke in others. You might give an account of the identity of a loved one in order to come to terms with his loss, as in a eulogy, or in other acts of mourning.[37] You might give an account of your own identity in order to clarify to yourself and to others (your view of) the nature and stakes of our shared situation, without necessarily expecting that this story will simply be accepted as the whole truth of the matter, or that—even if it were—it could serve as anything more than a preamble to the activity of political deliberation and judgment.[38] You might tell someone else who you are—loudly, perhaps—with the hope that by getting in his face you can complicate his *own* self-understanding, making it more difficult for him to go on living a certain kind of privilege unconsciously, but without expecting or even hoping to be locked in some sort of circle of mutual affirmation as a result. You might tell the world who you take yourself to be by publishing a manifesto, hoping that your story will draw an as yet unknown cast of others to join you in a political movement (whose specific aims you have not yet determined), and fully expecting that the resulting encounters will alter your sense of your own identity.[39]

In these cases and many others, identity is not being deployed as part of a practical syllogism; consequently, it does not require the kind of absolute fixity Laclau suggests we need to have if we are to be able to speak of identity at all. Indeed, in some of these cases, it seems possible that such absolute fixity—or even the illusion of it—could defeat the purposes to which these identifications are being put. And, as a consequence of *that*, it is unnecessary to imagine acknowledgment as a countervailing, negative moment in which we simply remind ourselves of the impossibility of our own attempts at closure, or work to undermine the very terms by which we proceed. Here, acknowledgment is already expressed in the shape of the language games and practices to which these accounts of identity belong: mourning, setting a scene, challenging or provoking, inviting . . . but *not* playing at being sovereign. And this suggests another possible component of a politics of acknowledgment: the redescription of various language games, and social and political practices, in ways that foreground the internal connections between the goods these games and practices provide, and the cultivation of an acceptance of practical finitude. What, in the case of *this* activity, counts as acknowledgment? And what does such acknowledgment contribute to the activity itself? This is not just a question of knowing what acknowledgment is; it is also a question of motivating it, of drawing ourselves and others toward it. (And, of course, it is not a matter of describing practices and games as they already are; sometimes we alter them as we go along.)

Let me conclude by suggesting one example that might illustrate both of these components of a politics of acknowledgment at once—the diagnosis of the contingent social and political sources of the desire for recognition; and the reinterpretation of a practice in ways that find a role for acknowledgment in it. If, as I have suggested, the pursuit of recognition is at least in part cultivated by (and centered around) the institutions of the putatively sovereign state, then we would do well to ask why the relationship between citizens and state institutions tends to be figured as a relationship of *recognition*. The answer, I suggest, has something to do with the way democratic legitimation proceeds under circumstances that preclude meaningful political action and participation for many citizens. If democratic theory's central premise is that the governed ought also to be the governors, then our democratic self-image labors under the weight of the fact that, in the name of self-government, we have created complex, powerful, and distant political institutions that often seem quite independent of our effective control, and to which we tend to relate relatively passively. In the face of this resiliently undemocratic distribution of political power, I suspect, we increasingly seek solace in an interpretation of the principle of democratic legitimacy that focuses on recognition rather than action: cultivating identification with the state may help to secure at least *de facto* democratic legitimation by enabling us to recognize these remote and alien institutions as *ours* (and vice versa)—while still doing little to render them more accountable to us. In other words, the experience of identification comes to supplant the experience of action as the ground of whatever sense of connection many people now have with the states that claim them.

But what is the alternative? In the history of democratic theory, such criticisms of the "democratic deficits" of large-scale representative governments and bureaucratic states often preface calls for the replacement of representative democracy or the bureaucratic state by something like direct popular rule, but while institutional reforms that move the distribution of political power and authority in democratic directions are surely possible in some arenas, such calls can easily often romanticize "the people" as a collective agent that one can imagine simply coming to occupy what Claude Lefort calls the "locus of power."[40] This is, I think, simply the democratic consummation of the fantasy of recognition, a dream of the moment at which ruler and ruled, seer and seen, become identical. One of its greatest expressions is Rousseau's description, in the *Letter to M. D'Alembert*, of a republican festival held out of doors, in which "each sees and loves himself in the others so that all will be better united"; another is Marx's anticipation of the day when "man" has "recognized [*erkannt*] and organized his own powers (*forces propres*) as social powers so that he no longer separates this social power, in the form of political power, from himself."[41]

Given the relationship I have tracked here between recognition and notions of mastery and control, however, perhaps what is needed is precisely to think about democratic power and action outside the frame of sovereignty. This might involve translating democracy's egalitarian impulses into a new idiom in which risk, loss, and vulnerability are seen as constitutive features of political life rather than as burdens to be overcome once and for all. This could mean, as Danielle Allen has suggested, reorienting democratic politics toward the problem of equitably distributing the sacrifices inevitably produced by political decisions over time and social space.[42] It could also mean reconceiving democracy as a pattern of mutual and interlocking relations of dependence among multiple loci of authority or concentrations of power.[43] And it could mean defining democratic citizenship not as the self-control of the people, but as a matter of taking part in the activity of politics, where taking part can refer not only to participation in authoritative deliberative and decision-making bodies, but also to a range of unofficial activities, both quotidian and extraordinary, through which authoritative acts are subjected to the unpredictable responses of those whose lives they touch.[44] The prospective rewards of democracy thus conceived are different from those of democracy understood as self-government. Such a version of democratic politics does not promise the pleasure of sovereignty, direct or vicarious; it promises, at best, the less grand and more tentative pleasure of potency—of simply having (and being carried along by) effects in the world, without necessarily being able to determine their trajectory.

Still, however much we may be able to substitute the pleasures of potency for the pleasures of sovereignty, the temptation of recognition will probably always be ineliminable; and indeed, as long as the social salience of identity persists, we would not want the desire for recognition to be eliminated, for—as we have seen—that desire has been responsible not only for danger and injury but also for progress and justice. A more modest hope for a non-sovereign practice of democracy, then, might lie in the multiplication and diffusion of the sites around which struggles for recognition are carried out, resisting the putatively sovereign state's implicit claim to hold a monopoly on the distribution of recognition and to be the ultimate arbiter of contests over identity. The point of such a pluralization would *not* be to enable a more accurate regime of recognition—as though the multiplication of sites of recognition (like the multiplication of pixels on a screen) could produce reflections of our identities that had finer resolution and crisper definition. Instead, such a pluralization might enable resistance to recognition's injustices by weakening the hold of any *single* exchange of recognition on our being: it may be safer and more conceivable to contest the terms of *one* exchange of recognition, or indeed to refuse that exchange altogether, if doing so does not amount to a kind of social death.[45] If we cannot do without the bonds of recognition, we also cannot do without the dark space between recognitions, which is the space of movement, of action, and of life.

A Note on the Cover

OVER THE YEARS that I have been writing this book, I have found myself reading and re-reading Aeschylus's *Oresteia*. At first, it was Hegel who led me back to Aeschylus. Later, I heard echoes of the *Oresteia* in the terms that often framed debates about identity in the 1990s: passionate tribalism versus sober citizenship, fragmentation versus common purpose; *pluribus* versus *unum*. Then, just as I was coming to see the concept of recognition as my unifying theme, a provocative day of theater sent me back to Aeschylus's play, persuaded that the *Oresteia* might not have "the happiest ending in all Greek tragedy" after all, and that its final scene, made newly complex for me, also captured something of what I hoped to say about recognition.[1]

Aeschylus's trilogy tells the story of the royal family of Argos—from Agamemnon's sacrifice of his daughter Iphigeneia; to Clytemnestra's revenge, in which she lures her husband down a path of blood-colored tapestries, ensnares him in his royal robes while he bathes, and slaughters him; to the return of Agamemnon's exiled son Orestes, who weaves a web of deception that brings Clytemnestra and her tyrannical lover Aegisthus to their deaths; to the pursuit of Orestes by his mother's terrible Erinyes, or Furies, who corner their quarry in Athens and sing their infamous binding song around him, tying him to (and tying him up with) his own deed. Here, the threads that hold families and cities together are twisted into snares, traps, and constraints: a king is bound, helpless, by the trappings of his own authority, and trusted words are made into weapons of guile, enchantment, and seduction.[2]

But the story is not quite over. Just when the Furies, having bound Orestes fast with their song in the Temple of Athena, are about to drink his blood, the goddess herself appears, jolting the story onto a different course by founding a new court, composed of Athenian jurors, to judge the controversy. With the help of Athena's tie-breaking vote, the jury acquits Orestes.[3] At first, the Furies refuse to accept the judgment of the tribunal, threatening instead to bring destruction raining down upon Athens. Athena tries to placate the Furies by offering them a secure and privileged sphere of influence within Athens, and with help from Peitho, goddess of persuasion, she wins them over. In the final scene, the tamed Furies utter prayers for prosperity and stability in Athens and are led, draped in ceremonial robes, to their new subterranean home.

These last scenes of the *Oresteia* constitute a classic instance of political recognition. Faced with an angry and powerful foe, Athena might well have responded by using violence to repel the threat and destroy the enemy. Rather than trying to suppress the Furies, however, Athena chooses a risky strategy of inclusion. She recognizes the Furies' distinctive contribution to society, grants them a corresponding measure of respect, and promises them a secure physical and social location within the community, hoping that they will reciprocate, agreeing to place their potent weapons in the service of Athens, its laws, and its newly founded court of justice. The gamble seems to work.

To many readers, this successful strategy of recognition seems to restore things to their proper functions, from language to regal garments. Athena's words to the Furies, unlike Clytemnestra's cunning speech to Agamemnon, constitute "a new and rational persuasion—one which is to be used on friends, not enemies, for good, not evil." When the Furies don ceremonial garments in the closing procession, "the robes which Clytemnestra used so blasphemously are now used properly to celebrate the establishment of a new and good order."[4] The moment of recognition between Athena and the Furies seems to mark a whole series of progressive transitions, from the uncontrolled pursuit of private vengeance to the rule of law; from blood loyalty to citizenship as the basis of social organization; from violence to reason; from uncertainty to security; from corruption to propriety. All in all, a "great advance in the history of civilization."[5]

There is something to this. There *is* a difference between Athena's generosity and, say, the hysterical, violent defensiveness with which the Creon of Sophocles' *Antigone* responds to the disruptive women who seem to threaten the integrity of the Theban body politic.[6] But it is too easy to stop there. Aeschylus's readers, exhausted like his characters by a seemingly endless chain of deceit and destruction, desperately *want* Athena's strategy of recognition to pay off: we long for ties of mutual recognition and shared affect that, for once, are not also shackles. But it is precisely this implication of our own desires in the process of interpretation that ought to make us hesitate before concluding that Aeschylus has given us what we want.

Consider again the example of Athena's persuasive speech to the Furies. Is Athena's speech really a completely different kind of use of language from the manipulative words of Clytemnestra, Orestes, and the Furies, as the conventional view of the *Oresteia* suggests? Are Athena's invocations of the Peitho, the goddess of persuasion, uncontaminated by the Peitho's association with seduction, bewitchment, bribery, and manipulation, both earlier in the *Oresteia* and elsewhere?[7] Or do these references to persuasion serve precisely to recall these associations, and to extend their significance into what might otherwise have seemed to be an unequivocally happy moment of reconciliation? Athena's appeal to the Furies, after all, begins not with a principled argument but a thinly veiled threat; she reminds the Furies that she is the only god who knows how to unlock Zeus's thunderbolts. And she continues by deploying an erotically charged vocabulary, asking the Furies to listen to the "sweet beguilement" of her voice; a few moments later, as this seductive spell takes effect, the Furies admit that Athena is likely to "have [her] way" with them.[8]

Or, again, take the example of the deep red robes that the newly tamed Furies wear during the closing procession. As classical scholars have noted, these robes (and other features of the final scene) seem to refer to the ceremonial garments worn by metics—resident foreigners—during the Panathenaic festivals.[9] The symbolism is apt: like metics, the Furies are outsiders who are incorporated into Athenian society while still retaining markers of their difference. Yet while the Furies' robes undoubtedly lend a joyous, celebratory air to the final scene by virtue of their association with the Panatheneia, it is not obvious that this is the *only* meaning the robes bear. Throughout the *Oresteia*, red and purple fabric has been associated with constraint and violence, from the path of textiles that leads Agamemnon into his palace, to the robe in which Clytemnestra ensnared her husband, staining it with his blood.[10] This symbolism, too, remains apt even at the end of the trilogy: as critics sensitive to the symbolic politics of gender in the *Oresteia* have shown, the episode of the domestication of the Furies allegorizes not only the foundation of Athenian democracy but also the exclusion of women from that democracy and the subordination of social spheres and forms of attachment associated with femininity.[11] Athena's seductive speech may be gentler than Creon's hysterical attacks, but her strategy of recognition still confines the Furies, both by restricting their sphere of influence to the household, and by physically fixing them in a subterranean chamber, not entirely unlike the cave in which Antigone is buried alive.[12]

Athena's recognition of the Furies contains the threat they pose to the Athenian *polis* by domesticating them, tying these *meta-oikoi*—which can mean both cohabitants (taking *meta-* in the sense of "with") and migrants or wanderers (taking *meta-* to suggest movement, as it does in *meta-pherein* and "metaphor")—to a particular physical location.[13] Likewise, many readers contain the threat posed to the dream of reconciliation by the earlier, darker episodes in the trilogy by controlling the movement of metaphor. These critics (sometimes) admit or even work to establish an equivalence of the Furies' garments with the murder robe, or of Athena's efforts at persuasion with those of Clytemnestra and

Orestes, but they insist that the equivalence can only work in one direction. The Furies' cloaks can redeem the sullied image of the robe, but cannot be contaminated by it; Athena's persuasive speech can restore Peitho to its proper function, but her integrity cannot be thrown into question by the similarity of her acts of persuasion to earlier seductions and deceptions. Here, as in Athens, movement is quashed by recognition—in this case, by critics' insistent claims to recognize the pure and proper character of the Furies' robes and Athena's speech.

Still, metaphors, like Furies, are not always so easily tamed. In 1994, I found myself at a production of the trilogy staged by François Rochaix at the American Repertory Theater in Cambridge, Massachussetts. Rochaix's version insisted upon the association of Peitho with seduction and manipulation from beginning to end: Athena's techniques of persuasion included serving wine to the famously abstemious Furies, who seemed too drunk to give meaningful consent when they eventually agreed to Athena's offer.[14] In Rochaix's closing procession, the Furies were led to the back of the stage, where they raised their glasses in a toast to the prosperity of Athens, and suddenly found themselves trapped behind a net that fell from above, of the same weave as the smaller prop that had been used to ensnare Agamemnon. The trapped Furies kept absolutely still, glasses still raised, as the lights dimmed.

Intrigued, I began reading more about the play, and, thanks to a footnote in David Luban's thoughtful essay "Some Greek Trials," I discovered that Peter Stein's 1980 production of the *Oresteia* at the Schaubühne am Halleschen Ufer in Berlin had also put an unconventional spin on the ceremonial garments that the Furies wear at the end of the *Eumenides*. As Luban reports, Stein's *Oresteia* "ended with the jurors escorting the Erinyes to chairs on the floor below the stage, then tying them to the chairs with the same purple cloth in which Clytemnestra had wrapped Agamemnon. They were tied tighter and tighter until they were completely immobilized." It is this equivocal final scene of a Fury doubly bound by recognition—honored *and* constrained, tied to the city *and* tied down within it—that appears on the cover of this book, thanks to Ruth Walz's compelling photograph.

"After the play," Luban adds, "women in the audience spontaneously arose to untie the Erinyes."[15]

Notes

INTRODUCTION

1. Fraser, *Justice Interruptus*, 11.

2. Taylor, "The Politics of Recognition," 24, 26.

3. Ibid., 50 (emphases added). On the continuity of this essay with Taylor's work on Hegel, see Rorty, "The Hidden Politics of Cultural Identification," 153–54.

4. Taylor, "The Politics of Recognition," esp. 51–73.

5. Rousseau, "Letter to M. D'Alembert," 126; quoted in ibid., 47–48.

6. Tully, *Strange Multiplicity*, 4–5.

7. An ontology, in this sense, is an implicit or explicit interpretation of the fundamental conditions of life in the social and political world, the kinds of things that exist there, and the range of possibilities that it bears. Cf. Taylor, "Cross-Purposes," 181; Connolly, *The Ethos of Pluralization*, chap. 1; and especially Stephen White, *Sustaining Affirmation*.

8. See Brown's powerful adaptation of Marx in *States of Injury*. Fraser's "Rethinking Recognition" and "Recognition without Ethics" raise different but analogous concerns.

9. Berlin, "The Pursuit of the Ideal," 15.

10. For another way of bringing together these two lines of thought, see Oliver, *Witnessing*.

11. Arendt, *The Human Condition*, 234.

12. Schlesinger, *The Disuniting of America*.

13. Young, "Ruling Norms and the Politics of Difference," 416; Bickford, "Anti-Anti-Identity Politics." Queer politics is an important contemporary counterexample; on its difference from the politics of recognition, see Warner, *The Trouble With Normal*, esp. chap. 3; Bower, "Queer Problems/Straight Solutions."

14. On clarity and responsibility, see Weber, "Science as a Vocation," 151–52; Brown, *Politics Out of History*.

CHAPTER ONE
FROM RECOGNITION TO ACKNOWLEDGMENT

1. Pitkin, *Fortune is a Woman*, 291.

2. Wittgenstein, *Philosophical Investigations*, par. 90 and passim; Pitkin, *Wittgenstein and Justice*.

3. On the "spatialization of temporality," see Shapiro's excellent discussion in *For Moral Ambiguity*, 113.

4. Hinsley, *Sovereignty*, 1; on the history of the concept see Onuf, *The Republican Legacy in International Thought*, chap. 5.

5. Arendt, *The Human Condition*, 234. For an analogous reading of the idea of state sovereignty as one example of a broader conception of sovereign agency,

see Orlie, *Living Ethically, Acting Politically*, esp. chaps. 1–2. On sovereign selfhood and its gendering, see Yeatman, "Justice and the Sovereign Self" and *Postmodern Revisionings of the Political*, chap. 4.

6. Berlin, "Two Concepts of Liberty," 131. This sense of "sovereignty" stands in a complicated relationship to another discourse stemming from Nietzsche, Bataille, and Derrida, in which "sovereignty" designates not control but unconditional expenditure; that is, action undertaken without expectation of reciprocal compensation. In "From Restricted to General Economy," Derrida contrasts this conception of sovereignty with the *Herrschaft* of Hegel's *Phenomenology* (259); in my terms, however, "sovereignty" and "mastery" are interchangeable. This is consistent with Derrida's point—that "sovereignty" in the sense of the capacity for unconditional expenditure cannot be achieved through the pursuit of mastery—but, as I argue in chap. 4, Hegel himself is at least intermittently a critic of the project of *Herrschaft* he describes. See also Bataille, "Hegel, Death, and Sacrifice"; Flay, "Hegel, Derrida, and Bataille's Laughter"; Judith Butler, "Commentary on Joseph Flay"; Borch-Jacobsen, "The Laughter of Being"; Noys, *Georges Bataille*, chap. 3. On Nietzsche see Richard White, *Nietzsche and the Problem of Sovereignty*.

7. These critiques often overlapped. See, among others, Pateman, *The Sexual Contract*; Benhabib, "The Generalized and the Concrete Other"; Sandel, *Liberalism and the Limits of Justice* (whence "unencumbered"); and Taylor, "Atomism" and "Nature and Scope of Distributive Justice." On *dominium* and state sovereignty see Burch, *"Property" and the Making of the International System*, 143–48; Onuf, *The Republican Legacy in International Thought*, 130–31; Kratochwil, "Sovereignty as *Dominium*."

8. See Sandel's distinction between the "voluntarist" and "cognitive" dimensions of agency: *Liberalism and the Limits of Justice*, 58–59, 152–53. Sandel's account of coming to self-knowledge is marked by a tension about which I say more in chap. 2, between the idea of identity as an authoritative ground of action, and the idea of identity as the *outcome* of action, including interaction with others, and thus knowable only in retrospect. The second pole of this tension is captured in Sandel's acknowledgment that self-knowledge is "less strictly private" than we might think: "a friend who knows me well" might "grasp something I have missed" or "[know] me better than I [know] myself" (181); yet Sandel undermines the radicalism of the point by casting interaction with others in cognitive terms (it's not *who I am* that is transformed by the other's response, but merely who I take myself to be) and by limiting the participants in these deliberations to "friends" (as if a stable distinction among friends, strangers, and enemies did not already depend upon certain unquestioned forms of self-knowledge, and as if those I take to be strangers and enemies could not grasp something about me that I have missed). For a related critique see Honig, *Political Theory and the Displacement of Politics*, chap. 6.

9. Taylor, "The Politics of Recognition" and *The Ethics of Authenticity*; Ferrara, "Authenticity and the Project of Modernity." For a different sense of "authenticity," see Larmore, *The Romantic Legacy*, 84–95.

10. Arendt, *The Human Condition*, 178–81. On Arendt, action, and identity see Bickford, *The Dissonance of Democracy*, 56–66; Honig, *Political Theory*

and the Displacement of Politics, 77–84; Orlie, "Forgiving Trespasses, Promising Futures."

11. Arendt, *The Human Condition*, 179. See also Arendt's denial that "expression" presses out something already inside (*Thinking*, 30); Honig, *Political Theory and the Displacement of Politics*, 79–80.

12. Arendt, *The Human Condition*, 184; see also Bickford, *The Dissonance of Democracy*, 61. On embodiment as a source (both acknowledged and denied by Arendt) of the nonsovereign character of action, see Zerilli, "The Arendtian Body," 179–84.

13. Arendt, *The Human Condition*, 193; see also 191–92.

14. Ibid., 234, 244.

15. Ibid., 234; on the substitution of making for acting see 220–30.

16. Ibid., 193. On this passage see Disch, *Hannah Arendt and the Limits of Philosophy*, 75–76, and below, chap. 3.

17. Arendt, *The Human Condition*, 193–94. On the dependence of the actor on the poet see Tsao, "Arendt Against Athens."

18. Young-Bruehl, *Hannah Arendt*, 461–62. Young-Bruehl focuses on Arendt's 1975 "Sonning Prize Speech"; other examples include her 1969 "Emerson-Thoreau Medal Lecture" and her Lessing Prize speech, "On Humanity in Dark Times."

19. Arendt, "Sonning Prize Speech," 14. I quote the typescript text of what appears to me to be the final version of the speech in the online version of the Hannah Arendt Papers; the text quoted in Young-Bruehl, *Hannah Arendt*, 462, differs slightly but inconsequentially.

20. This process can fruitfully be compared to the "fetishism of commodities," which Marx described as a process of mystification by which a "definite social relation between men . . . assumes . . . the fantastic form of a relation between things." Marx, *Capital*, 1:165. See also Joan Scott, "Multiculturalism and the Politics of Identity"; Connolly, *The Ethos of Pluralization*.

21. A similar, though not identical, use of "misrecognition" can be found in the work of Bourdieu, for whom recognition and misrecognition also have different objects: "recognition" refers to the conferral of legitimacy upon certain categories, while "misrecognition" refers to the failure to grasp the contingent relations of power out of which those categories arise; and the latter serves as the ground of the former (*Language and Symbolic Power*, 127; *The Logic of Practice*, 105–6). On my use, however, the object of misrecognition is not (or not only) a category or hierarchy but an agent's own condition of practical finitude.

22. This is true both for Taylor ("The Politics of Recognition," 37ff.) and for Honneth (e.g., *The Struggle for Recognition*, esp. chaps. 5–6), though in different ways.

23. One conveniently anthologized debate that shows how commonplace these distinctions are is Nussbaum et al., *For Love of Country*.

24. Beiner, "Introduction," 8.

25. Cf. Connolly, *The Ethos of Pluralization*, chap. 1, esp. 17–19. Connolly is one of the few who shifts out of the register of spatiality and into the register of temporality, particularly with his move from "pluralism" to "pluralization" (xiv).

26. For two different accounts of happiness and surprise that tie surprise in different ways to ordinariness, see Kateb, "Individuality and Egotism"; Vogler, "The Element of Surprise." The larger point overlaps with several critiques of reductive forms of individualism, including Flathman's account of the mysteriousness of the will in *Willful Liberalism*, Connolly's treatment of fundamentalized individualism in *The Ethos of Pluralization*, and Larmore's use of Stendahl to criticize the reduction of life to a "life-plan" in *The Romantic Legacy*, 86–95.

27. For different versions of the argument, see Judith Butler, "Universality in Culture"; Laclau, *Emancipations*; Butler, Laclau, and Žižek, *Contingency, Hegemony, Universality*; and Zerilli, "This Universalism Which Is Not One" and *Feminism and the Abyss of Freedom*.

28. I discuss this point at greater length in chap. 7.

29. Some of these terms are from Brubaker and Cooper's description of the "weak" conception of identity in "Beyond Identity," 11.

30. Honneth, *The Struggle for Recognition*, 126–27.

31. Tully, "Struggles over Recognition and Distribution."

32. Pirro, *Hannah Arendt and the Politics of Tragedy*; Euben, "Arendt's Hellenism." I discuss Arendt and tragedy in more detail in chap. 3.

33. One treatment of "recognition" in which the economistic language of distribution is especially prominent is Walzer, *Spheres of Justice*, chap. 11.

34. Taylor, "The Politics of Recognition," 26; Honneth, *The Struggle for Recognition*, 135.

35. This is also how Marx criticizes treatments of political economy that focus only on the distribution of goods as opposed to the shape of the social relations through which they are produced (see, e.g., the treatment of commodity fetishism in *Capital*, 1:165). Iris Young's critique of the "distributive paradigm" of justice makes a similar point (*Justice and the Politics of Difference*, chap. 1).

36. Fraser, "Recognition without Ethics," 26–27, 39 n. 5. The same point can be made in response to some critics of the politics of recognition: Oliver, for example, agrees that misrecognition is a matter of psychic distortion, but draws on Fanon to argue that the desire for recognition itself, which advocates of the politics of recognition understand as emancipatory, is an insidious effect of the distortion of the psychic life of oppressed people (*Witnessing*, 9; cf. chap. 1).

37. Fraser mentions this problem in "Rethinking Recognition," 112; I discuss it at greater length with respect to Taylor in chap. 2.

38. Fraser, "Recognition without Ethics," 24. A fuller statement of her position will appear in Fraser and Honneth, *Redistribution or Recognition?*

39. Ibid., 27. Fraser argues that this amounts to treating recognition as a matter of justice rather than ethics, but this rests on an untenable exclusion of all issues of moral psychology from the domain of justice; for a critique of Fraser on this point see Honneth, "Redistribution as Recognition."

40. Fraser, "Recognition without Ethics," 29. For critical discussion of Fraser's account of the relation of redistribution to recognition see Young, "Unruly Categories"; Fraser, "A Rejoinder to Iris Young"; Phillips, "From Inequality to Difference"; Judith Butler, "Merely Cultural"; Fraser, "Heterosexism, Misrecognition, and Capitalism"; and, most recently, Yar, "Beyond Nancy Fraser's 'Perspectival Dualism.'"

41. Fraser, "Recognition without Ethics," 29.

42. Ibid., 30.

43. Ibid., 31.

44. Fraser, *Justice Interruptus*, 30, 24; see also her forthcoming contribution to Fraser and Honneth, *Redistribution or Recognition?*

45. Fraser, *Justice Interruptus*, 28–31.

46. Another avenue open to Fraser would be to argue that "affirmation" and "transformation" are strategies appropriate to different kinds of groups: the former, to groups which have some identity of their own that the dominant majority has failed to respect; the latter, to groups that are themselves brought into existence *as* groups by an act of oppression or subordination. I have argued elsewhere (in a response to Carolin Emcke, who advances a version of this distinction) that such a distinction is untenable; see Emcke, "Between Choice and Coercion" and Markell, "The Recognition of Politics."

47. Fraser, "Recognition without Ethics," 33–34.

48. Cf. Warner's critique of the mapping of queerness onto: "casualness" as opposed to "intimacy," "sex with strangers" as opposed to "long-term commitment," "perverse pleasure" as opposed to "romantic love" (*The Trouble with Normal*, 73).

49. Warner, *The Trouble with Normal*, 96, 107 (and chap. 3 generally).

50. The first possibility seems implied by Honneth's characterization of struggles for recognition as the engine of the moral development of societies in history (see esp. part 3 of *The Struggle for Recognition*); the second possibility is commonplace in many versions of liberal multiculturalism (including Kymlicka's, which I discuss in chap. 6 below); for an example of the third see Gutmann, "Introduction," 23.

51. In addition to the discussion of the *Antigone* in chap. 3 below, see the treatments of *Oedipus Tyrannos* in Euben, *The Tragedy of Political Theory*, chap. 4; Segal, *Tragedy and Civilization*, chap. 7.

52. As will become clear in the discussion of Hegel's account of the master-slave relation in chap. 4, this does not deny that material incentives play a role in structures of social subordination: in many cases, the stabilization of intersubjective life through recognition will also pay material wages—for example, by insulating some people from the experience of certain kinds of labor at others' expense, or distributing the risk of material deprivation and impoverishment unequally across social space.

53. Du Bois's original discussion of the wages of whiteness was part of an analysis of the failure of cross-racial working-class solidarity in the American South (*Black Reconstruction*, 700–701). For discussion and elaboration see Roediger, *The Wages of Whiteness*; Charles Mills, *Blackness Visible*, esp. chap. 6; Olson, "The Du Boisian Alternative to the Politics of Recognition" and "The Democratic Problem of the White Citizen"; Cheryl Harris, "Whiteness as Property."

54. Arendt, *The Human Condition*, 234; on the relationship between plurality and the future, see 188–92.

55. See, e.g., Arendt, *The Origins of Totalitarianism*, 460–79; Canovan, *Hannah Arendt*, 25–28; on the rise of the social, Arendt, *The Human Condition*,

38–41. The assumption that threats to the political consist paradigmatically in efforts to destroy the political as such (rather than, say, the use of some axis of social differentiation to narrow the range of people with whom we are prepared to act politically) seems to me to be interconnected with Arendt's much-debated account of action as *entelecheia*, which has seemed to many readers to involve her in a "quest for political purity" in which the appearance of certain issues in politics (including but not limited to gender and sexuality) could only represent the socialization of the political and not the politicization of the social (Reinhardt, *The Art of Being Free*, 145; cf., among many others, Pitkin, "Justice" and *The Attack of the Blob* as well as many essays in Honig, ed., *Feminist Interpretations of Hannah Arendt*).

56. Seidman, *Difference Troubles*, 152 (glossing Fuss, *Essentially Speaking*, 103).

57. I discuss this point at greater length in chap. 7.

58. Warner, *Publics and Counterpublics*, 122; cf. his description of queer life as a form of sociability that "begins in an acknowledgment of all that is most abject and least reputable in oneself," including, importantly, the fact that sex is typically "an occasion for losing control" which therefore also risks becoming an occasion for shame; as well as the fact that people "commonly do not know their desires until they find them" (*The Trouble With Normal*, 35, 7).

59. This problem affects Oliver's critique of the politics of recognition in *Witnessing*; see, e.g., her account of recognition as essentially connected to the "abjection" or "exclusion" of otherness (10), or her claim that Taylor's model of recognition involves the "assimilation of difference into something familiar" (9, 44–46). The same problem also affects Michael Shapiro's critique of "nation-state time" in *For Moral Ambiguity*: although Shapiro begins by brilliantly criticizing the spatialization of issues of temporality (117), he subsequently performs a version of the same move he criticizes, shifting from a consideration of temporality as such to a consideration of multiple *and spatially differentiated* temporalities, and focusing on the ways in which these "diverse ways of being-in-time," borne by cultures or subcultures that "seek to establish a recognizable presence" in politics, are erased or incorporated by homogenizing nation-states (135).

60. This last possibility is explored in Connolly, *The Ethos of Pluralization* and "Pluralism, Multiculturalism and the Nation-State."

61. Not all movements that have travelled under the name of "multiculturalism" have been state-centric; nor have all been oriented toward recognition; see Chicago Cultural Studies Group, "Critical Multiculturalism." State-oriented multiculturalisms also have different histories in different places: in some cases, they have developed out of critical social movements that were not originally focused on securing official recognition; in other cases, multiculturalism itself has entered political discourse via state policy. See Bennett, ed., *Multicultural States*.

62. Stevens, *Reproducing the State*, 56ff.

63. Extremely useful exceptions (though most do not discuss "recognition" explicitly) include Brown, *States of Injury*; Minow, *Not Only for Myself*; Povinelli, "The State of Shame" (and now see her *The Cunning of Recognition*);

Neocleous, *Administering Civil Society*; Lloyd and Thomas, *Culture and the State*; Kastoryano, *Negotiating Identities*.

64. Duquette, "The Political Significance of Hegel's Concept of Recognition in the *Phenomenology*," 48; see also Patten, *Hegel's Idea of Freedom*, 129–35; Robert Williams, *Hegel's Ethics of Recognition*, chaps. 12–13.

65. For related though not identical accounts see Stevens, *Reproducing the State*; Habermas, "The European Nation-State"; Balibar, "The Nation Form"; Appadurai, "Full Attachment"; Markell, "Making Affect Safe for Democracy?"

66. I am focusing here on what international relations theorists call the domestic or "internal" face of sovereignty; see Wendt, *Social Theory of International Politics*, 206–7.

67. On the etymological relation between the political concept of the state and the idea of status or standing, see Skinner, "The State," 91ff.

68. Mitchell, "The Limits of the State," 78.

69. Ibid., 94–95. This does *not* mean that the state as a structural effect really comes to have all the features ascribed to the state as a thing: although the existence of states does involve the disproportionate concentration of power in certain institutions, for example, this does not make those institutions sovereign.

70. This can create some terminological hazards: for example, in what follows, I sometimes talk about the state as an agent that claims or seeks to defend its sovereignty; yet it is important to emphasize that "the state's claim" to sovereignty may be a claim spoken not only by the state itself, through its formal representatives, but also by anyone who identifies with the state (which is to say, anyone who is invested in *this* way of internally differentiating social life); not only in official deliberations, but also in unofficial public spheres.

71. See for example: Sassen, *Losing Control*; Held, "The Transformation of Political Community"; Camilleri and Falk, *The End of Sovereignty*.

72. Foucault, "Truth and Power," 121; see also "Two Lectures," 102.

73. Some international relations scholars suggest that this argument about globalization confuses sovereignty, as a matter of authority, with effective power: a state can still be sovereign even when it faces constraints on its ability to act as it wishes (Wendt, *Social Theory of International Politics*, 208; Krasner, *Sovereignty*, 10; Thomson, "State Sovereignty in International Relations"). But such a rigid distinction cannot be sustained: the reason sovereignty *matters* is that authority "confers power," conversely, the absence of effective control over a territory can undermine a state's claims to sovereign authority (Philpott, "Ideas and the Evolution of Sovereignty," 17; cf. Hinsley, *Sovereignty*, 17; on control as a criterion of sovereignty see Crawford, *The Creation of States in International Law*, 42–48). Thus many classical theorists of sovereignty—including Bodin and Hobbes—brought the connection between sovereignty and control into the foreground by defining sovereignty as a kind of *potestas* or power (Bodin, *On Sovereignty*, 1; Hobbes, *Leviathan*, 2.17 [Oakeshott 112]; cf. Walker, *Inside/Outside*, 165–66). The trouble here is that analysts on both sides of this debate typically approach sovereignty as a *state of affairs*—a state either is or isn't sovereign—rather than as a claim, desire, or project.

74. Foucault, "Two Lectures," 97.

75. Ibid., 102, 97.

76. Brown, *States of Injury*, 17. On governmentality, see Burchell, Gordon, and Miller, *The Foucault Effect*; Rose, *Powers of Freedom*; Barry, Osborne, and Rose, *Foucault and Political Reason*.

77. Brown, *States of Injury*, 28.

78. Lloyd and Thomas make a related suggestion that the modern state cannot be understood *simply* as "a contingently linked assemblage of institutions," for those institutions are still governed (at least on the level of cultural representation) by "a certain *idea* of the state," which guides those institutions and helps to determine the patterns of subject-formation that occur within them. *Culture and the State*, 4. Cf. Neocleous's critique of Foucault in *Administering Civil Society*, chap. 3.

79. James Scott, *Seeing Like a State*, 2.

80. Thus, in international politics, as Krasner has observed, systems of state sovereignty are frequently honored in the breach (*Sovereignty*, 24–25).

81. See the description of democratic despotism in Tocqueville, *Democracy in America*, 690–95.

82. My choice of the term "acknowledgment" is directly indebted to the work of Cavell and Tully, as well as to David Owen's exploration of the relations between these thinkers in "Cultural Diversity and the Conversation of Justice" and "Political Philosophy in a Post-Imperial Voice."

83. Tully, "Struggles over Recognition and Distribution," 477; "The Agonic Freedom of Citizens."

84. Tully, "Struggles over Recognition and Distribution," 479–80. This last image of players becoming attached to a game even through their losses is not Tully's, but it is suggested by his repeated description of political activity as a "game."

85. This is not to deny that some constitutional forms can insulate basic issues of political membership from some of the vicissitudes of majoritarian politics; but at the end of the day, such arrangements are themselves the outcomes of fundamentally political acts of constitutional founding, and are never *completely* insulated from the ongoing activity of politics understood in its broadest sense.

86. See Allen's analysis of democracy in terms of the fair distribution of loss and sacrifice in "Law's Necessary Forcefulness" and *Democratic Entanglements*.

87. The overlapping account of acknowledgment in Bentley and Owen, "Ethical Loyalties," seems to me to suffer, intermittently, from the same problem: while Bentley and Owen sometimes talk about acknowledgment as the surrender of "a particular kind of security in [one's own] commitments" (235), they also describe acknowledgment as something like the recognition of the validity or reasonability of other people's ways of reasoning or "kinds of reasons" (231), which, on my usage, puts us back in the register of recognition rather than acknowledgment.

88. Cavell, "Knowing and Acknowledging"; "The Avoidance of Love"; and part 4 of *The Claim of Reason*.

89. On Cavell and skepticism see Zerilli, "The Skepticism of *Willful Liberalism*"; Conant, "On Bruns, On Cavell."

90. Cavell, "Knowing and Acknowledging," 257; *The Claim of Reason*, 428.

91. Cavell, "Othello and the Stake of the Other," 141.

92. Honneth, "Invisibility," 110, 115. Honneth's use of "recognition" in this essay sometimes comes close to what I mean by "acknowledgment"—for example, in his claim that the act of recognition involves a "decentering" of the self (126), which he grounds in Kant's striking definition of "respect" as "the representation of a worth that infringes upon my self-love" (121, citing *Groundwork*, 14 n., [*Ak.* 401 n.]). Importantly, however, in this passage Kant also insists that "the object of respect is therefore *simply the law*, and indeed the law that we impose upon ourselves and yet as necessary in itself" (emphasis added). It is crucial that the recognition of others is mediated here by the apodictic recognition of the moral law, because this deprives Kant's passage of any serious suggestion of decentering: in respecting others I am merely following the incontestable command of my own will, and moreover respecting others precisely and only in virtue of the fact that they, like me, are rational beings. For a related discussion and critique of apodictic recognition in Kant, see Connolly, "Speed, Concentric Cultures, and Cosmopolitanism."

93. As Conant says, it aims to break with the whole "picture of knowledge" within which skeptics and antiskeptics have long been "locked together" in struggle ("On Bruns, On Cavell," 620–21).

94. See the formulations in *The Claim of Reason*, 389, 428–29; and "The Avoidance of Love," 278–79.

95. Cavell, "The Avoidance of Love," 274. Similarly, as Cavell suggests in *The Claim of Reason* in his discussion of the slaveowner who "sees certain human beings as slaves," what such a person is missing "is not something about slaves exactly, and not exactly about human beings. He is rather missing something about his connection with these people, his internal relation with them, so to speak" (376). This specific example of a failure of acknowledgment will return in chapter 4, when we turn to Hegel's account of the struggle for recognition and the master-slave relation.

96. Similar shifts are also performed or implied by Gooding-Williams, "Race, Multiculturalism and Democracy"; and Oliver, *Witnessing*, 2ff.

97. Cavell, *The Claim of Reason*, 434.

98. A similar slide occurs in Gooding-Williams's "Race, Multiculturalism, and Democracy," which draws a conception of recognition as self-recognition out of the work of Du Bois, but which does not guard sufficiently against the possibility of interpreting self-recognition as the recognition of one's own identity in Taylor's sense. For Gooding-Williams, self-recognition is a matter of "recognizing who *we* are, as distinct from recognizing that *they* have something valuable to say" (35); likewise, for Wolf (to whom Gooding-Williams attributes the distinction), it is a matter of "recogniz[ing] who we, as a community, are" ("Comment," 85).

99. David Owen and Aaron Ridley find something like acknowledgment in this sense at work in Nietzsche, reading the *Übermensch* not as a natural subspecies of humanity but as a cultural ideal, which consists in "the exercise and cultivation of the capacities and the disposition required to affirm the fact that chance and necessity are inevitable" ("Dramatis Personae," 151).

100. Cavell, "The Avoidance of Love," 309.

101. Rightly or wrongly, versions of this position have been attributed to Sartre (e.g., by Robert Williams, *Hegel's Ethics of Recognition*, 376; Honneth, *The Fragmented World of the Social*, 158–67) as well as Levinas (e.g., Sommer, *Proceed with Caution*, 27–30).

102. Zerilli, "The Skepticism of *Willful Liberalism*," esp. 49–52; Conant, "On Bruns, on Cavell," 628; cf. Sommer, *Proceed with Caution*, 6–7: "Vulnerability is no excuse for condemning language as untrustworthy, or for scoffing at its efforts to make connections between thought and things."

103. See Sommer, *Proceed with Caution*, chap. 1 and esp. 25.

104. See, e.g., Oliver, *Witnessing*, 18; for an excellent use of the example of racial injustice to spell out the meaning of witnessing, see her chap. 7.

105. Oliver uses these terms in the course of drawing out the contrast between recognition and witnessing in the introduction, chaps. 1 and 9, and the conclusion, esp. 3–15, 40–44, 208–24.

106. On alienation and the law see Honig, *Democracy and the Foreigner*, esp. chap. 5; on sacrifice, see Allen, "Law's Necessary Forcefulness" and *Democratic Entanglements*; on conflict and democratic politics see Markell, "Contesting Consensus"; Honig, "Dead Rights, Live Futures"; Allen, *Democratic Entanglements*; and Bickford, *The Dissonance of Democracy*. Bickford serves as an especially useful counterpoint to Oliver because she insists that owning up to the risk and threat of intersubjective life, rather than hoping to overcome it, is a precondition of living that life well (149ff.).

107. For an exemplary account of listening that finds in it something like what I am calling "acknowledgment," see Bickford, *The Dissonance of Democracy*, esp. chap. 5; for a similar account of "forgiving" see Orlie, "Forgiving Trespasses, Promising Futures."

CHAPTER TWO
THE DISTINGUISHING MARK

1. Taylor's essay was not the first work of postwar political thought to use the concept of recognition: Fanon (in *Black Skin, White Masks*) and Berlin (in "Two Concepts of Liberty") had already done so in the fifties. On Berlin and Taylor, see Abbey, *Charles Taylor*, 135ff.; on Fanon and Taylor see Oliver, *Witnessing*, chap. 1.

2. But see García Düttmann, *Between Cultures*, which opens with a perceptive account of the contradiction between recognition's "confirming" function and its "establishing" function (3–4).

3. As Honneth puts it, "while by cognizing a person we mean an identification of him as an individual that can gradually be improved upon, by 'recognizing' we refer to the expressive act through which this cognition is conferred with the positive meaning of an affirmation" ("Invisibility," 115). Honneth's insistence that recognition must involve something "added" to mere cognition (111) reflects the fact that in ordinary German usage there are actually three verbs—*erkennen*, *anerkennen*, and *wiedererkennen* (and their derivatives)—that can all fairly be translated by the English "to recognize" (and its derivatives). Recogni-

tion in the first, merely cognitive sense mentioned here—putting a name to a face, or simply perceiving something to be the case—is usually captured either by *wiedererkennen* or by *erkennen*, but not normally by *anerkennen*.

4. The distinction between these two uses of recognition is thus related to the distinction between the "constative" and "performative" uses of language; see Austin, *How to Do Things with Words*.

5. In international law the former view is called "declaratory" and the latter is called "constitutive." See Lauterpacht, *Recognition in International Law*, 2, 38–66; Crawford, *The Creation of States in International Law*, 16–25; Strang, "Contested Sovereignty," 22.

6. Taylor, "The Politics of Recognition," 30–31.

7. Appiah, "Identity, Authenticity, Survival," 149 (emphasis added).

8. For an early version of the criticism see ibid., 155; for a recent version of this charge, see Tempelman, "Constructions of Cultural Identity," 19–23.

9. Likewise, as others have observed, critiques of essentialism that treat it simply as a theoretical mistake—a failure to notice some fact about the social world—have proved oddly impotent, because they have failed to inquire into the sources of essentialism's practical appeal, which seems to persist even as theoretical anti-essentialism becomes a part of the conventional wisdom of social and political theory. See Calhoun, "Politics of Identity and Recognition," 198–99; Benhabib, "Democracy and Identity," 94; Michaels, "Race into Culture," 60–61 n. 39; Brubaker and Cooper, "Beyond Identity"; Suny, "Constructing Primordialism."

10. Constructionist language is easy to find in Taylor's discussions of identity, both in "The Politics of Recognition" and also *Sources of the Self*, e.g., 34–35, 46–47; for a defense of Taylor's account of identity against charges of essentialism, see Novotny, "'Taylor'-Made?" Neither Novotny nor constructionist critics of Taylor like Tempelman, however, inquire into the significance of the peculiar combination of essentialist and constructionist language Taylor employs.

11. Taylor, "The Politics of Recognition," 34, 25.

12. For example, Taylor ends one paragraph by saying that "by definition this [authentic] way of being cannot be socially derived, but must be inwardly generated." The next paragraph begins: "But in the nature of the case, there is no such thing as inward generation, monologically understood" (ibid., 32).

13. Taylor, "What is Human Agency"; *Sources of the Self*, chaps. 1–2. Importantly, this does not mean that human agents never engage in "weak" evaluation; his point is simply that human agency cannot be weakly evaluative all the way down.

14. Taylor, *Sources of the Self*, 27.

15. Ibid., 27–28.

16. Taylor, "The Politics of Recognition," 26.

17. Taylor, "Introduction," 1.

18. Taylor mentions these examples in the course of the "Introduction" and in chapters one and three of *Human Agency and Language*. Some of the same positions receive further critique in *Sources of the Self*, esp. chaps. 1–4.

19. Taylor, "Introduction," 4–5.

20. See Taylor's discussion of the oscillation in Marxist theory between a

"heroic" image of man as sovereign and a "scientific" account of the laws of history in *Hegel*, 546–58.

21. See, e.g., Taylor, "Atomism" and "Cross-Purposes"; for a parallel critique see Sandel, *Liberalism and the Limits of Justice*.

22. Taylor, "Introduction," 8.

23. Taylor discusses these features at some length in "Atomism" and "Cross-Purposes."

24. Taylor, "Introduction," 8.

25. Taylor, "Cross-Purposes."

26. Taylor, "Atomism," 197.

27. This connection is made explicit in Kymlicka's *Liberalism, Community and Culture*, which moves from a review of the liberal-communitarian debate into a discussion of minority rights and multiculturalism.

28. For some autobiographical comments that give a sense of these connections see Taylor, *Reconciling the Solitudes*, 136; "From Philosophical Anthropology to the Politics of Recognition," 109. For a systematic comparison of Taylor and Herder on the themes of language and nationalism, see Fox, "J. G. Herder and Charles Taylor."

29. On Taylor's account, not all designative theorists are necessarily naturalists: Hobbes, Locke, and Condillac were not naturalists, strictly speaking, because they did not assume a wholly external perspective on language, "but wanted to explain it very much from the inside, in terms of the agent's experience of self." Still, Taylor says, by treating the relationship of designation as unproblematic, these theorists *"prepared the way* for [the] elision [of the linguistic dimension] altogether in those modern behaviorist theories that try to explain thought and language strictly from the standpoint of the external observer" ("The Importance of Herder," 90, emphasis added).

30. Ibid., 80.

31. Taylor, "Language and Human Nature," 218.

32. Ibid., 220.

33. Taylor, "The Importance of Herder," 85.

34. Ibid., 84.

35. Ibid., 84–85 (emphasis added).

36. Ibid., 89.

37. Taylor, "Language and Human Nature," 225–26; "The Importance of Herder," 96–99.

38. Taylor, "Language and Human Nature," 226.

39. Ibid., 231.

40. Taylor, "Language and Human Nature," 232; cf. "The Importance of Herder," 97.

41. Taylor, "Language and Human Nature," 231.

42. Ibid., 215–47; "The Importance of Herder," 79–99. Herder's cultural pluralism is also deployed at pivotal points in "The Politics of Recognition" (30–32; 72); Taylor discusses the importance of Herder in an autobiographical register in "The Tradition of a Situation," 136.

43. Taylor, "The Importance of Herder," 87–89.

44. Curiously, while Taylor recounts this fable in his work on Herder's philosophy of language, he does not focus on the theme of recognition, either there or in his essay on the politics of recognition, which cites Herder's *Ideen zur Philosophie der Geschichte der Menschheit*, but not the *Essay*.

45. Stam, *Inquiries into the Origin of Language*, chap. 5.

46. Aarsleff, *From Locke to Saussure*, 146. Aarsleff argues that Herder's reputed originality has been vastly inflated, due to the failure of scholars to acknowledge Herder's misreading of one of his prime targets, Condillac's *Essay on the Origin of Human Knowledge*; for a similar critique of Herder's treatment of Süßmilch, see Kieffer, "Herder's Treatment of Süssmilch's Theory," 96–105.

47. Herder, *Abhandlung über den Ursprung der Sprache*, in vol. 5 of *Sämmtliche Werke*, 7, Gode 88. I did not discover Michael Forster's full translation of the *Abhandlung* until after this book went to press. I will therefore cite Suphan's German edition first, as the *Abhandlung*. Where a second page number is also given, it will refer to one of two partial English translations. "Gode" refers to Herder, "Essay on the Origin of Language," a partial translation by Alexander Gode. "Barnard" refers to a set of selections translated by F. M. Barnard in Herder, *J. G. Herder on Social and Political Culture*. Where only one number is given, the edition is Suphan's and the translation is my own.

48. Herder, *Abhandlung*, 18ff., Gode 99ff.

49. Ibid., 40–41, Gode 121.

50. Herder often returns to this figure, sometimes in explicitly biblical terms, sometimes not; see for example *The Spirit of Hebrew Poetry*, 1:128; *Outlines of a Philosophy of the History of Man*, 1:431; "Selections from *A Metacritique of the Critique of Pure Reason*," 100–101.

51. Herder, *Abhandlung*, 36–37, Gode 116–18 (translation modified).

52. Herder does not always distinguish in these pages between *anerkennen* and *erkennen*, and when he does, he says that a person "manifests reflection if he is able not only to discern [*erkennen*] all characteristics vividly or clearly, but if he can also *recognize and acknowledge* to himself [*bei sich anerkennen*] one or several of them as distinguishing characteristics," and calls this act of picking out the distinguishing characteristic an act of *Anerkenntnis*. Herder, *Abhandlung*, 35, Gode 116 (translation modified; "*anerkennen*" is emphasized in the original). Herder returns to the language of *Anerkennung* elsewhere, e.g., "Selections from *A Metacritique*," 100–101.

53. Eric MacGilvray, in a personal communication, has suggested that there might be an interesting difference between this scene and the politics of recognition among human beings, since there seems to be no sense in which the animal would be injured by the human's failure to recognize it properly. But the analogy is not so distant: as we shall see when we turn to the biblical echoes of Herder's scene, the failure to recognize an animal would both threaten humankind's divinely ordained sovereignty over nature and preclude that creature from fulfilling its God-given purpose, i.e., to be a "vassal" and "servant" to humanity (Herder, *Abhandlung*, 50, Gode 130–31). The "injury," if it can be called that, is of a very different sort, but that is because the identity is of a very different sort.

54. On this combination of passive receptivity and active construction in Herder's founding scene see Gaier, *Herders Sprachphilosophie und Erkenntniskritik*, 109–11.

55. This becomes particularly clear in some of Herder's subsequent engagements with the question of language origin, including the *Ideen* [which refers to the "divine gift of speech" (*Outlines*, 1:154)], many of which were meant to respond in part to criticisms of the *Essay* by Hamann and others defending the notion of divine origin. Herder, however, thought the *Essay* itself had not denied God's role in the origin of language, but merely insisted that God's role had been indirect: he had not given language to humankind already formed, but had enabled human beings to invent language themselves by using the divinely granted powers of speech and reflection to recognize the distinguishing marks of things, and name them. See e.g., Herder's letter to Hamann (August 1, 1772, in Hamann, *Briefwechsel*, 3:10; cited in Stam, *Inquiries into the Origin of Language*, 170.) Stam suggests Herder's defense is "disingenuous"; for a different view see Gaier, *Herders Sprachkritik*, 149–50. On the theological dimension of Herder's thought see Linker, "The Reluctant Pluralism of J. G. Herder"; Fox, "J. G. Herder and Charles Taylor."

56. Herder, *Abhandlung*, 50, Gode 131, quoting *Gen.* 2:19. This is Gode's translation of Herder's text, in which the biblical passage appears in what seems to be Herder's own German translation. As John Pizer notes, Herder also associates the origin of language with Adamic naming in a different text, the *Älteste Urkunde des Menschengeschlechts* (in vol. 7 of *Sämmtliche Werke*), which is an extended commentary on parts of *Genesis*. See Pizer, "Herder, Benjamin, and the 'Ursprung' of Language."

57. Herder, *Abhandlung*, 50, Gode 130–31. For echoes of the biblical notion of language as humankind's instrument of domination over nature, see *Outlines*, 431; *Spirit of Hebrew Poetry*, 128.

58. Herder, *Abhandlung*, 125, Barnard 165ff.; cf. *Outlines*, 1:427. Bauman and Briggs, "Language Philosophy as Language Ideology," 172–74, contains a concise discussion of these dynamics in Herder; but Bauman and Briggs wrongly conclude that Herder's account of linguistic and national plurality is altogether "affirmative in tone," and that "what for Locke is an impediment to true knowledge is for Herder a quality to be treasured" (174). As I shall suggest, Herder's attitude was more complex: while celebrating the capacity of *one* language to express the character of *one* nation, he also mourns the error and misunderstanding to which the plurality of languages has subjected humanity.

59. *Genesis* 11.

60. Herder, "On Diligence in the Study of Several Learned Languages," 29. Cf. Herder, *Abhandlung*, 132–33, Barnard 169.

61. Herder, *Älteste Urkunde des Menschengeschlechts*, in vol. 7 of *Sämmtliche Werke*, 41. My translation.

62. Herder, *Outlines*, 1:423. (The title of this work would better be translated *Ideas for a Philosophy of the History of Humankind*, and it is commonly known as the *Ideas* or *Ideen*, but I have used the title of the one complete English translation, from the turn of the nineteenth century.) On the theme of unity, diversity, and progress in the *Ideen*, see Muthu, *Enlightenment against Empire*,

chap. 6; on the same themes in "On Diligence," see Morton, *Herder and the Poetics of Thought*; and on the theological dimensions of Herder's progressivism see Linker, "Herder's Reluctant Pluralism"; Fox, "J. G. Herder and Charles Taylor."

63. Herder, *Outlines*, 1:222 (italics in original, spelling corrected).

64. Herder, "On Diligence," 30; *The Spirit of Hebrew Poetry*, 1:27; *Outlines*, 1:427.

65. Herder, *The Spirit of Hebrew Poetry*, 1:27; see also "Yet Another Philosophy of History," 43; *Outlines*, 1:19, 357, 427.

66. Herder, *Outlines*, 2:293–94; "Yet Another Philosophy of History," 38–40.

67. Bauman and Briggs, "Language Philosophy as Language Ideology," 185–94; Ergang, *Herder and the Foundations of Modern German Nationalism*, chap. 6.

68. Muthu, *Enlightenment against Empire*, chap. 6.

69. Morton, *Herder and the Poetics of Thought*, 108ff. (discussing "On Diligence"); *Outlines*, 2:294; see also "On Diligence," 33.

70. This invocation of misunderstanding should *not* be taken to mean that opacity is the natural order of things, or that mutual understanding is impossible; for a useful critique of a variant of that view (in terms of "incommensurability") see Stephen White's discussion of Taylor in *Sustaining Affirmation*, 54–55.

71. "Yet Another Philosophy of History," 38. Morton, in *Herder and the Poetics of Thought*, 144–46, has also noted a parallel between this passage and Herder's account of the origin of language in the *Essay*. Interestingly, Herder elsewhere draws explicit comparisons between nations and animals (as well as nations and plants): see *Outlines*, 1:108.

72. Herder, *Outlines*, 1:431.

73. Ibid., 1:166 (emphasis in original).

74. Taylor, "The Politics of Recognition," 35; see also "Two Theories of Modernity," 153ff.; "Modern Social Imaginaries," 95.

75. Taylor, "The Politics of Recognition," 34.

76. Taylor, "Modernity and Identity," 142 (emphasis added).

77. Taylor, "Modern Social Imaginaries," 95.

78. See Duby, *The Three Orders*; Moore, *The First European Revolution*; *The Formation of a Persecuting Society*. Even in his more detailed treatment in "Modern Social Imaginaries," Taylor seems to drain medieval society of its politics: in the premodern era, he says, violations of the (naturally and divinely sanctioned) social order were thought to be self-enforcing or self-correcting, through an agency beyond the human—"the course of things," "the assessment of time," and, presumably, the agency of God himself (95)—whereas in the modern era it is we humans who are responsible for realizing the norms instantiated in our different social imaginary (116). But this seems unable to account for the deployment of all-too-human power to enforce the terms or a particular social imaginary: were the men who burned heretics in eleventh-century France, for instance, passively awaiting the "assessment of time," or were they acting as its instruments?

79. Other examples include the ongoing contests over the ultimate priority of

sacred and secular authority; the rise of feudalism in the eleventh century and its subsequent (uneven) displacement by monarchical power; and the upheavals and possibilities for transformation generated by such phenomena as urbanization, the introduction of primogeniture, the proliferation of monastic orders, and the Crusades. On sacred and secular authority see the brief summary in Le Goff, *Medieval Civilization*, 95–97; or the longer documentary history in Tierney, *The Crisis of Church and State*. On feudalism, see Bloch, *Feudal Society*; Duby, *The Three Orders*; Le Goff, *Medieval Civilization*, esp. 90–95; on urbanization and primogeniture (as well as feudalism) see Moore, *The First European Revolution*. On the ways in which these and other social circumstances in the eleventh and twelfth centuries generated new opportunities to change social roles (as well as a fascination with the idea and experience of change itself) see Bynum, *Metamorphosis and Identity*, 26–27.

80. Taylor, "The Politics of Recognition," 32.

81. Taylor does not explicitly distinguish these two dimensions of the rise of modernity, but the distinction seems to be implied in, and required by, his explicit double use of the concept of authenticity, which—for him as for Herder—may refer either to the identity of an individual conceived of in opposition to the collectivity to which she belongs, or to the identity of the "culture-bearing people" as such, in which case the misrecognition of the group is, transitively, the misrecognition of each of its individual members as well ("The Politics of Recognition," 31).

82. Ibid., 32ff.

83. "*Völker*, like individuals, are required to extend mutual recognition to one another of their inevitable but complementary differences, because together they make up the whole chorale of humanity" (Taylor, "Modernity and Identity," 143).

84. Taylor, "The Importance of Herder, 97.

85. On the first two possibilities see Sommer, *Proceed with Caution*, chap. 1; on idioms, or "idiolects," see Flathman, *Willful Liberalism*, 216–21; *Reflections of a Would-Be Anarchist*, 27–30. These accounts suggest that Taylor is mistaken to say that, "put baldly, teleologically: we are meant to understand each other," and to associate mutual understanding with "growth" and "completion" ("Living with Difference," 216): if there is a *telos* to language then it includes both misunderstanding *and* understanding, which should be seen as each other's conditions rather than as stages in a developmental history.

86. Here I dissent from Stephen White's thoughtful chapter on Taylor in *Sustaining Affirmation*: while White argues that Taylor's work does provide an adequate ontological "prefiguration" of the existential condition of finitude, I believe Taylor's prefiguration of finitude is both incomplete (i.e., stronger in relation to the horizon of the past than in relation to that of the future) and uneven (i.e., while Taylor does prefigure our finitude in relation to the future, he does not do so consistently).

87. Taylor, "Language and Human Nature," 234. The same clauses are reproduced in a different order in "The Importance of Herder," 99.

88. Taylor, "The Politics of Recognition," 70 (and generally 66–73).

89. Ibid., 66ff.

90. Ibid., 66–67.

91. Ibid., 73. I am drawing here on Hanssen's critique of Taylor in "Ethics of the Other," 203–204, although I find more tension within Taylor's position than she does; for a similar criticism of the Gadamerian hermeneutics on which Taylor relies see Sommer, *Proceed with Caution*, 23–26.

92. For Taylor's explicit use of Herder in this context see "The Politics of Recognition," 72.

93. You might say that the act of recognition is a distinctive kind of speech act because it has a self-masking or self-obscuring character: the successful act of recognition *does* construct identities, but it does so precisely by seeming only to cognize them—or that "recognition" is a performative whose conditions of success or felicity include that it seem only to be a constative. On the idea of felicity and infelicity, see Austin, *How to Do Things with Words*, 13–14; and cf. García Düttmann, *Between Cultures*, 4. García Düttmann, however, too quickly characterizes this combination of performativity and constativity as "impossible," which risks foreclosing an investigation of the strategies by which actors negotiate the tension between performativity and constativity politically.

94. Taylor, *Sources of the Self*, 28.

95. See Taylor's account of the nature of practical reasoning in ibid., 71–75; cf. Stephen White's discussion in *Sustaining Affirmation*, 52–53.

96. Taylor, *Sources of the Self*, 47–48.

CHAPTER THREE
TRAGIC RECOGNITION

1. For this history, see Cave, *Recognitions*. For Aristotle's definition see *Poetics*, 1452a29–b8; on its importance to "the finest form of tragedy," *Poetics*, 1452b30–34. Except where otherwise noted, I use the translation in Bywater's edition of Aristotle, *On the Art of Poetry*, although I reverse his practice of capitalizing the first letters of such words as "tragedy" and "plot," and I change his rendering of *anagnôrisis* as "Discovery," substituting (the more common and more literal) "recognition." In working with the *Poetics* I have also benefited from the texts, translations, and/or commentaries contained in: Aristotle, *Poetics*, ed. Lucas; Halliwell, *The Poetics of Aristotle*; Else, *Aristotle's* Poetics; and Aristotle, *Poetics*, ed. and trans. Else.

2. Sophocles, *Oedipus The King*, 1068.

3. Aristotle, *Poetics*, 1452a29–32 (emphasis added). See also Goldhill, *Reading Greek Tragedy*, 85.

4. Arendt, *The Human Condition*, 234.

5. One reason I prefer "impropriety" to "unpredictability" is that the latter term is likely to be taken by many readers to refer exclusively to the unpredictability of causal processes. This is part of what Arendt means by unpredictability and also part of what I mean by impropriety, but, as I explain below, she and I also both aim to capture the fact that the description or meaning of an act itself is not under an agent's control. In this case, the unfamiliarity of the neologism may help to avoid misunderstandings to which Arendt's use of "unpredictability" could give rise.

6. Arendt, *The Human Condition*, 190–91, 197, 173.

7. Ibid., 193–94.

8. Ibid., 194. I was alerted to this point by Tsao, "Arendt against Athens," 107–8.

9. Arendt, *The Human Condition*, 197. As Tsao observes, Arendt is implicitly critical of the Periclean effort to make the *polis* into a scene of remembrance that would make poets and historians unnecessary ("Arendt against Athens," 113–16).

10. Tsao, "Arendt against Athens," 111; cf. Disch, *Hannah Arendt and the Limits of Philosophy*, 74–76.

11. This is the function she assigns equally to poetry, art, history, writing, and monument-building in *Human Condition* (173); it is also a prominent part of her account of tragic recognition in "On Humanity in Dark Times" (21). This is a running theme in Pirro, *Hannah Arendt and the Politics of Tragedy*; for succinct statements see 35–37; 88; 138.

12. Arendt, "On Humanity in Dark Times," 20–22; on the political importance of this second dimension of recognition as reconciliation, see Pirro, *Hannah Arendt and the Politics of Tragedy*, 139–42.

13. For a related account of the consequences of Arendt's simplification of "the Greeks" see Euben, "Arendt's Hellenism," 159. This suggests that, *pace* Tsao, the question is less whether Arendt was "for" or "against" the Greek understanding of action than *which* Greek understanding of action she was for; but Arendt's own rhetoric does make this question hard to pose.

14. Although this view is often associated with Hegel, his reading is actually more complex; see chap. 4, below.

15. Elshtain, "Antigone's Daughters," 53, 58–59.

16. Dietz, "Citizenship with a Feminist Face," 20, 29. I owe the device of framing the play through the opposition between Elshtain and Dietz to Bonnie Honig.

17. Judith Butler, *Antigone's Claim*, 2, 24.

18. Ibid., chap. 3; on the importance of the distinction between this sort of explicit prohibition and foreclosure, see Judith Butler, *Psychic Life of Power*, chap. 5.

19. As Butler observes, Antigone dies not by Creon's hand but her own, and treats her own fate as a foregone conclusion: *Antigone's Claim*, 27.

20. Ibid., 77–80. One trouble with this aspect of the interpretation is that Antigone explicitly recalls having publicly grieved the other members of her family (898–903), which makes it harder to read Polyneices' burial as the point of condensation of other, unavowed losses: in this instance, the incest taboo does not seem to have required so complete a foreclosure as Butler suggests; indeed, that taboo may have been *more* forgiving than Creon's own explicit prohibition.

21. Judith Butler, *Antigone's Claim*, 23–25; cf. 78–82.

22. Ibid., 77.

23. Ibid., 81; I say "inadvertantly" because Butler is elsewhere critical of this investment—for example, in her discussions of the politics of same-sex marriage: see Butler, Laclau, and Žižek, *Contingency, Hegemony, Universality*, 175ff.

24. Judith Butler, *Antigone's Claim*, 77; 77; 6; 23.

25. The first phrase is from Gellrich, *Tragedy and Theory*, xiii (Gellrich develops this argument at length with reference to Aristotle in chap. 2); the second is from Bernard Williams, *Shame and Necessity*, arguing that on this issue "Plato, Aristotle, Kant, Hegel are all on the same side" while "Sophocles and Thucydides" are on the other (163). Thanks to Peter Euben for pressing me to address this concern.

26. Aristotle, *Poetics*, 1451b32–52a10 and 1454a3–8, respectively; for discussion of these issues see Halliwell, *Aristotle's* Poetics, chap. 7. Murnaghan's "Sucking the Juice without Biting the Rind" reminds us not to idealize (or demonize) tragic practice as a site of untamed disorder: both tragedy *and* Aristotle's theorization of it, she argues, are caught between the conflicting imperatives of representing *and* distancing the terrible.

27. Gellrich, *Tragedy and Theory*, 104ff.

28. Ibid., 115.

29. Plato, *Republic*, 379b.

30. This also suggests a different way of reading Aristotle's preference for plots that turn on human *hamartia* rather than sheer contingency: the point of that preference is not to *deny* the place of contingency in human affairs, but to focus attention on the deadly intersection between contingency and the impossible pursuit of masterful agency.

31. Gellrich, *Tragedy and Theory*, 114–15.

32. Parenthetical citations of the *Antigone* refer to line numbers, and unless otherwise noted, quotations from the play follow Elizabeth Wyckoff's translation. For Greek text and textual commentary see Griffith's and Jebb's editions of the *Antigone*.

33. Polyneices' grievance is discussed in Aeschylus, *Seven Against Thebes*, 631–52, and Sophocles, *Oedipus at Colonus*, 1284–1307. On the death of the brothers see Aeschylus, *Seven Against Thebes*, 808–14.

34. On the conventional obligation to bury one's kin, see Lacey, *The Family in Classical Greece*, 148; on the legal obligation see Humphries, *The Family, Women, and Death*, 83.

35. On the legitimacy of the prohibition of burial, see Rosivach, "On Creon, *Antigone*, and Not Burying the Dead," 193–211; Hester, "Sophocles the Unphilosophical," 19–21, 55; Sourvinou-Inwood, "Assumptions and the Creation of Meaning," 137–38, esp. n. 20. It has been suggested that Creon overstepped his legitimate authority by at least implicitly prohibiting burial even outside Thebes (see Euben, *Corrupting Youth*, 155, and the sources in Rosivach, *supra*, 20). I am unconvinced that Creon's decree is meant to seem like an overstepping of his legitimate *territorial* authority, since the language of the edict (both in Creon's words at 204–7 and in Antigone's at 21–30) is explicit about *what* is prohibited and *to whom* the edict extends but makes no explicit claim to govern space outside of Thebes; moreover, while Polyneices' body has been left outside the city walls, Rosivach (*supra*, 208 n. 49) and Hester (*supra*, 20) both suggest that the body remains within Theban territory—as perhaps it must if the point of leaving him unburied is to let his disgraced body be seen by the townspeople (see Griffith's commentary to ll. 205–6 in *Antigone*, 162). Creon might with

more justice be faulted for failing to follow the practice of letting family members bury a traitor elsewhere, but as Griffith observes, that issue is never mentioned in the play (commentary to ll. 26–36 in *Antigone*, 127).

36. Kurtz and Boardman, *Greek Burial Customs*, 260; see also Sourvinou-Inwood, *'Reading' Greek Death*, 177–79; Holst-Warhaft, *Dangerous Voices*, chap. 4. Cf. Arendt, "On Humanity in Dark Times," 20–22, as well as Hegel's discussion of the work of immortalization performed by burial in *Phenomenology of Spirit*, 270–71.

37. See Freud, "Mourning and Melancholia"; Santner, *Stranded Objects*, chap. 1; Sacks, *The English Elegy*, chap. 1.

38. For some contemporary parallels, see Verdery, *The Political Lives of Dead Bodies*.

39. On the significance of *philos* and *ekhthros* in the *Antigone*, see Goldhill, *Reading Greek Tragedy*, 79–106, to whom I owe in particular the insight into the connection between *philia* and recognition (85), as well as Blundell, *Helping Friends and Harming Enemies*, 106–48; Konstan, "Greek Friendship," 82–85; Segal, *Tragedy and Civilization*, 185–86; and Neuburg, "How Like a Woman," 70–76.

40. See the sources in the preceding note as well as the relevant entries in Liddell and Scott, *A Greek-English Lexicon*. As this suggests, the idea that politics involves distinguishing friends and enemies is hardly the invention of Schmitt's *Concept of the Political*, though given the hostility that the mere mention of Schmitt's name can provoke, I should probably stress that Sophocles is ultimately critical of sovereign efforts to organize the political world into recognized friends and enemies (see below n. 105 and accompanying text).

41. Goldhill, *Reading Greek Tragedy*, 79–83.

42. See Jebb's note in his edition of *Antigone*, 10–11; Blundell, *Helping Friends and Harming Enemies*, 107 n. 5.

43. On the chthonian and Olympian in the context of the *Antigone*, see Segal, *Tragedy and Civilization*, 171.

44. Ibid., 183–84.

45. The question of the nature of kinship and its relation to gender was a live issue for the Greek audience: as Segal says, Antigone's use of matrilineal kinship words "reopens, on a personal level, the debate between Apollo and the Erinyes in Aeschylus's *Oresteia*," where the issue was precisely whether the father's seed or the mother's womb played a more important role in reproduction (ibid., 184).

46. See Foley, "Tragedy and Democratic Ideology," 146 n. 11 (responding to Sourvinou-Inwood, "Assumptions and the Creation of Meaning," 140). On the roles of men and women at funerals see Garland, *The Greek Way of Death*, chap. 3; Humphries, *The Family, Women and Death*, 83–88. There is controversy over whether "all three of you" refers to Oedipus, Jocasta, and Polyneices, or Oedipus, Jocasta, and Eteocles, but the point is valid either way; for two views see the commentaries to these lines in Jebb's and Griffith's editions (Jebb prefers Eteocles; Griffith, Polyneices). Besides, as Judith Butler points out, the use of ambiguous kinship language in the context of *this* family may be part of the point (*Antigone's Claim*, 77).

47. Segal, "The Female Voice and Its Contradictions," 66–72; "Lament and Closure in the *Antigone*," 120.

48. Jebb's translation; Wyckoff translates *philos kakos* as "a friend no friend."

49. See his statements to the chorus (484–85), to Antigone (525), and to Haemon (678–80).

50. Euben also argues that it is problematic to treat Creon and Antigone as simply "standing for" *polis* and *oikos*, etc. (*Corrupting Youth*, 154ff., 164ff.). However, Euben focuses on the ways in which Creon and Antigone fail to represent these terms from the beginning (for instance, by noting Creon's tyrannical behavior toward the chorus of elders even in his first speech [155], or Antigone's difference from Ismene even in the opening scene [166]), whereas I track the ways in which these failures of representation develop, becoming more acute and more obvious, across the course of the play—which has the advantage of highlighting the ways in which Antigone's and Creon's *attempts* at self- and other-recognition, however imperfect these attempts may be, nevertheless contribute to their fates.

51. Aristotle is referring here to the plot (*muthos*), which is the combination of the *pragmata*, which is usually translated as "incidents or events" but which is cognate with *praxis* (action) and certainly includes the *praxeis* of the actors (*prattontes*, meaning the agents in the story, not the Athenians who played them on stage). On Aristotle's vocabulary see Halliwell, *Aristotle's* Poetics, 138–42.

52. The translation of *êthos* as "character" can be misleading, because in English "character," especially in the context of drama, can have the minimal sense of "one of the people in the play" (in which case Aristotle's claim at 1450a23–24 that you can have tragedy without *êthos* would become nonsensical). It may be useful to note that, until the nineteenth century, the standard English translation of Aristotle's term *êthos*—in the *Poetics* as well as in the *Nicomachean Ethics* and the *Rhetoric*—was not "character" but "manners"; and that medieval (and later) Latin translations consistently rendered *êthos* as *mores*.

53. There is one obvious way in which the use of the term *êthos* in the *Poetics* departs from its meaning in the ethical writings: since the *Poetics* is a discussion of *mimêsis*, the term *êthos* sometimes takes on the sense of "dramatic characterization." But these uses are quite compatible: *êthos* in the sense of characterization seems simply to refer to those parts of the *mimêsis* that represent *êthos* in the ethical sense. See Halliwell, *Aristotle's* Poetics, 151ff.

54. Aristotle, *Metaphysics*, 1020a33; *Categories*, 8b25.

55. Aristotle, *Categories*, 8b27.

56. Sherman, *The Fabric of Character*, 1.

57. Chamberlain has shown that *êthos* originally referred to the "haunts" of an animal—that is, to the places where animals of a particular type were typically or characteristically found—and later came to refer to the regularities of behavior of human beings. Chamberlain also notes that "*êthos* comes from the Indo-European root *swedh*, see also in the Latin *suus* and *suesco*, meaning 'one's own' or 'proper'"; so we might say that something's *êthos* is just that

which leads it to do what is proper to it, as the sort of thing it is. "From 'Haunts' to 'Character,'" 97–108.

58. Aristotle, *Rhetoric*, 1388b31–34ff., 1408a25–31; see the discussion in Blundell, "*Êthos* and *Dianoia* Reconsidered," 164. As Chamberlain notes, *êthos* was sometimes used to refer to "the peculiarities which people of a certain *polis* acquire as a result of being brought up under its particular laws and customs" ("From 'Haunts' to 'Character,'" 101).

59. The *Poetics* itself says that *êthos* (here used in the at-one-remove sense of "characterization," or the dramatic depiction of "character"—on this see Halliwell, *Aristotle's* Poetics, 150–51) is that which "shows us the nature of a *prohairesis*" (1450b8–9, Halliwell's translation); certainly Antigone's and Creon's efforts to ground their actions in their identities show us aspects of the nature of their choices.

60. Sherman, *The Fabric of Character*, 1.

61. Going a step beyond Gellrich's claim (discussed above) that Aristotle's subordination of action to *êthos* in the ethical writings distorts his view of tragedy, this view takes seriously Aristotle's prioritization of action in the *Poetics*, but concludes from this that the *Poetics* must represent a sharp break from the ethical treatises.

62. Belfiore, *Tragic Pleasures*, 89.

63. On controversies surrounding the text of this passage see Nussbaum, *The Fragility of Goodness*, 378–79 and accompanying notes.

64. Halliwell, *Aristotle's* Poetics, 157; Nussbaum, *The Fragility of Goodness*, 379–82.

65. Amélie Rorty notes the echo of the discussion of happiness and misfortune in the *Ethics* in "The Psychology of Aristotelian Tragedy," 21 n. 14.

66. Aristotle performs this etymology with *êthikê* at *Nicomachean Ethics*, 1103a17–18, and with *êthos* at *Eudemian Ethics*, 1220a39–b1.

67. On the relationships among *dunamis*, *energeia*, *hexis*, and *praxis*, see Frank, "Democracy and Distribution," 795–96.

68. Aristotle, *Nicomachean Ethics*, 1100a10–1101b23. The epigraph to this essay, from Arendt's *Human Condition*, widens this idea, suggesting that *identity* cannot decisively be ascribed to a person while she is still acting into a contingent future. On vulnerability in Aristotle in general, see Nussbaum, *The Fragility of Goodness*, 380–82 and chaps. 11–12; Halliwell, *Aristotle's* Poetics, chap. 7; Rorty, "The Psychology of Aristotelian Tragedy"; Kosman, "Acting: *Drama* as the *Mimêsis* of *Praxis*," and Sherman, "*Hamartia* and Virtue."

69. See Nagel's discussion (in the context of an argument about luck and responsibility in ethics) of the apparently irresolvable split between the "internal" and "external" perspectives on our actions, in "Moral Luck," 37; cf. Kosman, "Acting," 65.

70. For a good reading Aristotle's account of responsibility, which stresses that he neither finds nor seeks to find some objective characteristic of an agent in virtue of which he can be said to have been either responsible or not, see Smiley, *Moral Responsibility and the Boundaries of Community*, chap. 2.

71. On the inferiority of tragic plots based on "mere chance," see Aristotle, *Poetics*, 1452a1–11; good discussions can be found in Sherman, "*Hamartia* and

Virtue"; Rorty, "The Psychology of Aristotelian Tragedy"; and Yack, *The Problems of a Political Animal*, chap. 8.

72. This is the source of action's impropriety that Arendt emphasizes; see Arendt, *The Human Condition*, 190–93, 233–34; *Between Past and Future*, 169–71; cf. Rorty, "The Psychology of Aristotelian Tragedy," 11.

73. Benhabib calls this the "interpretive indeterminacy" of action (*Critique, Norm, and Utopia*, 88–89; 136).

74. Nussbaum, *The Fragility of Goodness*, chap. 12; see also Yack, *The Problems of a Political Animal*, chap. 8.

75. This suggests a connection between Aristotle's claim about the priority of action to character and his requirement of "necessity or probability" in tragedy. Frede rightly suggests that the requirement of necessity or probability can be rendered compatible with tragedy's focus on unexpected reversals if we attribute to Aristotle the view that "the poet's task [is] to present the unusual as necessary or at least as likely," and she finds this view reflected in Aristotle's concession that "the unlikely can be the likely" (1456a24–25, 1461b15) ("Necessity, Chance, and 'What Happens for the Most Part' in Aristotle's *Poetics*," 209–10). But it's unclear what that maxim can mean, and its paradoxical sound has led other commentators to dismiss it as a "*jeu d'esprit*" (Else, *Aristotle's* Poetics, 551). Belfiore suggests that this maxim can be taken seriously if we assume Aristotle is using "likely" (*eikos*) in two different senses: "*apparently* likely" and "*actually* likely" (*Tragic Pleasures*, 120). But there is another possibility. The requirement of necessity or probability in tragedy is itself double, for it applies both to character and to action: the poet should write "so that whenever such-and-such a personage says or does such-and-such a thing, it shall be the probable or necessary outcome of his character; and whenever this incident follows on that, it shall be either the necessary or probable consequence of it" (1454a33–36). Perhaps, then, the two senses of *eikos* at play in the maxim "the unlikely can be the likely" are actually "*eikos* with respect to character" and "*eikos* with respect to action." That reading is consistent with the examples of "probable improbabilities" Aristotle uses at 1456a19–25: in the cases of the "clever villain (e.g., Sisyphus) deceived" and the "brave wrongdoer worsted," the improbability is an improbability with respect to the *êthos* of the agent, and while Aristotle does not flesh out the examples enough for us to be sure, it seems plausible that what has happened in these cases is that the probabilities of action (or interaction, as Frede nicely stresses) have overtaken the probabilities of character—just as they should, if tragedy is an imitation not of persons but of action.

76. On the ode, see Euben, *Corrupting Youth*, 171–76; Goheen, *The Imagery of Sophocles'* Antigone, 53–56.

77. Goheen, *The Imagery of Sophocles'* Antigone, 141 n. 1 (and accompanying discussion at 53).

78. As Nussbaum puts it, "if one listened only to Antigone, one would not know that a war had taken place or that anything called 'city' was ever in danger" (*The Fragility of Goodness*, 63–64).

79. As Euben observes, in the course of the play Antigone moves from "the enclosure of the most immediate family," in her opening conversation with Ismene, to "the public world" in her final speech to the chorus of citizens (*Cor-*

rupting Youth, 168). It's important to note, however, that while Antigone both steps and is thrust *into* political space, she never quite takes up the vocabulary *of* politics: her act is not framed as a political challenge to Creon, though it becomes one despite her.

80. Although Creon nominally acknowledges that Antigone's disobedience is an instance of disorder within the *oikos*, he does so only in order to *deny* that Antigone's kinship ought to influence his action, and to reinforce his subordination of all other concerns to political rule. To permit disobedience among relatives, Creon says, would compel him to permit it in the city at large; thus, enforcing the edict against Antigone is *just another instance* of ensuring "justice in the *polis*" (662).

81. On this as an expression of specifically filial devotion, see Nussbaum, *The Fragility of Goodness*, 62; O'Brien, *Guide to Sophocles' Antigone*, 77. On the military language, see Jebb's note to line 640 and O'Brien, *Guide to Sophocles' Antigone*, 79, from which the quoted words are taken.

82. On Antigone's treatment of Ismene see Blundell, *Helping Friends and Harming Enemies*, 111–15.

83. Tracking the distinction between blood ties and marriage ties in the *Antigone*, Neuburg suggests that Antigone's lament is an example of a conflict between plural values: "Antigone will never get to have a marriage-family," Neuburg observes, because "she is going to die for the sake of her blood-family: her two roles in the world, daughter and sister on the one hand, wife and mother on the other, have come into apparently irreconcilable conflict." Neuburg, however, overlooks the fact that, because marriage ties and blood ties are not only distinct but *also* interdependent, Antigone's deed *also* undermines her identification with the principle of kinship through blood by depriving her of the opportunity to bear children. See Neuburg, "How Like a Woman," 66–67; also Murnaghan, "*Antigone* 904–20 and the Institution of Marriage," 192–207; and Sorum, "Family in Sophocles' *Antigone* and *Electra*," 206.

84. For a subtle discussion of Creon's tyranny, see Euben, *Corrupting Youth*, 153–64. Euben suggests, contra those who think Creon "stands for the city," that Creon cannot "be identified with 'the city' or maleness" (154); but such an argument over whether Creon does or does not "stand for" the *polis* is beside the point in the same way as arguments (e.g., between Elshtain and Dietz) over whether the Antigone "stands for" the *oikos*: only by focusing on action in addition to character can we make sense of the fact that Creon both expresses apparently sincere commitments to good governance and political *philia* in his opening speech, and, through his action, comes to betray or undermine those commitments (in ways that, as Euben rightly notes, are already anticipated by some features Creon's first speech).

85. Segal, "Lament and Closure in the *Antigone*," 131.

86. See Griffith's commentary in Sophocles, *Antigone*, 129 (commentary to ll. 35–36); on the dependence of stoning on citizen cooperation, see Allen, *The World of Prometheus*, 208–9.

87. The notion that the Theban citizenry quietly sympathizes with Antigone is repeated by Haemon at 690–95, raising the tantalizing question of whether Antigone really did expect to die: might she have been banking on the sympathy

of the Theban citizens to rescue her from a form of punishment that Creon was powerless to carry out on his own? On Creon's dependence, see Allen, *The World of Prometheus*, 209.

88. For the former hypothesis see Allen, *The World of Prometheus*, 209; on the latter, see the discussions in Sophocles, *Antigone*, ed. Griffith, 253–54; and Sophocles, *Antigone*, ed. Jebb, 144.

89. The idea that this exchange somehow makes matters worse for Antigone is supported by Creon's speech at 473ff., in which he takes particular offense at the fact that she not only did the deed but is now boasting of it to him; indeed, her boasts are the immediate occasion for his first explicit expression of a crisis of masculinity (480–85).

90. Particularly after Haemon, unwisely, begins mocking his father (740–41). The idea that Creon's plans for Antigone are, at this point, still unclear is brought home by Creon's subsequent command that Antigone be brought out of the house so that she can die then and there, in Haemon's presence. This cruel response to his son's mockery is thwarted by Haemon's sudden departure (758–61).

91. Vermeule notes that in Sophocles' description the cave has all the architectural features of a bronze-age chamber tomb, which was itself called an "*oikos for the dead*"; see *Aspects of Death in Early Greek Art and Poetry*, 54. See also Rehm, *Marriage to Death*, chap. 4, and Seaford, "The Imprisonment of Women in Greek Tragedy," 76–90. On the propriety of enclosure as a form of punishment for women, see Allen, *The World of Prometheus*, 208–9.

92. In fact, Sophocles has already introduced the theme of the difference between the actor and the significance of the act in another episode involving a messenger: the guard who first informs Creon that Polyneices' corpse has been buried is initially suspected of having committed the crime himself, though he protests that he "never did the deed" (321).

93. Arendt, *The Human Condition*, 184. Arendt specifically mentions the use of messengers within tragedy as an illustration of the gap between the perspective of the actor and the perspective of the narrator in *Between Past and Future*, 45.

94. Aristotle, *Poetics*, 1452a29–32.

95. Thus I dissent from John Jones's effort to correct the overemphasis on character in the interpretation of tragedy by claiming that "the text makes it plain that we can't" read *anagnôrisis* as the recognition of an individual's identity (*On Aristotle and Greek Tragedy*, 15–16). As the examples indicate, there is some sense in which it is impossible *not* to say that recognition is the recognition of a person (on this see Else, *Aristotle's Poetics: The Argument*, 352–53); the point is that this is not the recognition of a coherent practical identity in the sense (and with the unambiguously positive valence) presupposed by the politics of recognition.

96. On the suddenness of *peripeteia*, see Else, *Aristotle's Poetics*, 345; Else persuasively interprets *peripeteia* as a subset of *metabolê* at 343.

97. On the importance of this phrase and its connection to *peripeteia* and *anagnôrisis*, see Else, *Aristotle's Poetics*, 329ff.; Halliwell, *Aristotle's Poetics*, 212.

98. Thus Halliwell's gloss of this gap as the "disparity between the knowledge

or intentions of the dramatic characters and the underlying nature of their actions" is too restrictive, insofar as it suggests that the nature of one's action is something "underlying" it, i.e., something that could have been known in advance, if only we were sufficiently attentive or aware (*Aristotle's* Poetics, 212).

99. On the grammatical splitting see Griffith's commentary to ll. 368–71.

100. For a related discussion of this part of the Ode (though not in terms of *anagnôrisis*) see Euben, *Corrupting Youth*, 175. This suggests that Sophocles is, in a sense, an insightful critic before the fact of modern efforts to resuscitate the friend/enemy distinction as the organizing principle of politics.

101. See Patricia Mills, *Woman, Nature and Psyche*, 28–29.

CHAPTER FOUR
THE ABDICATION OF INDEPENDENCE

1. Hegel, *Phenomenology of Spirit*, 111–19. All subsequent references to the *Phenomenology* in this chapter will be in parentheses, by page number of the Miller translation.

2. Fukuyama, *The End of History and the Last Man*, 152.

3. Ibid., 200–202.

4. Taylor, "The Politics of Recognition," 50.

5. See, *inter alia*, Honneth, *The Struggle for Recognition* and *The Fragmented World of the Social*; Robert Williams, *Recognition* and *Hegel's Ethics of Recognition*; Siep, *Anerkennung als Prinzip der Praktischen Philosophie*; Wildt, *Autonomie und Anerkennung*; Habermas, "Labor and Interaction"; H. S. Harris, "The Concept of Recognition in Hegel's Jena Manuscripts."

6. Kojève's lectures were attended by, among others, Merleau-Ponty, Lacan, Levinas, Sartre, and Bataille; his lecture notes were published in France in 1947 and a selection from them was later translated into English as Kojève, *Introduction to the Reading of Hegel*. For philosophical studies of this reception of Hegel, see Judith Butler, *Subjects of Desire*, and Roth, *Knowing and History*. For an historical outline, see Heckman's "Introduction" to Jean Hyppolite, *Genesis and Structure of Hegel's Phenomenology of Spirit*.

7. See Honneth, *The Fragmented World of the Social*, chap. 9, and *The Struggle for Recognition*, chap. 7; Robert Williams, *Hegel's Ethics of Recognition*, chaps. 1, 15; for a moderate defense of Kojève, see Jurist, *Beyond Hegel and Nietzsche*, 196–200.

8. The phrase is Patten's (*Hegel's Idea of Freedom*, 133); the most extensive reconstruction along these lines is Robert Williams, *Hegel's Ethics of Recognition*; and see also Neuhouser, *Foundations of Hegel's Social Theory*, e.g., 14.

9. Among recent interpreters, Robert Williams and Jurist have also identified relationships between the themes of tragedy and recognition in Hegel. For Williams, particular relationships of recognition may be called "tragic" if they fail in a certain way to achieve the ideal of reciprocity, collapsing instead into conflict, struggle, and loss; the case of Antigone and Creon is one example, and the case of conflict in international relations is another (*Recognitions*, 200–206; *Hegel's Ethics of Recognition*, 357–63). But the fact that some relations of rec-

ognition are "tragic" in this way does not exclude the possibility that others may transcend the conditions of tragedy; for Williams, recognition "at the level of the individual nation-state" (361) may be such an example. Yet this reading too quickly compartmentalizes the force of tragedy in Hegel's understanding of recognition, as I argue in chap. 5. Jurist is rightly critical of just this tendency to compartmentalization in Williams and others, and he implies that there is a tragic moment to Hegel's view of recognition *as such* (*Beyond Hegel and Nietzsche*, 87ff., 188). Jurist is also the scholar who has done the most to draw connections between Hegelian recognition and Aristotelian-tragic *anagnôrisis* (see especially his "Hegel's Concept of Recognition"), and his recent effort to bring Nietzsche and Hegel closer together by stressing the former's neglected appreciation of sociality and the latter's neglected appreciation of individuality and even "narcissism" is important (*Beyond Hegel and Nietzsche*). On Jurist's reading of Hegel, however, what turns out to be crucial about tragedy (and about the relationship between recognition and *anagnôrisis*) is that it teaches us that recognition is a kind of self-knowledge (*Beyond Hegel and Nietzsche*, 77), where self-knowledge includes both the "narcissistic" knowledge of oneself as self-identical, and the knowledge of oneself as related to others. But because Jurist equates narcissism with a certain kind of individualism, he then claims that the challenge of recognition is just the familiar challenge of integrating individuality with community: "Mutual recognition occurs between consciousnesses who regard each other as free and equal. This provides a path for the individual to belong to society, where a strong bond is affirmed yet individuality is not obliterated" (*Beyond Hegel and Nietzsche*, 190). On my reading, by contrast, tragedy points to a different axis of tension: not the tension between oneself as an individual and oneself as belonging to a larger community, but a cross-cutting tension between the acknowledgment of the openness and contingency of human interaction on the one hand, and the denial of that openness and contingency on the other hand through the pursuit of recognition—either of oneself *qua* individual or of oneself *qua* community member, or both.

10. On similar divisions in the context of Hegel's engagement with tragedy, see Dennis Schmidt, *On Germans and Other Greeks*, chap. 3; de Beistegui, "Hegel: or the tragedy of thinking"; Menke, *Tragödie im Sittlichen*, e.g., 23–25. For a reading that casts Hegel more straightforwardly in opposition to Sophocles, see Connolly, *Political Theory and Modernity*, chap. 4 and 185–89.

11. On the tragic structure of Hegel's phenomenological exposure of various "crises" of spirit, see Dennis Schmidt, *On Germans and Other Greeks*, 90, and especially Menke, *Tragödie im Sittlichen*, although I think Menke's emphasis on "necessity" in his account of the tragic risks overlooking the significance of the contingency of the future (and its denial) in tragedy.

12. See Hegel's characterization of this triad in *Philosophy of Right*, sec. 33. Unless otherwise noted, quotations from this text are drawn from Nisbet's translation, *Elements of Hegel's Philosophy of Right*.

13. One of the best reconstructions of this voice, which makes it seem far less threatening than familiar caricatures of Hegel as a proto-totalitarian, is Michael Hardimon's *Hegel's Social Philosophy*.

14. On the relation between these two parts of the *Philosophy of Right*, see Robert Williams, *Hegel's Ethics of Recognition*, 112–22, responding to Ilting, "The Structure of Hegel's *Philosophy of Right*."

15. Robert Williams notes the belatedness of recognition in tragedy (*Recognition*, 204) but suggests that belatedness is merely the symptom of an incompletely developed form of *Sittlichkeit*, rather than a general feature of recognition (reflecting a general condition of human action). This does not mean that every social interaction is bound to lead to irreconcilable conflict and catastrophic reversal à la *Antigone*, but it is acknowledgment, not recognition, that is most likely to forestall that result. In the *Antigone*, as I have suggested, it is Antigone's and Creon's pursuit of recognition that blinds them to the impropriety of action; and this failure of acknowledgment magnifies the consequences of action's impropriety, which is most shattering and catastrophic for precisely those actors who are most deeply invested in the project of becoming sovereign.

16. Speight refers to this as the "retrospectivity" of agency in Hegel (*Hegel, Literature, and the Problem of Agency*, chap. 2 and *passim*).

17. See, e.g., Pinkard, *Hegel's Phenomenology*, 339–43; Neuhouser, *Foundations of Hegel's Social Theory*, 274; something of the same idea also seems to be suggested by Pippin, *Modernism as a Philosophical Problem*, 166. These moves with respect to Hegel echo Tully's move with respect to the contemporary politics of recognition; see his "Struggles over Recognition and Distribution," my "The Recognition of Politics," and my discussion in chap. 1 above.

18. Hegel, *Philosophy of Right*, 23; Sophocles, *Antigone*, 1348–53; Pinkard invokes the preface in support of his open-ended reading of Hegel in *Hegel's Phenomenology*, 339.

19. For another more radical reading of the implications of the ending of the preface, see Pippin, "Hegel and Institutional Rationality," 17ff.

20. Winckelmann, "Thoughts on the Imitation of the Painting and Sculpture of the Greeks," 42.

21. On Hegel's *Gymnasium* activities and interests see H. S. Harris, *Hegel's Development*, vol. 1, chap. 1. For more extensive (and comprehensive) treatments of the theme of tragedy in Hegel, see the sources in notes 9–10 as well as Finlayson, "Conflict and Reconciliation in Hegel's Theory of the Tragic"; Gellrich, *Tragedy and Theory*; Menke, *Tragödie im Sittlichen*; Pöggeler, "Hegel und die griechische Tragödie"; Speight, *Hegel, Literature, and the Problem of Agency*.

22. Hegel, *Aesthetics*, 2:1218. For examples of the early allusions to the *Oresteia*, see "Spirit of Christianity," 224–30; "Natural Law," 151–52.

23. See Pinkard, *Hegel's Phenomenology*, 135; Pippin, "You Can't Get There from Here," 74–75.

24. The classic English-language survey of Hellenophilia in German letters remains E. M. Butler, *The Tyranny of Greece over Germany*. For an example of Hegel's early infatuation with an idealized image of Greece, see "The Tübingen Essay," a 1793 fragment that contrasts the alienating tendency of "positive" religion with the folk religion of ancient Greece; and for different accounts of Hegel's gradual break with his early Hellenism, see Pöggeler, "Hegel und die griechische Tragödie"; and Shklar, "Hegel's 'Phenomenology.'"

25. E.g., Steiner, *Antigones*, 43–51; Hester, "Sophocles the Unphilosophical," 14ff.

26. Patricia Mills, *Woman, Nature, and Psyche*, 35; see also the slightly different version of this discussion of the *Antigone* in the anthology edited by Mills, *Feminist Interpretations of G. W. F. Hegel*.

27. Characterizations of its genre have varied. On the *Phenomenology* as epic, see Shklar, *Freedom and Independence*, 7; as tragedy, see Shklar, *Freedom and Independence*, 10; as comedy, Rose, *Mourning Becomes the Law*, 72–76, and Judith Butler, "Commentary on Joseph Flay," 174–78; as *Bildungsroman*, Judith Butler, *Subjects of Desire*, 17.

28. One of the most significant examples of this inattentiveness to the internal structure of Hegel's text is the characterization of his famous passage about the "intuitiveness" and "unconsciousness" of the sister's devotion to the law of the family (274) *as a description of Antigone*. Thus Patricia Mills, for instance, criticizes Hegel for *overlooking* the fact that Antigone's deed is the result of a conscious choice and not an unconscious intuition (*Woman, Nature, and Psyche*, 32; see also the similar moves in Chanter's reading of Hegel and Irigaray in *The Ethics of Eros*, 80–126). But the relevant passage occurs in the first section of Hegel's reading, *before* particular individuals and their deeds—Antigone and Creon—come on the scene.

29. I hardly mean to defend every component of Hegel's account of Greek *Sittlichkeit* as an accurate statement, either textually or historically, of the background to the *Antigone*. For instance, Hegel's reconstruction of the priority of the relation of sister to brother at 274–75 still seems tendentious, and probably reflects a modern idealization of sorority more than anything else (on this see Steiner, *Antigones*, 12–15).

30. I have changed Miller's translation from "his own authority" to "its own authority"; there is no warrant for the masculine pronoun in the text, which simply refers to "das innerliche Fürsichsein," and which occurs more broadly in the context of a discussion of "das sittliche Bewußtsein."

31. Robert Williams, *Recognition*, 203. This reading also fits most easily with Williams's and others' broader effort to draw out an ideal of successful recognition from Hegel: if the trouble with the *Antigone* is simply that Antigone and Creon have incomplete understandings of the whole (perhaps because the whole itself is as yet incompletely developed or internally articulated), this leaves open the prospect that we might come to identify ourselves in more complete and satisfactory ways as parts of a (more fully developed) totality, overcoming the tragic "contradiction between the known and the unknown" manifest in Antigone's and Creon's acts.

32. This account of action echoes Hegel's earlier discussion, in "The Spirit of Christianity," of the role of the deed in Aeschylus's *Oresteia*: "It is the deed itself which has created a law whose domination now comes on the scene" (230).

33. For important discussions of the retrospectivity of agency and the exposure of action to unintended consequences in Hegel, see Speight, *Hegel, Literature, and the Problem of Agency*, chap. 2; and Gauthier, *Hegel and Feminist Social Criticism*, chap. 1.

34. Speight, *Hegel, Literature, and the Problem of Agency*, 47–48; see also McCumber's account of the importance of the future in "Dialectical Identity."

35. Hyppolite, *Genesis and Structure of Hegel's Phenomenology of Spirit*, 339, hints at this sort of parallel between Hegel's treatment of tragedy and his treatment of sense-certainty by citing the following passage from the *Philosophy of History* as a gloss on Hegel's characterization of Greek ethical life as "immediate": "[The Greeks] did not know the abstraction of a state, which our understanding considers essential; their goal was the vital native land, this Athens, this Sparta, these temples, these altars, this manner of living together, this milieu of citizens, these mores, these habits." The passage, in a different translation, can be found in Hegel, *Philosophy of History*, 253; Hyppolite does not comment on the indexicals.

36. Cf. Arendt, commenting on Koyré's reading of Hegel: "His central thesis is that Hegel's 'greatest originality' resides in his 'insistence on the future, the primacy ascribed to the future over the past.' We would not find this surprising if it were not said about Hegel" (*Willing*, 40).

37. I owe this observation to Seyla Benhabib.

38. On the structure of the *Phenomenology* and especially on the significance of the problematic chapter on "Reason," see Pippin, "You Can't Get There from Here"; Pinkard, *Hegel's Phenomenology*, 79–81.

39. Pinkard, *Hegel's Phenomenology*, 113–19. Curiously, given his interest in authenticity, Taylor does not discuss this portion of the *Phenomenology* in his survey of that book in *Hegel*: the place for such a discussion would be at 168, but Taylor jumps ahead into a discussion of the final form of individuality in the chapter ("reason as testing laws," or, roughly, Kantian practical reason).

40. Hegel, *Phenomenology of Spirit*, 240 (par. 401): "The individual who is going to act seems, therefore, to find himself in a circle in which each moment already presupposes the other, and thus he seems unable to find a beginning, because he only gets to know his original nature, which must be his End, *from the deed*, while, in order to act, he must have that End beforehand." Hegel adds, hilariously: "But for that very reason he has to start immediately."

41. On this see Pinkard, *Hegel's Phenomenology*, 118; Pippin, "You Can't Get There from Here," 75, although Pippin does not specifically focus on plurality as a source of the phenomenon of unintended results and consequences.

42. See here the reconstructions of Hyppolite, *Genesis and Structure of Hegel's Phenomenology of Spirit*, 156–62, and Pinkard, *Hegel's Phenomenology*, 50.

43. Kojève, *Introduction to the Reading of Hegel*, 4.

44. My reconstruction of this sentence follows the excellent account of Pinkard, *Hegel's Phenomenology*, 52–53.

45. Pinkard, *Hegel's Phenomenology*, 52 (emphasis added). Pinkard's use of the term "abdication" is extremely helpful and I have used it throughout this section; but see n. 53 below.

46. Hegel, *Phenomenology of Spirit*, 110 (par. 175).

47. For the sake of consistency, I have altered Miller's translation from "lord" and "bondsman" to "master" and "slave" here and in subsequent quotations. Some critics have argued that this latter translation of *Herr* and *Knecht* leads to

interpretive errors by "replac[ing] the feudal terms of Hegel's analysis (to which the English 'serfdom' is appropriate) with a notion of slavery resonant with both the world of ancient Greece and the heritage of European colonialism" (Osborne, *The Politics of Time*, 72; cf. Rockmore, *Cognition*, 66), but for compelling recent arguments tying Hegel's text rather directly to Aristotle's treatment of slavery in the *Politics* and to modern colonial slavery, see, respectively, Bull, "Slavery and the Multiple Self, esp. 103ff., and Buck-Morss, "Hegel and Haiti."

48. Because the German word for self-consciousness (*Selbstbewußtsein*) is neuter while *Herr* and *Knecht* are gendered masculine, Miller's English translation of the *Phenomenology* refers to master and slave as "he" but to self-consciousness as "it." I have followed this convention in this chapter for the purpose of maintaining consistency between my text and the material I quote.

49. Taylor, *Hegel*, 154 (and see also Taylor's more recent gloss on Hegel in "The Politics of Recognition," 50); McCumber, *Poetic Interaction*, 40. Similar glosses of Hegel's point can be found in, *inter alia*, Kain, "Self-Consciousness, the Other, and Hegel's Dialectic of Recognition," 111–12; Smith, *Hegel's Critique of Liberalism*, 118–19; Franco, *Hegel's Philosophy of Freedom*, 90; Patten, *Hegel's Idea of Freedom*, 127–28; Fukuyama, *The End of History and the Last Man*, 194.

50. In this vision of equality, *everyone* gets to occupy the position of "master"—it is, as Michael Walzer has noted, a vision of a "society of misters," where "mister," an alteration of "master," serves the universalized form of what had previously been a title of differential honor. See Walzer, *Spheres of Justice*, 251–52.

51. That indeterminacy is, of course, why surrender, especially unconditional surrender, is risky—a risk that historical practices of "surrender" often seek to mitigate by converting the moment of surrender into a moment of recognition, in which the cessation of hostilities leads directly into the assumption of a new set of agreed-upon social roles. On the meaning of surrender and its relationship to recognition see Wagner-Pacifici, "Prolegomena to a Paradigm."

52. Because these phrases occur after Hegel has made his transition from the struggle to the master-slave relation, it is often assumed that they refer *only* to the psychological experience of the slave in that concrete social form; but it's impossible to make sense of Hegel's account of one self-consciousness's motivation to surrender without taking them to refer back to the scene of struggle as well, as Hegel seems to do at 115 (par. 189). On this dual meaning, see Jurist, *Beyond Hegel and Nietzsche*, 162; Robert Williams is also good on this point: *Hegel's Ethics of Recognition*, 61–62.

53. The literature is generally unclear on the character of this act of submission. Kojève, for example, sometimes does stress the character of the slave's "fear of death" as a confrontation of his own finitude (*Introduction to the Reading of Hegel*, 47–48), but at other times Kojève perpetuates the view of the slave's "recognition" as primarily other directed and only secondarily a matter of self-knowledge (8). Hyppolite describes the slave's consciousness as involving "recognition of his own dependence," but seems to regard this as a feature of the slave's experience only *after* his submission (*Genesis and Structure of Hegel's Phenomenology of Spirit*, 175) as does Connolly in *Political Theory and Moder-*

nity (95). Others describe the act of submission in ways wholly opposed to my reading. Pinkard, despite his helpful use of the term "abdication," glosses this abdication as one self-consciousness "accept[ing] the other's point of view as the truth" (*Hegel's Phenomenology*, 59), which obscures the self-regarding moment of the act; and Dallmayr says that "the stronger party subdues the weaker party and forces the latter to labor as a slave"—probably a more accurate historical account of the genesis of slavery, but not faithful to Hegel's text (*G. W. F. Hegel*, 67). The author who most strongly emphasizes the self-regarding character of recognition in Hegel is Jurist (in *Beyond Hegel and Nietzsche* and "Hegel's Concept of Recognition"), but he tends to gloss the "self-knowledge" involved in recognition as the knowledge of oneself as the bearer of a certain identity, rather than as the knowledge of one's own ontological condition of finitude, which is a different matter. Finally, this act of abdication is similar in certain respects to what Robert Williams, following Ludwig Siep, identifies as one of the four aspects of Hegelian recognition: *Freigabe*, or "release," in which one "allow[s] the other to go free," renouncing attempts to dominate or control the other (*Hegel's Ethics of Recognition*, 84; cf. 21 and *Recognitions*, 155). But Williams's conception of *Freigabe* is not clearly identified as a renunciation of the desire to find confirmation of one's independence, and perhaps for this reason, Williams underestimates the tension between recognition as *Freigabe* and recognition as the achievement of satisfaction through union with others in a larger whole, which (as I am arguing) is the continuation by other means of the very desire that is supposed to be *renounced* in *Freigabe*. Indeed, Williams sometimes lets the self-regarding, abdicative character of *Freigabe* slip away, glossing it as the affirmation or recognition of others in their difference (*Hegel's Ethics of Recognition*, 84, 333). But as we shall see in the next chapter, *that* posture can be as problematically oriented toward sovereignty, and hence also as dominative, as the simpler attempt to eliminate otherness through assimilation.

54. This paragraph has been prompted in part by the comments of an anonymous reader for Princeton University Press, and in thinking through the point I have been aided by Stephen White's treatment of finitude as death in *Sustaining Affirmation*, 132–36 (discussing Taylor's critique of Connolly) as well as by Villa's account of the divergence between Arendt and Heidegger around the relative importance of mortality among the various aspects of the human condition (*Arendt and Heidegger*, chap. 4, esp. 141).

55. The terminology is drawn from the famous treatment of "death [as] Dasein's *ownmost* possibility" in Heidegger, *Being and Time*, 304–11. On the influence of Hegel on this strand of twentieth-century thought (via Kojève) see Roth, *Knowing and History*, esp. chap. 5; on Heidegger's reading of Hegel around this theme see Taminiaux, *Heidegger and the Problem of Fundamental Ontology*, chap. 4 and 202–6.

56. Arendt, *The Human Condition*, 193–94.

57. Stephen White, *Sustaining Affirmation*, 135. I agree with White that the idea of mortality is not necessarily tied to this sovereign posture—and I certainly agree that this posture is not Connolly's—but unlike White, I think this suggests that we should not equate finitude with mortality, for our responses to the

condition of mortality may be inflected in importantly different ways depending upon what else we include (or fail to include) in our figurations of human finitude.

58. For a related account of how plurality inflects mortality see Villa, *Arendt and Heidegger*, 141.

59. On the relationship between Hegelian recognition and tragic *anagnôrisis*, see Jurist, "Hegel's Concept of Recognition," but also n. 9 above.

60. Allusions to Hegel's story can, for example, be discerned in the work of W. E. B. Du Bois as early as his Harvard commencement address, "Jefferson Davis as a Representative of Civilization," and more famously in *The Souls of Black Folk*; on Du Bois and Hegel see Zamir, *Dark Voices*; Gooding-Williams, "Philosophy of History and Social Critique in *The Souls of Black Folk*" and "Race, Multiculturalism, and Democracy"; and Bull, "Slavery and the Multiple Self." Other important treatments of modern (and, sometimes, ancient) slavery, colonialism, and their legacies that either explicitly discuss or echo Hegel include Fanon, *Black Skin, White Masks*; Patterson, *Slavery and Social Death*, esp. 97–101; Genovese, *Roll, Jordan, Roll*; Davis, *The Problem of Slavery in the Age of Revolution*, 557–64; Binder, "Mastery, Slavery, and Emancipation" (together with responses in the same issue by Kendall Thomas and Jonathan Bush); Buck-Morss, "Hegel and Haiti." Among the crucial texts for the Marxist reading of the episode are Kojève, *Introduction to the Reading of Hegel*; Lukàcs, *The Young Hegel*; and Marcuse, *Reason and Revolution*. For some feminist uses (and refusals) of the story, see Beauvoir, *The Second Sex*, e.g. 64–65; Benjamin, *The Bonds of Love*, chap. 2; Gauthier, *Hegel and Feminist Social Criticism*; Patricia Mills, *Woman, Nature, and Psyche*; "Hegel and the 'Woman Question'"; and many of the essays in Patricia Mills, ed., *Feminist Interpretations of G. W. F. Hegel*.

61. "As a universal form of the World-Spirit, Stoicism could only appear on the scene in a time of universal fear and bondage." (121).

62. Marx, *Capital*, 1:198 (emphasis added).

63. This results in the exclusion of one commodity from the "ranks" or "world" of commodities, a kind of denial of the status of "citizen of that world" that Marx attributes to other commodities (*Capital*, 159–62; 155).

64. Cf. Zerilli, *Signifying Woman*, which traces the role that the figure of the "disorderly woman" plays in the management of the experience of anxiety or chaos in the work of Rousseau, Burke, and Mill.

65. I have altered Miller's translation of "die ewige Ironie des Gemeinwesens" here and elsewhere to accord with common usage (Miller has "the everlasting irony [in the life] of the community").

66. For other readings that find the potential for (different) feminist critiques in these passages, see Irigaray, "The Eternal Irony of the Community"; Ravven, "Has Hegel Anything to Say to Feminists."

67. Hegel, *Philosophy of Right*, secs. 165–66.

68. Ibid., sec. 166 (addition). The "additions" to the text are drawn from two sets of students' lecture notes.

69. Robert Williams, for example, says that there is "no reason in principle why [woman] may not have a public vocation, even if Hegel seems to confine

her ethical substantiality to the family in the *Philosophy of Right*" (*Hegel's Ethics of Recognition*, 225); similarly, Ravven asserts that "nothing in the Hegelian philosophic approach would seem to necessitate this extraordinary lapse in the empathic understanding of women" ("Has Hegel Anything to Say to Feminists," 239). Neuhouser and Franco confront the issue at somewhat greater length, acknowledging that (as Neuhouser says) to reject Hegel's view of gender difference "is to deny a nontrivial element of Hegel's account" (Neuhouser, *Foundations of Hegel's Social Theory*, 275; cf. Franco, *Hegel's Philosophy of Freedom*, 244–47), but concluding that all of the ethically important functions Hegel assigns to the family can be performed without endorsing sexual inequality. Neuhouser and Franco's arguments are persuasive enough, but as I shall try to show, Hegel's ideology of sexual inequality is tied to the rest of his political thought in other ways as well: in particular, by the ways in which that ideology serves as the condition of the possibility of a satisfying regime of recognition among the (male) participants in the Hegelian public sphere.

70. Patricia Mills arrives at similar conclusions by a different route (and, in particular, one that takes the reading of the *Antigone* in the *Phenomenology* to be continuous with the treatment in the *Philosophy of Right*); see "Hegel's *Antigone*."

71. For an exception, see Judith Butler's subtle reading of this last part of Hegel's account in *Antigone's Claim*, 36.

72. See Patricia Mills, "Hegel's *Antigone*," 77.

73. Interestingly, in a portion of the 1805–1806 Jena *Philosophy of Spirit* on the concept of the will, Hegel distinguishes between the will as power and drive, and the will as the guiding and manipulation of a power located elsewhere: in this latter mode, called "cunning," Hegel said, "the will becomes feminine" (*Hegel and the Human Spirit*, 104). He adds that one crucial mode of operation of "cunning" is to "watc[h] something accomplish its own destruction by its own efforts," or to "compel others to be what they are," revealing themselves in their contradictions, which can often take place through "silence," the "worst, vilest cunning" (104). Fascinatingly, this mode of operation is also precisely the one Hegel ascribes to phenomenology, in opposition to "dogmatism," in the Preface to the *Phenomenology*: Hegel's sort of science is "the cunning which, while seeming to abstain from activity, looks on and watches how determinateness, with its concrete life, just where it fancies it is pursuing its own self-preservation and particular interest, is in fact doing the very opposite" (33). The tacit gendering of the activity of philosophy in Hegel's work deserves further investigation.

74. Detienne and Vernant, *Cunning Intelligence and Greek Culture and Society*, 321 n. 78; cf. 13.

75. This possibility is especially plausible given that, in the pages leading up to his discussion of "womankind," Hegel has been as much concerned with the background conflict between Polyneices and Eteocles as with the action of the *Antigone* itself: there is no reason to assume that he confined his references to only one of the available textual sources that dealt with the story in question.

76. As Hegel says in the remarks to *Philosophy of Right*, sec. 261, "particular interests should certainly not be set aside, let alone suppressed; on the contrary,

they should be harmonized with the universal, so that both they themselves and the universal are preserved."

77. For the former function, see *Philosophy of Right*, sec. 290 (addition); for the latter, see secs. 255 (addition).

78. For the former function, see *Philosophy of Right*, sec. 301 (remark); for the latter, see sec. 315 (and addition).

79. Marx, "Critique of Hegel's Doctrine of the State," 152. See also the subtle and detailed reconstruction of Cohen and Arato in *Civil Society and Political Theory*, chap. 2.

80. Hegel, *Philosophy of Right*, sec. 166 (addition). I have combined elements of Knox's and Nisbet's translations here, for while Nisbet's is generally more literal, I think Knox's "who knows how?" better captures Hegel's meaning than Nisbet's "imperceptibly." The original reads: "Die Bildung der Frauen geschieht, man weiß nicht wie, gleichsam durch die Atmosphäre der Vorstellung, mehr durch das Leben also durch das Erwerben von Kenntnissen."

81. Hegel, *Philosophy of Right*, secs. 314, 315.

82. Robert Williams, *Hegel's Ethics of Recognition*, 27; Honneth, *The Struggle for Recognition*, 62.

83. For a similar sort of response to Williams see Jurist, *Beyond Hegel and Nietzsche*, 188.

84. Robert Williams, *Recognition*, 170; *Hegel's Ethics of Recognition*, 10. In his first book, Williams referred to this as the distinction between Hegel's "eidetics" and "empirics" of intersubjectivity (*Recognition*, 15–16); in his more recent work he also calls this the distinction between the "ontological" and "ontic" levels of analysis (*Hegel's Ethics of Recognition*, 373).

85. Robert Williams, *Hegel's Ethics of Recognition*, 11. Williams *does* say that "despite Hegel's affirmation of reciprocal recognition, recognition retains negative aspects" (3). As his reconstruction of Hegel's *Philosophy of Right* proceeds, however, it becomes clear that Williams does not regard these "negative aspects" as part of the ontological structure of recognition *as such*; rather, he compartmentalizes them, attributing them only to *some* concrete forms of recognition (such as master and slave, or the "system of needs" in civil society), and not others (such as love or the state).

86. Indeed, if anything, Williams himself inadvertently performs the same reductionism he criticizes in Sartre and Kojève, who he says "fai[l] to see that for Hegel recognition has an ontological structure capable of supporting a wider range of instantiations than master/slave, conflict, and domination" (373). But "conflict" and "domination" are not *instantiations* of recognition, they are themselves general structures that can be instantiated in a variety of ways, and so to show (as Williams does) that master-slave is not the only possible instantiation of recognition is not yet to show that any other instantiation of recognition is free of conflict or domination.

87. Robert Williams, *Hegel's Ethics of Recognition*, 376; cf. Honneth, *The Fragmented World of the Social*, 158–67.

88. See Arendt, "Concern With Politics in Recent European Philosophical Thought," 436–40.

89. Honneth, *The Fragmented World of the Social*, 161.

90. Ibid., 165.

91. For readings that defend Hegel against these charges, see, among many others, Robert Williams, *Hegel's Ethics of Recognition*; Gordon, "Hegel and the Politics of Difference"; Neuhouser, *Foundations of Hegel's Social Theory*; Patten, *Hegel's Idea of Freedom*; Jurist, *Beyond Hegel and Nietzsche*; Hardimon, *Hegel's Social Philosophy*.

92. Neuhouser, *Foundations of Hegel's Social Theory*, 15.

93. Robert Williams, *Hegel's Ethics of Recognition*, 327ff.; cf. Hardimon, *Hegel's Social Philosophy*, 39–41 (on "otherness").

94. Robert Williams, *Hegel's Ethics of Recognition*, 219–26 and 380–89.

95. For a good statement of the importance of the mediation of social institutions in the achievement of successful relations of recognition, see Patten, *Hegel's Idea of Freedom*, 129–35.

CHAPTER FIVE
DOUBLE BINDS

1. Hegel, *Philosophy of Right*, sec. 270 (note). Unless otherwise noted, quotations from this text are taken from Nisbet's translation, *Elements of Hegel's Philosophy of Right*.

2. See for example Tunick, "Hegel on Political Identity and the Ties that Bind"; Robert Williams, *Hegel's Ethics of Recognition*, 327ff. (discussed in more detail below); for an earlier defense of Hegel on the subject of pluralism see Avineri, *Hegel's Theory of the Modern State*, 167–75.

3. This sense of otherness was more prominent in Williams's first book, *Recognition: Fichte and Hegel on the Other*, where his central target seemed to be a reading of Hegel as a hard-core metaphysical idealist for whom all otherness is to be understood *ontologically* as an effect of a self-positing, self-developing ego.

4. Robert Williams, *Hegel's Ethics of Recognition*, 327, 333.

5. Ibid., 333.

6. Despite their differences, Hegel's "struggle for recognition" closely resembles Hobbes's "time of war, where every man is enemy to every man" (*Leviathan*, chap. 13); likewise, the idea of a state mediating among equally dependent self-consciousnesses brings to mind the covenant of mutual submission to a sovereign that founds Hobbes's commonwealth (chap. 17). Yet Hegel also charged that contractarian theory remained unable to overcome the domination that marked the relationship between master and slave; instead, he claimed, it merely displaced the locus of domination from relations among individuals to the relation between the individual and the state, which always remained "external" and therefore basically coercive. ("On the Scientific Ways of Treating Natural Law," 112–14.) On Hegel and Hobbes, see Strauss, *The Political Philosophy of Hobbes*, 57–58; Siep, "Hegels Auseinandersetzung mit Hobbes in den Jenaer Schriften," of which a selection has been translated as Siep, "The Struggle for Recognition"; and Honneth, *The Struggle for Recognition*, chaps. 1–3.

7. Hegel, *Philosophy of Mind*, 172 (*Zusatz* to sec. 432, emphasis added).

8. Duquette, "The Political Significance of Hegel's Concept of Recognition in the *Phenomenology*," 48; see also Patten, *Hegel's Idea of Freedom*, 129–35; Robert Williams, *Hegel's Ethics of Recognition*, chaps. 12–13.

9. See, e.g., Taylor, "Democratic Exclusion."

10. Marx, "Critique of Hegel's Doctrine of the State," 141.

11. Robert Williams, *Hegel's Ethics of Recognition*, 332 n. 130.

12. Marx, "On the Jewish Question," esp. 30–33.

13. Brown, *States of Injury*, ix, 28; for the explicit use of Marx see chap. 5, esp. 109–14. See also her "Rights and Identity in Late Modernity"; "Revaluing Critique"; "Suffering Rights as Paradoxes"; and *Politics Out of History*, esp. chap. 2.

14. Brown, *States of Injury*, 100–103.

15. For a good account see Carlebach, *Karl Marx and the Radical Critique of Judaism*, 65–69 (on the policy proposal); 82–85 (on Hermes); 125–47 (on Bauer's essay).

16. This is Marx's reading of Bauer in "On the Jewish Question," 29. Although he defended what Marx would call "merely" political emancipation, Bauer did not claim that religion should be left alone to thrive in the private sphere. Rather, he thought that the political deinstitutionalization of orthodox Christianity would hasten the progressive self-transformation of Christianity into universal philosophical *Wissenschaft*—i.e., the self-abolition of religion as it has conventionally been understood. On Bauer's theological views see Toews, *Hegelianism*, chap. 9.

17. Marx, "On the Jewish Question," 31.

18. The quoted passages are in ibid., 31; on religion and alienation see 32 ("Religion is simply the recognition of man in a roundabout fashion; that is, through an intermediary. . . . Christ is the intermediary to whom man attributes all his own divinity and all his religious *bonds*.") and cf. Feuerbach, "The Essence of Christianity," 153–55.

19. Marx, "On the Jewish Question," 33.

20. Brown, "Revaluing Critique," 475; cf. *States of Injury*, 56; "Rights and Identity in Late Modernity," 97–101.

21. Marx, "On the Jewish Question," 33.

22. Brown, *States of Injury*, 109, 114; cf. "Revaluing Critique," 473.

23. Marx, "Critique of Hegel's Doctrine of the State," 137. Two Marxian scholars who have recently, in different ways, drawn out this strand of Marx's thinking about the state-civil society relationship are Paul Thomas, *Alien Politics*; and Neocleous, *Administering Civil Society*.

24. Marx, "On the Jewish Question," 45.

25. Here I depart slightly from Paul Thomas's *Alien Politics*, which treats the "Critique" of Hegel and "On the Jewish Question" together as the sources of an undogmatic alternative to the reductionist view of the state articulated by Marx between 1846 and 1850, which subsequently (and unfortunately) became hegemonic within Marxist theory. Without denying what Thomas persuasively shows—that "On the Jewish Question" begins to articulate a powerful alternative to the ruling-class theory of the state—I do *also* find important and consequential premonitions of Marx's later reductionism in the same essay.

26. Marx, "On the Jewish Question," 46.

27. Ibid., 33, 45. Indeed, Marx's verb for "restrain" here is *fesseln*, which should immediately recall the "fetters," *Fesseln*, of the 1859 "Preface" to the *Contribution to the Critique of Political Economy*, 21.

28. Marx, "On the Jewish Question," 52. Brown does not follow Marx down this path; see e.g., *States of Injury*, 103 n. 13.

29. These terms are from Brown, "Revaluing Critique," 473 and 475; and *States of Injury*, 109. Brown acknowledges that states *do* intervene in this way, especially as loci of disciplinary power (see e.g., *States of Injury*, 17, 58) but she does not suggest that this behavior is tied to the state's legitimacy needs. As I have suggested in chap. 1, I suspect that this has as much to do with her insistence on separating the state from the notion of sovereignty as with the influence of Marx.

30. "In achieving what Marx refers to as their political abolition, the social power of these elements [such as race or gender] is removed from political view and from political redress" (Brown, "Revaluing Critique," 475).

31. "Schreiben der Juden-Gemeinde zu Königsberg in Preußen an den König," November 25, 1808, in Freund, *Emanzipation der Juden in Preußen*, 2:401–2.

32. Though the movement that began in 1781 is commonly called a movement for "emancipation," Katz shows that the term itself was not commonly used in discussions of the status of European Jews until 1828 (its first appearance being in the German form *Emanzipierung* in 1816); the term seems to have been transplanted from English debates about the removal of restrictions against officeholding by Catholics. Katz, "The Term 'Jewish Emancipation,'" 114–17.

33. Dohm, *Über die bürgerliche Verbesserung der Juden*. For the general course of emancipation, see Meyer, *German-Jewish History in Modern Times*, vol. 2; Vital, *A People Apart*; Rürup, "Jewish Emancipation and Bourgeois Society"; Sorkin, *The Transformation of German Jewry*, chap. 1; Mosse, "From 'Schutzjuden' to 'Deutsche Staatsbürger jüdischen Glaubens.'"

34. Quoted in Sheehan, *German History, 1770–1866*, 51.

35. On the course of revolutionary emancipation see the last chapter of Hertzberg, *The French Enlightenment and the Jews*; Birnbaum, "Between Social and Political Assimilation."

36. See Rürup, "Jewish Emancipation and Bourgeois Society," 74–75; Sorkin, *The Transformation of Germany Jewry*, 28–29; On the intellectual influence of the principles of the Revolution on German reformers see chap. 6 of Sheehan, *German History*.

37. "Edikt betreffend die bürgerlichen Verhältnisse der Juden in dem Preußischen Staate," March 11, 1812, in Huber, *Dokumente zur deutschen Verfassungsgeschichte*, 1:45–47 (hereafter "Edikt").

38. Ibid., 45–47.

39. On the Jewish response to the edict, see Fischer, *Judentum, Staat und Heer in Preußen im frühen 19. Jahrhundert*, 26–29. Surviving evidence of contemporary reaction represents educated opinion in the larger, urban Jewish communities, which had led the movement for emancipation (and for assimilation); on the elite bias of much surviving documentary evidence, see the "Introduction" to Lowenstein, *The Mechanics of Change*.

40. "Schreiben der Aeltesten der Berliner Judenschaft an Hardenberg," March 12, 1812, in Freund, *Emanzipation der Juden in Preußen*, 2:451–52.

41. Quoted in Brann, *Schlesiche Judenheit* , 18.

42. Sorkin, *The Transformation of German Jewry*, 110.

43. Rürup, "The Tortuous and Thorny Path to Legal Equality," 15.

44. The Edict of 1812 had important implications not only for Prussian Jews, but for all Prussians, for it was one of a series of proclamations, beginning no later than the promulgation of the *Allgemeines Landrecht* of 1794, that helped to consolidate the territorial integrity and sovereignty of the Prussian state as well as the collective identity of its citizens. Before the Edict of 1812 *no* subjects of the Prussian king had the legal status of citizens of the state (*Staatsbürger*); their privileges and responsibilities to the state were mediated wholly through citizenship in municipalities or provinces or through membership in the traditional *Stände*—the "estates" or "corporations," which included the nobility and peasantry as well as guilds and professional organizations. Ironically, though their hold on their new status was precarious, Jews became citizens while their fellow Germans remained, for the moment, subjects. On the *Allgemeines Landrecht* see Brubaker, *Citizenship and Nationhood in France and Germany*, 57ff.; Koselleck, *Preußen Zwischen Reform und Revolution*, chap. 1. On the comparative status of Jewish and non-Jewish Germans, see Mosse, "From 'Schutzjuden' to 'Deutsche Staatsbürger jüdischen Glaubens,'" 93. Brubaker dates the statewide codification of citizenship to the 1842 "Law on the acquisition and loss of the quality of a Prussian subject," but even this requires qualification, for while the 1842 law does nationalize *membership* in the Prussian state—*Staatsangehörigkeit*—it does not employ the concept of state citizenship (*Staatsbürgerschaft*), but refers to Prussians instead as subjects (*Untertanen*) ("Gesetz über die Erwerbung und den Verlust der Eigenschaft als preußischer Unteran sowie über den Eintritt in fremde Staatsdienste," December 31, 1842, in Lichter, *Die Staatsangehörigkeit nach deutschem und ausländischem Recht*, 521–24).

45. Baron, "Newer Approaches to Jewish Emancipation," 57.

46. Dohm, *Über die bürgerliche Verbesserung der Juden*, 35.

47. Sorkin, *The Transformation of German Jewry*, 23–28, gives a relatively detailed summary of Dohm's argument.

48. Ibid., 28, discusses two typical anti-Jewish responses to Dohm.

49. Sorkin, *The Transformation of German Jewry*, 91.

50. Quoted in Aschheim, *Brothers and Strangers*, 12.

51. Rürup, "The Tortuous and Thorny Path to Legal Equality," 7.

52. Jacob Katz has traced this expression and its variants back to discussions of the religious liberties of the Huguenots in seventeenth-century France after the Edict of Nantes, and also discusses its subsequent application to Jesuits and Freemasons. See "A State Within a State," 124–153.

53. Dohm, *Über die bürgerliche Verbesserung der Juden*, 26.

54. Ibid., 28.

55. See Katz's discussion of an anonymous pamphlet entitled *Verhältnis der Juden und der Christen* in "A State within a State," 145–46.

56. "Immediatvorlage Schroetters an den König," November 20, 1808, in Freund, *Emanzipation der Juden in Preußen*, 2:209.

57. Ibid., 209.

58. The quotation (given more fully in the epigraph to this chapter) comes from Kriminalrat F. Brand; reported in Jolowicz, *Geschichte der Juden in Königsberg in Preußen*, 119. Freund (*Emanzipation der Juden in Preußen*, 1:126ff.) doubts Brand's account of the preparation of the first draft of the emancipation edict, but Brann points out that the inconsistencies Freund finds in Brand's recollections do not directly cast doubt on the substance of the anecdote about his conversation with Schrötter. Brann, *Die schlesische Judenheit*, 16.

59. See "Edikt," sec. 6, which states that "Jews who violate the instructions in § 2 and 3 shall be regarded and treated as foreign Jews [*fremde Juden*]." On the precise legal relation between these conditions and the status of citizenship, see Rönne and Simon, *Früheren und gegenwärtigen Verhältnisse der Juden*, 274 n. 1.

60. "Edikt," secs. 2–3. On the permanent surname as a technique through which the state seeks to render its population "legible," see Scott, Tehranian, and Mathias, "Production of Legal Identities Proper to States" (discussing Jewish emancipation at 16–17); on the state and naming practices in the same period in France, see Noiriel, "Identification of the Citizen." On naming practices and identity documents as instruments of recognition see Caplan, "'This or That Particular Person.'"

61. See for instance sec. 15 of Brand's draft, "Der Brand'sche Entwurf," in Freund, *Emanzipation der Juden in Preußen*, 2:222.

62. See "Edikt," 45. Similar linguistic transformations took place among Jews. Sorkin notes that the "overwhelming preoccupation to establish that the Jews were no longer a political group can also be seen in the change made in the *Sulamith*'s subtitle in 1810. The journal's original subtitle read, 'A Journal for the Promotion of Culture and Humanity within the Jewish Nation' (*unter der jüdischen Nation*). At the beginning of its third year the last words of the subtitle became 'among the Israelites' (*unter den Israeliten*)" (*The Transformation of German Jewry*, 101). See also H. D. Schmidt, "The Terms of Emancipation, 1781–1812," 31.

63. See Graetz, "From Corporate Community to Ethnic-Religious Minority, 1750–1830," 71; Holeczek, "Judenemanzipation in Preußen," 150. For the provision, see "Edikt," secs. 20–21, 30. Sec. 21 allows unspecified exceptions for cases in private law in which religious practice demands use of a specific legal provision or form, though it does not return authority in such cases to the rabbis.

64. Sorkin, *The Transformation of German Jewry*, 137.

65. Marx, "On the Jewish Question," 32. This should not be taken to mean that the edict *simply* or *unilaterally* transformed a national identity into a religious one; only that it was one important force pressing in that direction.

66. See Rose, "Ahasverus and the Destruction of Judaism," chap. 2 of *German Question/Jewish Question*; Hasan-Rokem and Dundes, eds., *Wandering Jew*.

67. The figure comes from Richarz's introduction to *Jewish Life in Germany*, 3.

68. For instance, a substantial number of Jews migrated into Germany and western Europe from the east during and after the Thirty Years' War. See Shul-

vass, *From East to West*, chaps. 1–2. On local expulsions in the sixteenth and seventeenth centuries, see Sorkin, *The Transformation of German Jewry*, 44.

69. See Arendt, *The Origins of Totalitarianism*, 16–18; Sheehan, *German History*, 33–34.

70. On the history and size of this emigration before 1800, see Shulvass, *From East to West*.

71. "Edikt," secs. 34–35. On patterns of occupation of immigrants, see Shulvass, *From East to West*, passim.

72. See Hardenberg's instructions of June 25, 1812, printed in Rönne and Simon, *Früheren und gegenwärtigen Verhältnisse der Juden*, 267. In the decades following emancipation, the Prussian "Passports and Aliens Police" apparently regarded Jews—whom they took to be essentially itinerant—with great suspicion. See Lüdtke, *Police and State in Prussia, 1815–1850*, 81, 91–92, 110.

73. Quoted in Katz, "A State Within a State," 139–40, quoting Fichte, *Beiträge zur Berichtigung der Urteile des Publikums über die Französische Revolution*, 129–30.

74. Fichte, *Beiträge*, 130 (my translation).

75. Robert Williams, *Hegel's Ethics of Recognition*, 332 n. 130.

76. The section on "objective spirit" from the 1817 Heidelberg *Encyclopaedia* is published in Hegel, *Vorlesungen über Rechtsphilosophie, 1818–1831*; transcripts from the 1817–1818 lectures are published in Hegel, *Vorlesungen über Naturrecht und Staatswissenschaft*; transcripts from the 1818–1819 lectures are published in Hegel, *Vorlesungen über Rechtsphilosophie, 1818–1831*, vol. 1; transcripts from the 1819–1820 lectures are published in Hegel, *Philosophie des Rechts: Die Vorlesung von 1819/20 in einer Nachschrift*.

77. On the 1819 riots, the publication history of Fries's pamphlet, and its readings in beerhouses, see Sterling, "Anti-Jewish Riots in Germany in 1819," esp. 116 n. 44.

78. Yovel, *Dark Riddle*, 45.

79. See the definition given in "The Positivity of the Christian Religion," 71.

80. Hegel, "The Spirit of Christianity," 190–91.

81. Ibid., 199–200.

82. For accounts of these transformations see Steven Smith, "Hegel and the Jewish Question" and *Spinoza, Liberalism, and the Question of Jewish Identity*, 185–96; Emil Fackenheim, *Encounters between Judaism and Modern Philosophy*, chap. 3.

83. Hegel, *Lectures on the Philosophy of Religion*, 2:154. For good accounts of the continuities between Hegel's youthful and mature positions, see Yovel's *Dark Riddle* as well as the earlier article "Hegels Begriff der Religion und die Religion der Erhabenheit."

84. Hegel, "The Spirit of Christianity," 190–91.

85. Hegel, *Phenomenology of Spirit*, 117 (par. 194).

86. Hegel, *Lectures on the Philosophy of Religion*, 2:442.

87. Ibid., 447.

88. Hegel, "The Spirit of Christianity," 192. Derrida discusses this passage in *Glas*, 48–50 (left column).

89. Hegel, *Lectures on the Philosophy of Religion*, 2:156. Emphasis added.

90. Hegel, "The German Constitution," 21.
91. Hegel, *Philosophy of Right*, sec. 278; on the monarch, see secs. 279–82.
92. Hegel, "The German Constitution," 101.
93. Hegel, "The Spirit of Christianity," 182.
94. Ibid., 186.
95. Ibid.
96. Hegel, *Lectures on Natural Right and Political Science*, 298.
97. Ibid., 298.
98. Yovel (*Dark Riddle*, 94) argues that "Hegel draws a line between the patronizing toleration he recommends for the Quakers and the outright equality he demands for the Jews. Toleration for him is an act of grace which depends on the good will and strength of the state suffering the 'anomaly.' When these conditions cease to exist, toleration has no place. But the Jews must be more than tolerated; they should be given equal rights *on principle*, regardless of the circumstances." I dissent from Yovel here for two reasons. First, Hegel's note is constructed in such a way that the case of the Jews (*like* the case of the Quakers) seems to be an *example* of the claim that "only if the state is strong in other respects can it overlook and tolerate such anomalies, relying above all on the power of custom and the inner rationality of its institutions to reduce and overcome the discrepancy if the state does not strictly enforce its rights in this respect," for Hegel then proceeds, without signaling any sort of break, to move directly into a consideration of the case of the Jews; indeed, that consideration begins with the statement that Jewish emancipation is "contrary to formal right," which establishes a continuity with, not a break from, the preceding sentence about the state strictly enforcing its rights. Second, Yovel implies that Hegel's retort that "the Jews are primarily *human beings*" marks an argument from abstract, universal principle; yet as Hegel goes on to indicate, the point of reminding us that the Jews are human beings is to ground what is effectively a psychological argument about the proper strategic approach to assimilation.
99. Hegel, *Philosophy of Right*, sec. 270.
100. Ibid., sec. 270 (note). Thus, while I agree with McCumber's claim in "Dialectical Identity" that Hegel's own thought can be used to criticize "static" models of identity, it seems unwarranted to attribute to Hegel the idea that Jews should be emancipated because, as Jews, they are participants in a historical dynamic of dialectical identity-formation: the footnote on emancipation is, to the contrary, one of the places at which Hegel himself turns away from the most valuable implications of his own thought. See McCumber, "Dialectical Identity."
101. Hegel, *Philosophy of Right* sec. 270 (note); sec. 268.
102. On the controversy see Meyer, "The Religious Reform Controversy in the Berlin Jewish Community, 1814–1823"; Geiger, *Geschichte der Juden in Berlin*, 1:165–68 and especially (for documentary evidence) 2:210–34. The following account relies heavily on Meyer's work in this article and the sources noted in the next note.
103. For this background see Meyer, ed., *German-Jewish History in Modern Times*, vol. 1; Meyer, *Response to Modernity*; Meyer, *German Political Pressure*

and Jewish Religious Response; Sorkin, *The Transformation of German Jewry*; Katz, *Out of the Ghetto*.

104. See the excerpt from Friedländer's reform proposal in Geiger, *Geschichte der Juden in Berlin*, 2:211; and the summary of the proposal in Meyer, *Response to Modernity*, 44–45.

105. The quoted language is from the King's order, reprinted in Geiger, *Geschichte der Juden in Berlin*, 2:219–20; see Meyer, "The Religious Reform Controversy," 141–42.

106. Reprinted in Geiger, *Geschichte der Juden in Berlin*, 2:219–20.

107. Kabinets-Ordre of December 9, 1823, reprinted in Rönne and Simon, *Früheren und Gegenwärtigen Verhältnisse der Juden*, 93; cf. Meyer, "The Religious Reform Controversy," 150.

108. According to Hardenberg's instructions of June 25, 1812 concerning the implementation of the edict, Jews legally resident in Prussia as of March 24, 1812 would receive certificates declaring that "in conformity with section 4 of the decree of 11 March 1812 it is hereby certified that N.N. and his descendents are adopted as Royal Prussian denizens and citizens and everywhere to be respected" (Bering, *The Stigma of Names*, 32, citing Rönne and Simon, *Die früheren und gegenwärtigen Verhältnisse der Juden*, 268).

109. In 1818, for example, the Ministry of the Interior and Police instructed the department of police in Aachen that its jurisdiction included "general security, roads, construction, food and health, markets, weights and measures, trade and industry, passes and aliens, fire regulations together with poor relief, lunatic asylums, censorship, and Jewish matters." See Lüdtke, *Police and State in Prussia*, 42.

110. See Bering, *The Stigma of Names*, 34, quoting Humboldt's opinion on Schrötter's draft of an emancipation edict, July 17, 1809, printed in Freund, *Emanzipation der Juden in Preußen*, 2:275. I have altered the translation of Humboldt.

111. Bering, *The Stigma of Names*, 50. Bering tells the fascinating story of the king's effort to ensure the purity of Christian names in detail in chap. 5.

112. Katz, *Out of the Ghetto*, 86.

113. Quoted in Katz, "A State within a State," 147; emphasis added. See also Aschheim's discussion of various characterizations of the assimilated Jew as deceiver in *Brothers and Strangers*, 63ff.

114. For a non-Hegelian version of the same point, see Gilman, *Jewish Self-Hatred*, 3.

115. The most important of Arendt's texts on this theme are the essays in part 1 of *The Jew as Pariah*; *Rahel Varnhagen*; and part 2 of *The Origins of Totalitarianism*. See also Mendes-Flohr, *German Jews*.

116. Arendt, *The Jew as Pariah*, 110–11.

117. Arendt, *The Origins of Totalitarianism*, 67.

118. Quoted in Arendt, *Rahel Varnhagen*, 13.

119. Aschheim, *Brothers and Strangers*, 11–12.

120. On the effects of changing patterns of language use on ties among Jews in different states, see Freimark, "Language Behavior and Assimilation," 173,

and Katz, *Out of the Ghetto*, 214–15. H. D. Schmidt considers the disappearance of the Hebrew-language journal of the Haskalah, *Me'asef*, "symbolical of the disestablishment of Hebrew amongst the German Jews," and notes that *Me'asef* printed the Edict of 1812 on its "last pages . . . before it closed down." See "The Terms of Emancipation, 1781–1812," 41.

121. Wertheimer, *Unwelcome Strangers*, 132 and chap. 7 generally; see also Aschheim, *Brothers and Strangers*, 55.

122. Taylor, "The Politics of Recognition," 37–38.

123. Ibid., 43. Thanks to Will Kymlicka for posing this response directly to an earlier version of this chapter.

124. On these developments see Aschheim, *Brothers and Strangers*, esp. chaps. 6, 8.

125. Hegel, *Philosophy of Right*, sec. 185.

126. Hegel, "The German Constitution," 13; cf. Marx, "On the Jewish Question," 34.

127. Hegel, *Philosophy of Right*, sec. 260 (addition); sec. 261 (remark).

128. E.g., Marx, "Critique of Hegel's Doctrine of the State," 117–18 (on the Constitution), 141 (on the Estates); 197 (on representation).

129. See the ending paragraphs of "On the Jewish Question," 46.

130. Marx, "Excerpts from James Mill," 278. Thanks to James Der Derian for pointing me to this text.

CHAPTER SIX
THE SLIPPERY SLOPE

1. Roger Cohen, "Call for 'Guiding Culture,'" 10.

2. Sorkin, *The Transformation of German Jewry*, 20; see also Rürup, "Jewish Emancipation and Bourgeois Society," 69–72.

3. Cf. Povinelli, "The State of Shame," 578–81. This argument is indebted to work of several scholars who have pointed to the function of multiculturalism as a state project and as an instrument of national fantasy, often though not always in the Australian context; including Povinelli, "The State of Shame" and now *The Cunning of Recognition*; Hage, *White Nation*; Cowlishaw, "Disappointing Indigenous People"; Stratton and Ang, "Multicultural Imagined Communities"; Goldberg, "Introduction"; and Chicago Cultural Studies Group, "Critical Multiculturalism."

4. While in this chapter I use "multiculturalism" and "multicultural recognition" synonymously to refer to practices and theories which involve, or are justified in terms of, the recognition or accommodation of a person or group *qua* bearer of a distinctive cultural identity, the word "multiculturalism" itself has been used to refer to a wider range of political and theoretical projects; see Chicago Cultural Studies Group, "Critical Multiculturalism," for a discussion (and as an example).

5. Taylor, "The Politics of Recognition," 31; 42.

6. Sewell, "The Concept(s) of Culture," 39; on the place of this view in the history of anthropology see Kuper, *Culture*; for critiques and alternatives see Clifford and Marcus, *Writing Culture*; Clifford, *The Predicament of Culture*;

Ortner, ed., *The Fate of "Culture"*; Johnson, "Why Respect Culture"; Wedeen, "Conceptualizing Culture."

7. One of the strongest statements of this view is in Margalit and Halbertal, "Liberalism and the Right to Culture," 498–99.

8. Clifford, *The Predicament of Culture*, 338; cf. Sewell's discussion of the turn to "practice" in the study of culture in "The Concept(s) of Culture," 46–55, and the other sources in n. 6 above.

9. Cf. Honig's definition of culture as a "living, breathing system for the distribution and enactment of agency, power and privilege" ("'My Culture Made Me Do It,'" 39).

10. Recognition tends to appear in Kymlicka's work as the "symbolic" good provided by multiculturalism, rather than as the overarching justificatory framework in which multiculturalism as a whole is situated, as in Taylor's essay; see, e.g., *Finding Our Way*, 55–57; *Politics in the Vernacular*, 40–41.

11. Kymlicka, *Finding Our Way*, 23; 4.

12. These include *Liberalism, Community, and Culture* (1989); *Multicultural Citizenship* (1995); *Finding Our Way* (1998); and *Politics in the Vernacular* (2001).

13. Kymlicka, *Multicultural Citizenship*, 26–33; an expanded list appears in *Finding Our Way*, 42.

14. Kymlicka, *Multicultural Citizenship*, 2.

15. Taylor, "Cross-Purposes," 181.

16. Taylor, "Introduction," 1; see above, chaps. 1 and 2.

17. This is my own extremely condensed summary of one strand of argument in the first five chapters of Kymlicka, *Liberalism, Community, and Culture*.

18. See for example the sweeping attacks on "culture" in Bromwich, "Culturalism, the Euthanasia of Liberalism" and Kateb, "Notes on Pluralism"; a similar view seems to inform Okin's "Is Multiculturalism Bad for Women?"

19. This is, I think, roughly Taylor's position in "The Politics of Recognition"; for more on this see chapter 2 above.

20. Kymlicka, *Multicultural Citizenship*, 83.

21. Ibid., 101–5; 171.

22. Ibid., 84.

23. Ibid., 84. Kymlicka criticizes the view that people don't have a right to their *own* culture on the grounds that it "treats the loss of one's culture as similar to the loss of one's job," i.e., as the loss of a replaceable external resource (84); but his objection to the analogy is not that culture is not external in that way; it is, rather, that switching cultures is more costly than switching jobs. On the significance of treating culture as property, see Handler, "On Having a Culture" and "Who Owns the Past?"; Coombe, *The Cultural Life of Intellectual Properties*.

24. Kymlicka, *Multicultural Citizenship*, 85.

25. Ibid.

26. Ibid., 89–90.

27. Ibid., 87.

28. Ibid., 87–88.

29. Ibid., 104; the earlier distinction is in *Liberalism, Community, and Cul-*

ture, 166–67. For a sense of why Kymlicka adopts these distinctions, see Waldron, "Minority Cultures and the Cosmopolitan Alternative," 786–88, arguing that Kymlicka's stress (in *Liberalism, Community and Culture*) on the "security" or "stability" of culture contradicts his liberal commitment to autonomy. For excellent critique of the earlier distinction (which I think is still applicable to its successor) see Tomasi, "Kymlicka, Liberalism, and Respect for Cultural Minorities," 586–95; Johnson's critique in "Why Respect Culture," 416, does not separate the two distinctions but is incisive about both of them at once.

30. Johnson, "Why Respect Culture," 416.

31. E.g., Kymlicka, *Politics in the Vernacular*, 1, 4, 23; *Multicultural Citizenship*, 10. My point here, I should stress, is *not* to criticize Kymlicka for his choice of audience.

32. See Kymlicka, *Finding Our Way*, 4–5.

33. Kymlicka, *Multicultural Citizenship*, 75.

34. See, e.g., ibid., 82.

35. Ibid., 2.

36. Influential statements of the critique can be found in Schlesinger, *The Disuniting of America*; Gitlin, *The Twilight of Common Dreams*; and Gwyn, *Nationalism Without Walls*; for other discussions of the issue see among many others Phillips, "Why Worry About Multiculturalism"; Spinner-Halev, "Cultural Pluralism and Partial Citizenship"; Beiner, "Introduction"; Habermas, "Struggles for Recognition in the Democratic Constitutional State"; Walzer, *What It Means to Be an American*; Miller, *On Nationality*; Rockefeller, "Comment."

37. Kymlicka, *Multicultural Citizenship*, 174–75; cf. *Politics in the Vernacular*, 36; "Comments on Shachar and Spinner-Halev," 120; *Finding Our Way*, 4–5. This audience is also concerned that multiculturalism will entail the acceptance of illiberal cultural practices, including those that involve the oppression of women; I discuss this point later. See Kymlicka, *Multicultural Citizenship*, chap. 8; *Finding Our Way*, chap. 4; "Comment on Shachar and Spinner-Halev."

38. Kymlicka, *Multicultural Citizenship*, 50.

39. Kymlicka, *Finding Our Way*, 57.

40. See especially Kymlicka, *Multicultural Citizenship*, chap. 9; *Finding Our Way*, chaps. 1–3.

41. Kymlicka, *Multicultural Citizenship*, 192.

42. Kymlicka, *Finding Our Way*, 4.

43. Ibid., 22–23, 38.

44. Ibid., 55. Kymlicka offers no evidence that the successful integration of Catholics was due to, as he says, "the growing recognition that immigrants are only seeking fair terms of integration." Often, successful integration is messier and less principled—as, for example, when it is secured through the embrace of whiteness and white supremacy (see, e.g., Roediger, *The Wages of Whiteness*, chap. 6; Ignatiev, *How the Irish Became White*).

45. See, e.g., the discussion of racism in Kymlicka, *Finding Our Way*, 81 and esp. 195 n. 24.

46. Ibid., 61; Kymlicka, *Multicultural Citizenship*, 179; *Finding Our Way*, 61.

47. These descriptions occur in the space of four pages: Kymlicka, *Multicultural Citizenship*, 177–180; cf. *Finding Our Way*, chap. 3.

48. For an excellent example see Flathman, *Reflections of a Would-Be Anarchist*, esp. chap. 5.

49. For an exploration of this problem through a treatment of Habermas and "constitutional patriotism," see Markell, "Making Affect Safe for Democracy?"

50. Kymlicka, *Politics in the Vernacular*, 59. In this passage, Kymlicka seems to be making two closely related points: first, that the slippery slope concern presupposes that there are not stable distinctions between types of group (e.g., national minorities and immigrant groups), and, second, that the slippery slope concern presupposes that "*each group* has infinitely flexible needs and aspirations" (59, emphasis added).

51. See, e.g., Gwyn, *Nationalism without Walls*, chap. 11 (this is one of the critiques of multiculturalism to which Kymlicka is responding in *Finding Our Way*).

52. Kymlicka, *Politics in the Vernacular*, 25; *Multicultural Citizenship*, 92–93.

53. See for example Hegel, *Philosophy of Right*, secs. 184–85 and remark to sec. 255; Durkheim, *Division of Labor in Society* and "Individualism and the Intellectuals."

54. This idea parallels, and draws on, Bonnie Honig's account in *Democracy and the Foreigner* of the ways in which the symbolic politics of foreignness serves as a site onto which democratic citizens displace analogous problems, including their own experience of the alienness of the law.

55. On official apologies, see Levy, *The Multiculturalism of Fear*, chap. 8; Trouillot, "Abortive Rituals."

56. Povinelli, "The State of Shame," 583–87. My treatment of shame here was inspired by Povinelli's as well as by Berlant, "The Subject of True Feeling"; and Cowlishaw, "Disappointing Indigenous People."

57. Povinelli, "The State of Shame," 582.

58. On this point see Trouillot's discussion of the temporality of apologies in "Abortive Rituals," 174ff.

59. Kymlicka, *Politics in the Vernacular*, 59.

60. Kymlicka, *Multicultural Citizenship*, 18.

61. Ibid., 76.

62. Ibid., 19.

63. Kymlicka, *Politics in the Vernacular*, 25 n. 18.

64. Ibid., 25.

65. For two different accounts of the headscarves affair, see Galeotti, "Citizenship and Equality," and Moruzzi, "A Problem with Headscarves" (along with the accompanying response by Galeotti and a rejoinder by Moruzzi). For a detailed reconstruction of the context of the event and the various threads of political response, see Elaine Thomas, "Competing Visions of Citizenship and Integration."

66. Kymlicka, *Multicultural Citizenship*, 31. Moruzzi usefully explains that the Persian word *chador*, which names a "long, cloak-like Iranian garment," is quite inappropriate to the case, which involved North African immigrants

wearing headscarves, or (in French) *foulards* ("A Problem With Headscarves," 655).

67. Importantly, given the way Kymlicka has justified the right to culture, even a hypothetical multicultural claim made by a member of one modernized liberal culture who had emigrated to another would still need to be anchored *not* in the thinness and pluralism of his or her original culture but in what it rules out; i.e., in the constraining function that it shares with the "thick" cultures it had supposedly left behind.

68. Cf. Stratton and Ang, "Multicultural Imagined Communities," 156 (referring to the multicultural national imaginary in Australia as an involving an idea of a "managed unity-in-diversity").

69. This is what Walzer calls liberalism's "art of separation" ("Liberalism and the Art of Separation," 315); cf. Rawls's discussion of the distinction between our "public" or "institutional" identities and our "noninstitutional or moral" identities in *Political Liberalism*, 30–31.

70. James Scott, *Seeing Like a State*, 2–3 and *passim*.

71. Kymlicka, *Finding Our Way*, 57.

72. See Povinelli, "The State of Shame," 582; and thanks to Candace Vogler on this point.

73. I have substituted "headscarf" for Kymlicka's "*chador*" here; see n. 66 above.

74. Elaine Thomas, "Competing Visions of Citizenship," 168, 172.

75. Elaine Thomas observes that they "said relatively little on their own behalf" ("Competing Visions of Citizenship," 175); Moruzzi says they seem never to have been quoted in the national press and were almost always referred to by their first names only ("A Problem with Headscarves," 668 n. 14).

76. On these possibilities and others, see Moruzzi, "A Problem With Headscarves"; Elaine Thomas, "Competing Visions of Citizenship."

77. Honig, *Democracy and the Foreigner*, 97–98.

78. Cowlishaw, "Disappointing Indigenous People."

79. Kymlicka, "Comments on Shachar and Spinner-Halev," 113–14.

80. At their most diffuse, these criticisms take the form of fairly general worries about the mentality of deference to "cultural tradition" that multiculturalism supposedly involves, and usually involve appeals to such familiar cases as the cluster of practices known collectively as "female genital mutilation" (FGM), or the treatment of women by the Taliban. More sophisticated versions of the criticism focus on specific legal and political accommodations, ranging from the successful use of "cultural defenses" in rape and murder cases to the extension of autonomy in family and personal law to groups whose legal traditions work to enforce the subordination of women. One of the most extensively developed versions of the critique can be found in the recent work of Susan Moller Okin, including the title essay in *Is Multiculturalism Bad For Women?*, as well as "Feminism and Multiculturalism: Some Tensions," and "Feminism, Women's Human Rights, and Cultural Differences." In addition to the responses to Okin in *Is Multiculturalism Bad For Women?*, other important work here includes Coleman, "Individualizing Justice through Multiculturalism"; Volpp, "Talking 'Culture'"; Nussbaum, *Sex and Social Justice*; Shachar, *Multicultural Jurisdic-*

tions; Deveaux, "Conflicting Equalities"; Carens, *Culture, Citizenship, and Community*, chap. 6; Spinner-Halev, "Feminism, Multiculturalism, Oppression, and the State."

81. Kymlicka, "Liberal Complacencies," 34.

82. As Bonnie Honig points out, Okin's critique of multiculturalism accepts rather than interrogates the claim "my culture made me do it," granting "culture" an authority and univocality it does not have, notwithstanding the efforts of some cultural agents to *represent* culture as simply requiring a particular course of action. See Honig, "'My Culture Made Me Do It,'" 36–37.

83. As Povinelli explains, the Australian Supreme Court's decision in *Mabo and Others v. The State of Queensland* keys Aboriginal land rights to the maintenance of "traditional customs, beliefs and practices" ("The State of Shame," 587); see also the examples in Minow, *Not Only For Myself*, chap. 3.

84. Most recently in the American war on Afghanistan: see Hirschkind and Mahmood, "Feminism, the Taliban, and Politics of Counter-Insurgency."

85. This does not mean that "judging other cultures" is impossible; but, as Linda Zerilli has elegantly argued, it does mean that framing the question that way tends to reproduce an unhelpful opposition between those who think such judgment is straightforward and those who think such judgment is impossible. Acknowledging the possibility *and* difficulty of judgment in such cases requires treating them not as encounters between self-enclosed totalities, but as encounters between agents differently situated on a (nevertheless continuous) cultural terrain; from this latter perspective, the problem of judgment in these cases turns out not to be fundamentally different from the problem of political judgment in general (*Feminism and the Abyss of Freedom*).

86. Kymlicka does not perform this reduction—I suspect he would also be critical of it—yet his framework seems to me to encourage it in ways he does not acknowledge. For example, in his description of the sort of public conversation that ought to happen around the "limits of tolerance" in Canada (exemplified by a debate over *hijab* in the Québec schools) it is noteworthy that the *only* thing the non-Muslim Québécois are supposed to have learned from the process was that "not all Muslims support keeping women locked up in the house; not all Muslims support talaq divorces and clitoridectomy," and so on; and that it was therefore safe to accept *hijab* in the schools because doing so "was not going to mean accepting those other practices" (*Finding Our Way*, 69). They learned, in short, to make more accurate discriminations between Muslims whose beliefs do not violate non-Muslim "Canadian institutions and principles" (61) and those whose beliefs do; but there is no sense here that such a conversation might have involved anything like a questioning and subtler reconstruction of the Québécois' interpretations and judgments of the various practices in question, or an interrogation of the sources of their own earlier stereotypes.

87. This stress on doing could be contrasted with Hage's distinction between a (problematic) multiculturalism of "having," which positions white Australians as the active possessors of objectified, passive "diversity," and a (good) multiculturalism of "being," which would break down this asymmetry by acknowledging that "we *are* diversity" (*White Nation*, 139–40): this move, I think, does not go quite far enough.

CONCLUSION
TOWARD A POLITICS OF ACKNOWLEDGMENT

1. Sophocles, *Antigone*, 594.

2. On the double binds of redemptive language see Warner, "What Like a Bullet Can Undeceive?"

3. See among others Goldhill, "The Great Dionysia and Civic Ideology"; "The Audience of Athenian Tragedy"; Cartledge, "'Deep Plays'"; Euben, "Introduction"; *The Tragedy of Political Theory*, chap. 1; *Corrupting Youth*, chaps. 2, 6.

4. Euben, *Corrupting Youth*, 147.

5. Stephen White, *Sustaining Affirmation*, 11, 69–70.

6. E.g., Plato, *Republic* 331e (Polemarchus's definition); cf. Aristotle's discussion of "partial" justice, *Nicomachean Ethics* 1130a–1131a; Rawls, *A Theory of Justice*, 10–11. Although I shall speak of this idea of justice as concerned with equality, it is obviously proportional rather than absolute equality that I have in mind.

7. Young, *Justice and the Politics of Difference*, 21–22.

8. Ibid., 26.

9. Ibid., 23.

10. This is the sort of injustice that Rancière refers to as a "fundamental miscount" of those who have a part in the city (*Disagreement*, 6); which Derrida, in *The Politics of Friendship*, marks by repeatedly punctuating his discussion of friends with the question "how many of us are there?" (1); and which Connolly, in his account of the "politics of becoming," identifies by distinguishing between constituencies that have already made it onto the "public register of justice" and "protean movements" that exist "below the threshold at which the formal practice of justice kicks in" (*Why I Am Not a Secularist*, 10).

11. My use of the language of "avoidance" here draws on Cavell's "The Avoidance of Love"; for a discussion of Cavell see chap. 1.

12. Cf. Rancière's discussion of democracy as a matter of the equality of "anyone at all" (*Disagreement*, 16).

13. Arendt, "Emerson-Thoreau Medal Lecture," 1.

14. Arendt's understanding of "welcoming" is thus somewhat different from Iris Young's account of "greeting," which she casts as the "virtuous form of the communication mode that the *Gorgias* presents as the vice of flattery." As such, greeting is tailored to the "particularity" of others, and often includes "introductory speeches that name the others with honorific titles, acknowledge the greatness of their achievements and ideals, and so on"; as such, it seems to me to be a species of recognition, not acknowledgment (*Intersecting Voices*, 70).

15. Such an evasion is even more clearly evident in Arendt's Lessing Prize essay, "On Humanity in Dark Times"; for an excellent discussion see Disch, "On Friendship in 'Dark Times.'"

16. Kymlicka, *Finding Our Way*, 48.

17. Ibid., 48–49.

18. Ibid., 97–100. Kymlicka reads "Queer Nation" simply as a separatist nationalist self-description; for a different view of the "label" see Berlant and Freeman, "Queer Nationality."

19. For an exemplary critique of marriage as an institution of privilege, see Warner, *The Trouble With Normal*, chap. 3.

20. Ibid., 35, 2.

21. Ibid., 7.

22. Laclau, "The Impossibility of Society," 90.

23. Laclau, "Deconstruction, Pragmatism, Hegemony," 56; see also ibid., 90.

24. Laclau, "The Impossibility of Society," 90; see also "Death and Resurrection of the Theory of Ideology," 302 n. 7; Laclau and Mouffe, *Hegemony and Socialist Strategy*, 112.

25. Laclau, "Why Do Empty Signifiers Matter to Politics," 45

26. Marx, "Contribution to the Critique of Hegel's Philosophy of Right: Introduction," 64.

27. Laclau, "Why Do Empty Signifiers Matter to Politics," 46; Laclau, "Universalism, Particularism, and the Question of Identity," 34; Laclau and Mouffe, *Hegemony and Socialist Strategy*, 190.

28. Laclau, "Deconstruction, Pragmatism, Hegemony," 59.

29. "Incompletion and provisionality belong to the essence of democracy" (Laclau, "Beyond Emancipation," 16).

30. Laclau, "Death and Resurrection of the Theory of Ideology," 302; "The Impossibility of Society," 90.

31. Norval, "Frontiers in Question," 69 (focusing specifically on the difference between the sort of identity that emerges out of "family resemblances" and the sort that emerges out of the establishment of boundaries). For exemplary invocations of Wittgenstein see Laclau and Mouffe, "Post-Marxism Without Apologies," 109; *Hegemony and Socialist Strategy*, 111.

32. Wittgenstein, *Philosophical Investigations*, par. 103 (speaking here of the ideal of nonvague expressions of rules).

33. Conant, "On Bruns, On Cavell," 621; see Cavell, *The Claim of Reason*, 46 (saying that he "tak[es] the very raising of the question of knowledge in a certain form, or spirit, to constitute skepticism, regardless of whether a philosophy takes itself to have *answered* the question affirmatively or negatively").

34. Wittgenstein, *Philosophical Investigations*, pars. 133 (on therapy) and 109 (on bewitchment).

35. Ibid., par. 101.

36. Ibid., par. 83; for other examples see pars. 23, 27, 33, 66. My reading of the tone of these passages was provoked by Cavell's description of the stifling feeling of Wittgenstein's description of the "primitive language" of the builder and his assistant in par. 2; see "Notes and Afterthoughts," 146ff.

37. It is true that the function of mourning is closely tied to agency, but not in the same way that Antigone's demand for recognition in the face of the *prohibition* of mourning had been: it does not determine what you are to do, but rather prepares you to brave the world of action again, precisely in its indeterminacy.

38. See here Iris Young's account of social difference as a resource ofr democratic communication: *Inclusion and Democracy*, esp. 115–20.

39. Cf. Bickford, "Anti-Anti-Identity Politics," esp. 122 (on the political uses of understandings of identity as "created"); for an example of an approach to "race" that seems to me to resist sovereign deployments of race as identity in this way, see Guinier and Torres, *The Miner's Canary*.

40. Lefort, "The Question of Democracy," 13. For a related discussion see my "Making Affect Safe For Democracy?"

41. Marx, "On the Jewish Question," 46 (translation modified).

42. On democratic politics as a matter of the equitable distribution of loss and sacrifice, see Allen, *Democratic Entanglements*.

43. For an interesting application of this idea in the context of multicultural politics, see Shachar, *Multicultural Jurisdictions*.

44. On democratic action as a matter of "taking rights and liberties rather than waiting for them to be granted by a sovereign power," see Honig, *Democracy and the Foreigner*, 99.

45. On this point see Judith Butler's critique of Althusser in *The Psychic Life of Power*, 129–31.

AFTERWORD
A NOTE ON THE COVER

1. Stanford, *Greek Tragedy and the Emotions*, 163. My reading of the *Oresteia* is indebted to several excellent treatments of the play, including Allen, *The World of Prometheus*, 18–24; Euben, *The Tragedy of Political Theory*, chap. 3; Goldhill, *Language, Sexuality, Narrative* and "The Language of Tragedy"; Luban, "Some Greek Trials"; Rocco, "Democracy and Discipline in Aeschylus's *Oresteia*"; and Tussman, "The Orestes Case."

2. On anxiety over language's potential opacity as a central concern of the *Oresteia*, see Goldhill, *Reading Greek Tragedy*, chap. 1. On the connections between the "weaving" of a linguistic deceit and the textile imagery of the *Oresteia*, see Jenkins, "The Ambiguity of Greek Textiles"; McClure, "Clytemnestra's Binding Spell"; and Morrell, "The Fabric of Persuasion."

3. I bracket the persistent scholarly controversy about the size of the jury and the significance of Athena's vote. See Sommerstein's discussion in Aeschylus, *Eumenides*, 222ff.

4. Rabinowitz, "From Force to Persuasion," 183, 185; for other progressivist readings see Dodds, "Morals and Politics in the 'Oresteia,'" 31; Kitto, *Form and Meaning in Drama*, 86; Kuhns, *The House, the City, and the Judge*; Podlecki, *Political Background of Aeschylean Tragedy*, 77–81; Winnington-Ingram, "A Religious Function of Greek Tragedy," 23, and *Studies in Aeschylus*, chaps. 4–8.

5. Meier, *The Greek Discovery of Politics*, 91; for an extensive catalog of antitheses operating in the play see Zeitlin, "The Dynamics of Misogyny," 111–12.

6. See Segal, "Lament and Closure in *Antigone*," 119–20.

7. On these assocations see Buxton, *Persuasion in Greek Tragedy*, 49–52, 63–66; despite his capacious view of the range of meanings of the term, Buxton, like others, reads the final scene as an instance of "frank and open" persuasion

uncontaminated by the earlier appearances of the term (105–113; cf. E. T. Owen, *The Harmony of Aeschylus*, 129).

8. Aeschylus, *Eumenides*, 827–28; 886, 900. On the ambiguity resulting from Athena's use of threats see David Cohen, "The Theodicy of Aeschylus," 138–39; Luban, "Some Greek Trials," 317–18; Rocco, "Democracy and Discipline," 162–63. On Athena's seductive language, see Buxton, *Persuasion in Greek Tragedy*, 51–52, and esp. 111; Gewirtz, "Aeschylus' Law," 1053.

9. Athena addresses the Furies as *metoikoi* at *Eumenides*, 1011; on the meaning and translation of *metoikos*, see Whitehead, *The Ideology of the Athenian Metic*, 6–7; on the association with the Panatheneia, see Bowie, "Religion and Politics in Aeschylus' *Oresteia*," 27–28, though Bowie, like many others, suggests that the reference to the Panathenaic robe works simply to *counteract* the long association of the red robe with "entrapment and death" (28); likewise Jenkins, "The Ambiguity of Greek Textiles," 118; Goheen, "Aspects of Dramatic Symbolism," 122–25.

10. Rocco, "Democracy and Discipline," 159, draws the parallel between the Furies' robes and the path of textiles, and admirably refuses to assume that the Furies' robes remain uncontaminated by the association.

11. The essential work here is Zeitlin, "The Dynamics of Misogyny"; see also related discussions in Rocco, "Democracy and Discipline"; Saxonhouse, "Aeschylus' *Oresteia*."

12. On the sphere of influence see Aeschylus, *Eumenides*, 894–95 ("no *oikos* shall be prosperous without your will"); on the confinement, see 804–805, 1023; and Flaumenhaft, "Seeing Justice Done," 38–39.

13. Whitehead, *Ideology of the Athenian Metic*, 6.

14. Rochaix here takes a liberty with the text, but remains faithful to its spirit: the Furies are noted for demanding wineless libations; see e.g., Aeschylus, *Eumenides*, 106–109, and Vidal-Naquet, "Hunting and Sacrifice in Aeschylus' *Oresteia*," 157–58; the Furies themselves complain elsewhere in the *Eumenides* about an earlier case in which Apollo persuaded the Fates with wine (723–28).

15. Luban, "Some Greek Trials," 318 n. 135. On this production see Wiegenstein, *Über Theater, 1966–1986*, 178–86.

Works Cited

Aarsleff, Hans. *From Locke to Saussure: Essays on the Study of Language and Intellectual History*. Minneapolis: University of Minnesota Press, 1982.

Abbey, Ruth. *Charles Taylor*. Princeton: Princeton University Press, 2000.

Aeschylus. *Eumenides*. Ed. Alan H. Sommerstein. Cambridge: Cambridge University Press, 1989.

———. *Seven Against Thebes*. Trans. David Grene. In *The Complete Greek Tragedies*, ed. David Grene and Richmond Lattimore. Vol. 1, *Aeschylus*. Chicago: University of Chicago Press, 1959.

———. *Seven Against Thebes*. Ed. G. O. Hutchinson. Oxford: Clarendon Press, 1985.

Allen, Danielle. *Democratic Entanglements: Rhetoric, Distrust, and Sacrifice*. Forthcoming.

———. "Law's Necessary Forcefulness: Ralph Ellison vs. Hannah Arendt on the Battle of Little Rock." *Oklahoma City University Law Review* 26, no. 3 (Fall 2001): 857–95.

———. *The World of Prometheus: The Politics of Punishing in Democratic Athens*. Princeton: Princeton University Press, 2000.

Appadurai, Arjun. "Full Attachment." *Public Culture* 10, no. 2 (Winter 1998): 443–49.

Appiah, K. Anthony. "Identity, Authenticity, Survival: Multicultural Societies and Social Reproduction." In *Multiculturalism: Examining the Politics of Recognition*, ed. Amy Gutmann. Princeton: Princeton University Press, 1994.

Arendt, Hannah. "The Concept of History." In *Between Past and Future: Eight Exercises in Political Thought*. New York: Penguin, 1968.

———. "Concern with Politics in Recent European Philosophical Thought." In *Essays in Understanding, 1930–1954*, ed. Jerome Kohn. New York: Harcourt Brace and Co., 1994.

———. "Emerson-Thoreau Medal Lecture." American Academy of Arts and Sciences, April 9, 1969. Box 73, The Hannah Arendt Papers, Manuscript Division, Library of Congress, Washington, D.C. (consulted via web at http://memory.loc.gov/ammem/arendthtml/arendthome.html).

———. *The Human Condition*. Chicago: University of Chicago Press, 1958.

———. *The Jew as Pariah: Jewish Identity and Politics in the Modern Age*. Ed. Ron H. Feldman. New York: Grove Press, 1978.

———. "On Humanity in Dark Times: Thoughts about Lessing." In *Men in Dark Times*. New York: Harvest/HBJ, 1968.

———. *The Origins of Totalitarianism*. New ed. with added prefaces. New York: Harvest/HBJ, 1973.

———. *Rahel Varnhagen: The Life of a Jewish Woman*. Revised ed. Trans. Richard and Clara Winston. New York: Harcourt Brace Jovanovich, 1974.

———. "Sonning Prize Speech." Copenhagen, Denmark, April 18, 1975. Box

78, Hannah Arendt Papers, Manuscript Division, Library of Congress, Washington, D.C. (consulted via web at http://memory.loc.gov/ammem/arendthtml/arendthome.html).

———. *Thinking*. Vol. 1 of *The Life of the Mind*. New York: Harcourt Brace Jovanovich, 1978.

———. *Willing*. Vol. 2 of *The Life of the Mind*. New York: Harcourt Brace Jovanovich, 1978.

Aristotle. *Aristotle's Poetics*. Ed. and trans. Gerald F. Else. Ann Arbor: University of Michigan Press, 1970.

———. *The "Art" of Rhetoric*. Trans. John Henry Freese. Cambridge, MA: Harvard University Press, 1926.

———. *Categories*. Trans. E. M. Edghill. In *The Basic Works of Aristotle*, ed. Richard McKeon. New York: Random House, 1941.

———. *Eudemian Ethics*. Trans. H. Rackham. In *Aristotle*. Vol. 20, *The Athenian Constitution; The Eudemian Ethics; On Virtues and Vices*. Cambridge, MA: Harvard University Press, 1981.

———. *Metaphysics*. Trans. W. D. Ross. In *The Basic Works of Aristotle*, ed. Richard McKeon. New York: Random House, 1941.

———. *Nicomachean Ethics*. Ed. and trans. Martin Ostwald. Upper Saddle River, NJ: Prentice-Hall, 1999.

———. *On the Art of Poetry*. Ed. and trans. Ingram Bywater. Oxford: Clarendon Press, 1909.

———. *Poetics*. Ed. D. W. Lucas. Oxford: Clarendon Press, 1972.

Aschheim, Steven E. *Brothers and Strangers: The East European Jew in German and German Jewish Consciousness, 1800–1923*. Madison: University of Wisconsin Press, 1982.

Austin, J. L. *How to Do Things with Words*. 2nd ed. Ed. J. O. Urmson and Marina Sbisà. Cambridge, MA: Harvard University Press, 1975.

Avineri, Shlomo. *Hegel's Theory of the Modern State*. Cambridge: Cambridge University Press, 1972.

Balibar, Étienne. "The Nation Form: History and Ideology." In *Race, Nation, Class: Ambiguous Identities*, by Étienne Balibar and Immanuel Wallerstein. London: Verso, 1991.

Baron, Salo W. "Newer Approaches to Jewish Emancipation." *Diogenes*, no. 29 (Spring 1960): 56–81.

Barry, Andrew, Thomas Osborne, and Nikolas Rose, eds. *Foucault and Political Reason: Liberalism, Neo-Liberalism, and Rationalities of Government*. Chicago: University of Chicago Press, 1996.

Bataille, Georges. "Hegel, Death, and Sacrifice." In *The Bataille Reader*, ed. Fred Botting and Scott Wilson. Oxford: Blackwell, 1997.

Bauman, Richard, and Charles L. Briggs. "Language Philosophy as Language Ideology: John Locke and Johann Gottfried Herder." In *Regimes of Language: Ideologies, Polities, and Identities*, ed. Paul V. Kroskrity. Santa Fe, NM: School of American Research Press, 2000.

de Beauvoir, Simone. *The Second Sex*. Ed. and trans. H. M. Parshly. New York: Vintage Books, 1989.

Beiner, Ronald. "Introduction." In *Theorizing Citizenship*, ed. Ronald Beiner. Albany: SUNY Press, 1995.

de Beistegui, Miguel. "Hegel, or the Tragedy of Thinking." In *Philosophy and Tragedy*, ed. Miguel de Beistegui and Simon Sparks. London: Routledge, 2000.

Belfiore, Elizabeth S. *Tragic Pleasures: Aristotle on Plot and Emotion*. Princeton: Princeton University Press, 1992.

Benhabib, Seyla. *Critique, Norm, and Utopia: A Study of the Foundations of Critical Theory*. New York: Columbia University Press, 1986.

———. "Democracy and Identity: In Search of the Civic Polity." *Philosophy and Social Criticism* 24, nos. 2–3 (April 1998): 85–100.

———. "The Generalized and the Concrete Other." Chap. 5 in *Situating the Self: Gender, Community, and Postmodernism in Contemporary Ethics*. New York: Routledge, 1992.

Benjamin, Jessica. *The Bonds of Love: Psychoanalysis, Feminism, and the Problem of Domination*. New York: Pantheon Books, 1988.

Bennett, David, ed. *Multicultural States: Rethinking Difference and Identity*. London: Routledge, 1998.

Bentley, Russell, and David Owen. "Ethical Loyalties, Civic Virtue and the Circumstances of Politics." *Philosophical Explorations* 4, no. 3 (September 2001): 223–39.

Bering, Dietz. *The Stigma of Names: Antisemitism in German Daily Life, 1812–1933*. Trans. Neville Plaice. Cambridge: Polity Press, 1992.

Berlant, Lauren. "The Subject of True Feeling: Pain, Privacy, and Politics." In *Cultural Studies and Political Theory*, ed. Jodi Dean. Ithaca: Cornell University Press, 2000.

Berlant, Lauren, and Elizabeth Freeman. "Queer Nationality." In *Fear of a Queer Planet: Queer Politics and Social Theory*, ed. Michael Warner. Minneapolis: University of Minnesota Press, 1993.

Berlin, Isaiah. "The Pursuit of the Ideal." In *The Crooked Timber of Humanity: Chapters in the History of Ideas*. New York: Alfred A. Knopf, 1991.

———. "Two Concepts of Liberty." In *Four Essays on Liberty*. Oxford: Oxford University Press, 1969.

Bickford, Susan. "Anti-Anti-Identity Politics: Feminism, Democracy, and the Complexities of Citizenship." *Hypatia* 12, no. 4 (Fall 1997): 111–31.

———. *The Dissonance of Democracy: Listening, Conflict, and Citizenship*. Ithaca: Cornell University Press, 1996.

Binder, Guyora. "Mastery, Slavery, and Emancipation." *Cardozo Law Review* 10, nos. 5–6 (March–April 1989): 1435–80.

Birnbaum, Pierre. "Between Social and Political Assimilation: Remarks on the History of Jews in France." In *Paths of Emancipation: Jews, States, and Citizenship*, ed. Pierre Birnbaum and Ira Katznelson. Princeton: Princeton University Press, 1995.

Bloch, Marc. *Feudal Society*. 2 vols. Trans. L. A. Manyon. Chicago: University of Chicago Press, 1964.

Blundell, Mary Whitlock. "*Êthos* and *Dianoia* Reconsidered." In *Essays on Aristotle's* Poetics, ed. Amélie Oksenberg Rorty. Princeton: Princeton University Press, 1992.

———. *Helping Friends and Harming Enemies: A Study in Sophocles and Greek Ethics*. Cambridge: Cambridge University Press, 1989.

Bodin, Jean. *On Sovereignty: Four Chapters from* The Six Books of the Commonwealth. Ed. and trans. Julian H. Franklin. Cambridge: Cambridge University Press, 1992.

Borch-Jacobsen, Mikkel. "The Laughter of Being." In *Bataille: A Critical Reader*, ed. Fred Botting and Scott Wilson. Oxford: Blackwell, 1998.

Bourdieu, Pierre. *Language and Symbolic Power*. Ed. John B. Thompson. Trans. Gino Raymond and Matthew Adamson. Cambridge, MA: Harvard University Press, 1991.

———. *The Logic of Practice*. Trans. Richard Nice. Stanford: Stanford University Press, 1990.

Bower, Lisa. "Queer Problems/Straight Solutions: The Limits of a Politics of 'Official Recognition.'" In *Playing with Fire: Queer Politics, Queer Theories*, ed. Shane Phelan. New York: Routledge, 1997.

Bowie, A. M. "Religion and Politics in Aeschylus' *Oresteia*." *Classical Quarterly* 43, no. 1 (1993): 10–31.

Brann, M. *Die schlesische Judenheit vor und nach dem Edikt vom 11. März 1812*. Breslau: Köbnersche Verlagsbuchhandlung, 1913.

Bromwich, David. "Culturalism, the Euthanasia of Liberalism." *Dissent* (Winter 1995): 89–102.

Brown, Wendy. *Politics Out of History*. Princeton: Princeton University Press, 2001.

———. "Revaluing Critique: A Response to Kenneth Baynes." *Political Theory* 28, no. 4 (August 2000): 469–79.

———. "Rights and Identity in Late Modernity." In *Identities, Politics, and Rights*, ed. Austin Sarat and Thomas R. Kearns. Ann Arbor: University of Michigan Press, 1995.

———. *States of Injury: Power and Freedom in Late Modernity*. Princeton: Princeton University Press, 1995.

———. "Suffering Rights as Paradoxes." *Constellations* 7, no. 2 (June 2000): 230–41.

Brubaker, Rogers. *Citizenship and Nationhood in France and Germany*. Cambridge, MA: Harvard University Press, 1992.

Brubaker, Rogers, and Frederick C. Cooper. "Beyond 'Identity.'" *Theory and Society* 29, no. 1 (February 2000): 1–47.

Buck-Morss, Susan. "Hegel and Haiti." *Critical Inquiry* 26, no. 4 (Summer 2000): 821–65.

Bull, Malcolm. "Slavery and the Multiple Self." *New Left Review*, no. 231 (September–October 1998): 94–131.

Burch, Kurt. *"Property" and the Making of the International System*. Boulder: Lynne Rienner Publishers, 1998.

Burchell, Graham, Colin Gordon, and Peter Miller. *The Foucault Effect: Studies in Governmentality*. Chicago: University of Chicago Press, 1991.

Butler, E. M. *The Tyranny of Greece over Germany*. Boston: Beacon Press, 1958.

Butler, Judith. *Antigone's Claim: Kinship Between Life and Death*. New York: Columbia University Press, 2000.

———. "Commentary on Joseph Flay's 'Hegel, Derrida, and Bataille's Laughter.'" In *Hegel and His Critics: Philosophy in the Aftermath of Hegel*, ed. William Desmond. Albany: SUNY Press, 1989.

———. "Merely Cultural." *New Left Review* 227 (January–February 1998): 33–44.

———. *The Psychic Life of Power: Theories in Subjection*. Stanford: Stanford University Press, 1997.

———. *Subjects of Desire: Hegelian Reflections in Twentieth-Century France*. New York: Columbia University Press, 1987.

———. "Universality in Culture." In *For Love of Country: Debating the Limits of Patriotism*, by Martha C. Nussbaum et al. Boston: Beacon Press, 1996.

Butler, Judith, Ernesto Laclau, and Slavoj Žižek. *Contingency, Hegemony, Universality: Contemporary Dialogues on the Left*. London: Verso, 2000.

Buxton, R. G. A. *Persuasion in Greek Tragedy: A Study of Peitho*. Cambridge: Cambridge University Press, 1982.

Bynum, Caroline Walker. *Metamorphosis and Identity*. New York: Zone Books, 2001.

Calhoun, Craig. "The Politics of Identity and Recognition." In *Critical Social Theory: Culture, History, and the Challenge of Difference*. Oxford: Blackwell, 1995.

Camilleri, Joseph A., and Jim Falk. *The End of Sovereignty? The Politics of a Shrinking and Fragmenting World*. Aldershot: Edward Elgar, 1992.

Canovan, Margaret. *Hannah Arendt: A Reinterpretation of Her Political Thought*. Cambridge: Cambridge University Press, 1992.

Caplan, Jane. "'This or That Particular Person': Protocols of Identification in Nineteenth-Century Europe." In *Documenting Individual Identity: The Development of State Practices in the Modern World*, ed. Jane Caplan and John Torpey. Princeton: Princeton University Press, 2001.

Carens, Joseph H. *Culture, Citizenship, and Community: A Contextual Exploration of Justice as Evenhandedness*. Oxford: Oxford University Press, 2000.

Carlebach, Julius. *Karl Marx and the Radical Critique of Judaism*. London: Routledge & Kegan Paul, 1978.

Cartledge, Paul. "'Deep Plays': Theatre as Process in Greek Civic Life." In *The Cambridge Companion to Greek Tragedy*, ed. P. E. Easterling. Cambridge: Cambridge University Press, 1997.

Cave, Terence. *Recognitions: A Study in Poetics*. Oxford: Clarendon Press, 1990.

Cavell, Stanley. "The Avoidance of Love: A Reading of *King Lear*." In *Must We Mean What We Say? A Book of Essays*. Cambridge: Cambridge University Press, 1976.

———. *The Claim of Reason: Wittgenstein, Skepticism, Morality, and Tragedy*. Oxford: Oxford University Press, 1979.

———. "Knowing and Acknowledging." In *Must We Mean What We Say? A Book of Essays*. Cambridge: Cambridge University Press, 1976.

———. "Notes and Afterthoughts on the Opening of Wittgenstein's *Investigations*." In *Philosophical Passages: Wittgenstein, Emerson, Austin, Derrida*. Oxford: Blackwell, 1995.

Cavell, Stanley. "Othello and the Stake of the Other." In *Disowning Knowledge in Six Plays of Shakespeare*. Cambridge: Cambridge University Press, 1977.

Chamberlain, Charles. "From 'Haunts' to 'Character': The Meaning of *Êthos* and its Relation to Ethics." *Helios*, n.s. 11, no. 2 (Winter 1984): 97–108.

Chanter, Tina. *The Ethics of Eros: Irigaray's Rewriting of the Philosophers*. New York: Routledge, 1995.

Chicago Cultural Studies Group. "Critical Multiculturalism." In *Multiculturalism: A Critical Reader*, ed. David Theo Goldberg. Oxford: Basil Blackwell, 1994.

Clifford, James. *The Predicament of Culture: Twentieth-Century Ethnography, Literature, and Art*. Cambridge, MA: Harvard University Press, 1988.

Clifford, James, and George E. Marcus, eds. *Writing Culture: The Poetics and Politics of Ethnography*. Berkeley: University of California Press, 1986.

Cohen, David. "The Theodicy of Aeschylus: Justice and Tyranny in the Oresteia." *Greece and Rome* 33, no. 2 (October 1986): 129–141.

Cohen, Jean L., and Andrew Arato. *Civil Society and Political Theory*. Cambridge, MA: MIT Press, 1992.

Cohen, Roger. "Call for 'Guiding Culture' Rekindles Political Debate in Germany." *The New York Times* (November 5, 2000): 10.

Coleman, Doriane Lambelet. "Individualizing Justice Through Multiculturalism: The Liberals' Dilemma." *Columbia Law Review* 96, no. 5 (June 1996): 1093–1167.

Conant, James. "On Bruns, On Cavell." *Critical Inquiry* 17 (Spring 1991): 616–34.

Connolly, William E. *The Ethos of Pluralization*. Minneapolis: University of Minnesota Press, 1995.

———. "Pluralism, Multiculturalism, and the Nation-State: Rethinking the Connections." *Journal of Political Ideologies* 1, no. 1 (February 1996): 53–73.

———. *Political Theory and Modernity*. 2nd ed. Ithaca: Cornell University Press, 1993.

———. "Speed, Concentric Cultures, and Cosmopolitanism." *Political Theory* 28, no. 5 (October 2000): 596–618.

———. *Why I Am Not a Secularist*. Minneapolis: University of Minnesota Press, 1999.

Coombe, Rosemary J. *The Cultural Life of Intellectual Properties: Authorship. Appropriation and the Law*. Durham: Duke University Press, 1998.

Cowlishaw, Gillian. "Disappointing Indigenous People: Violence and the Refusal of Help." *Public Culture* 15, no. 1 (Winter 2003): 103–25.

Crawford, James. *The Creation of States in International Law*. Oxford: Clarendon Press, 1979.

Dallmayr, Fred. *G. W. F. Hegel: Modernity and Politics*. Newbury Park: Sage Publications, 1993.

Davis, David Brion. *The Problem of Slavery in the Age of Revolution, 1770–1823*. Ithaca: Cornell University Press, 1975.

Derrida, Jacques. *Glas*. Trans. John P. Leavey, Jr., and Richard Rand. Lincoln: University of Nebraska Press, 1986.

———. "From Restricted to General Economy: A Hegelianism without Reserve." In *Writing and Difference*, trans. Alan Bass. Chicago: University of Chicago Press, 1978.

———. *The Politics of Friendship*. Trans. George Collins. London: Verso, 1997.

Detienne, Marcel, and Jean-Pierre Vernant. *Cunning Intelligence in Greek Culture and Society*. Trans. Janet Lloyd. Chicago: University of Chicago Press, 1991.

Deveaux, Monique. "Conflicting Equalities? Cultural Group Rights and Sex Equality." *Political Studies* 48, no. 3 (June 2000): 522–39.

Dietz, Mary G. "Citizenship with a Feminist Face: The Problem with Maternal Thinking." *Political Theory* 13, no. 1 (February 1985): 19–37.

Disch, Lisa Jane. *Hannah Arendt and the Limits of Philosophy*. Ithaca: Cornell University Press, 1994.

———. "On Friendship in 'Dark Times.'" In *Feminist Interpretations of Hannah Arendt*, ed. Bonnie Honig. University Park: Pennsylvania State University Press, 1995.

Dodds, E. R. "Morals and Politics in the *Oresteia*." *Proceedings of the Cambridge Philological Society* 186 (1960): 19–31.

Dohm, Christian Wilhelm. *Über die bürgerliche Verbesserung der Juden*. Berlin: Nicolai, 1781.

Du Bois, W. E. B. *Black Reconstruction: An Essay Toward a History of the Part Which Black Folk Played in the Attempt to Reconstruct Democracy in America, 1860–1880*. Philadelphia: Albert Saifer, n.d.

———. "Jefferson Davis as a Representative of Civilization." In *Against Racism: Unpublished Essays, Papers, Address, 1887–1961*. Ed. Herbert Aptheker. Amherst: University of Massachusetts Press, 1985.

———. *The Souls of Black Folk*. New York: Vintage Books, 1990.

Duby, Georges. *The Three Orders: Feudal Society Imagined*. Trans. Arthur Goldhammer. Chicago: University of Chicago Press, 1980.

Duquette, David. "The Political Significance of Hegel's Concept of Recognition in the *Phenomenology*." *Bulletin of the Hegel Society of Great Britain*, no. 29 (Spring–Summer 1994): 38–54.

Durkheim, Émile. *The Division of Labor in Society*. Trans. W. D. Halls. New York: Free Press, 1984.

———. "Individualism and the Intellectuals." In *On Morality and Society*, ed. Robert N. Bellah. Chicago: University of Chicago Press, 1973.

Else, Gerald F. *Aristotle's* Poetics: *The Argument*. Cambridge, MA: Harvard University Press, 1967.

Elshtain, Jean Bethke. "Antigone's Daughters." *democracy* 2, no. 2 (April 1982): 46–59.

Emcke, Carolin. "Between Choice and Coercion." *Constellations* 7, no. 4 (December 2000): 483–95.

Ergang, Robert Reinhold. *Herder and the Foundations of German Nationalism*. New York: Columbia University Press, 1931.

Euben, J. Peter. "Arendt's Hellenism." In *The Cambridge Companion to Hannah Arendt*, ed. Dana Villa. Cambridge: Cambridge University Press, 2000.

Euben, J. Peter. *Corrupting Youth: Political Education, Democratic Culture, and Political Theory*. Princeton: Princeton University Press, 1997.

———. "Introduction." In *Greek Tragedy and Political Theory*, ed. J. Peter Euben. Berkeley: University of California Press, 1986.

———. *The Tragedy of Political Theory: The Road Not Taken*. Princeton: Princeton University Press, 1990.

Fackenheim, Emil L. *Encounters between Judaism and Modern Philosophy*. New York: Schocken Books, 1980.

Fanon, Franz. *Black Skin, White Masks*. Trans. Charles Lam and Mark Mann. New York: Grove Press, 1967.

Ferrara, Alessandro. "Authenticity and the Project of Modernity." *European Journal of Philosophy* 2, no. 3 (December 1994): 241–73.

Feuerbach, Ludwig. "The Essence of Christianity." In *The Young Hegelians: An Anthology*, ed. Lawrence S. Stepelevich. Cambridge: Cambridge University Press, 1983.

Fichte, Johann Gottlieb. *Beiträge zur Berichtigung der Urteile des Publikums über die Französische Revolution*. Leipzig: Reclam, n.d.

Finlayson, J. G. "Conflict and Reconciliation in Hegel's Theory of the Tragic." *Journal of the History of Philosophy* 37, no. 3 (July 1999): 493–520.

Fischer, Horst. *Judentum, Staat und Heer in Preußen im frühen 19. Jahrhundert: Zur Geschichte der staatlichen Judenpolitik*. Tübingen: J.C.B. Mohr, 1968.

Flathman, Richard E. *Reflections of a Would-Be Anarchist*. Minneapolis: University of Minnesota Press, 1998.

———. *Willful Liberalism: Voluntarism and Individuality in Political Theory and Practice*. Ithaca: Cornell University Press, 1992.

Flaumenhaft, Mera J. "Seeing Justice Done: Aeschylus's *Oresteia*." In *The Civic Spectacle: Essays on Drama and Community*. London: Rowman and Littlefield, 1994.

Flay, Joseph C. "Hegel, Derrida, and Bataille's Laughter." In *Hegel and His Critics: Philosophy in the Aftermath of Hegel*, ed. William Desmond. Albany: SUNY Press, 1989.

Foley, Helene. "Tragedy and Democratic Ideology: The Case of Sophocles' *Antigone*." In *History, Tragedy, Theory: Dialogues on Athenian Drama*, ed. Barbara Goff. Austin: University of Texas Press, 1995.

Foucault, Michel. "Truth and Power." In *Power/Knowledge: Selected Interviews and Other Writings, 1972–77*, ed. Colin Gordon. New York: Pantheon Books, 1980.

———. "Two Lectures." In *Power/Knowledge: Selected Interviews and Other Writings, 1972–1977*, ed. Colin Gordon. New York: Pantheon Books, 1980.

Fox, Russell Arben. "J. G. Herder and Charles Taylor on Language, Identity and National Community." Paper presented at the 2001 Annual Meeting of the Midwest Political Science Association, Chicago, IL (April 19–22, 2001).

Franco, Paul. *Hegel's Philosophy of Freedom*. New Haven: Yale University Press, 1999.

Frank, Jill. "Democracy and Distribution: Aristotle on Just Desert." *Political Theory* 26, no. 6 (December 1998): 784–802.

Fraser, Nancy. "Heterosexism, Misrecognition, and Capitalism: A Response to Judith Butler." *Social Text* 52–53 (Fall–Winter 1997): 279–89.

———. *Justice Interruptus: Critical Reflections on the "Postsocialist" Condition*. New York: Routledge, 1997.

———. "Recognition without Ethics?" *Theory, Culture & Society* 18, nos. 2–3 (April–June 2001): 21–42.

———. "A Rejoinder to Iris Young." *New Left Review* 223 (May–June 1997): 126–29.

———. "Rethinking Recognition." *New Left Review* 3 (May–June 2000): 107–120.

Fraser, Nancy, and Axel Honneth. *Redistribution or Recognition? A Philosophical Exchange*. Trans. Joel Golb. London: Verso Books, forthcoming.

Frede, Dorothea. "Necessity, Chance, and 'What Happens for the Most Part' in Aristotle's *Poetics*." In *Essays on Aristotle's Poetics*, ed. Amélie Oksenberg Rorty. Princeton: Princeton University Press, 1992.

Freimark, Peter. "Language Behavior and Assimilation: The Situation of the Jews in Northern Germany in the First Half of the Nineteenth Century." *Leo Baeck Institute Year Book* 24 (1979): 157–77.

Freud, Sigmund. "Mourning and Melancholia." In *Collected Papers*. Vol. 4. Trans. Joan Riviere. New York: Basic Books, 1959.

Freund, Ismar. *Die Emanzipation der Juden in Preußen*. 2 vols. Berlin: Poppelauer, 1912.

Fukuyama, Francis. *The End of History and the Last Man*. New York: Free Press, 1992.

Fuss, Diana. *Essentially Speaking: Feminism, Nature, and Difference*. New York: Routledge, 1989.

Gaier, Ulrich. *Herders Sprachphilosophie und Erkenntniskritik*. Stuttgart: Frommann-Holzboog, 1988.

Galeotti, Anna Elisabetta. "Citizenship and Equality: The Place for Toleration." *Political Theory* 21, no. 4 (November 1993): 585–605.

García Düttmann, Alexander. *Between Cultures: Tensions in the Struggle for Recognition*. Trans. Kenneth B. Woodgate. London: Verso, 2000.

Garland, Robert. *The Greek Way of Death*. Ithaca: Cornell University Press, 1985.

Gauthier, Jeffrey A. *Hegel and Feminist Social Criticism: Justice, Recognition, and the Feminine*. Albany: SUNY Press, 1997.

Geiger, Ludwig. *Geschichte der Juden in Berlin*. 2 vols. in 1. Berlin: Guttentag, 1871.

Gellrich, Michelle. *Tragedy and Theory: The Problem of Conflict Since Aristotle*. Princeton: Princeton University Press, 1988.

Genovese, Eugene D. *Roll, Jordan, Roll: The World the Slaves Made*. New York: Pantheon Books, 1974.

Gewirtz, Paul. "Aeschylus' Law." *Harvard Law Review* 101 (1988): 1043–55.

Gilman, Sander L. *Jewish Self-Hatred: Anti-Semitism and the Hidden Language of the Jews*. Baltimore: Johns Hopkins University Press, 1986.

Gitlin, Todd. *The Twilight of Common Dreams: Why America is Wracked by Culture Wars*. New York: Metropolitan Books, 1995.

Goheen, Robert F. "Aspects of Dramatic Symbolism: Three Studies in the 'Oresteia.'" *American Journal of Philology* 76, no. 2 (April 1955): 113–37.

———. *The Imagery of Sophocles' Antigone: A Study of Poetic Language and
Structure*. Princeton: Princeton University Press, 1951.

Goldberg, David Theo. "Introduction: Multicultural Conditions." In *Multiculturalism: A Critical Reader*, ed. David Theo Goldberg. Oxford: Blackwell,
1994.

Goldhill, Simon. "The Audience of Athenian Tragedy." In *The Cambridge Companion to Greek Tragedy*, ed. P. E. Easterling. Cambridge: Cambridge University Press, 1997.

———. "The Great Dionysia and Civic Ideology." In *Nothing to Do with Dio-
nysos? Athenian Drama in its Social Context*, ed. John J. Winkler and Froma
I. Zeitlin. Princeton: Princeton University Press, 1990.

———. "The Language of Tragedy: Rhetoric and Communication." In *The
Cambridge Companion to Greek Tragedy*, ed. P. E. Easterling. Cambridge:
Cambridge University Press, 1997.

———. *Language, Sexuality, Narrative: The Oresteia*. Cambridge: Cambridge
University Press, 1984.

———. *Reading Greek Tragedy*. Cambridge: Cambridge University Press, 1986.

Gooding-Williams, Robert. "Philosophy of History and Social Criticism in *The
Souls of Black Folk*." *Social Science Information* 26, no. 1 (March 1987):
99–114.

———. "Race, Multiculturalism and Democracy." *Constellations* 5, no. 1 (March
1998): 18–41.

Gordon, Rupert. "Hegel and the Politics of Difference." Paper presented at the
Annual Meeting of the American Political Science Assoiation (Washington,
D.C., August 31–September 3, 2000).

Graetz, Michael. "From Corporate Community to Ethnic-Religious Minority,
1750–1830." *Leo Baeck Institute Year Book* 37 (1992): 71–82.

Guinier, Lani, and Gerald Torres. *The Miner's Canary: Enlisting Race, Resisting
Power, Transforming Democracy*. Cambridge, MA: Harvard University Press,
2002.

Gutmann, Amy. "Introduction." In *Multiculturalism: Examining the Politics of
Recognition*, ed. Amy Gutmann. Princeton: Princeton University Press, 1994.

Gwyn, Richard. *Nationalism Without Walls: The Unbearable Lightness of
Being Canadian*. Toronto: McClelland & Stewart, 1995.

Habermas, Jürgen. "The European Nation-State: On the Past and Future of Sovereignty and Citizenship." In *The Inclusion of the Other: Studies in Political
Theory*, ed. Ciaran Cronin and Pablo De Greiff. Cambridge, MA: MIT Press,
1998.

———. "Labor and Interaction: Remarks on Hegel's Jena *Philosophy of Mind*."
In *Theory and Practice*. Trans. John Viertel. Boston: Beacon Press, 1973.

———. "Struggles for Recognition in the Democratic Constitutional State." In
The Inclusion of the Other, ed. and trans. Ciaran Cronin. Cambridge, MA:
MIT Press, 1998.

Hage, Ghassan. *White Nation: Fantasies of White Supremacy in a Multicultural
Society*. New York: Routledge, 2000.

Halliwell, Stephen. *Aristotle's* Poetics. London: Duckworth, 1986.

―――. *The Poetics of Aristotle: Translation and Commentary*. Chapel Hill: University of North Carolina Press, 1987.

Hamann, Johann Georg. *Briefwechsel*. Ed. Walther Ziesemer and Arthur Henkel. 7 vols. Wiesbaden: Insel, 1955–79.

Handler, Richard. "On Having a Culture: Nationalism and the Preservation of Quebec's Patrimoine." In *Objects and Others: Essays on Museums and Material Culture,* ed. George Stocking. Madison: University of Wisconsin Press, 1985.

―――. "Who Owns the Past? History, Cultural Property and the Logic of Possessive Individualism." In *The Politics of Culture*, ed. Brett Williams. Washington, D.C.: Smithsonian Institution, 1991.

Hanssen, Beatrice. "Ethics of the Other." In *Critique of Violence: Between Poststructuralism and Critical Theory*. London: Routledge, 2000.

Hardimon, Michael O. *Hegel's Social Philosophy: The Project of Reconciliation*. Cambridge: Cambridge University Press, 1994.

Harris, Cheryl. "Whiteness as Property." *Harvard Law Review* 106 (June 1993): 1707–91.

Harris, Henry S. "The Concept of Recognition in Hegel's Jena Manuscripts." In *Hegel in Jena*, ed. Dieter Henrich and Klaus Düsing. *Hegel-Studien*, Beiheft 20. Bonn: Bouvier Verlag Herbert Grundmann, 1980.

―――. *Hegel's Development*. Vol. 1, *Toward the Sunlight, 1770–1801*. Oxford: Oxford University Press, 1972.

Hasan-Rokem, Galit, and Alan Dundes, eds. *The Wandering Jew: Essays in the Interpretation of a Christian Legend*. Bloomington: Indiana University Press, 1986.

Hegel, Georg Wilhelm Friedrich. *Aesthetics: Lectures on Fine Art*. 2 vols. Trans. T. M. Knox. Oxford: Clarendon Press, 1975.

―――. *Elements of Hegel's Philosophy of Right*. Ed. Allen W. Wood. Trans. H. B. Nisbet. Cambridge: Cambridge University Press, 1991.

―――. "The German Constitution." In *Political Writings*, ed. Laurence Dickey and H. B. Nisbet. Trans. H. B. Nisbet. Cambridge: Cambridge University Press, 1999.

―――. *Hegel and the Human Spirit*. Ed. and trans. Leo Rauch. Detroit: Wayne State University Press, 1983.

―――. *Hegel's Phenomenology of Spirit*. Trans. A. V. Miller. Oxford: Oxford University Press, 1977.

―――. *Hegel's Philosophy of Mind*. Trans. William Wallace and A. V. Miller. Oxford: Clarendon Press, 1971.

―――. *Hegel's Philosophy of Right*. Trans. T. M. Knox. Oxford: Clarendon Press, 1942.

―――. *Lectures on Natural Right and Political Science*. Ed. Staff of the Hegel Archives. Trans. J. Michael Stewart and Peter C. Hodgson. Berkeley: University of California Press, 1995.

―――. *Lectures on the Philosophy of Religion*. 3 vols. Ed. Peter C. Hodgson. Trans. R. F. Brown et al. Berkeley: University of California Press, 1984–87.

―――. "On the Scientific Ways of Treating Natural Law." In *Political Writ-*

ings, ed. Laurence Dickey and H. B. Nisbet. Trans. H. B. Nisbet. Cambridge: Cambridge University Press, 1999.

———. *Philosophie des Rechts: Die Vorlesung von 1819/20 in einer Nachschrift*. Ed. Dieter Henrich. Frankfurt: Suhrkamp Verlag, 1983.

———. *Philosophy of History*. Trans. J. Sibree. New York: Dover Publications, 1956.

———. "The Positivity of the Christian Religion." In *Early Theological Writings*, ed. and trans. Richard Kroner and T. M. Knox. Philadelphia: University of Pennsylvania Press, 1971.

———. "The Spirit of Christianity and its Fate." In *Early Theological Writings*, ed. and trans. Richard Kroner and T. M. Knox. Philadelphia: University of Pennsylvania Press, 1971.

———. "The Tübingen Essay." In *Three Essays, 1793–1795*, ed. and trans. Peter Fuss and John Dobbins. Notre Dame, IN: University of Notre Dame Press, 1984.

———. *Vorlesungen über Naturrecht und Staatswissenschaft*. Ed. C. Becker, W. Bonsiepen et al. Hamburg: Felix Meiner Verlag, 1983.

———. *Vorlesungen über Rechtsphilosophie, 1818–1831*. Ed. Karl-Heinz Ilting. 4 vols. Stuttgart: Frommann-Holzboog, 1973.

———. *Werke*. 20 vols. Frankfurt: Suhrkamp Verlag, 1986.

Heidegger, Martin. *Being and Time*. Trans. John Macquarrie and Edward Robinson. New York: Harper and Row, 1962.

Held, David. "The Transformation of Political Community: Rethinking Democracy in the Context of Globalization." In *Democracy's Edges*, ed. Ian Shapiro and Casiano Hacker-Cordón. Cambridge: Cambridge University Press, 1999.

Herder, Johann Gottfried. "Essay on the Origin of Language." Trans. Alexander Gode. In Jean-Jacques Rousseau and Johann Gottfried Herder, *On the Origin of Language*. Chicago: University of Chicago Press, 1966.

———. "On Diligence in the Study of Several Learned Languages." In *Selected Early Works, 1764–1767*, ed. Ernest A. Menze and Karl Menges. Trans. Ernest A. Menze with Michael Palma. University Park: Pennsylvania State University Press, 1992.

———. *J. G. Herder on Social and Political Culture*. Ed. and trans. F. M. Barnard. Cambridge: Cambridge University Press, 1969.

———. *Outlines of a Philosophy of the History of Man*. Trans. T. Churchill. 2nd ed. 2 vols. London: J. Johnson, 1803.

———. *Sämmtliche Werke*. Ed. Bernhard Suphan. 33 vols. Berlin: Wiedmannsche Buchhandlung, 1877–1913.

———. "Selections from *A Metacritique of the Critique of Pure Reason*." In *Metacritique: The Linguistic Assault on German Idealism*, ed. and trans. Jere Paul Surber. Amherst, NY: Humanity Books, 2001.

———. *The Spirit of Hebrew Poetry*. Trans. James Marsh. 2 vols. Burlington: Edward Smith, 1833. Reprint: 2 vols. in 1. Naperville, IL: Aleph Press, 1971.

———. "Yet Another Philosophy of History." In *Against Pure Reason: Writings on Religion, Language, and History*. Ed. and trans. Marcia Bunge. Minneapolis: Fortress Press, 1993.

Hertzberg, Arthur. *The French Enlightenment and the Jews*. New York: Columbia University Press, 1968.

Hester, D. A. "Sophocles the Unphilosophical: A Study in the *Antigone*." *Mnemosyne*, 4th ser., 24 (1971): 11–59.

Hinsley, F. H. *Sovereignty*. 2nd ed. Cambridge: Cambridge University Press, 1986.

Hirschkind, Charles, and Saba Mahmood. "Feminism, the Taliban, and Politics of Counter-Insurgency." *Anthropological Quarterly* 75, no. 2 (Spring 2002): 339–54.

Hobbes, Thomas. *Leviathan*. Ed. Michael Oakeshott. Oxford: Basil Blackwell, 1955.

Holeczek, Heinz. "Die Judenemanzipation in Preußen." In *Die Juden als Minderheit in der Geschichte*, ed. Bernd Martin and Ernst Schulin. Munich: Deutscher Taschenbuch Verlag, 1981.

Holst-Warhaft, Gail. *Dangerous Voices: Women's Laments and Greek Literature*. London: Routledge, 1992.

Honig, Bonnie. "Dead Rights, Live Futures: A Reply to Habermas's 'Constitutional Democracy.'" *Political Theory* 29, no. 6 (December 2001): 792–805.

———. *Democracy and the Foreigner*. Princeton: Princeton University Press, 2001.

———. "'My Culture Made Me Do It.'" In *Is Multiculturalism Bad For Women?*, by Susan Moller Okin et al. Ed. Joshua Cohen, Matthew Howard, and Martha C. Nussbaum. Princeton: Princeton University Press, 1999.

———. *Political Theory and the Displacement of Politics*. Ithaca: Cornell University Press, 1993.

Honig, Bonnie, ed. *Feminist Interpretations of Hannah Arendt*. University Park: Pennsylvania State University Press, 1995.

Honneth, Axel. *The Fragmented World of the Social: Essays in Social and Political Philosophy*. Ed. Charles W. Wright. Albany: SUNY Press, 1995.

———. "Invisibility: On the Epistemology of 'Recognition.'" *The Aristotelian Society Supplementary Volume* (2001): 111–26.

———. "Redistribution as Recognition: A Response to Nancy Fraser." in *Redistribution or Recognition? A Philosophical Exchange*, by Nancy Fraser and Axel Honneth. Trans. Joel Golb. London: Verso Books, forthcoming.

———. *The Struggle for Recognition: The Moral Grammar of Social Conflicts*. Trans. Joel Anderson. Cambridge, MA: MIT Press, 1996.

Huber, Ernst Rudolf. *Dokumente zur deutschen Verfassungsgeschichte*. 5 vols. Stuttgart: Kohlhammer, 1961.

Humphries, S. C. *The Family, Women, and Death: Comparative Studies*. 2nd ed. Ann Arbor: University of Michigan Press, 1993.

Hyppolite, Jean. *Genesis and Structure of Hegel's Phenomenology of Spirit*. Trans. Samuel Cherniak and John Heckman. Evanston: Northwestern University Press, 1974.

Ignatiev, Noel. *How the Irish Became White*. New York: Routledge, 1995.

Ilting, K.-H. "The Structure of Hegel's *Philosophy of Right*." In *Hegel's Political*

Philosophy: Problems and Perspectives, ed. Z. A. Pelczynski. Cambridge: Cambridge University Press, 1971.

Irigaray, Luce. *Speculum of the Other Woman*. Trans. Gillian C. Gill. Ithaca: Cornell University Press, 1985.

Jenkins, I. D. "The Ambiguity of Greek Textiles." *Arethusa* 18, no. 2 (Fall 1985): 109–32.

Johnson, James. "Why Respect Culture?" *American Journal of Political Science* 44, no. 3 (July 2000): 405–18.

Jolowicz, H. *Geschichte der Juden in Königsberg in Preußen*. Posen: Joseph Jolowicz, 1867.

Jones, John. *On Aristotle and Greek Tragedy*. London: Chatto & Windus, 1962.

Jurist, Elliot L. *Beyond Hegel and Nietzsche: Philosophy, Culture, and Agency*. Cambridge, MA: MIT Press, 2000.

———. "Hegel's Concept of Recognition." *The Owl of Minerva* 19, no. 1 (Fall 1987): 5–22.

Kain, Philip J. "Self-Consciousness, The Other and Hegel's Dialectic of Recognition: Alternative to a Post-Modern Subterfuge." *Philosophy and Social Criticism* 24, no. 5 (September 1998): 105–26.

Kant, Immanuel. *Groundwork of the Metaphysics of Morals*. Ed. and trans. Mary Gregor. Cambridge: Cambridge University Press, 1997.

Kastoryano, Riva. *Negotiating Identities: States and Immigrants in France and Germany*. Trans. Barbara Harshav. Princeton: Princeton University Press, 2002.

Kateb, George. "Individuality and Egotism." In *Skepticism, Individuality, and Freedom: The Reluctant Liberalism of Richard Flathman*, ed. Bonnie Honig and David R. Mapel. Minneapolis: University of Minnesota Press, 2002.

———. "Notes on Pluralism." *Social Research* 61, no. 3 (Fall 1994): 511–37.

Katz, Jacob. "A State Within a State: The History of an Anti-Semitic Slogan." In *Zur Assimilation und Emanzipation der Juden: Ausgewählte Schriften*. Darmstadt: Wissenschaftliche Buchgesellschaft, 1982.

———. "The Term 'Jewish Emancipation': Its Origin and Historical Impact." In *Zur Assimilation und Emanzipation der Juden: Ausgewählte Schriften*. Darmstadt: Wissenschaftliche Buchgesellschaft, 1982.

———. *Out of the Ghetto: The Social Background of Jewish Emancipation, 1770–1870*. Cambridge, MA: Harvard University Press, 1973.

Kieffer, Bruce. "Herder's Treatment of Süssmilch's Theory of the Origin of Language in the *Abhandlung über den Ursprung der Sprache*: A Re-evaluation." *The Germanic Review* 53, no. 3 (Summer 1978): 96–105.

Kitto, H. D. F. *Form and Meaning in Drama: A Study of Six Greek Plays and of Hamlet*. 2nd ed. London: Methuen, 1964.

Kojève, Alexandre. *Introduction to the Reading of Hegel*. Ed. Allan Bloom. Trans. James H. Nichols, Jr. Ithaca: Cornell University Press, 1980.

Konstan, David. "Greek Friendship." *American Journal of Philology* 117 (1996): 71–94.

Koselleck, Reinhart. *Preußen Zwischen Reform und Revolution: Allgemeines*

Landrecht, Verwaltung, und soziale Bewegung von 1791 bis 1848. Stuttgart: Ernst Klett Verlag, 1967.

Kosman, Aryeh. "Acting: *Drama* as the *Mimêsis* of *Praxis*." In *Essays on Aristotle's* Poetics, ed. Amélie Oksenberg Rorty. Princeton: Princeton University Press, 1992.

Krasner, Stephen D. *Sovereignty: Organized Hypocrisy*. Princeton: Princeton University Press, 1999.

Kratochwil, Friedrich. "Sovereignty as *Dominium*: Is There a Right of Humanitarian Intervention?" In *Beyond Westphalia: State Sovereignty and International Intervention*, ed. Gene M. Lyons and Michael Mastanduno. Baltimore: The Johns Hopkins University Press, 1995.

Kuhns, Richard. *The House, the City, and the Judge: The Growth of Moral Awareness in the* Oresteia. Indianapolis: Bobbs-Merrill, 1962.

Kuper, Adam. *Culture: The Anthropologists' Account*. Cambridge, MA: Harvard University Press, 1999.

Kurtz, Donna C., and John Boardman. *Greek Burial Customs*. London: Thames and Hudson, 1971.

Kymlicka, Will. "Comments on Shachar and Spinner-Halev: An Update from the Multiculturalism Wars." In *Multicultural Questions*. Ed. Christian Joppke and Steven Lukes. Oxford: Oxford University Press, 1999.

———. *Finding Our Way: Rethinking Ethnocultural Relations in Canada*. Toronto: Oxford University Press, 1998.

———. "Liberal Complacencies." In *Is Multiculturalism Bad For Women?*, by Susan Moller Okin, et al. Ed. Joshua Cohen, Matthew Howard, and Martha C. Nussbaum. Princeton: Princeton University Press, 1999.

———. *Liberalism, Community, and Culture*. Oxford: Clarendon Press, 1989.

———. *Multicultural Citizenship: A Liberal Theory of Minority Rights*. Oxford: Clarendon Press, 1995.

———. *Politics in the Vernacular: Nationalism, Multiculturalism and Citizenship*. Oxford: Oxford University Press, 2001.

Lacey, W. K. *The Family in Classical Greece*. Auckland: University of Auckland, 1980.

Laclau, Ernesto. "Beyond Emancipation." In *Emancipation(s)*. London: Verso, 1996.

———. "Death and Resurrection of the Theory of Ideology." *MLN* 112, no. 3 (April 1997): 297–321.

———. "Deconstruction, Pragmatism, Hegemony." In *Deconstruction and Pragmatism*, by Simon Critchley et al. Ed. Chantal Mouffe. London: Routledge, 1996.

———. "The Impossibility of Society." In *New Reflections on the Revolution of Our Time*. London: Verso, 1990.

———. "Universalism, Particularism, and the Question of Identity." In *Emancipation(s)*. London: Verso, 1996.

———. "Why Do Empty Signifiers Matter to Politics?" In *Emancipation(s)*. London: Verso, 1996.

Laclau, Ernesto, and Chantal Mouffe. *Hegemony and Socialist Strategy: Towards a Radical Democratic Politics*. London: Verso, 1985.

Laclau, Ernesto, and Chantal Mouffe. "Post-Marxism without Apologies." In *New Reflections on the Revolution of Our Time*, by Ernesto Laclau. London: Verso, 1990.

Larmore, Charles. *The Romantic Legacy*. New York: Columbia University Press, 1996.

Lauterpacht, H. *Recognition in International Law*. Cambridge: Cambridge University Press, 1947.

Lefort, Claude. "The Question of Democracy." In *Democracy and Political Theory*. Trans. David Macey. Minneapolis: University of Minnesota Press, 1988.

Le Goff, Jacques. *Medieval Civilization, 400–1500*. Trans. Julia Barrow. Oxford: Blackwell, 1989.

Levy, Jacob T. *The Multiculturalism of Fear*. Oxford: Oxford University Press, 2000.

Lichter, Matthias. *Die Staatsangehörigkeit nach deutschem und ausländischem Recht*. 2nd ed. Berlin: Carl Heymanns Verlag, 1955.

Liddell, Henry George, and Robert Scott. *A Greek-English Lexicon*. 9th ed., rev. Henry Stuart Jones and Roderick McKenzie. Oxford: Oxford University Press, 1968.

Linker, Damon. "The Reluctant Pluralism of J. G. Herder." *Review of Politics* 62, no. 2 (Spring 2000): 267–93.

Lloyd, David, and Paul Thomas. *Culture and the State*. New York: Routledge, 1998.

Lowenstein, Steven M. *The Mechanics of Change: Essays in the Social History of German Jewry*. Atlanta: Scholars Press, 1992.

Luban, David. "Some Greek Trials." In *Legal Modernism*. Ann Arbor: University of Michigan Press, 1994.

Lüdtke, Alf. *Police and State in Prussia, 1815–1850*. Trans. Pete Burgess. Cambridge: Cambridge University Press, 1989.

Lukács, Georg. *The Young Hegel: Studies in the Relations Between Dialectics and Economics*. Trans. Rodney Livingstone. Cambridge, MA: MIT Press, 1976.

Marcuse, Herbert. *Reason and Revolution: Hegel and the Rise of Social Theory*. New York: Humanities Press, 1954.

Margalit, Avishai, and Moshe Halbertal. "Liberalism and the Right to Culture." *Social Research* 61, no. 3 (Fall 1994): 491–510.

Markell, Patchen. "Contesting Consensus: Rereading Habermas on the Public Sphere." *Constellations* 3, no. 3 (1997): 377–400.

———. "Making Affect Safe for Democracy? On 'Constitutional Patriotism.'" *Political Theory* 28, no. 1 (February 2000): 38–63.

———. "The Recognition of Politics: A Comment on Emcke and Tully." *Constellations* 7, no. 4 (December 2000): 496–506.

Marx, Karl. *Capital*. Vol. 1. Trans. Ben Fowkes. New York: Vintage Books, 1977.

———. "Contribution to the Critique of Hegel's Philosophy of Right: Introduction." In *The Marx-Engels Reader*, by Karl Marx and Friedrich Engels. Ed. Richard C. Tucker. 2nd ed. London: W. W. Norton, 1978.

———. *A Contribution to the Critique of Political Economy*. Ed. Maurice Dobb. Trans. S. W. Ryazanskaya. New York: International Publishers, 1970.

———. "Critique of Hegel's Doctrine of the State." In *Early Writings*, trans. Rodney Livingstone and Gregor Benton. London: Penguin Books, 1992.

———. "Excerpts from James Mill's *Elements of Political Economy*." In *Early Writings*. Trans. Rodney Livingstone and Gregor Benton. London: Penguin Books, 1992.

———. *Die Frühschriften*. Ed. Siegfried Landshut. Stuttgart: Alfred Kröner Verlag, 1971.

———. "On the Jewish Question." In *The Marx-Engels Reader*, by Karl Marx and Friedrich Engels. Ed. Richard C. Tucker. 2nd ed. London: W. W. Norton, 1978.

McClure, Laura. "Clytemnestra's Binding Spell (*Ag.* 958–974)." *The Classical Journal* 92, no. 2 (December 1996–January 1997): 123–40.

McCumber, John. "Dialectical Identity in a 'Post-Critical' Era: A Hegelian Reading." *South Atlantic Quarterly* 94, no. 4 (Fall 1995): 1145–60.

———. *Poetic Interaction: Language, Freedom, Reason*. Chicago: University of Chicago Press, 1989.

Meier, Christian. *The Greek Discovery of Politics*. Trans. David McLintock. Cambridge, MA: Harvard University Press, 1990.

Mendes-Flohr, Paul. *German Jews: A Dual Identity*. New Haven: Yale University Press, 1999.

Menke, Christoph. *Tragödie im Sittlichen: Gerechtigkeit und Freiheit nach Hegel*. Frankfurt am Main: Suhrkamp, 1996.

Meyer, Michael A. *German Political Pressure and Jewish Religious Response in the Nineteenth Century*. New York: Leo Baeck Institute, 1981.

———"The Religious Reform Controversy in the Berlin Jewish Community, 1814–1823." *Leo Baeck Institute Year Book* 24 (1979): 139–55.

———. *Response to Modernity: A History of the Reform Movement in Judaism*. Detroit: Wayne State University Press, 1995.

———, ed. *German-Jewish History in Modern Times*. Vol. 1, *Tradition and Enlightenment: 1600–1780*. New York: Columbia University Press, 1996.

———, ed. *German-Jewish History in Modern Times*. Vol. 2, *Emancipation and Acculturation: 1780–1871*. New York: Columbia University Press, 1997.

Michaels, Walter Benn. "Race into Culture: A Critical Genealogy of Cultural Identity." In *Identities*, ed. Kwame Anthony Appiah and Henry Louis Gates, Jr. Chicago: University of Chicago Press, 1995.

Miller, David. *On Nationality*. Oxford: Oxford University Press, 1995.

Mills, Charles W. *Blackness Visible: Essays on Philosophy and Race*. Ithaca: Cornell University Press, 1998.

Mills, Patricia Jagentowicz. *Woman, Nature, and Psyche*. New Haven: Yale University Press, 1987.

Mills, Patricia Jagentowicz, ed. *Feminist Interpretations of G. W. F. Hegel*. University Park: Pennsylvania State University Press, 1996.

———. "Hegel and the 'Woman Question.'" In *The Sexism of Social and Political Theory: Women and Reproduction from Plato to Nietzsche*, ed. Lorenne M. G. Clark and Lynda Lange. Toronto: University of Toronto Press, 1979.

———. "Hegel's *Antigone*." In *Feminist Interpretations of G. W. F. Hegel*, ed. Patricia Jagentowicz Mills. University Park: Pennsylvania State University Press, 1996.

Minow, Martha. *Not Only for Myself: Identity, Politics, and the Law.* New York: New Press, 1997.

Mitchell, Timothy. "The Limits of the State: Beyond Statist Approaches and their Critics." *American Political Science Review* 85, no. 1 (March 1991): 77–96.

Moore, R. I. *The First European Revolution, c. 970–1215.* Oxford: Blackwell, 2000.

———. *The Formation of a Persecuting Society: Power and Deviance in Western Europe, 950–1250.* Oxford: Blackwell, 1990.

Morrell, Kenneth Scott. "The Fabric of Persuasion: Clytemnestra, Agamemnon, and the Sea of Garments." *The Classical Journal* 92, no. 2 (December 1996–January 1997): 141–65.

Morton, Michael. *Herder and the Poetics of Thought: Unity and Diversity in On Diligence in Several Learned Languages.* University Park: Pennsylvania State University Press, 1989.

Moruzzi, Norma Claire. "A Problem with Headscarves: Contemporary Complexities of Political and Social Identity." *Political Theory* 22, no. 4 (November 1994): 653–72.

Mosse, Werner E. "From '*Schutzjuden*' to '*Deutsche Staatsbürger jüdischen Glaubens*': The Long and Bumpy Road of Jewish Emancipation in Germany." In *Paths of Emancipation: Jews, States, and Citizenship,* ed. Pierre Birnbaum and Ira Katznelson. Princeton: Princeton University Press, 1995.

Murnaghan, Sheila. "*Antigone* 904–20 and the Institution of Marriage." *American Journal of Philology* 107, no. 2 (Summer 1986): 192–207.

———. "Sucking the Juice without Biting the Rind: Aristotle and Tragic Mimêsis." *New Literary History* 26, no. 4 (Autumn 1995): 755–73.

Muthu, Sankar. *Enlightement against Empire.* Princeton: Princeton University Press, 2003.

Nagel, Thomas. "Moral Luck." In *Mortal Questions.* Cambridge: Cambridge University Press, 1979.

Neocleous, Mark. *Administering Civil Society: Towards a Theory of State Power.* London: Macmillan Press, 1996.

Neuburg, Matt. "How Like a Woman: Antigone's 'Inconsistency.'" *Classical Quarterly* 40, no. 1 (1990): 54–76.

Neuhouser, Frederick. *Foundations of Hegel's Social Theory: Actualizing Freedom.* Cambridge, MA: Harvard University Press, 2000.

Nietzsche, Friedrich. *Human, All Too Human.* Trans. R. J. Hollingdale. Cambridge: Cambridge University Press, 1986.

Noiriel, Gérard. "The Identification of the Citizen: The Birth of Republican Civil Status in France." In *Documenting Individual Identity: The Development of State Practices in the Modern World,* ed. Jane Caplan and John Torpey. Princeton: Princeton University Press, 2001.

Norval, Aletta J. "Frontiers in Question." *Filosofski Vestnik* 18, no. 2 (1997): 51–75.

Novotny, Kristin M. "'Taylor'-Made? Feminist Theory and the Politics of Identity." *Women and Politics* 19, no. 3 (1998): 1–19.

Noys, Benjamin. *Georges Bataille: A Critical Introduction.* London: Pluto Press, 2000.

Nussbaum, Martha C. *The Fragility of Goodness: Luck and Ethics in Greek Tragedy and Philosophy*. Cambridge: Cambridge University Press, 1986.

———. *Sex and Social Justice*. New York: Oxford University Press, 1999.

Nussbaum, Martha C., et al. *For Love of Country: Debating the Limits of Patriotism*. Ed. Joshua Cohen. Boston: Beacon Press, 1996.

O'Brien, Joan V. *Guide to Sophocles' Antigone*. Carbondale: Southern Illinois University Press, 1978.

Okin, Susan Moller. "Feminism and Multiculturalism: Some Tensions." *Ethics* 108, no. 4 (July 1998): 661–84.

———. "Feminism, Women's Human Rights, and Cultural Differences." *Hypatia* 13, no. 2 (Spring 1998): 32–52.

———. "Is Multiculturalism Bad for Women?" In *Is Multiculturalism Bad For Women?*, by Susan Moller Okin et al. Ed. Joshua Cohen, Matthew Howard, and Martha C. Nussbaum. Princeton: Princeton University Press, 1999.

——— et al. *Is Multiculturalism Bad For Women?* Ed. Joshua Cohen, Matthew Howard, and Martha C. Nussbaum. Princeton: Princeton University Press, 1999.

Oliver, Kelly. *Witnessing: Beyond Recognition*. Minneapolis: University of Minnesota Press, 2001.

Olson, Joel. "The Democratic Problem of the White Citizen." *Constellations* 8, no. 2 (June 2001): 163–83.

———. "The Du Boisian Alternative to the Politics of Recognition." Paper presented at the Annual Meeting of the American Political Science Association (Washington, D.C., August 31–September 3, 2000).

Onuf, Nicholas Greenwood. *The Republican Legacy in International Thought*. Cambridge: Cambridge University Press, 1998.

Orlie, Melissa A. "Forgiving Trespasses, Promising Futures." In *Feminist Interpretations of Hannah Arendt*, ed. Bonnie Honig. University Park: Pennsylvania State University Press, 1995.

———. *Living Ethically, Acting Politically*. Ithaca: Cornell University Press, 1997.

Ortner, Sherry B., ed. *The Fate of "Culture": Geertz and Beyond*. Berkeley: University of California Press, 1999.

Osborne, Peter. *The Politics of Time: Modernity and Avant-Garde*. London: Verso, 1995.

Owen, David. "Cultural Diversity and the Conversation of Justice: Reading Cavell on Political Voice and the Expression of Consent." *Political Theory* 27, no. 5 (October 1999): 579–96.

———. "Political Philosophy in a Post-Imperial Voice." *Economy and Society* 28, no. 4 (November 1999): 520–49.

Owen, David, and Aaron Ridley. "Dramatis Personae: Nietzsche, Culture, and Human Types." In *Why Nietzsche Still? Reflections on Drama, Culture, and Politics*, ed. Alan D. Schrift. Berkeley: University of California Press, 2000.

Owen, E. T. *The Harmony of Aeschylus*. Toronto: Clarke, Irwin, 1952.

Pateman, Carole. *The Sexual Contract*. Stanford: Stanford University Press, 1988.

Patten, Alan. *Hegel's Idea of Freedom*. Oxford: Oxford University Press, 1999.

Patterson, Orlando. *Slavery and Social Death: A Comparative Study*. Cambridge, MA: Harvard University Press, 1982.

Phillips, Anne. "From Inequality to Difference: A Severe Case of Displacement?" *New Left Review* 224 (July–August 1997): 143–53.

———. "Why Worry about Multiculturalism?" *Dissent* (Winter 1997): 57–63.

Philpott, Daniel. "Ideas and the Evolution of Sovereignty." In *State Sovereignty: Change and Persistence in International Relations*, ed. Sohail H. Hashmi. University Park: Pennsylvania State University Press, 1997.

Pinkard, Terry. *Hegel's Phenomenology: The Sociality of Reason.* Cambridge: Cambridge University Press, 1994.

Pippin, Robert B. "Hegel and Institutional Rationality." *Southern Journal of Philosophy* 39 (2001): 1–25.

———. *Modernism as a Philosophical Problem: On the Dissatisfactions of European High Culture.* Cambridge, MA: Basil Blackwell, 1991.

———. "You Can't Get There From Here." In the *Cambridge Companion to Hegel*, ed. Frederick C. Beiser. Cambridge: Cambridge University Press, 1993.

Pirro, Robert C. *Hannah Arendt and the Politics of Tragedy.* DeKalb: Northern Illinois University Press, 2001.

Pitkin, Hanna Fenichel. *The Attack of the Blob: Hannah Arendt's Concept of the Social.* Chicago: University of Chicago Press, 1998.

———. *Fortune is a Woman: Gender and Politics in the Thought of Niccolò Machiavelli.* Berkeley: University of California Press, 1984.

———. "Justice: On Relating Private and Public." *Political Theory* 9, no. 3 (August 1981): 327–52.

———. *Wittgenstein and Justice: On the Significance of Ludwig Wittgenstein for Social and Political Thought.* New ed. Berkeley: University of California Press, 1993.

Pizer, John. "Herder, Benjamin, and the 'Ursprung' of Language." *Carleton Germanic Papers* 16 (1988): 31–46.

Plato. *Republic.* Trans. G. M. A. Grube. Revised by C. D. C. Reeve. Indianapolis: Hackett, 1992.

Podlecki, Anthony J. *The Political Background of Aeschylean Tragedy.* Ann Arbor: University of Michigan Press, 1966.

Pöggeler, Otto. "Hegel und die griechische Tragödie." In *Hegels Idee einer Phänomenologie des Geistes.* 2nd ed. Freiburg: Verlag Karl Alber, 1993.

Povinelli, Elizabeth A. *The Cunning of Recognition: Indigenous Alterity and the Making of Australian Multiculturalism.* Durham: Duke University Press, 2002.

———. "The State of Shame: Australian Multiculturalism and the Crisis of Indigenous Citizenship." *Critical Inquiry* 24, no. 2 (Winter 1998): 575–610.

Rabinowitz, Nancy S. "From Force to Persuasion: Aeschylus' *Oresteia* as Cosmogonic Myth." *Ramus* 10, no. 2 (1981): 159–91.

Rancière, Jacques. *Disagreement: Politics and Philosophy.* Trans. Julie Rose. Minneapolis: University of Minnesota Press, 1999.

Ravven, Heidi M. "Has Hegel Anything to Say to Feminists?" In *Feminist Interpretations of G. W. F. Hegel*, ed. Patricia Jagentowicz Mills. University Park: Pennsylvania State University Press, 1996.

Rawls, John. *Political Liberalism*. New York: Columbia University Press, 1993.

———. *A Theory of Justice*. Cambridge, MA: Harvard University Press, 1971.

Rehm, Rush. *Marriage to Death: The Conflation of Wedding and Funeral Rituals in Greek Tragedy*. Princeton: Princeton University Press, 1994.

Reinhardt, Mark. *The Art of Being Free: Taking Liberties with Tocqueville, Marx, and Arendt*. Ithaca: Cornell University Press, 1997.

Richarz, Monika. *Jewish Life in Germany: Memoirs from Three Centuries*. Trans. Stella P. Rosenfeld and Sidney Rosenfeld. Bloomington: Indiana University Press, 1991.

Rocco, Christopher. "Democracy and Discipline in Aeschylus's *Oresteia*." In *Tragedy and Enlightenment: Athenian Political Thought and the Dilemmas of Modernity*. Berkeley: University of California Press, 1997.

Rockefeller, Steven C. "Comment." In *Multiculturalism: Examining the Politics of Recognition*, ed. Amy Gutmann. Princeton: Princeton University Press, 1994.

Rockmore, Tom. *Cognition: An Introduction to Hegel's* Phenomenology of Spirit. Berekeley: University of California Press, 1997.

Roediger, David R. *The Wages of Whiteness: Race and the Making of the American Working Class*. London: Verson, 1991.

Rönne, Ludwig von, and Heinrich Simon. *Die früheren und gegenwärtigen Verhältnisse der Juden in den sämmtlichen Landestheilen des Preußischen Staates*. Breslau: Aderholtz, 1843.

Rorty, Amélie Oksenberg. "The Hidden Politics of Cultural Identification." *Political Theory* 22, no. 1 (February 1994): 152–66.

———. "The Psychology of Aristotelian Tragedy." In *Essays on Aristotle's* Poetics, ed. Amélie Oksenberg Rorty. Princeton: Princeton University Press, 1992.

Rose, Gillian. *Mourning Becomes the Law: Philosophy and Representation*. Cambridge: Cambridge University Press, 1996.

Rose, Nikolas. *Powers of Freedom: Reframing Political Thought*. Cambridge: Cambridge University Press, 1999.

Rose, Paul Lawrence. *German Question/Jewish Question: Revolutionary Antisemitism from Kant to Wagner*. Princeton: Princeton University Press, 1990.

Rosivach, Vincent J. "On Creon, *Antigone*, and Not Burying the Dead." *Rheinisches Museum für Philologie* 126, nos. 3–4 (1983): 193–211.

Roth, Michael S. *Knowing and History: Appropriations of Hegel in Twentieth-Century France*. Ithaca: Cornell University Press, 1988.

Rousseau, Jean-Jacques. "Letter to M. D'Alembert on the Theatre." In *Politics and the Arts*, ed. and trans. Allan Bloom. Ithaca: Cornell University Press, 1968.

Rürup, Reinhard. "Jewish Emancipation and Bourgeois Society." *Leo Baeck Institute Year Book* 14 (1969): 67–91.

———. "The Tortuous and Thorny Path to Legal Equality: 'Jew Laws' and Emancipatory Legislation in Germany from the Late Eighteenth Century." *Leo Baeck Institute Year Book* 31 (1986): 3–33.

Sacks, Peter M. *The English Elegy: Studies in the Genre from Spenser to Yeats*. Baltimore: The Johns Hopkins University Press, 1985.

Sandel, Michael J. *Liberalism and the Limits of Justice*. Cambridge: Cambridge University Press, 1982.

Santner, Eric L. *Stranded Objects: Mourning, Memory and Film in Postwar Germany*. Ithaca: Cornell University Press, 1990.

Sassen, Saskia. *Losing Control: Sovereignty in an Age of Globalization*. New York: Columbia University Press, 1996.

Saxonhouse, Arlene. "Aeschylus' *Oresteia*: Misogyny, Philogyny and Justice." *Women and Politics* 4, no. 2 (Summer 1984): 11–32.

Schlesinger, Arthur M., Jr. *The Disuniting of America: Reflections on a Multicultural Society*. New York: Norton, 1993.

Schmidt, Dennis J. *On Germans and Other Greeks: Tragedy and Ethical Life*. Bloomington: Indiana University Press, 2001.

Schmidt, H. D. "The Terms of Emancipation, 1781–1812: The Public Debate in Germany and its Effect on the Mentality and Ideas of German Jewry." *Leo Baeck Institute Year Book* 1 (1956): 28–47.

Schmitt, Carl. *The Concept of the Political*. Trans. George Schwab. Chicago: University of Chicago Press, 1996.

Scott, James C. *Seeing Like a State: How Certain Schemes to Improve the Human Condition Have Failed*. New Haven: Yale University Press, 1998.

Scott, James C., John Tehranian, and Jeremy Mathias. "The Production of Legal Identities Proper to States: The Case of the Permanent Family Surname." *Comparative Studies in Society and History* 44, no. 1 (January 2002): 4–44.

Scott, Joan W. "Multiculturalism and the Politics of Identity." In *The Identity in Question*, ed. John Rajchman. New York: Routledge, 1995.

Seaford, Richard. "The Imprisonment of Women in Greek Tragedy." *Journal of Hellenic Studies* 110 (1990): 76–90.

Segal, Charles. "The Female Voice and Its Contradictions: From Homer to Tragedy." In *Religio Graeco-Romana: Festschrift für Walter Pötscher*, ed. Joachim Dalfen et al. *Grazer Beiträge*, supp. 5. Graz: Institut für Klassische Philologie, 1993.

———. "Lament and Closure in *Antigone*." In *Sophocles' Tragic World: Divinity, Nature, Society*. Cambridge, MA: Harvard University Press, 1995.

———. *Tragedy and Civilization: An Interpretation of Sophocles*. Cambridge, MA: Harvard University Press, 1981.

Seidman, Steven. *Difference Troubles: Queering Social Theory and Sexual Politics*. Cambridge: Cambridge University Press, 1997.

Sewell, William H., Jr. "The Concept(s) of Culture." In *Beyond the Cultural Turn: New Directions in the Study of Society and Culture*, ed. Victoria E. Bonnell and Lynn Hunt. Berkeley: University of California Press, 1999.

Shachar, Ayelet. *Multicultural Jurisdictions: Cultural Differences and Women's Rights*. Cambridge: Cambridge University Press, 2001.

Shapiro, Michael J. *For Moral Ambiguity: National Culture and the Politics of the Family*. Minneapolis: University of Minnesota Press, 2001.

Sheehan, James J. *German History, 1770–1866*. Oxford: Clarendon Press, 1989.

Sherman, Nancy. *The Fabric of Character: Aristotle's Theory of Virtue*. Oxford: Clarendon Press, 1989.

———. "*Hamartia* and Virtue." In *Essays on Aristotle's* Poetics, ed. Amélie Oksenberg Rorty. Princeton: Princeton University Press, 1992.

Shklar, Judith N. *Freedom and Independence: A Study of the Political Ideas of Hegel's* Phenomenology of Mind. Cambridge: Cambridge University Press, 1976.

———. "Hegel's 'Phenomenology': An Elegy for Hellas." In *Hegel's Political Philosophy: Problems and Perspectives*, ed. Z. A. Pelczynski. Cambridge: Cambridge University Press, 1971.

Shulvass, Moses A. *From East to West: The Westward Migration of Jews from Eastern Europe during the Seventeenth and Eighteenth Centuries*. Detroit: Wayne State University Press, 1971.

Siep, Ludwig. *Anerkennung als Prinzip der praktischen Philosophie: Untersuchungen zu Hegels Jenaer Philosophie des Geistes*. Freiburg: Karl Alber Verlag, 1979.

———. "Hegels Auseinandersetzung mit Hobbes in den Jenaer Schriften." *Hegel-Studien* 9 (1974): 155–207.

———. "The Struggle for Recognition: Hegel's Dispute with Hobbes in the Jena Writings." Trans. Charles Dudas. In *Hegel's Dialectic of Desire and Recognition: Texts and Commentary*, ed. John O'Neill. Albany: SUNY Press, 1996.

Skinner, Quentin. "The State." In *Political Innovation and Conceptual Change*, ed. Terence Ball, James Farr, and Russell L. Hanson. Cambridge: Cambridge University Press, 1989.

Smiley, Marion. *Moral Responsibility and the Boundaries of Community: Power and Accountability from a Pragmatic Point of View*. Chicago: University of Chicago Press, 1992.

Smith, Steven B. "Hegel and the Jewish Question: In Between Tradition and Modernity." *History of Political Thought* 12, no. 1 (Spring 1991): 87–106.

———. *Hegel's Critique of Liberalism: Rights in Context*. Chicago: University of Chicago Press, 1989.

———. *Spinoza, Liberalism, and the Question of Jewish Identity*. New Haven: Yale University Press, 1997.

Sommer, Doris. *Proceed with Caution, When Engaged by Minority Writing in the Americas*. Cambridge, MA: Harvard University Press, 1999.

Sophocles. *Antigone*. Trans. Elizabeth Wyckoff. In David Grene and Richmond Lattimore, eds. *The Complete Greek Tragedies*. Vol. 2, *Sophocles*. Chicago: University of Chicago Press, 1959.

———. *Antigone*. Ed. Mark Griffith. Cambridge: Cambridge University Press, 1999.

———. *The Antigone*. Part 3 of *The Plays and Fragments*, ed. R. C. Jebb. 3rd ed. Cambridge: Cambridge University Press, 1900.

———. *Oedipus at Colonus*. Trans. Robert Fitzgerald. In David Grene and Richmond Lattimore, eds. *The Complete Greek Tragedies*. Vol. 2, *Sophocles*. Chicago: University of Chicago Press, 1959.

Sophocles. *Oedipus the King*. Trans. David Grene. In David Grene and Richmond Lattimore, eds. *The Complete Greek Tragedies*. Vol. 2. *Sophocles*. Chicago: University of Chicago Press, 1959.

Sorkin, David. *The Transformation of German Jewry, 1780–1840*. New York: Oxford University Press, 1987.

Sorum, Christina Elliot. "The Family in Sophocles' *Antigone* and *Electra*." *Classical World* 75, no. 4 (March–April 1982): 201–11.

Sourvinou-Inwood, Christiane. "Assumptions and the Creation of Meaning: Reading Sophocles' *Antigone*." *Journal of Hellenic Studies* 109 (1989): 134–48.

———. *'Reading' Greek Death: To the End of the Classical Period*. Oxford: Clarendon Press, 1995.

Speight, Allen. *Hegel, Literature, and the Problem of Agency*. Cambridge: Cambridge University Press, 2001.

Spinner-Halev, Jeff. "Cultural Pluralism and Partial Citizenship." In *Multicultural Questions*, ed. Christian Joppke and Stephen Lukes. Oxford: Oxford University Press, 1999.

———. "Feminism, Multiculturalism, Oppression, and the State." *Ethics* 112, no. 1 (October 2001): 84–113.

Stam, James H. *Inquiries into the Origin of Language: The Fate of a Question*. New York: Harper and Row, 1976.

Stanford, W. B. *Greek Tragedy and the Emotions: An Introductory Study*. London: Routledge and Kegan Paul, 1983.

Steiner, George. *Antigones*. Oxford: Clarendon Press, 1984.

Sterling, Eleanore O. "Anti-Jewish Riots in Germany in 1819: A Displacement of Social Protest." *Historia Judaica* 12, pt. 2 (October 1950): 105–42.

Stevens, Jacqueline. *Reproducing the State*. Princeton: Princeton University Press, 1999.

Strang, David. "Contested Sovereignty: The Social Construction of Colonial Imperialism." In *State Sovereignty as Social Construct*, ed. Thomas J. Biersteker and Cynthia Weber. Cambridge: Cambridge University Press, 1996.

Stratton, Jon, and Ien Ang. "Multicultural Imagined Communities: Cultural Difference and National Identity in the USA and Australia." In *Multicultural States: Rethinking Difference and Identity*, ed. David Bennett. London: Routledge, 1998.

Strauss, Leo. *The Political Philosophy of Hobbes: Its Basis and Genesis*. Trans. Elsa M. Sinclair. Chicago: University of Chicago Press, 1936.

Suny, Ronald Grigor. "Constructing Primordialism: Old Histories for New Nations." *Journal of Modern History* 73, no. 4 (December 2001): 862–96.

Taminiaux, Jacques. *Heidegger and the Problem of Fundamental Ontology*. Ed. and trans. Michael Gendre. Albany: SUNY Press, 1991.

Taylor, Charles. "Atomism." In *Philosophy and the Human Sciences*. Vol. 2 of *Philosophical Papers*. Cambridge: Cambridge University Press, 1985.

———. "Cross-Purposes: The Liberal-Communitarian Debate." In *Philosophical Arguments*. Cambridge, MA: Harvard University Press, 1995.

———. "Democratic Exclusion (and Its Remedies?)" In *Citizenship, Diversity, and Pluralism: Canadian and Comparative Perspectives*, ed. Alan C. Cairns et al. Montreal: McGill-Queen's University Press, 1999.

———. "From Philosophical Anthropology to the Politics of Recognition: An Interview with Charles Taylor." Interview by Philippe de Lara. *Thesis Eleven*, no. 52 (February 1998): 103–12.

————. *The Ethics of Authenticity*. Cambridge, MA: Harvard University Press, 1992.

————. *Hegel*. Cambridge: Cambridge University Press, 1975.

————. "The Importance of Herder." In *Philosophical Arguments*. Cambridge, MA: Harvard University Press, 1995.

————. "Introduction." In *Philosophical Papers*. 2 vols. Cambridge: Cambridge University Press, 1985.

————. "Language and Human Nature." In *Human Agency and Language*. Vol. 1 of *Philosophical Papers*. Cambridge: Cambridge University Press, 1985.

————. "Living with Difference." In *Debating Democracy's Discontent: Essays on American Politics, Law, and Public Philosophy*, ed. Anita L. Allen and Milton C. Regan, Jr. Oxford: Oxford University Press, 1998.

————. "Modern Social Imaginaries." *Public Culture* 14, no. 1 (Winter 2002): 91–124.

————. "Modernity and Identity." In *Schools of Thought: Twenty-Five Years of Interpretive Social Science*, ed. Joan W. Scott and Debra Keates. Princeton: Princeton University Press, 2001.

————. "The Nature and Scope of Distributive Justice." In *Philosophy and the Human Sciences*. Vol. 2 of *Philosophical Papers*. Cambridge: Cambridge University Press, 1985.

————. "The Politics of Recognition." In *Multiculturalism: Examining the Politics of Recognition*, ed. Amy Gutmann. Princeton: Princeton University Press, 1994.

————. *Reconciling the Solitudes: Essays on Canadian Federalism and Nationalism*. Ed. Guy Laforest. Montreal: McGill-Queen's University Press, 1993.

————. *Sources of the Self: The Making of The Modern Identity*. Cambridge, MA: Harvard University Press, 1989.

————. "The Tradition of a Situation." In *Reconciling the Solitudes: Essays on Canadian Federalism and Nationalism*. Ed. Guy Laforest. Montreal: McGill-Queen's University Press, 1993.

————. "Two Theories of Modernity." *Public Culture* 11, no. 1 (Winter 1999): 153–74.

————. "What is Human Agency?" In *Human Agency and Language*. Vol. 1 of *Philosophical Papers*. Cambridge: Cambridge University Press, 1985.

Tempelman, Sasja. "Constructions of Cultural Identity: Multiculturalism and Exclusion." *Political Studies* 47, no. 1 (March 1999): 17–31.

Thomas, Elaine R. "Competing Visions of Citizenship and Integration in France's Headscarves Affair." *Journal of European Area Studies* 8, no. 2 (2000): 167–85.

Thomas, Paul. *Alien Politics: Marxist State Theory Retrieved*. New York: Routledge, 1994.

Thomson, Janice E. "State Sovereignty in International Relations: Bridging the Gap Between Theory and Empirical Research." *International Studies Quarterly* 39 (1995): 213–33.

Tierney, Brian. *The Crisis of Church and State, 1050–1300*. Englewood Cliffs, NJ: Prentice-Hall, 1964.

Tocqueville, Alexis de. *Democracy in America*. Ed. J. P. Mayer. Trans. George Lawrence. New York: Harper Collins, 1988.

Toews, John Edward. *Hegelianism: The Path Toward Dialectical Humanism, 1805–1841.* Cambridge: Cambridge University Press, 1985.

Tomasi, John. "Kymlicka, Liberalism, and Respect for Cultural Minorities." *Ethics* 105 (April 1995): 580–603.

Trouillot, Michel-Rolph. "Abortive Rituals: Historical Apologies in the Global Era." *Interventions* 2, no. 2 (2000): 171–86.

Tsao, Roy T. "Arendt Against Athens: Rethinking *The Human Condition.*" *Political Theory* 30, no. 1 (February 2002): 97–123.

Tully, James. "The Agonic Freedom of Citizens." *Economy and Society* 28, no. 2 (May 1999): 161–82.

———. *Strange Multiplicity: Constitutionalism in an Age of Diversity.* Cambridge: Cambridge University Press, 1995.

———. "Struggles over Recognition and Distribution." *Constellations* 7, no. 4 (December 2000): 469–82.

Tunick, Mark. "Hegel on Political Identity and the Ties that Bind." In *Beyond Liberalism and Communitarianism: Studies in Hegel's* Philosophy of Right, ed. Robert R. Williams. Albany: State University of New York Press, 2001.

Tussman, Joseph. "The Orestes Case." In *The Burden of Office: Agamemnon and Other Losers.* Vancouver: Talonbooks, 1989.

Verdery, Katherine. *The Political Lives of Dead Bodies: Reburial and Postsocialist Change.* New York: Columbia University Press, 1999.

Vermeule, Emily. *Aspects of Death in Early Greek Art and Poetry.* Berkeley: University of California Press, 1979.

Vidal-Naquet, Pierre. "Hunting and Sacrifice in Aeschylus' *Oresteia.*" In *Myth and Tragedy in Ancient Greece,* by Jean-Pierre Vernant and Pierre Vidal-Naquet. Trans. Janet Lloyd. New York: Zone Books, 1988.

Villa, Dana R. *Arendt and Heidegger: The Fate of the Political.* Princeton: Princeton University Press, 1996.

Vital, David. *A People Apart: The Jews in Europe, 1789–1939.* Oxford: Oxford University Press, 1999.

Vogler, Candace. "The Element of Surprise." Unpublished manuscript.

Volpp, Leti. "Talking 'Culture': Gender, Race, Nation, and the Politics of Multiculturalism." *Columbia Law Review* 96 (October 1996): 1573–1617.

Wagner-Pacifici, Robin. "Prolegomena to a Paradigm: Narratives of Surrender." *Qualitative Sociology* 24, no. 2 (2001): 269–81.

Waldron, Jeremy. "Minority Cultures and the Cosmopolitan Alternative." *University of Michigan Journal of Law Reform* 25 (1992): 751–93.

Walker, R. B. J. *Inside/Outside: International Relations as Political Theory.* Cambridge: Cambridge University Press, 1993.

Walzer, Michael. "Liberalism and the Art of Separation." *Political Theory* 12, no. 3 (August 1984): 315–30.

———. *Spheres of Justice: A Defense of Pluralism and Equality.* New York: Basic Books, 1983.

———. *What It Means to Be an American: Essays on the American Experience.* New York: Marsilio, 1992.

Warner, Michael. *Publics and Counterpublics.* Cambridge, MA: MIT Press, 2002.

———. *The Trouble with Normal: Sex, Politics, and the Ethics of Queer Life.* Cambridge, MA: Harvard University Press, 1999.

———. "What Like a Bullet Can Undeceive?" *Public Culture* 15, no. 1 (Winter 2003): 41–54.

Weber, Max. "Science as a Vocation." In *From Max Weber: Essays in Sociology*, ed. and trans. H. H. Gerth and C. Wright Mills. New York: Oxford University Press, 1958.

Wedeen, Lisa. "Conceptualizing Culture: Possibilities for Political Science." *American Political Science Review* 96, no. 4 (December 2002): 713–28.

Wendt, Alexander. *Social Theory of International Politics.* Cambridge: Cambridge University Press, 1999.

Wertheimer, Jack. *Unwelcome Strangers: East European Jews in Imperial Germany.* New York: Oxford University Press, 1987.

White, Richard J. *Nietzsche and the Problem of Sovereignty.* Urbana: University of Illinois Press, 1997.

White, Stephen K. *Sustaining Affirmation: The Strengths of Weak Ontology in Political Theory.* Princeton: Princeton University Press, 2000.

Whitehead, David. *The Ideology of the Athenian Metic.* Cambridge: Cambridge Philological Society, 1977.

Wiegenstein, Roland H. *Über Theater, 1966–1986.* Zürich: Ammann Verlag, 1987.

Wildt, Andreas. *Autonomie und Anerkennung: Hegels Moralitätskritik im Lichte seiner Fichte-Rezeption.* Stuttgart: Klett-Cotta, 1982.

Williams, Bernard. *Shame and Necessity.* Berkeley: University of California Press, 1993.

Williams, Robert R. *Hegel's Ethics of Recognition.* Berkeley: University of California Press, 1997.

———. *Recognition: Fichte and Hegel on the Other.* Albany: SUNY Press, 1992.

Winckelmann, Johann Joachim. "Thoughts on the Imitation of the Painting and Sculpture of the Greeks." Trans. H. B. Nisbet. In *German Aesthetic and Literary Criticism: Winckelmann, Lessing, Hamann, Herder, Schiller, and Goethe*, ed. H. B. Nisbet. Cambridge: Cambridge University Press, 1985.

Winnington-Ingram, R. P. "A Religious Function of Greek Tragedy." *Journal of Hellenic Studies* 74 (1954): 16–24.

———. *Studies in Aeschylus.* Cambridge: Cambridge University Press, 1983.

Wittgenstein, Ludwig. *Philosophical Investigations.* Trans. G. E. M. Anscombe. New York: Macmillan, 1953.

Wolf, Susan. "Comment." In *Multiculturalism: Examining the Politics of Recognition*, ed. Amy Gutmann. Princeton: Princeton University Press, 1994.

Yack, Bernard. *The Problems of a Political Animal: Community, Justice, and Conflict in Aristotelian Political Thought.* Berkeley: University of California Press, 1993.

Yar, Majid. "Beyond Nancy Fraser's 'Perspectival Dualism.'" *Economy and Society* 30, no. 3 (August 2001): 288–303.

Yeatman, Anna. "Justice and the Sovereign Self." In *Justice and Identity: Antipodean Practices*, ed. Margaret Wilson and Anna Yeatman. Wellington: Bridget Williams Books, 1995.

———. *Postmodern Revisionings of the Political*. London: Routledge, 1994.

Young, Iris Marion. "Gender as Seriality." In *Intersecting Voices: Dilemmas of Gender, Political Philosophy, and Policy*. Princeton: Princeton University Press, 1997.

———. *Justice and the Politics of Difference*. Princeton: Princeton University Press, 1990.

———. "Ruling Norms and the Politics of Difference: A Comment on Seyla Benhabib." *Yale Journal of Criticism* 12, no. 2 (1999): 415–21.

———. "Unruly Categories: A Critique of Nancy Fraser's Dual Systems Theory." *New Left Review* 222 (March–April 1997): 147–60.

Young-Bruehl, Elisabeth. *Hannah Arendt: For Love of the World*. New Haven: Yale University Press, 1982.

Yovel, Yirmiyahu. *Dark Riddle: Hegel, Nietzsche, and the Jews*. University Park: Pennsylvania State University Press, 1998.

———. "Hegels Begriff der Religion und die Religion der Erhabenheit." *Theologie und Philosophie* 51, no. 4 (1976): 512–37.

Zamir, Shahood. *Dark Voices: W. E. B. Du Bois and American Thought, 1888–1903*. Chicago: University of Chicago Press, 1995.

Zeitlin, Froma. "The Dynamics of Misogyny: Myth and Mythmaking in the *Oresteia*." In *Playing the Other: Gender and Society in Classical Greek Literature*. Chicago: University of Chicago Press, 1996.

Zerilli, Linda M. G. "The Arendtian Body." In *Feminist Interpretations of Hannah Arendt*, ed. Bonnie Honig. University Park: Pennsylvania State University Press, 1995.

———. *Feminism and the Abyss of Freedom*. Chicago: University of Chicago Press, forthcoming.

———. *Signifying Woman: Culture and Chaos in Rousseau, Burke, and Mill*. Ithaca: Cornell University Press, 1994.

———. "The Skepticism of *Willful Liberalism*." In *Skepticism, Individuality, and Freedom: The Reluctant Liberalism of Richard Flathman*, ed. Bonnie Honig and David R. Mapel. Minneapolis: University of Minnesota Press, 2002.

———. "This Universalism Which Is Not One." *Diacritics* 28, no. 2 (1998): 3–20.

Žižek, Slavoj. *The Sublime Object of Ideology*. London: Verso, 1989.

Index

12, 16, 22–24, 101; tension between cognitive and constructive senses of, 39–42, 48–49, 58–59; transformative vs. affirmative, 19–21, 23, 199n.46

religion: controversy over nineteenth-century reform of Jewish, 144–45; Edict of 1812 (Prussia) regarding Jewish, 135–36, 137; Hegel's characterization of Jewish, 139–42; Marx on Jewish emancipation as separation of state and, 131; Marx on relation between political state and, 128; public holidays and, 181

Rhetoric (Aristotle), 76

"right to culture": Kymlicka's arguments on agency and, 155, 156–61, 239n.23, 242n.67; rhetoric of multiculturalism and, 161–65

Rochaix, François, 193

Rousseau, Jean-Jacques: *Confessions*, 102; *Letter to M. D'Alembert*, 188

Rürup, Reinhard, 133, 134

same-sex marriage, 20–21

Sandel, Michael, 196n.8

Sartre, Jean-Paul, 92, 119, 120

Schlesinger, Arthur, 6

Scott, James, 153, 170

Segal, Charles, 72–73

"sense-certainty," Hegel's account of, 101–2

Seven Against Thebes (Aeschylus), 116–17

Sewell, William, 154

Shapiro, Michael, 195n.3, 200n.59

Sherman, Nancy, 75, 77

social ontology, 4

"societal culture," 168–69

society: distinction between the state and, 27, 129–30; medieval notion of three orders of, 54, 209n.78, 209–10n.79; naturalism on individual as independent of, 44

Sophocles: human aspiration tracked in dramas of, 21; Oedipus the King's recognition scene by, 62. See also *Antigone* (Sophocles)

Sorkin, David, 133, 134, 153

sovereignty: concept of not limited to states, 11; defining, 10–11, 196n.6; Foucault's critique of power as, 28–30; Hegel's defense of Jewish emancipation as means to, 138–43; identity and, 12–13;

language and pursuit of, 46–47; politics of recognition as pursuit of, 11–12, 14; of state, 10–11, 25–32, 124–27, 138–43, 170–71, 201n.70; Taylor on aspiration to, 46–47, 53; as unconditional expenditure, 196n.6

the state: distinction between society and, 27, 129–30; Hegel on, 117–18, 124–26, 141–43; identity and, 125–27, 152–53, 175–76; as inherently a site of subordination, 32; Marx on, 129–31, 150; monocultural vs. multicultural versions of, 152–53; as object of identification, 125–27; as participant in politics of recognition, 25–32, 117–18, 123–31, 137–38, 141–43, 152–53; *Phenomenology* on, 25; *Philosophy of Right* notion of, 26, 117–18, 124–25, 142; politics of recognition approached through sovereignty and, 11, 15, 30–32; recognition and, 25–32; role in multicultural recognition by, 25–28, 30–31, 170; sovereignty of, 10–11, 25–32, 124–27, 138–43, 170–71, 201nn.70, 73; understood as linked assemblage of institutions, 202n.78. See also nation-state

States of Injury (Brown), 29–30, 127–31, 195n.8

Stein, Peter, 193

Stevens, Jacqueline, 25

"the struggle for recognition" (*Kampf um Anerkennung*), 2, 103–5

Süßmilch, Johann Peter, 47, 48

subordination: *Antigone's* representation of female, 72–74, 81–82, 113, 114, 115–16; as consequence of politics of recognition, 112–13, 146–51, 173–76; Hegel's antifeminism and, 113–18; Hegel's diagnosis of, 96, 108–13; implications of Hegel's master-slave approach for, 112–13; Marx's analysis of, 109–10; misread as mere ignorance, 163; misread as mere inequality, 182; role of material incentives in, 199n.52; rooted in failure of acknowledgment, 112–13, 119–20, 121, 164; sources of, 21–24; state as inherently site of, 32. *See also* domination; master-slave relationship

surprise, 15, 24, 36, 58, 198n.26